Women's Experience in America
An Historical Anthology

edited by

Esther Katz

Anita Rapone

Transaction Books
New Brunswick (U.S.A.) and London (U.K.)

Library of Congress Catalog Number: 79-64179
ISBN: 0-87855-668-0 (paper)
Printed in the United States of America

Library of Congress Cataloging in Publication Data

Main entry under title:

Women's experience in America.

 Bibliography: p.
 1. Women—United States—History—Addresses, essays, lectures. 2.
Women—United States—Social conditions—Addresses, essays, lectures. 3.
Women—United States—Biography—Addresses, essays, lectures. I. Katz,
Esther. II. Rapone, Anita.
HQ1410.W67   301.41′2′0973   79-64179
ISBN 0-87855-668-0

CONTENTS

Women's Experience in America
An Historical Anthology

Introduction:

American Women
and Domestic Culture:
An Approach to Women's History

Esther Katz and Anita Rapone

In the past decade, women's history has emerged as one of the most vital fields of historical inquiry, and has raised broad conceptual and methodological issues. One primary concern of historians in this field has been to develop analytical approaches appropriate to the unique position of women in history. To date, the dominant approach has, like much traditional history however, stressed economic roles as the key explanatory factor for changes in status. Thus, the most prevalent theory is that the position of American women improved in the preindustrial colonial period and began to decline with the growth of industrialization of the late eighteenth-early nineteenth century. After a brief evaluation of this theory as an interpretation for the history of women, we propose to offer an alternative approach based on an analysis of gender-based social structures.

Proponents of this status decline thesis have based their analysis of women's economic status on two factors: occupational diversity among women and their role in the family economy. Since by the nineteenth century, women had become less active in both respects, the colonial period has been viewed as a relative "golden age" for women. While acknowledging that the colonists transported their patriarchal notions of family and community with them to the New World, historians have asserted that the exigencies of creating a society in the wilderness made the lives of women less rigid and confined. They argued that the relative fluidity of colonial society along with the shortage of labor and the family-centered economy elevated the economic status of women through what one historian referred to as a "democratic attitude toward work." Women were found working in a variety of commercial enterprises as traders, merchants, tavern and innkeepers, and skilled craftsmen and artisans.[1]

By the late eighteenth century, however, women not only faced increasing resistance to their nondomestic work, but when employed had fewer occupational choices than in the colonial period. For example, women were systematically excluded from newly professionalizing fields by the introduction of required educational training from which they were barred. Women even lost dominance in obstetrics—a field which had traditionally been theirs. A similar pattern is apparent in their commercial activities which became limited to marginal ventures such as small dry goods shops and boardinghouses. While women lost professional and business opportunities, the shortage of male workers opened other areas of employment for them in the newly emerging factories. However, the introduction of women into factory work only contributed to the deterioration of their economic position. Because they were considered temporary workers who would leave the factory upon marriage, women's wages were low and job advancement limited.[2]

The second component used in the status decline thesis to analyze the position of women is their level of productivity in the family economy. Historians have argued that, because the preindustrial colonial economy was centered in the home, the economic contribution of women was as essential as that of men to family survival. They concluded that women's central role in economic production provided them with a sense of self-worth and social prestige and improved their position in society. With the transition from a subsistence to a market economy, the status of women began to decline. As men expanded their activities into the marketplace, the work of women in the home lost prestige since it produced no income for the family. Consequently, women themselves lost status because the work they did lost status.[3]

Exponents of the status decline thesis, then, have argued that by the nineteenth century women were largely excluded from the public world of money and power, and confined to the private world of the household. Furthermore, they added, middle class women began to benefit from the growing wealth of their men, and they were able to increase their leisure time by hiring other women to relieve them of many household chores and childcare responsibilities. As women's roles both within the home and in the public world became more ornamental, a new ideal of womanhood began to emerge—the nineteenth-century "lady." The ideology of femininity that accompanied this new role model directed women to be pure, pious, submissive and domestic. This has been interpreted as an ideology of confinement and isolation appropriate to the exclusion of women from economic activity.[4]

The status decline thesis poses a number of problems. First, it depends on the assumption that social status is derived from labor value; but historical exceptions undermine its validity. For example, the work done by slaves and indentured servants too was an essential economic contribution; yet their status was low. Therefore, there is no necessary reason to assume that, because women's work was essential to family survival, their status was relatively high. Furthermore, this approach minimizes the strength of the doctrine of female subordination in the colonial period. Finally, it overlooks both the fact that sex role divisions transcend economic change and that these divisions themselves contribute to changes in social structure.

A more productive approach for analyzing the position of women in society is to examine the social structures which govern their interactions with that society. Such an examination reveals that in colonial society, women were more severely circumscribed than is indicated by an analysis of work roles. Because the primary socioeconomic unit was the patriarchal family, women were dependent on men—fathers, husbands, sons—to define their relationship to society. Only women without male family heads were able to relate to social institutions directly, but, rather than enjoying greater freedom and opportunity, many of these women suffered because they lacked male protection and legitimacy. According to a recent study, widows in eighteenth-century Massachusetts were frequently forced to live in reduced circumstances, for they did not have the funds and legal rights to manage the properties entrusted to them.[5] Many widows were older women without the wealth that would provide a compensatory inducement to prospective husbands and were therefore unable to ease their plight by remarriage. In many cases they had no recourse but to personally petition the courts for expanded property and contractual rights. Since widows were forced to act individually rather than collectively, any benefits they acquired were pragmatic exceptions which sustained the subordinate legal and economic position of women generally. Their successes at these efforts, then, must be interpreted not so much as an indication of the improved status of women in colonial society, but as evidence of the harshness of their economic and social position.

In early New England, the social behavior of women was regulated by the church oligarchy and by male family heads who were accountable for the behavior of their wives and children. Any woman who attempted to increase her autonomy was defined as deviant. One of the most articulate challengers was Anne Hutchinson, whose role in the Antinomian controversy created a multi-level crisis.[6] Not only did she upset the family hierarchy by asserting her spiritual independence, but by minimizing the role of the male clergy, she undermined the basis of both religious and secular authority. Perhaps most threatening of all was her ability to attract large numbers of female supporters and to inspire women to similar challenges. The sexual nature of the hostility toward Anne Hutchinson and her female supporters indicates that their major crime was their deviance from prevailing norms of female thought and behavior. The inability of these women to successfully defend themselves from this sexual attack illustrates their vulnerability in a society governed by exclusively male-dominated social structures.

By the nineteenth century, with the polarization of society into male and female spheres, women acquired more power to determine their own lives and to affect their society. While men were developing an individualized competitive market culture, women created a collective domestic culture through which they were able to relate directly to society. An analysis of the inner workings of this domestic culture suggests that the separation of home and work constituted a positive development for women since it allowed them to derive satisfaction and benefits from a society based on clearly defined segregated sex roles.[7] By formulating the character and functions of women as distinctly separate from men, domestic culture and ideology provided women with self-respect, a unifying sense of shared purpose, and the ability to act collectively.

A key component of this culture was the system of female friendships through which women shared the values and experiences associated with their ascribed domestic roles and the stages of the female life cycle. These friendships took on even greater importance because the rigid role separation of the sexes led to an emotional segregation which severely limited the intimacy between men and women. Thus, these friendships carried an emotional intensity that did not extend to relationships with men.[8] The value women placed on female community is evident in their unhappiness over its breakdown. Women on the westward migration, for example, perceived the blurring of the rigid sex role separation of tasks as a threat to the integrity of their female domain and persistently attempted to reestablish their domestic culture.[9]

This female domestic culture provided a foundation for the extension of women's activities into the male-dominated public world. The moral superiority attributed to women through the ideology of womanhood provided legitimacy for their efforts to organize collectively to promote social causes. The innate piety associated with women justified the expansion of their familial religious duties to include missionary and church-related charitable activities. Recognition of their particular suitability for good works allowed women the opportunity to develop a wide range of voluntary associations through which they imposed their shared values on reform movements. A notable example of women's impact was the establishment of female moral reform societies which shifted the emphasis of the movement against prostitution from the protection of young men to the defense and uplifting of female prostitutes. Their aggressive attacks on the double standard reflected their willingness to use their sexually defined powers and rights to openly control male behavior. Such female voluntary associations not only extended the impact of domestic culture, but also intensified gender identification among women. They constituted a major form of social structure in the female community. In a highly mobile society, the existence of such organizations throughout the nation added to the ability of the female culture to transcend rapid social change.[10]

The growth of female education was also related to the rise of a domestic culture. The early female academies and seminaries which were designed to prepare women for their domestic responsibilities reflected the increased status of those roles. Furthermore, the segregation of women into a separate educational system designed specifically for their lives as women reinforced the female consciousness that characterized the domestic sphere. These female schools were another structure through which women formed supportive, close and lasting attachments that further strengthened gender identification.[11]

The influence of the domestic culture is also apparent in women's efforts to forge a new profession for themselves—nursing.[12] Just as women legitimized their involvement in reform by emphasizing their piety and purity, women based their efforts to care for the sick and wounded in the Civil War on their maternal and nurturing qualities. Through their conflict with army officers and doctors over the control of nursing, women established their right to join the medical profession and, after the war, succeeded in establishing accredited nursing schools. Their success reflects their willingness to use the power they derived from the domestic culture to further expand their sphere of influence.

In the nineteenth century, women's domestic roles derived status, significance and power from this supporting female culture; by the twentieth century, however, this culture was disintegrating. A key factor in this disintegration was the rejection of intimate female friendships as an acceptable form of social interaction by the medical and psychological community which viewed these relationships as deviant.[13] Psychologists and theorists such as G. Stanley Hall, Havelock Ellis and most notably Sigmund Freud formulated women's sexual needs exclusively in terms of heterosexual and heterosocial relationships and assumed that, because of the limitations on heterosexual contact, women in the nineteenth century were sexually frustrated and emotionally disturbed. Their analysis clearly devalued any form of close female relationships, while encouraging a wider range of male-female associations. Furthermore, this marked emphasis on female heterosexual fulfillment along with changing social mores thrust women into a competitive sexual marketplace.[14] The intimacy of childhood associations with female family members and friends was increasingly eroded as young girls entered the dating culture where a premium was placed on their ability to attract male attention. Thus the system of supportive female friendships was replaced in the twentieth century by competitive, isolating male-centered behavior.

The integrity of the domestic culture was further undermined by economic growth which drew women out of the female-dominated home environment. As increasing numbers of young women in the twentieth century took jobs in offices and shops, they entered a heterosexual work environment which inhibited close female attachments. Unlike the sororial atmosphere of the early Lowell factories, for example, in the twentieth-century office setting, women were encouraged to vie with each other not only for male attention, but for job advancement as well.[15]

Another factor in this cultural disintegration was expanding urbanization, which not only weakened familial ties, but provided institutional replacements for many of the functions previously served by the system of female rituals. The supportive role of the female community in pregnancy and childbirth, for example, was taken over by the urban hospital. Similarly, as socializing roles of mothers in preparing their daughters for the responsibilities of marriage and motherhood lessened, young women had to rely on impersonal advice on courtship, marriage and motherhood provided by mass media.

Another manifestation of the disintegration of female culture was the demise of those reform organizations which were based on gender identification and, to varying degrees, on an ideology of female moral superiority. The early settlement houses were conscious communities of women who assumed that their unique female qualities provided them with true social vision. The woman's rights movement encompassed similarly oriented reform groups as well as those groups seeking to improve the position of their sex. By the 1920s, however, the sense of female dedication had disappeared as many women joined the male-dominated Progressive reform movement. The settlement houses, for example, lost that special sense of calling embodied in the concept of the residential community, as younger workers, especially men, began to see themselves as professionals and preferred to maintain separate homes of their own. Woman's rights groups too suffered from the loss of a female cultural identity and even though organizationally well developed, lost their sustaining sense of purpose. Though they had mustered a tenuous merger over the suffrage issue, their victory left them fragmented and disorganized. Their failure to develop a bloc vote and their persistent conflict over the Equal Rights Amendment reflect the extent to which women had lost their ideological and cultural basis of unity.[16]

As a result of this breakdown of the domestic culture, women in the twentieth century lacked the supportive cultural framework to give prestige and social significance to their domestic roles. With the loss of female intimacy, women became exclusively dependent on their relationships with men not only for their economic well-being but for their emotional fulfillment as well. As the twentieth-century home became centered on the husband, the separate male and female spheres were transformed into male-defined public and private spheres. As women lost their autonomous domestic culture and their position in society became marginal, integration into the male world became imperative. The position of women in the twentieth century, then, must be compared with that of men.

When the political status of women is measured against that of men, it becomes clear that women were not integrated into the political structure despite their attainment of suffrage. The weakened gender identification that resulted from the undermining of female culture prevented the creation of an effective female voting bloc. This failure of a significant women's vote to emerge after 1920, along with resistance to their election to public office and their participation in any of the decision-making structures of political parties, effectively consigned women to a marginal role in the political process.[17]

Another major aspect of equality is economic status. While the number of working women continued to grow in the twentieth century, the majority were concentrated in low status, low paying white collar and service occupations, and underrepresented in higher level management and professional jobs. In 1970, for example, though women were 38.0 percent of the work force, they were only 9.2 percent of the medical doctors, 4.8 percent of the lawyers, 4.0 percent of the physicists and astronomers, and 1.6 percent of the engineers.[18] The differential between male and female wages constitutes another form of inequality. As of 1974, for example, the median income for all female workers was still only fifty-seven percent of that of male workers, while women college graduates averaged lower incomes than men with only high school diplomas.[19] This pattern reflects the persistence of widespread economic discrimination throughout the century.

The legitimacy of women as paid workers is undermined by the assumption that their primary social roles are to serve as wives and mothers. The justification for occupational and wage discrimination has been based on the view that women workers are less committed to their jobs. Furthermore, women face role conflicts that inhibit their career advancement. If married women, for example, work outside the home, it is not an alternative to their domestic functions, but an addition to them. Finally, because the social status of women is low, the status of all female-associated occupations is also low. Thus, in 1957, in industries where women comprised more than fifty percent of the labor force, the industry paid a wage well below the national average.[20] Similarly, professions dominated by women, such as teaching, nursing, librarianship and social work, all have lower status and wages than male-dominated professions.[21]

The twentieth century, then, emerges as a period of transition, for women continue to face the persistence of sex role divisions. They lack the validation and support of a strong domestic culture and have not yet achieved full integration into male-dominated social structures.

NOTES

1. The standard source on occupational diversity among colonial women is Elisabeth A. Dexter, *Colonial Women of Affairs: Women in Business and the Professions in America Before 1776,* 2nd. ed., revised (Boston: Houghton Mifflin Company, 1931). See also, Julia Cherry Spruill, *Women's Life and Work in the Southern Colonies* (Chapel Hill: University of North Carolina Press, 1938) and Edith Abbott, *Women in Industry* (New York: D. Appleton & Co., 1928), chap. 1. The quotation is from Dexter, p. 183.

2. For a treatment of the loss of business and professional opportunities among women, see especially Elisabeth A. Dexter, *Career Women of America 1776-1840* (Francestown, N.H.: Marshall Jones Co., 1950) and Gerda Lerner, "The Lady and the Mill Girl: Changes in the Status of Women in the Age of Jackson," *Midcontinent American Studies Journal* 10 (Spring 1969): 5-15. Lerner places particular emphasis on the social differences between the increasingly homebound, middle-class "lady" and the exploited "mill girl." For a further articulation of the declining status of female factory workers, see Gerda Lerner, ed., *The Female Experience: An American Documentary* (Indianapolis: The Bobbs-Merrill Company, Inc., 1977), pp. xxx–xxxii.

3. Mary Ryan, *Womanhood in America From Colonial Times to the Present* (New York: New Viewpoints, 1975), pp. 21-135, includes the shift from a subsistence to a cash crop economy as an underlying cause for status decline among women; Lerner, *The Female Experience,* pp. xxviii–xxx; Joan Hoff Wilson, "The Illusion of Change: Women and the American Revolution," in *The American Revolution,* ed. Alfred F. Young (DeKalb, Ill.: Northern Illinois Press, 1976), pp. 336-445, see especially, pp. 393-400.

4. Barbara Welter, "The Cult of True Womanhood: 1820-1860," *American Quarterly* 18 (Summer 1966): 151-74, suggests that the prescriptive literature of the time presented the idealized woman as a "hostage in the home." Gerda Lerner, "The Lady and the Mill Girl," and Mary Ryan, *Womanhood in America,* pp. 106-35, interpret this ideology as evidence of woman's declining status in the nineteenth century.

5. Alexander Keyssar, "Widowhood in Eighteenth-Century Massachusetts: A Problem in the History of the Family," *Perspectives in American History* 8 (1974): 83-119.

6. Ben Barker-Benfield, "Anne Hutchinson and the Puritan Attitude Toward Women," *Feminist Studies* I (1972): 65-96; Lyle Koehler, "The Case of the American Jezebels: Anne Hutchinson and Female Agitation During the Years of the Antinomian Turmoil, 1636-1640," *William and Mary Quarterly* 30 (1974): 55-78.

7. Barbara Sicherman, "American History," *Signs: Journal of Women in Culture and Society* 1 (1974): 461-87, suggests that one new trend in women's history is the emphasis on the positive aspects of women's sphere. Daniel Scott Smith, "Family Limitation, Sexual Control, and Domestic Feminism in Victorian America," *Feminist Studies* 1 (1973): 40-57, has argued that in the nineteenth century the status of women was

derived from their domestic roles, which were the vehicle for positive
social change and increased social status for women.

8. Nancy F. Cott, *The Bonds of Womanhood: "Woman's Sphere" in New England, 1780-1835* (New Haven: Yale University Press, 1977), pp. 160-96; Carroll Smith-Rosenberg, "The Female World of Love and Ritual: Relations between Women in Nineteenth-Century America," *Signs: Journal of Women in Culture and Society* 1 (1975): 1-29.

9. Johnny Faragher and Christine Stansell, "Women and Their Families on the Overland Trail, 1842-1867," *Feminist Studies* 2 (1975): 150-66.

10. For analyses of women's voluntary activities, see: Nancy F. Cott, *Bonds of Womanhood*, pp. 126-59; Keith Melder, "The Beginnings of the Women's Rights Movement in the United States, 1800-1840" (unpublished Ph.D. dissertation, Yale University, 1964) and "Ladies Bountiful: Organized Women's Benevolence in Early Nineteenth-Century America," *New York History* XLVIII (1967): 231-54; Carroll Smith-Rosenberg, "Beauty, the Beast and the Militant Woman: A Case Study in Sex Roles and Social Stress in Jacksonian America," *American Quarterly* 23 (1971): 562-84.

11. For a discussion of gender identification and education, see: Jill Conway, "Perspectives on the History of Women's Education in the United States," *History of Education Quarterly* 14 (1974): 1-12; Nancy F. Cott, *Bonds of Womanhood*, pp. 101-25. The early ideological debate on female education is discussed by Linda Kerber, "Daughters of Columbia: Educating Women for the Republic, 1787-1805," in *The Hofstadter Aegis: A Memorial*, eds. Stanley Elkins and Eric McKitrick (New York: Alfred A. Knopf, Inc., 1974), pp. 36-59.

12. Ann Douglas Wood, "The War Within a War: Women Nurses in the Union Army," *Civil War History* 18 (1972): 197-212. For analyses of other occupations associated with specifically female characteristics, see: Joan Burstyn, "Catharine Beecher and the Education of American Women," *New England Quarterly* 47 (1974): 386-403; Dee Garrison, "The Tender Technicians: The Feminization of Public Librarianship, 1876-1905," *Journal of Social History* 6 (1972-73): 131-59; R. Laurence Moore, "The Spiritualist Medium: A Study of Female Professionalism in Victorian America," *American Quarterly* 27 (1975): 200-21; Kathryn Kish Sklar, *Catharine Beecher: A Study in American Domesticity* (New Haven: Yale University Press, 1973); Ann Douglas Wood, "The 'Scribbling Women' and Fanny Fern: Why Women Wrote," *American Quarterly* 23 (1971): 3-24.

13. Carroll Smith-Rosenberg suggests that once such intimate female friendships are viewed as instances of "latent homosexuality," they become "the indication of a disease in progress—seeds of pathology which belie the reality of an individual's heterosexuality." ("The Female World of Love and Ritual," p. 28).

14. Mary Ryan, *Womanhood in America*, pp. 287-95.

15. For a discussion of the strength of the female community in the Lowell mills, see Thomas Dublin, "Women, Work, and the Family: Female Operatives in the Lowell Mills, 1830-1860," *Feminist Studies* 3 (1975): 30-39.

16. For a basic history of the woman's rights movement, see Eleanor Flex-

ner, *Century of Struggle: The Woman's Rights Movement in the United States* (New York: Atheneum, 1968). On women in the settlement movement, see: Jill Conway, "Women Reformers and American Culture, 1870–1930," *Journal of Social History* 5 (1971–72): 164–77; John P. Rousmaniere, "Cultural Hybrid in the Slums: The College Woman and the Settlement House, 1889-1894," *American Quarterly* 22 (1970): 45–66. For one interpretation of the ultimate failure of the woman's rights movement, see William L. O'Neill, *Everyone Was Brave: The Rise and Fall of Feminism in America* (Chicago: Quadrangle Books, Inc., 1969); see also his explanation of the demise of the settlement houses, pp. 249-51. For an analysis of women's reform activities in the 1920s, see J. Stanley Lemons, *The Woman Citizen: Social Feminism in the 1920's* (Urbana: University of Illinois Press, 1973).

17. In addition to O'Neill, see also William H. Chafe, *The American Woman: Her Changing Social, Economic, and Political Roles, 1920-1970* (New York: Oxford University Press, 1972), pp. 25-47, 112-32.

18. Percentages are calculated from numbers given in U.S. Bureau of the Census, *1970 Census of Population: Characteristics of the Population,* Vol. 1, Part 1, Sect. 2 (Washington, D.C.: U.S. Government Printing Office, 1973) Table 221, p. 718.

19. U.S. Bureau of the Census, *A Statistical Portrait of Women in the U.S.* (Washington, D.C.: U.S. Government Printing Office, 1976), p. 45.

20. William H. Chafe, *The American Woman,* p. 185.

21. For discussions of twentieth-century female occupational patterns among women and sex discrimination, see especially Chafe, *American Woman;* Robert W. Smuts, *Women and Work in America* (New York, Schocken Books, 1971). For analyses of women and the professions, see: Cynthia Fuchs Epstein, *Woman's Place: Options and Limits in Professional Careers* (Berkeley: University of California Press, 1971); Frank Stricker, "Cookbooks and Law Books: The Hidden History of Career Women in Twentieth-Century America," *Journal of Social History* 10 (1976): 1-19.

SELECTED READINGS

Arts in Society, "Women and the Arts." (Spring-Summer 1974).

Baxandall, Rosalyn, Linda Gordon and Susan Reverby, eds. *America's Working Women: A Documentary History, 1600-Present.* New York: Vintage, 1976.

Carroll, Berenice, ed. *Liberating Women's History: Theoretical and Critical Essays.* Urbana: University of Illinois Press, 1976.

Cott, Nancy F., ed. *Root of Bitterness: Documents of the Social History of American Women.* New York: E.P. Dutton & Co., Inc., 1972.

Brownlee, W. Eliot and Mary H. Brownlee, eds. *Women in the American Economy: A Documentary History, 1675-1927.* New Haven: Yale University Press, 1976.

Gerstenberger, Donna and Carolyn Allen. "Women Studies/American Studies, 1970-1975." *American Quarterly* 29 (1977): 263-79.

Gordon, Ann D., Mari Jo Buhle and Nancy E. Schrom. "Women in American Society." *Radical America* 5 (July-Aug. 1971).
History of Education Quarterly, "Reinterpreting Women's Education." (Spring 1974).
Journal of Presbyterian History, "Women and the Presbyterian Church." (Summer 1974).
Lerner, Gerda, ed. *The Female Experience: An American Documentary.* Indianapolis: The Bobbs-Merrill Co., Inc., 1977.
Ryan, Mary P. *Womanhood in America: From Colonial Times to the Present.* New York: New Viewpoints, 1975.
Sicherman, Barbara. "Review Essay: American History." *Signs: Journal of Women in Culture and Society* 1 (Winter 1975): 461–86.

WOMEN IN
COLONIAL SOCIETY

Seventeenth-century settlers in the New World brought Old World social patterns which clearly defined male and female roles. They transplanted the English model of woman as politically, socially and legally subordinate to man. The assumption of woman's inferior status had its roots in Christian tradition, particularly in St. Paul's injunctions against assertiveness and independence in women. While colonies varied in their political and socioeconomic patterns, the settlers had in common a high degree of religious commitment. The extent to which Protestant doctrine affected social organization was evident in New England colonies, like Massachusetts Bay where religious conformity was deemed essential to community survival. The Puritan settlement attempted to create a society based on the ideal of a "priesthood of all believers," a concept which did not extend to women. In the Puritan hierarchy, as men were subordinate to God, so were women subordinate to men. Though eligible for salvation, women were excluded from theological debate and decision-making. In fact, in 1633 the Reverend John Cotton requested that women applying for church membership not be examined in a public confession because this violated Pauline doctrine. In a Puritan oligarchy, religious proscriptions against women were also political proscriptions. Women were cut off from the political prerogatives of the elect, and therefore from any significant public role. Episodic attempts to deviate from those proscriptions were quickly silenced.

The most articulate challenger was Anne Hutchinson, a proselytizer for the Antinomians who believed in salvation through grace rather than good works. In the article by Lyle Koehler, the social origins and implications of this challenge are analyzed in relation to the subordinate position of women in Puritan society.

In the discussion of the response of Puritan leadership to the Hutchinson challenge, the Koehler selection illuminates the importance of the patriarchal family in colonial America. The preindustrial family was a self-sufficient unit, in which the wife, as household manager, was responsible for the production of food and other essential goods. In some cases, this meant supervising a large staff of servants or slaves. Furthermore, she was responsible for the education and early religious training of the children. Since colonial society was based largely on family units, the presence of women was a prerequisite for the growth and continuance of the community.

During the initial stages of settlement, it seemed that women might fare better in the New World than they had in the Old. This was most evident in early landholding practices. In Maryland, for example, female members of large English families were in some instances granted manorial rights over thousands of acres. Some women came to Virginia as indentured servants, often on the promise of land. In several New England towns, although most women arrived in family units, small lots were set aside for unmarried women. In Pennsylvania, women were offered seventy-five acres of land. However, within a few years, as more and more women arrived, these opportunities were withdrawn by virtually every colony. Women were once again excluded from control and ownership of the primary form of wealth.

Just as the colonies offered women land to encourage the multiplication of family units, they also made legal provisions for women in the event the family unit was dissolved through the death of the husband. For example, Massachusetts Bay established the principle of dower rights, a widow's claim to a portion of her husband's estate. However, she was only entitled to the use or profits of this real property before it passed on to the children at her death. While a widow gained some economic independence, this practice was designed both to keep her from becoming a public charge and to preserve the property for her husband's heirs. But by the eighteenth century, the inadequacy of dowers to support widows led to an important, if limited, innovation. The Keyssar selection, using quantitative data, discusses the legal steps taken by some widows to secure total control over this property. The article further indicates that it was primarily through widowhood that colonial women assumed an independent economic identity.

The position of women in the colonial period must be understood in the context of a society in which the family was the socioeconomic unit. While there were early innovations that offered opportunities to women, these were primarily designed to encourage the foundation and survival of families. These were limited at best, and gradually disappeared as colonial society was no longer endangered by a shortage of women. Only later when communities were faced with the potential public dependency of widows, did women gain any further economic concessions. The transplanted tradition of female subordination had as tenacious a hold in the New World as it had in the Old.

SELECTED READINGS

Barker-Benfield, Ben. "Anne Hutchinson and the Puritan Attitude Toward Women," *Feminist Studies* 1 (Fall 1972): 65–96.

Benson, Mary Sumner. *Women in Eighteenth-Century America: A Study of Opinion and Social Usage.* New York: Columbia University Press, 1935.

Berger, Paul and Stephen Nissenbaum. *Salem Possessed: The Social Origins of Witchcraft.* Cambridge, Mass.: Harvard University Press, 1974.

Cott, Nancy F. "Divorce and the Changing Status of Women in Eighteenth-Century Massachusetts," *William and Mary Quarterly* 3d Ser., 33 (October 1976): 586-614.

Demos, John. "Underlying Themes in the Witchcraft of Seventeenth-Century New England," *American Historical Review* 75 (June 1970): 1311–26.

Dexter, Elisabeth A. *Colonial Women of Affairs: Women in Business and the Professions in America Before 1776.* 2nd ed., rev. Boston: Houghton Mifflin Company, 1931.

Kerber, Linda K. "Daughters of Columbia: Educating Women for the Republic, 1787-1805," in *The Hofstadter Aegis: A Memorial,* ed. Stanley Elkins and Eric McKitrick. New York: Alfred A. Knopf, 1974, pp. 36–59.

Moller, Herbert. "Sex Composition and Correlated Culture Patterns of Colonial America," *William and Mary Quarterly* 3rd Ser. 2 (April 1945): 113-53.

Smith, Daniel Scott, "The Demographic History of Colonial New England," *Journal of Economic History* 32 (March 1972): 165-83.

Smith, Daniel Scott. "Parental Power and Marriage Patterns: An Analysis of Historical Trends in Hingham, Mass." *Journal of Marriage and the Family* 35 (August 1973): 419-28.

Spruill, Julia Cherry. *Women's Life and Work in the Southern Colonies.* Chapel Hill: University of North Carolina Press, 1938.

Thompson, Roger. *Women in Stuart England and America: A Comparative Study.* London: Routledge and Kegan Paul, 1974.

Weisberg, D. Kelly. " 'Under Greet Temptations Heer': Women and Divorce in Puritan Massachusetts." *Feminist Studies* 2 (1975): 183–93.

Wells, Robert V. "Family Size and Fertility Control in Eighteenth-Century America: A Study of Quaker Families." *Population Studies* 25 (1971): 73–82.

Wells, Robert V. "Quaker Marriage Patterns in a Colonial Perspective." *William and Mary Quarterly* 3d Ser. 29 (July 1972): 415–42.

Wilson, Joan Hoff. "The Illusion of Change: Women and the American Revolution," in *The American Revolution* ed. Alfred F. Young. DeKalb, Illinois: Northern Illinois Press, 1976, pp. 336–445.

The Case of the American Jezebels: Anne Hutchinson and Female Agitation During the Years of Antinomian Turmoil, 1636-1640

Lyle Koehler

Between 1636 and 1638 Massachusetts boiled with controversy, and for more than three centuries scholars have attempted to define and redefine the nature, causes, and implications of that controversy. Commentators have described the rebellious Antinomians as "heretics of the worst and most dangerous sort" who were guilty of holding "absurd, licentious, and destructive" opinions,[1] as "a mob scrambling after God, and like all mobs quickly dispersed once their leaders were dealt with,"[2] and as the innocent victims of "inexcusable severity and unnecessary virulence."[3] Other narrators have called the most famous Antinomian, Anne Hutchinson, a "charismatic healer, with the gift of fluent and inspired speech,"[4] another St. Joan of Arc,[5] a rebel with a confused, bewildered mind,[6] and a woman "whose stern and masculine mind ... triumphed over the tender affections of a wife and mother."[7]

Almost without exception, these critics and defenders of Ms. Hutchinson and the Antinomians have dealt specifically with Antinomianism as a religious movement and too little with it as a social movement.[8] Emery Battis has traced the occupational status of 190 Antinomians and Antinomian sympathizers to examine the secular as well as the religious aspects of the controversy, but his work suffers from one major oversight: only three of his rebels are female.[9] As Richard S. Dunn has rightly observed, "The role of women in colonial life continues to be neglected," [10] and only one colonial specialist, Michael J. Colacurcio, has been much concerned with women as Antinomians. Colacurcio has argued that sexual tensions were central to the Antinomian controversy, but it is not his primary concern to describe the nature of those tensions. Rather, he focuses on Anne Hutchinson as a "type" of Hawthorne's scarlet lady, Hester Prynne.[11] Dunn's appeal, "We need another view of Ms. Hutchinson," [12] still entices.

That Anne Hutchinson and many other Puritan women should at stressful times rebel, either by explicit statement or by implicit example, against the role they were expected to fulfill in society is readily understandable, since that role, in both old and New England, was extremely limiting. The model English woman was weak, submissive, charitable, virtuous, and modest. Her mental and physical activity was limited to keeping the home in order, cooking, and bearing and rearing children, although she might occasionally serve the community as a nurse or midwife. She was urged to avoid books and intellectual exercise, for such activity might overtax her weak mind, and to serve her husband willingly, since she was by nature his inferior.[13] In accordance with the Apostle Paul's doctrine, she was to hold her tongue in church and be careful not "to teach, nor to usurp authority over the man, but to be in silence." [14]

In their letters, lectures, and historical accounts many of the Bay Colony men and some of the women showed approval of modest, obedient, and submissive females. Governor John Winthrop's wife Margaret was careful to leave such important domestic matters as place of residence to her husband's discretion, even when she had a preference of her own. She was ashamed because she felt that she had "no thinge with in or with out" worthy of him and signed her letters to him "your faythfull and obedient wife" or "your lovinge and obedient wife." Lucy Downing, Winthrop's sister, signed her chatty letters to her brother, "Your sister to commaund." Elizabeth, the wife of Winthrop's son John, described herself in a letter to her husband as "thy eaver loveing and kinde wife to comande in whatsoeaver thou plesest so long as the Lord shall bee plesed to geve me life and strenge." [15]

Winthrop himself was harshly critical of female intellect. In 1645 he wrote that Ann Hopkins, wife of the governor of Connecticut, had lost her understanding and reason by giving herself solely to reading and writing. The Massachusetts statesman commented that if she "had attended her household affairs, and such things as belong to women, and not gone out of her way and calling to meddle in such things as are proper for men, whose minds are stronger, etc. she had kept her wits, and might have improved them usefully and honorably in the place God had set her." Earlier he had denounced Anne Hutchinson as "a woman of a haughty and fierce carriage, of a nimble wit and active spirit, and a very voluble tongue, more bold than a man, though in understanding and judgement, inferiour to many women." [16]

Winthrop echoed the expectations of the male-dominated society in which he lived, in much the same way as the New England propagandist William Wood and Anne Hutchinson's ministerial accusers did. In 1634 Wood praised the Indian women's "mild carriage and obedience to their husbands," despite his realization that Indian men were guilty of "churlishness and inhumane behavior" toward their wives. Reverend John Cotton arrived in Boston in 1633 and soon requested that women desiring church membership be examined in private since a public confession was "against the apostle's rule and not fit for a women's modesty." At a public lecture less than a year later Cotton explained that the apostle directed women to wear veils in church only when "the custom of the place" considered veils "a sign of the women's subjection." Cambridge minister Thomas Shepard, one of Anne Hutchinson's most severe critics, commended his own wife for her "incomparable meekness of spirit, toward myself especially," while Hugh Peter, a Salem pastor and another of Ms. Hutchinson's accusers, urged his daughter to respect her feminine meekness as "Womans Ornament." [17]

The female role definition that the Massachusetts ministers and magistrates perpetuated severely limited the assertiveness, the accomplishment, the independence, and the intellectual activity of Puritan women. Bay Colony women who might resent such a role definition before 1636 had no ideological rationale around which they could organize the expression of their frustration—whatever their consciousness of the causes of that frustration. With the marked increase of Antinomian sentiment in Boston and Anne Hutchinson's powerful example of resistance, the distressed females were able—as this article will attempt to demonstrate—to channel their frustration into a viable theological form and to rebel openly against the perpetuators of the spiritual and secular status quo. Paradoxically enough, the values that Antinomians embraced minimized the importance of individual action, for they believed that salvation could be demonstrated only by the individual feeling God's grace within.

The process of salvation and the role of the individual in that process was, for the Puritan divines, a matter less well defined. The question of the relative importance of good works (i.e., individual effort) and grace (i.e., God's effort) in preparing man for salvation and concerned English Puritans from their earliest origins, and clergymen of old and New England attempted to walk a broad, although unsure, middle ground between the extremes of Antinomianism and Arminianism. But in 1636 Anne Hutchinson's former mentor and the new teacher of the Boston church, John Cotton, disrupted the fragile theological balance and led the young colony into controversy when he "warned his listeners away from the specious comfort of preparation and re-emphasized the covenant of grace as something in which God acted alone and unassisted." [18] Cotton further explained that a person could become conscious of the dwelling of the Holy Spirit within his soul and directed the Boston congregation "not to be afraid of the word *Revelation.*" [19] The church elders, fearing that Cotton's "Revelation" might be dangerously construed to invalidate biblical law, requested a clarification of his position.

While the elders debated with Cotton the religious issues arising out of his pronouncements, members of Cotton's congregation responded more practically and enthusiastically to the notion of personal revelation by ardently soliciting converts to an emerging, loosely-knit ideology which the divines called pejoratively Antinomianism, Opinionism, or Familism.[20] According to Thomas Weld, fledgling Antinomians visited new migrants to Boston, "especially, men of note, worth, and activity, fit instruments to advance their designe." Antinomian principles were defended at military trainings, in town meetings, and before the court judges. Winthrop charged the Opinionists with causing great disturbance in the church, the state, and the family, and wailed, "All things are turned upside down among us." [21]

The individual hungry for power could, as long as he perceived his deep inner feeling of God's grace to be authentic, use that feeling to consecrate his personal rebellion against the contemporary authorities. Some Boston merchants used it to attack the accretion of political power in the hands of a rural-dominated General Court based on land instead of capital. Some "ignorant and unlettered" men used it to express contempt for the arrogance of "black-coates that have been at the Ninneversity." [22] Some women, as we will see, used it to castigate the authority of the magistrates as guardians of the state, the ministers as guardians of the church, and their husbands as guardians of the home. As the most outspoken of these women, Anne Hutchinson diffused her opinions among all social classes by means of contacts made in the course of her profession of midwifery and in the biweekly teaching sessions she held at her home. Weld believed that Ms. Hutchinson's lectures were responsible for distributing "the venome of these [Antinomian] opinions into the very veines and vitalls of the People in the Country." [23]

Many women identified with Ms. Hutchinson's rebellious intellectual stance and her aggressive spirit. Edward Johnson wrote that "the weaker Sex" set her up as "a Priest" and "thronged" after her. John Underhill reported he daily heard a "clamor" that "New England men usurp over their wives, and keep them in servile subjection." Winthrop blamed Anne for causing "divisions between husband and wife . . . till the weaker give place to the stronger, otherwise it turnes to open contention," and Weld charged the Antinomians with using the yielding, flexible, and tender women as "an Eve, to catch their husbands also." One anonymous English pamphleteer found in Antinomianism a movement "somewhat like the Trojan horse for rarity" because "it was covered with womens aprons, and bolstered out with the judgement and deep discerning of the godly and reverent." [24]

From late 1636 through early 1637 female resistance in the Boston church reached its highest pitch. At one point, when pastor John Wilson rose to preach, Ms. Hutchinson left the congregation and many women followed her out of the meetinghouse. These women "pretended many excuses for their going out," an action which made it impossible for the authorities to convict them of contempt for Wilson. Other rebels did, however, challenge Wilson's words as he spoke them, causing Weld to comment, "Now the faithfull Ministers of Christ must have dung cast on their faces, and be no better than Legall Preachers, Baals Priests, Popish Factors, Scribes, Pharisees, and Opposers of Christ himselfe." [25]

Included among these church rebels were two particularly active women, Jane (Mrs. Richard) Hawkins and milliner William Dyer's wife Mary, both of whom Winthrop found obnoxious. The governor considered the youthful Ms. Dyer to be "of a very proud spirit," "much addicted to revelations," and "notoriously infected with Ms. Hutchinson's errors." Ms. Dyer weathered Winthrop's wrath and followed Anne to Rhode Island, but her "addictions" were not without serious consequence. Twenty-two years later she would return to Boston and be hanged as a Quaker.[26] The other of Hutchinson's close female associates, Jane Hawkins, dispensed fertility potions to barren women and occasionally fell into a trance-like state in which she spoke Latin. Winthrop therefore denounced her as "notorious for familiarity with the devill," and the General Court, sharing his apprehension, on March 12, 1638, forbade her to question "matters of religion" or "to meddle" in "surgery, or phisick, drinks, plaisters, or oyles." Ms. Hawkins apparently disobeyed this order, for three years later the Court banished her from the colony under the penalty of a severe whipping or such other punishment as the judges thought fit.[27]

Other women, both rich and poor, involved themselves in the Antinomian struggle. William Coddington's spouse, like her merchant husband, was "taken with the familistical opinions." [28] Mary Dummer, the wife of wealthy landowner and Assistant Richard Dummer, convinced her husband to move from Newbury to Boston so that she might be closer to Ms. Hutchinson.[29] Mary Oliver, a poor Salem calenderer's wife, reportedly exceeded Anne "for ability of speech, and appearance of zeal and devotion" and, according to Winthrop, might "have done hurt, but that she was poor and had little acquaintance [with theology]." Ms. Oliver held the "dangerous" opinions that the church was managed by the "heads of the people, both magistrates and ministers, met together," instead of the people themselves, and that anyone professing faith in Christ ought to be admitted to the church and the sacraments. Between 1638 and 1650 she appeared before the magistrates six times for remarks contemptuous of ministerial and magisterial authority and experienced the stocks, the lash, the placement of a cleft stick on her tongue, and imprisonment. One of the Salem magistrates became so frustrated with Ms. Oliver's refusal to respect his authority that he seized her and put her in the stocks without a trial. She sued him for false arrest and collected a minimal ten shillings in damages. Her victory was short-lived, however, and before she left Massachusetts in 1650 she had managed to secure herself some reputation as a witch.[30]

Mary Oliver and the other female rebels could easily identify with the Antinomian ideology because its theological emphasis on the inability of the individual to achieve salvation echoed the inability of women to achieve recognition on a sociopolitical level. As the woman realized that she could receive wealth, power, and status only through the man, her father or her husband, so the Antinomian realized that he or she could receive grace only through God's beneficence. Thus, women could have found it appealing that in Antinomianism *both* men and women were relegated vis-à-vis God to the status that women occupied in Puritan society vis-à-vis men, that is, to the status of malleable inferiors in the hands of a higher being. All power, then, emanated from God, raw and pure, respecting no sex, rather than from male authority figures striving to interpret the Divine Word. Fortified by a consciousness of the Holy Spirit's inward dwelling, the Antinomians could rest secure and self-confident in the belief that they were mystic participants in the transcendent power of the Almighty, a power far beyond anything mere magistrates and ministers might muster. Antinomianism could not secure for women such practical earthly powers as sizable estates, professional success, and participation in the church and civil government, but it provided compensation by reducing the significance of these powers for the men. Viewed from this perspective, Antinomianism extended the feminine experience of humility to both sexes, which in turn paradoxically created the possibility of feminine pride, as Anne Hutchinson's dynamic example in her examinations and trials amply demonstrated.

Anne Hutchinson's example caused the divines much frustration. They were chagrined to find that she was not content simply to repeat to the "Simple Weomen" [31] the sermons of John Wilson, but that she also chose to interpret and even question the content of those sermons. When she charged that the Bay Colony ministers did not teach a covenant of grace as "clearly" as Cotton and her brother-in-law, John Wheelwright, she was summoned in 1636 to appear before a convocation of the clergy. At this convocation and in succeeding examinations, the ministers found particularly galling her implicit assertion that she had the intellectual ability necessary to judge the truth of their theology. Such an assertion threatened their self-image as the intellectual leaders of the community and the spokesmen for a male-dominated society. The ministers and magistrates therefore sharply criticized Anne for not fulfilling her ordained womanly role. In September 1637 a synod of elders resolved that women might meet "to pray and edify one another," but when one woman "in a prophetical way" resolved questions of doctrine and expounded Scripture, then the meeting was "disorderly." At Anne's examination on November 7 and 8, Winthrop began the interrogation by charging that she criticized the ministers and maintained a "meeting and an assembly in your house that hath been condemned by the general assembly as a thing not tolerable nor comely in the sight of God nor fitting for your sex." Later in the interrogation, Winthrop accused her of disobeying her "parents," the

magistrates, in violation of the Fifth Commandment, and pater-
nalistically told her, "We do not mean to discourse with those of your
sex." Hugh Peter also indicated that he felt Anne was not fulfilling the
properly submissive, nonintellectual feminine role. He ridiculed her
choice of a female preacher of the Isle of Ely as a model for her own
behavior and told her to consider "that you have stept out of you
place, *you have rather bine a Husband than a Wife and a preacher than
a Hearer; and a Magistrate than a Subject.*" [32]

When attacked for behavior inappropriate to her sex, Ms. Hutchinson did not hesitate to demonstrate that she was the intellectual equal
of her accusers. She tried to trap Winthrop when he charged her with
dishonoring her "parents": "But put the case Sir that I do fear the
Lord and my parents, may not I entertain them that fear the Lord
because my parents will not give me leave?" To provide a biblical
justification for her teaching activities, she cited Titus's rule (2:3-4)
"that the elder women should instruct the younger." Winthrop ordered
her to take that rule "in the sense that elder women must instruct the
younger about their business, and to love their husbands." But Anne
disagreed with this interpretation, saying, "I do not conceive but that it
is meant for some publick times." Winthrop rejoined, "We must . . .
restrain you from maintaining this course," and she qualified, "If you
have a rule for it from God's word you may." Her resistance infuri-
ated the governor, who exclaimed, "We are your judges, and not you
ours." When Winthrop tried to lure her into admitting that she taught
men, in violation of Paul's proscription, Anne replied that she
throught herself justified in teaching a man who asked her for instruction, and added sarcastically, "Do you think it not lawful for me to
teach women and why do you call me to teach the court?" [33]

Anne soon realized that sarcastic remarks would not persuade the
court of the legitimacy of her theological claims. Alternatively, therefore, she affected a kind of modesty to cozen the authorities at the
same time that she expressed a kind of primitive feminism through
double-entendre statements and attacked the legitimacy of Paul's idea
of the nonspeaking, nonintellectual female churchmember. When the
Court charged her with "prophesying," Anne responded, "The Men of
Berea are commended for examining *Pauls* Doctrine; wee do no more
[in our meetings] but read the notes of our teachers Sermons, and then
reason of them by searching the Scriptures." [34] Such a statement was
on one level an "innocent" plea to the divines that the women were
only following biblical prescription. On another level it was an attack
on the ministers for presuming to have the final word on biblical
interpretation. On yet a third level, since she focused on "Pauls Doc-

trine" and reminded men that they should take another look at that teaching, her statement was a suggestion that ministerial attitudes toward women ought to be reexamined.

At another point Anne responded to Winthrop's criticism with a similar statement having meaning on three levels. The governor had accused her of traducing the ministers and magistrates and, when summoned to answer this charge, of saying that "the fear of man was a snare and therefore she would not be affeared of them." She replied, "They say I said the fear of man is a snare, why should I be afraid. When I came unto them, they urging many things unto me and I being backward to answer at first, at length this scripture came into my mind 29th Prov. 15. The fear of man bringeth a snare, but who putteth his trust in the Lord shall be safe." [35] Once again, her response was phrased as an "innocent" plea to God to assuage her fears, while at the same time it implied that God was on her side in opposition to the ministers and magistrates. Her statement also told women that if they trusted in God they need not fear men, for such fear trapped them into being "backward" about reacting in situations of confrontation with men.

Anne, although aware of the "backwardness" of women as a group, did not look to intensified group activity as a remedy for woman's downtrodden status. Her feminism consisted essentially of the subjective recognition of her own strength and gifts and the apparent belief that other women could come to the same recognition. A strong, heroic example of female self-assertiveness was necessary to the development of this recognition of one's own personal strength. Anne chose the woman preacher of the Isle of Ely as her particular heroic model; she did, Hugh Peter chided, "exceedingly magnifie" that woman "to be a Womane of 1000 hardly any like to her." Anne could thus dissociate herself from the "divers worthy and godly Weomen" of Massachusetts and confidently deride them as being no better than "soe many Jewes," unconverted by the light of Christ.[36] Other Bay Colony women who wished to reach beyond the conventional, stereotypic behavior of "worthy and godly Weomen" attached themselves to the emphatic example of Anne and to God's ultimate power in order to resist the constraints which they felt as Puritan women.

Fearful that Ms. Hutchinson's example might be imitated by other women, the divines wished to catch her in a major theological error and subject her to public punishment. Their efforts were not immediately successful. Throughout her 1637 examination Anne managed to parry the verbal thrusts of the ministers and magistrates by replying to their many questions with questions of her own, forcing them to justify

their positions from the Bible, pointing out their logical inconsistencies, and using innuendo to cast aspersions upon their authoritaria-
nism. With crucial assistance from a sympathetic John Cotton, she left
the ministers with no charge to pin upon her. She was winning the
debate when, in an apparently incautious moment, she gave the authorities the kind of declaration for which they had been hoping.
Raising herself to the position of judge over her accusers, she asserted,
"I know that for this you goe about to doe to me, God will ruine you
and your posterity, and this whole State." Asked how she knew this,
she explained, "By an immediate revelation." [37] With this statement
Anne proved her heresy to the ministers and they then took steps to
expose her in excommunication proceedings conducted before the
Boston church. The divines hoped to expel a heretic from their midst,
to reestablish support for the Puritan way, to prevent unrest in the
state and the family, and to shore up their own anxious egos in the
process.

The predisposition of the ministers to defame Ms. Hutchinson before the congregation caused them to ignore what she was actually
saying in her excommunication trial. Although she did describe a relationship with Christ closer than anything Cotton had envisioned, she
did not believe that she had experienced Christ's Second Coming in
her own life. Such a claim would have denied the resurrection of the
body at the Last Judgment and would have clearly stamped her as a
Familist.[38] Ms. Hutchinson's accusers, ignoring Thomas Leverett's re-
minder that she had expressed belief in the resurrection, argued that if
the resurrection did not exist, biblical law would have no validity nor
the marriage covenant any legal or utilitarian value. The result would
be a kind of world no Puritan could tolerate, a world where the basest
desires would be fulfilled and "foule, groce, filthye and abominable"
sexual promiscuity would be rampant. Cotton, smarting from a psychological slap Anne had given him earlier in the excommunication
proceedings [39] and in danger of losing the respect of the other ministers, admonished her with the words "though I have not herd, nayther
do I thinke, you have bine unfaythfull to your Husband in his Marriage Covenant, *yet that will follow upon it.*" By referring to "his"
marriage covenant Cotton did not even accord Anne equal participation in the making of that covenant. The Boston teacher concluded his
admonition with a criticism of Anne's pride: *"I have often feared the
highth of your Spirit and being puft up with your owne parts."* [40]

Both the introduction of the sexual issue into the trial and Cotton's
denunciation of Ms. Hutchinson must have had the effect of curbing
dissent from the congregation. Few Puritans would want to defend

Anne in public when such a defense could be construed as supporting promiscuity. Since Cotton had earlier been sympathetic to the Antinomian cause and had tried to save Anne at her 1637 examination, his vigorous condemnation of her must have confused her following. Cotton even went so far as to exempt the male Antinomians from any real blame for the controversy when he characterized Antinomianism as a women's delusion. He urged that women, like children, ought to be watched, reproved Hutchinson's sons for not controlling her theological ventures, and called those sons "Vipers ... [who] *Eate through the very Bowells of your Mother,* to her Ruine." Cotton warned the Boston women "to looke to your selves and to take heed that you reaceve nothinge for Truth which hath not the stamp of the Word of God [as interpreted by the ministers] ... for you see she [Anne] is but a Woman and *many unsound and dayngerous principles are held by her."* Thomas Shepard agreed that intellectual activity did not suit women and warned the congregation that Anne was likely "to seduce and draw away many, Espetially simple Weomen of her owne sex." [41]

The female churchmembers, who would have had good reason to resent the clergy's approach, could not legitimately object to the excommunication proceedings because of Paul's injunction against women speaking in church. Lacking a clearly-defined feminist consciousness and filled with "backward" fear, the women could not refuse to respect that injunction, even though, or perhaps because, Anne had been presented to the congregation as the epitome of despicableness, as a woman of simple intellect, and as a liar, puffed up with pride and verging on sexual promiscuity. This caricature of Anne did not, however, prevent five men, including her brother-in-law Richard Scott and Mary Oliver's husband Thomas, from objecting to her admonition and excommunication. Cotton refused to consider the points these men raised and dismissed their objections as rising out of their own self-interest or their natural affection for Anne. [42]

In Anne's excommunication proceedings the ministers demonstrated that they had found the means necessary to deal effectively with this rebellious woman and a somewhat hostile congregation. At her examination and her excommunication trial Anne attempted to place the ministers on the defensive by questioning them and forcing them to justify their positions while she explained little. She achieved some success in the 1637 trial, but before her fellow churchmembers she found it difficult to undercut the misrepresentation of her beliefs and the attack on her character. Perhaps fearing the banishment which had been so quickly imposed on her associate, John Wheelwright, she recanted, but even in her recantation she would not totally compromise her position. She expressed sorrow for her errors of expression but admitted no errors in judgment and assumed no appearance of humiliation. When Wilson commanded her *"as a Leper to withdraw your selfe out of the Congregation,"* Anne rose, walked to the meetinghouse door, accepted Mary Dyer's offered hand, and turned to impugn her accusers' power: "The Lord judgeth not as man judgeth, better to be cast out of the Church then to deny Christ." [43]

During the year and a half following Ms. Hutchinson's excommunication, the Massachusetts ministers and magistrates prosecuted several other female rebels. In April 1638 the Boston church cast out Judith Smith, the maidservant of Anne's brother-in-law, Edward Hutchinson, for her "obstinate persisting" in "sundry Errors." On October 10 of the same year the Assistants ordered Katherine Finch to be whipped for "speaking against the magistrates, against the Churches, and against the Elders." Less than a year later Ms. Finch again appeared before the Assistants, this time for not carrying herself "dutifully to her husband," and was released upon promise of reformation. In September 1639 the Boston church excommunicated Phillip(a?) Hammond "as a slanderer and revyler both of the Church and Common Weale." Ms. Hammond, after her husband's death, had resumed her maiden name, operated a business in Boston, and argued in her shop and at public meetings "that Mrs. Hutchinson neyther deserved the Censure which was putt upon her in the Church, nor in the Common Weale." The Boston church also excommunicated two other women for partially imitating Anne Hutchinson's example: Sarah Keayne was found guilty in 1646 of "irregular prophesying in mixed assemblies," and Joan Hogg nine years later was punished "for her disorderly singing and her idleness, and for saying she is commanded of Christ so to do." [44]

The Salem authorities followed Boston's example in dealing with overly assertive women. In late 1638 the Salem church excommunicated four of Roger Williams's former followers: Jane (Mrs. Joshua) Verin, Mary Oliver, servant Margery Holliman, and widow Margery Reeves. These women had consistently refused to worship with the congregation, and the latter two had denied that the churches of the Bay Colony were true churches.[45] Yet another woman, Dorothy Talby, who was subject to a different kind of frustration, troubled the Essex County magistrates by mimicking Anne Hutchinson's proclamation of "immediate revelation" to justify her personal rebellion. In October 1637 the county court ordered her chained to a post "for frequent laying hands on her husband to the danger of his life, and contemning the authority of the court," and later ordered her whipped for "misdemeanors against her husband." Later, according to Winthrop, she claimed a "revelation from heaven" instructing her to kill her husband and children and then broke the neck of her three-year-old daughter, Difficult. At her execution on December 6, 1638, Ms. Talby continued her defiance by refusing to keep her face covered and expressing a desire to be beheaded, as "it was less painful and less shameful." [46]

Dorothy Talby was one of an increasing number of women to appear before the General Court and the Court of Assistants, an increase which seemed to reflect both a greater rebelliousness in women and a hardening of magisterial attitudes. In the first five years of Puritan settlement only 1.7 percent of the persons convicted of criminal offenses by the Deputies and the Assistants were women. During and after the years of the Antinomian controversy the percentage of female offenders was significantly higher—6.7 percent from 1635 to 1639 and 9.4 percent from 1640 to 1644. If Charles E. Banks's enumeration of 3,505 passengers from ship lists is representative of the more than 20,000 persons who came to Massachusetts between 1630 and 1639, it can be assumed that the number of women did not increase proportionately to the number of men. Banks's ship lists reveal that 829 males and 542 females came to Massachusetts between 1630 and 1634, a number which increased in the next five years to 1,279 males and 855 females. The percentage of females increased only .6 percent, from 39.5 percent between 1630 and 1634 to 40.1 percent between 1635 and 1639.[47] These comparative figures suggest that by 1640 the magistrates could no longer afford to dismiss with verbal chastisement females found guilty of drunkenness, cursing, or premarital fornication.[48]

The magistrates not only used the threat of a humiliating courtroom appearance and possible punishment to keep female rebels quiet but also levied very stringent penalties on male Antinomian offenders. Anne Hutchinson's son-in-law William Collins was sentenced to pay a £100 fine for charging the Massachusetts churches and ministers with being anti-Christian and calling the king of England the king of Babylon. Anne's son Francis, who had accompanied Collins to Boston in 1641, objected to the popular rumor that he would not sit at the same table with his excommunicated mother and feeling that the Boston church was responsible, called that church "a strumpet." The church excommunicated Francis and the Assistants fined him £40, but neither he nor Collins would pay the stipulated amounts (even when those fines were reduced to £40 and £20) and therefore spent some time in jail.[49]

Besides prosecuting Antinomian sympathizers in church and court, the Massachusetts ministers and magistrates carefully watched new ministers, lest they deliver "some points savoring of familism," [50] and justified the emergent orthodox position in their sermons and publications. Of these publications, which were directed at audiences both in New and old England, John Cotton's *Singing of Psalmes a Gospel-Ordinance* most significantly asserted the traditional feminine role-response. The Boston teacher, apparently with Ms. Hutchinson in mind, told his readers that "the woman is more subject to error than a man" and continued, "It is not permitted to a woman to speak in the Church by way of propounding questions though under pretence of desire to learn for her own satisfaction; but rather it is required she should ask her husband at home. For under pretence of questioning for learning sake, she might so propound her question as to teach her teachers; or if not so, yet to open a door to some of her own weak and erroneous apprehensions, or at least soon exceed the bounds of womanly modesty." Cotton explained that a woman could speak in church only when she wished to confess a sin or to participate in singing hymns.[51]

Other Bay Colony leaders popularized the idea that the intellectual woman was influenced by Satan and was therefore unable to perform the necessary functions of womanhood. Weld described Mary Dyer's abortive birth as "a woman child, a fish, a beast, and a fowle, all woven together in one, and without an head," and wrote of Anne Hutchinson's probable hydatidiform mole as "30. monstrous births . . . none at all of them (as farre as I could ever learne) of humane shape." [52] According to Winthrop's even more garish account of Mary Dyer's child, the stillborn baby had a face and ears growing upon the shoulders, a breast and back full of sharp prickles, female sex organs on the rear and buttocks in front, three clawed feet, no forehead, four horns above the eyes, and two great holes upon the back.[53] Wheelwright wrote from his new home in Exeter to attack the governor's farfetched description of these births. That clergyman called Winthrop's monsters "a monstrous conception of his brain, a spurious issue of his intellect," and told that governor that he should know better "*then to delude the world with untruths.* [For] I question not his learning, etc. but I admire his certainty or rather impudence: did the man obtestricate [obstetricate]?" [54]

Despite Wheelwright's effort, Weld's opinion that "as she had vented mishapen opinions, so she must bring forth deformed monsters" impressed the people of the Bay Colony, a people who believed that catastrophic occurrences were evidences of God's displeasure. Some Massachusetts residents viewed the births as the products of both the women's "mishapen opinions" and their supposed promiscuity. Edward Johnson and Roger Clap lamented the "phantasticall madnesse" of those who would hold "silly women laden with their lusts" in higher esteem than "those honoured of Christ, indued with power and authority from him to Preach." A rumor reached England that Henry Vane had crossed the Atlantic in 1637 with Ms. Dyer and Ms. Hutchinson and had "debauched both, and both were delivered of monsters."⁵⁵ It was also widely rumored that three of the Antinomian women, Anne Hutchinson, Jane Hawkins, and Mary Oliver, had sold their souls to Satan and become witches. Anne in particular "gave cause of suspicion of witchcraft" after she easily converted to Antinomianism one new male arrival in Rhode Island.⁵⁶

The promotion of the belief that the Antinomian female leaders were witches filled with aberrant lusts and unable to live as proper women was accompanied by an attack on the masculinity of some of the Antinomian men. Although Anne's husband, William, had been a prosperous landowner, a merchant, a deputy to the General Court, and a Boston selectman, Winthrop described him as a "man of very mild temper and weak parts, and wholly guided by his wife." Clap also felt that William Hutchinson and the other Antinomian men were deficient in intellect and judgment. He expressed surprise that any of the men in the movement had "strong parts."⁵⁷

While Massachusetts gossip focused on disordered Antinomian births, lusty Antinomian women, and weak Antinomian men, Winthrop and Cotton tried to convince their English and New England readers that public opinion had been solidly behind Ms. Hutchinson's excommunication. Winthrop contended that "diverse women" objected to this rebel's example and would have borne witness against her "if their modesty had not restrained them." Cotton supported the governor's claim by construing the relative silence at Anne's church trial to mean that the "whole body of the Church (except her own son) consented with one accord, to the publick censure of her, by admonition first, and excommunication after." By asserting this falsehood and ignoring Leverett's admission that many churchmembers wished to stay Anne's excommunication, Cotton made it appear that any person who complained about her censure was contradicting the near-unanimous opinion of the congregation.⁵⁸

The effort to discredit the Antinomians and Antinomian sentiment in the Bay Colony was quite successful. By the late 1640s Antinomianism, in a practical sense, was no longer threatening; the ministers and magistrates had managed to preserve a theological system they found congenial. "*Sanctification* came to be in some Request again; and there were *Notes* and *Marks* given of a good Estate."⁵⁹ The position of Massachusetts women within the religious system remained essentially unchanged, while in Rhode Island and nearby Providence Plantations the status of women was somewhat improved. In Providence and Portsmouth the men listened to the wishes of the women and protected the "liberty" of women to teach, preach, and attend services of their choosing. When Joshua Verin, one of the original settlers at Providence, restrained his wife Jane from attending religious services at Roger Williams's home, a town meeting considered the matter. John Greene argued before the townsmen that if men were allowed to restrain their wives, "all the women in the country would cry out." William Arnold rejoined that God had ordered the wife to be subject to her husband and that such a commandment should not be broken merely to please women. According to Winthrop, the townsmen "would have censured Verin, [but] Arnold told them, that it was against their own order, for Verin did that he did out of conscience; and their order was, that no man should be censured for his conscience." Winthrop neglected to record that the town meeting did disfranchise Verin until he declared that he would not restrain his wife's "libertie of conscience," nor did Winthrop mention that Verin had "trodden" his wife "under foot tyrannically and brutishly," endangering her life. After his censure, Verin returned to Salem, and Roger Williams urged Winthrop to prevent this "boisterous and desperate" young man from hauling "his wife with ropes to Salem, where she must needs be troubled and troublesome." [60]

After Anne Hutchinson's arrival and throughout the remainder of the century, women taught and preached in public in Rhode Island. Johnson wrote that in 1638 "there were some of the female sexe who (deeming the Apostle Paul to be too strict in not permitting a room [woman] to preach in the publique Congregation) taught notwithstanding ... having their call to this office from an ardent desire of being famous." According to Johnson, Anne Hutchinson, "the grand Mistresse of them all, ... ordinarily prated every Sabbath day, till others, who thirsted after honour in the same way with her selfe, drew away her Auditors." [61] This prating was more purposive than Johnson might have been willing to admit, for Anne soon involved herself in a new controversy, this one springing out of the resentment of many of the poorer inhabitants of the settlement toward Judge (Governor) William Coddington's autocratic rule, his land allotment policy, and his efforts to establish a church resembling closely the Massachusetts example.[62] Allying herself with Samuel Gorton, a religious freethinker and a defender of justice for all men, "rich or poore, ignorant or learned," Anne began to attack the legitimacy of *any* magistracy. Together, she and Gorton managed to foment the rebellion of April 28, 1639, in which the Portsmouth inhabitants formed a new body politic, ejected Coddington from power, and chose William Hutchinson to replace him. William, however, also did not believe in magistracy and soon refused to occupy the office of judge. Coddington, who had fled south with his followers to found Newport, then claimed the judgeship by default, was recognized by the Massachusetts authorities, and proceeded to administer the affairs of Rhode Island.[63] Gorton and at least eleven others responded to Coddington's resumption of power by plotting armed rebellion against him and were ultimately banished from the colony. Anne broke with the Gortonists over that issue, and she and William joined the Newport settlement.[64]

William Hutchinson died at Newport in 1640, and for much of that year Anne was silent. By 1641, however, she had come out of mourning and, according to Winthrop, turned anabaptist. She and "divers" others supported passive resistance to authority, "denied all magistracy among Christians, and maintained that there were no churches since those founded by the apostles and evangelists, nor could any be." [65] Such opinions achieved enough popularity in Rhode Island to contribute to the dissolution of the church at Newport,[66] although not enough to remove Coddington from power. Disgruntled and fearing that Massachusetts would seize the Rhode Island settlements, Anne sought refuge in the colony of New Netherland in 1642, but her stay there was not long. In August 1643 she, William Collins, two of her sons, and three of her daughters were killed by Indians who had quarreled with her Dutch neighbors.[67]

The Massachusetts clergy rejoiced. Not only had God destroyed the "American Jesabel," [68] but the Lord's vengeance had descended upon her sons and daughters, the poisoned seed. Peter Bulkeley spoke for all the Massachusetts ministers when he concluded, "Let her damned heresies shee fell into ... and the just vengeance of God, by which shee perished, terrifie all her seduced followers from having any more to doe with her leaven." [69] But her "seduced followers" were horrified only at the reaction of the Puritan clergy. Anne's sister, Katherine Scott, commented that the Bay Colony authorities "are drunke with the blod of the saints," and Anne's former Portsmouth neighbor, Randall Holden, blamed those same authorities for forcing Anne first to Rhode Island and ultimately to her death. He reminded them of her partially successful struggle against authority: "you know ... your great and terrible word magistrate is no more in its original, that masterly or masterless which hath no great lustre in our ordinary acceptation." [70]

Impervious to such protests, the Bay Colony divines considered Anne Hutchinson's death to be the symbolic death of Antinomianism. To these divines she had been the incarnation of the Antinomian evil, and their accounts of the Antinomian stress in Boston accented *her* beliefs, *her* activities, and *her* rebelliousness. The ministers were not as concerned with the important roles played by Coddington, Wheelwright, Vane, and the other male Antinomian leaders because none of these men threatened the power and status structure of society in the concrete way that Anne Hutchinson did. Anne was clearly not, as the ministers might have wished, a submissive quiet dove, content to labor simply in the kitchen and the childbed. She was witty, aggressive, and intellectual. She had no qualms about castigating in public the men who occupied the most authoritative positions. She claimed the right to define rational, theological matters for herself and by her example spurred other women to express a similar demand. Far from bewildered, she thwarted her accusers with her intellectual ability. Perceiving her as a threat to the family, the state, the religion, and the status hierarchy, the Puritan authorities directed their antagonism against Anne's character and her sex. By doing so, they managed to salve the psychological wounds inflicted by this woman who trod so sharply upon their male status and their ministerial and magisterial authority. Their method had a practical aspect as well; it helped restore respect for the ministry and curb potential dissent.

Anne's ability to attract large numbers of women as supporters caused the ministers and magistrates some worry but little surprise, since they believed that women were easily deluded. They chided Anne for choosing a female preacher as a role model and refused to attribute any merit to her at times subtle, at times caustic intellectual ability. They could see only the work of Satan in Anne's aggressiveness and not the more human desire for equal opportunity and treatment which this rebel never hesitated to assert by example in the intellectual skirmishes she had with her accusers throughout her trials. The double oppression of life in a male-dominated society, combined with biological bondage to her own amazing fertility, could not destroy her self-respect. Because of the theologically based society in which she lived, it was easy for her to ally herself with God and to express her self-confidence in religious debates with the leading intellectual authorities. Neither Anne's rebellion nor the rebellion of her female followers was directed self-consciously against their collective female situation or toward its improvement. Specific feminist campaigns for the franchise, divorce reform, female property ownership after marriage, and the like would be developments of a much later era. For

Anne Hutchinson and her female associates Antinomianism was simply an ideology through which the resentments they intuitively felt could be focused and actively expressed.

NOTES

1. John A. Albro, ed., *The Works of Thomas Shepard,* I (New York, 1967 [orig. publ. n.p., 1853]), cxvi–cxvii.
2. Darrett B. Rutman, *Winthrop's Boston: Portrait of a Puritan Town, 1630–1649* (Chapel Hill, N.C., 1965), p. 121.
3. John Stetson Barry, *The History of Massachusetts. The Colonial Period* (Boston, 1855), p. 261.
4. Andrew Sinclair, *The Emancipation of the American Woman* (New York, 1966), p.23.
5. Edith Curtis, *Anne Hutchinson: A Biography* (Cambridge, Mass., 1930), pp. 72–73.
6. Emery Battis, *Saints and Sectaries: Anne Hutchinson and the Antinomian Controversy in the Massachusetts Bay Colony* (Chapel Hill, N.C., 1962), pp. 9, 50–56, 90, admits that Ms. Hutchinson had a "prodigious memory and keen mind," but he believes that she was "wracked with unbearable doubt" as a result of her inability to find a male "mental director." Her husband could not fulfill this need, for he "seems to have lacked the power to provide adequate support and direction for his wife." Ms. Hutchinson's rebellion, according to Battis, grew out of this need for male guidance and was accentuated by the fact that she was experiencing menopause and felt that "her own inadequacy was at least in part responsible" for the death of two of her children. Of these many reasons for Ms. Hutchinson's restlessness, Battis substantiates only his conclusion that she was undergoing menopause. His argument is weakened, however, by anthropological research which ties the psychological distress of menopause to the loss of self-esteem that middle-aged women experience in societies where their status deteriorates at menopause. See Joan Solomon, "Menopause: A Rite of Passage," *Ms.* I (Dec. 1972): 18. Puritan New England was clearly not such a society, for elderly women could serve as deaconesses and, since they were free from the materialistic proclivities of youth, could furnish venerable examples for younger women. See Benjamin Colman, *The Duty and Honour of Aged Women. A Sermon on the Death of Madam Abigail Foster* (Boston, 1711), pp. 11–30.
7. Peter Oliver, *The Puritan Commonwealth. An Historical Review of the Puritan Government in Massachusetts in its Civil and Ecclesiastical Relations* . . . (Boston, 1856), p. 181.
8. Anne Hutchinson and the Antinomians have been treated sympathetically in Charles Francis Adams, *Three Episodes of Massachusetts History* (Boston, 1892); Brooks Adams, *The Emancipation of Massachusetts* (Boston, 1887); Winnifred King Rugg, *Unafraid: A Life of Anne Hutchinson* (Boston, 1930); Theda Kenyon, *Scarlet Anne* (New York, 1939); Vernon Louis Parrington, *Main Currents in American Thought: The Colonial Mind* (New York, 1927); Eleanor Flexner, *Century*

of Struggle: The Woman's Rights Movement in the United States (Cambridge, Mass., 1959); Elisabeth Anthony Dexter, *Colonial Women of Affairs: A Study of Women in Business and the Professions before 1776* (Boston, 1924); Sinclair, *Emancipation of American Woman;* Rufus M. Jones, *The Quakers in the American Colonies* (New York, 1911); Curtis, *Anne Hutchinson;* Barry, *History of Massachusetts.* Critics of Anne and the Antinomians include Henry Martyn Dexter, *As to Roger Williams, and His "Banishment" from the Massachusetts Plantation; with a Few Further Words Concerning the Baptists, the Quakers, and Religious Liberty* (Boston, 1873); George E. Ellis, "Life of Anne Hutchinson with a Sketch of the Antinomian Controversy in Massachusetts," in *The Library of American Biography,* ed. Jared Sparks, 2d Ser., VI (Boston, 1849); John Gorham Palfrey, *A Compendious History of the First Century of New England* . . . (Boston, 1872); Thomas Jefferson Wertenbaker, *The First Americans 1607–1690* (New York, 1927); Oliver, *Puritan Commonwealth;* Rutman, *Winthrop's Boston.* More balanced treatments are Edmund S. Morgan, *The Puritan Dilemma: The Story of John Winthrop* (Boston, 1958), and Battis, *Saints and Sectaries.*

9. Battis, *Saints and Sectaries,* pp. 249–307. The three women whom Battis lists as Antinomians are Anne Hutchinson, Jane Hawkins, and Mary Dyer.

10. "The Social History of Early New England," *American Quarterly* 24 (1972): 677.

11. "Footsteps of Anne Hutchinson: The Context of *The Scarlet Letter,*" *ELH* 39 (1972): 459–94.

12. Dunn, "Social History of Early New England," *American Quarterly* 24 (1972): 677.

13. Studies of early seventeenth-century English attitudes about women appear in Georgiana Hill, *Women in English Life from Mediaeval to Modern Times* (London, 1896); M. Phillips and W.S. Tomkinson, *English Women in Life and Letters* (London, 1926); Gamaliel Bradford, *Elizabethan Women* (Boston, 1936); Doris Mary Stenton, *The English Woman in History* (London, 1957).

14. I Tim. 2:11–12. St. Paul told the Corinthians: "Let your women keep silence in the churches; for it is not permitted unto them to speak; but they are commanded to be under obedience, as also saith the law. And if they will learn any thing, let them ask their husbands at home; for it is a shame for women to speak in the church" (I Cor. 14:34–35).

15. Margaret Winthrop to John Winthrop, 1624–1630, *The Winthrop Papers* (Boston, 1929–1944), I, 354–55; II, 165, 199; Lucy Downing to John Winthrop, 1636–1640, Massachusetts Historical Society, *Collections,* 5th Ser., I (Boston, 1871), 20, 25, 27; Elizabeth Winthrop to John Winthrop, ca. June 1636, *Winthrop Papers,* III, 267.

16. James Kendall Hosmer, ed., *Winthrop's Journal: "History of New England," 1630–1649,* Original Narratives of Early American History (New York, 1908), II, 225; John Winthrop, *A Short Story of the Rise, reign and ruine of the Antinomians, Familists and Libertines* in *The Antinomian Controversy, 1636–1638: A Documentary History,* ed. David D. Hall (Middletown, Conn., 1968), p. 263.

17. William Wood, *New Englands Prospect* . . . (London, 1634), pp. 121–22;

Hosmer, ed., *Winthrop's Journal*, I, 107, 120; Michael McGiffert, ed., *God's Plot: The Paradoxes of Puritan Piety, Being the Autobiography and Journal of Thomas Shepard* (Amherst, Mass., 1972), p. 70; Hugh Peter, *A Dying Father's Last Legacy to An Only Child: Or, Mr. Hugh Peter's Advice to His Daughter* . . . (Boston, 1717), p. 22.

18. Morgan, *Puritan Dilemma*, p. 137. McGiffert's introduction to Shepard's autobiography and journal contains a discussion of the Puritans' problems with assurance. See McGiffert, ed., *God's Plot*, pp. 1–32. Puritan attitudes toward the preparation process are treated comprehensively and perceptively in Norman Pettit, *The Heart Prepared: Grace and Conversion in Puritan Spiritual Life* (New Haven, Conn., 1966).

19. John Cotton, *A Treatise of the Covenant of Grace, as it is despensed to the Elect Seed, effectually unto Salvation* (London, 1671), p. 177. 'Cotton's subsequent debate with the other ministers appears in Hall, ed., *Antinomian Controversy*, pp. 24–151.

20. The Familists or Family of Love, a sect which originated in Holland about 1540 and spread to England, gained a largely undeserved reputation for practicing promiscuity. Antinomianism was associated in the Puritan mind with the licentious orgies that accompanied the enthusiasm of John Agricola in sixteenth-century Germany. Opinionism was a term often used for any theology that the divines disliked. James Hastings, ed., *Encyclopaedia of Religion and Ethics* (New York, 1908–1926), I, 581–82; V, 319; IX, 102.

21. Thomas Weld, "The Preface," to Winthrop, *Short Story* in Hall, ed., *Antinomian Controversy*, pp. 204, 208–09; Winthrop, *Short Story*, ibid., p. 253.

22. J. Franklin Jameson, ed., *Johnson's Wonder-Working Providence, 1628–1651*, Original Narratives of Early American History (New York, 1910), p. 127.

23. Weld, "Preface," to Winthrop, *Short Story*, in Hall, ed., *Antinomian Controversy*, p. 207.

24. Jameson, ed., *Johnson's Wonder-Working Providence*, p. 132; John Underhill, *Newes from America; or A New and Experimentall Discoverie of New England* . . . (London, 1638), reprinted in Mass. Hist. Soc., *Colls.*, 3d Ser., VI (Boston, 1837), 5; Winthrop, *Short Story*, in Hall, ed., *Antinomian Controversy*, 253; Weld, "Preface," to Winthrop, *Short Story*, ibid., pp. 205–06; *Good News from New England: with An exact Relation of the first planting that Countrey* (1648), reprinted in Mass. Hist. Soc., *Colls.*, 4th Ser., I (1852), 206.

25. John Cotton, *The Way of Congregational Churches Cleared*, in Hall, ed., *Antinomian Controversy*, p. 423, and Weld, "Preface," to Winthrop, *Short Story*, ibid., p. 209.

26. Hosmer, ed., *Winthrop's Journal*, I, 266; Winthrop, *Short Story*, in Hall, ed., *Antinomian Controversy*, p. 281; Horatio Rogers, "Mary Dyer Did Hang Like a Flag," in *The Quaker Reader*, ed. Jessamyn West (New York, 1962), pp. 168–75.

27. Jameson, ed., *Johnson's Wonder-Working Providence*, p. 132; Winthrop, *Short Story*, in Hall, ed., *Antinomian Controversy*, p. 281; Nathaniel B. Shurtleff, ed., *Records of the Governor and Company of the Massachusetts Bay in New England, 1628–1641* (Boston, 1853), I, 224, 329.

28. Hosmer, ed., *Winthrop's Journal*, I, 270.
29. "The Rev. John Eliot's Record of Church Members, Roxbury, Massachusetts," in *A Report of the Boston Commissioners, Containing the Roxbury Land and Church Records* (Boston, 1881), p. 77.
30. Hosmer, ed., *Winthrop's Journal*, I, 285-86; George Francis Dow, ed., *Records and Files of the Quarterly Courts of Essex County, Massachusetts, 1636-1656*, I (Salem, Mass., 1911), 12, 138, 180, 182-83, 186; John Noble, ed., *Records of the Court of Assistants of the Colony of the Massachusetts Bay, 1630-1644*, II (Boston, 1904), 80, hereafter cited as *Assistants Records*; Sidney Perley, *History of Salem, Massachusetts, 1638-1670*, II (Salem, Mass., 1926), 50; Thomas Hutchinson, *The Witchcraft Delusion of 1692* (Boston, 1870), p. 6.
31. "A Report of the Trial of Mrs. Anne Hutchinson before the Church in Boston," in Hall, ed., *Antinomian Controversy*, p. 365.
32. Hosmer, ed., *Winthrop's Journal*, I, 234; "The Examination of Mrs. Anne Hutchinson at the Court at Newtown," in Hall, ed., *Antinomian Controversy*, pp. 312-14, 318; "Trial of Anne Hutchinson before Boston church," ibid., pp. 380, 382-83.
33. "Examination of Mrs. Hutchinson at Newtown," in Hall, ed., *Antinomian Controversy*, pp. 313-16.
34. Winthrop, *Short Story*, ibid., p. 268.
35. "Examination of Mrs. Hutchinson at Newtown," ibid., p. 330.
36. "Trial of Anne Hutchinson before Boston church," ibid., p. 380. That Ms. Hutchinson chose a woman preacher as a model for her rebellious behavior, instead of the more popular "Spirit-mystic" and "apostle of Ely," William Sedgwick, indicates that Anne had some level of feminist self-awareness and suggests that she was not greatly in need of specifically male guidance. Cotton expressed the view that she was far from satisfied with his guidance. "Mistris *Hutchinson* seldome resorted to mee," he wrote, "and when she did come to me, it was seldome or never (that I can tell of) that she tarried long. I rather think, she was loath to resort much to me, or, to conferre long with me, lest she might seeme to learne somewhat from me." Cotton, *Congregational Churches Cleared*, ibid., p. 434. Cotton's testimony may not be completely accurate, as he was writing to wash the Antinomian stain off his own hands.

   Little is know about Anne Hutchinson's role-model, the woman of Ely. Thomas Edwards, a contemporary Puritan divine, remarked that "there are also some women preachers in our times, who keep constant lectures, preaching weekly to many men and women. In Lincolnshire, in Holland and those parts [i.e., the parts about Holland in Lincolnshire] there is a woman preacher who preaches (it's certain), and 'tis reported also she baptizeth, but that's not so certain. *In the Isle of Ely (that land of errors and sectaries) is a woman preacher also."* See his *Gangraena* ... (London, 1646), Pt. ii, 29, quoted in Battis, *Saints and Sectaries*, 43n.
37. Winthrop, *Short Story*, in Hall, ed., *Antinomian Controversy*, p. 273, and "Examination of Mrs. Hutchinson at Newtown," ibid., p. 337.
38. A good discussion of the theological issues surrounding resurrection is provided in Jesper Rosenmeier, "New England's Perfection: The Image of Adam and the Image of Christ in the Antinomian Crisis, 1634 to 1638," *William and Mary Quarterly*, 3d. Ser., 27 (1970): pp. 435-59.

Rosenmeier depicts Ms. Hutchinson too explicitly as a Familist without supplying sufficient evidence.

39. Ms. Hutchinson had responded to an argument of Cotton's with the rejoinder, "I desire to hear God speak this and not man." "Trial of Anne Hutchinson before Boston church," in Hall, ed., *Antinomian Controversy,* pp. 358, 362, 355.

40. Ibid., p. 372. See Battis, *Saints and Sectaries,* 52n.

41. "Trial of Anne Hutchinson before Boston church," in Hall, ed., *Antinomian Controversy,* pp. 369, 370, 365.

42. Ibid., pp. 385–87, 366–68.

43. Ibid., pp. 378, 388, and Winthrop, *Short Story,* ibid., p. 307.

44. Richard D. Pierce, ed., *The Records of the First Church in Boston, 1630–1868,* I, in Colonial Society of Massachusetts, *Publications,* XXXIX (Boston, 1961), 22, 25; *Assistants Records,* II, 78, 82; Emil Oberholzer, Jr., *Delinquent Saints: Disciplinary Action in the Early Congregational Churches of Massachusetts* (New York, 1956), p. 85; "The Diaries of John Hull," American Antiquarian Society, *Archaelogia Americana,* III (Worcester, Mass., 1857), 192n.

45. Joseph B. Felt, *Annals of Salem, Massachusetts,* II (Salem, Mass., 1845), 573, 576, and Charles Henry Pope, *The Pioneers of Massachusetts* (Boston, 1900), p. 382.

46. Dow, ed., *Essex County Court Records,* I, 6, 9; *Assistants Records,* II, 78; "A Description and History of Salem by the Rev. William Bentley," Mass. Hist. Soc., *Colls.,* 1st Ser., VI (Boston, 1799), 252; Hosmer, ed., *Winthrop's Journal,* I, 282–83; Felt, *Annals of Salem,* II, 420. The attitude of Dorothy Talby's husband may have contributed to the release of her violent inclinations, for on July 1, 1639, he was censured by the Salem church for "much pride and unnaturalness to his wife." Perley, *History of Salem,* II, 52.

47. The author has calculated the percentage of female offenders from the *Assistants Records* and the percentage of male and female arrivals in New England from the ship lists in Charles Edward Banks, *The Planters of the Commonwealth: A Study of the Emigrants and Emigrations in Colonial Times . . .* (Boston, 1930). The increase in female offenders may not seem very significant at first glance. However, if the sex distribution of the Massachusetts population remained stable between 1630 and 1644, which is a big assumption, a z-score comparison of the 1630 to 1634 and the 1635 to 1639 populations yields a result statistically significant at the five percent level. A comparison of the 1630 to 1634 and the 1640 to 1644 populations yields an even more astounding result which is significant at the one percent level. There is a one percent statistical probability that the increase in female offenders from 1630 to 1644 is due only to chance.

48. Before 1641 the Deputies and Assistants did not prosecute women for fornication or lascivious behavior unless those women were considered "whores" or "sluts." Premarital sexual activity was believed to be sinful, but the male was considered the active, initiatory agent and the female the passive, yielding participant. As a result of this guiding conceptualization, only two women but seventeen men were convicted of fornication or enticement to fornication between 1630 and 1639. After the assertiveness of many women in the Antinomian unrest had proven to the authorities

that women must be held more accountable for their actions, the magistrates began to prosecute both male and female fornicators, including for the first time women who had become pregnant and then married the fathers of their children. Between 1640 and 1644 eighteen men and ten women were punished for premarital sexual activities. *Assistants Records*, II, *passim;* Shurtleff, ed., *Mass. Bay Records,* I, II, *passim.*

49. *Assistants Records,* II, 109; Hosmer, ed., *Winthrop's Journal,* II, 38–40; John Cotton to Francis Hutchinson, Mass. Hist. Soc., *Colls.,* 2d Ser., X (1823), 186. In 1633 the Assistants fined Capt. John Stone £100 for assaulting Justice Roger Ludlow and calling him a "just ass." Four years later Robert Anderson was fined £50 for "contempt," but no other reviler of authority was fined more than £20. *Assistants Records,* II, 35, 66.

50. In 1639 the authorities criticized the Rev. Hanserd Knowles for holding "some of Mrs. Hutchinson's opinions" and two years later forced the Rev. Jonathan Burr to renounce certain errors which, wrote Winthrop, "savor[ed] of familism." Hosmer, ed., *Winthrop's Journal,* I, 295; II, 22–23.

51. "Psalm-Singing a Godly Exercise" [*Singing of Psalmes a Gospel-Ordinance* . . . (London, 1650)], in *A Library of American Literature From the Earliest Settlement to the Present Time,* I, eds., Edmund Clarence Stedman and Ellen MacKay Hutchinson (New York, 1891), 266.

52. Weld, "Preface," to Winthrop, *Short Story,* in Hall, ed., *Antinomian Controversy,* p. 214. Dr. Paul A. Younge's diagnosis of Ms. Hutchinson's "30. monstrous births" as a hydatidiform mole, a uterine growth which frequently accompanies menopause is adopted in Battis, *Saints and Sectaries,* p. 346.

53. Winthrop, *Short Story,* in Hall, ed., *Antinomian Controversy,* pp. 280–81.

54. Charles H. Bell, ed., *John Wheelwright: His Writings, Including His Fast-Day Sermon, 1637, and His Mercurius Americanus, 1645; with a Paper upon the Genuineness of the Indian Deed of 1629, and a Memoir* (Boston, 1876), pp. 195–96.

55. Weld, "Preface," to Winthrop, *Short Story,* in Hall, ed., *Antinomian Controversy,* p. 214; Jameson, ed., *Johnson's Wonder-Working Providence,* p. 28; "Roger Clap's Memoirs," in *Chronicles of the First Planters of the Colony of Massachusetts Bay, from 1623-1636,* ed. Alexander Young (Boston, 1846), p. 360; "From Majr. Scott's mouth," Mass. Hist. Soc., *Proceedings,* 1st Ser., XIII (1873-1875), 132. John Josselyn, a British traveler, wrote that he was surprised to find "a grave and sober person" who told him about Mary Dyer's "monster" on his first visit to Massachusetts in 1639. See his *An Account of Two Voyages to New-England* . . . (London, 1675), pp. 27–28.

56. Hosmer, ed., *Winthrop's Journal,* II, 8.

57. Ibid., I, 299, and "Clap's Memoirs," in Young, ed., *First Planters of Massachusetts,* p. 360.

58. Winthrop, *Short Story,* in Hall, ed., *Antinomian Controversy,* p. 307, and Cotton, *Congregational Churches Cleared,* ibid., p. 420.

59. George H. Moore, "Giles Firmin and His Various Writings," *Historical Magazine,* 2d Ser., III (1868), 150, quoting Giles Firmin, Πανομργια, a *brief review of Mr. Davis's Vindication: giving no satisfaction* . . . (London, 1693).

60. Hosmer, ed., *Winthrop's Journal*, I, 286–87; John Russell Barlett, ed., *Records of the Colony of Rhode Island and Providence Plantations, in New England, 1636–1663*, I (Providence, R.I., 1856), 16; Roger Williams to John Winthrop, May 22, 1638, in John R. Bartlett, ed., *The Complete Writings of Roger Williams* (New York, 1963 [orig. publ. Providence, R.I., 1874]), 95–96; Williams to Winthrop, Oct. 1638, ibid., p. 124.

61. Jameson, ed., *Johnson's Wonder-Working Providence*, p. 186.

62. Howard M. Chapin, *Documentary History of Rhode Island*, II (Providence, R.I., 1916), 68, 84. Coddington controlled the dispensation of land titles because the original deed to Rhode Island was issued in his name.

63. Edward Winslow, *Hypocrisie Unmasked: A true Relation of the Proceedings of the Governour and Company of the Massachusetts against Samuel Gorton* . . . (London, 1646), p. 44, 54–55, 67; Hosmer, ed., *Winthrop's Journal*, I, 297, 299; Chapin, *History of Rhode Island*, II, 56–57; William Coddington to John Winthrop, Dec. 9, 1639, *Winthrop Papers*, IV, 160–61; Robert Baylie, *A Dissuasive from the Errours of the Time* . . . (London, 1645), p. 150.

64. Chapin, *History of Rhode Island*, II, 68, and Winslow, *Hypocrisie Unmasked*, pp. 53, 83.

65. Hosmer, ed., *Winthrop's Journal*, II, 39.

66. Thomas Lechford, *Plain Dealing: or, Newes from New-England* . . . (London, 1642), reprinted in Mass. Hist. Soc., *Colls.*, 3d Ser., III (Boston, 1833), 96.

67. "Letter of Randall Holden, Sept. 15th, 1643," ibid., I (1825), 13, and Samuel Niles, "A Summary Historical Narrative of the Wars in New-England with the French and Indians, in the several Parts of the Country," ibid., VI (1837), 201.

68. Winthrop, *Short Story*, in Hall, ed., *Antinomian Controversy*, p. 310.

69. Perry Miller, *The New England Mind: The Seventeenth Century* (New York, 1939), p. 391. Increase Mather saw the hand of God at work again when Anne's son Edward died from Indian wounds in 1675. "It seems to be an observable providence," Mather observed, "that so many of that family die by the hands of the uncircumcised." "Diary of Increase Mather, 1674–87," Mass. Hist. Soc., *Procs.*, 2d Ser., XIII (1900), 400.

70. Katherine Scott to John Winthrop, Jr., 1658, Mass. Hist. Soc., *Colls.*, 5th Ser., I (1871), 96–97, and "Letter of Randall Holden, Sept. 15th, 1643," ibid., 3d Ser., I (1825), 13–15.

Widowhood in Eighteenth-Century Massachusetts: A Problem in the History of the Family

Alexander Keyssar

I

In the society of colonial New England, where the family was the principal unit of social organization and economic production, the death of a married man was, potentially, an event of considerable consequence. In addition to the immediate emotional strains of grief and loss, such a death placed the surviving members of a household in a set of new relations to one another, to property, and to the law. The widow of the deceased, of course, lived at the center of the changes in family life. Although her precise situation depended upon factors such as age, wealth, and family size, a widow, no longer the dependent partner in a marriage, had to adjust to new needs and circumstances. The responsibility for her economic support was shifted to different shoulders. The total labor available to the household was reduced, and patterns of authority within the family were altered. As a woman, a widow possessed legal rights which, although expanding in the eighteenth century, were much more limiting than those possessed by men.[1]

Widowhood, clearly, was a possible source of social and economic problems for the members of a newly incomplete family.

According to traditional accounts of family life in the colonies, however, the problems actually generated by widowhood were very few. Potential dislocations were avoided by one simple and widespread phenomenon: widows remarried, rapidly and, if necessary repeatedly. Widowhood was of short duration, and adult women spent little time living outside a complete household, needing independent rights as women. The traditional history offers a model of marriage in early New England that incorporates this view of widowhood. The colonists married early and married often. Many young women died due to childbirth and overwork; their husbands remarried as soon as they could locate a partner.[2] A woman might become a widow by the premature death of her husband or, more likely, if, as a second or third wife, she were considerably younger than her spouse. According to this model, there would be many more widowers than widows. The Puritan emphasis on living in families, coupled with the preponderance of adult men in the society, created a high demand for all marriageable women.

Still another factor, historians have claimed, contributed to the rapid remarriage of widows. Puritan marriage was largely an economic affair, as any reader of Samuel Sewall's diary must know, and widows were at a premium because of their wealth, their "thirds" almost always being larger than any portion that a maiden daughter might inherit.[3] Indeed, it seems that the judge's diary has been the principal source of information about marriage in eighteenth-century Massachusetts, and one can hardly find a discussion of widowhood which does not recount Sewall's financial haggling with the widows Denison and Winthrop.[4] In the eighteenth century, when women were no longer numerically scarce in eastern New England, widows, due to their wealth, were presumably able to cope with the problems of their new status by rapidly exchanging it for another marriage.

In recent years, however, a few historians have begun to challenge the traditional version of family life and history in colonial New England. Using the methods of historical demography, their studies suggest that seventeenth- and eighteenth-century New Englanders married in their mid-twenties rather than in their teens, that individual households tended to be nuclear rather than extended, and that various aspects of family life were deeply influenced by the changing pressures of population upon the available land resources.[5] Philip Greven, in his detailed study of Andover, Massachusetts, has found that marriages broken by an early death were the exception rather than the rule and that remarriage was not nearly as widespread a phenomenon as had been believed.[6] If the conclusions which Greven and others have derived from local studies are applicable to larger areas of New England, then the outlines of the life and history of the Puritan family must be redrawn.

For instance, if widows did not commonly remarry, then the potential problems of a woman living outside a complete household may have been actual and sustained problems. Death, and thus widowhood, are natural crises, but the impact of and response to these crises vary with the demographic, social, and economic environment. How did widows and their children survive? How did the family, the community, and the political authorities of the colony respond to the problems of widowhood? What was the legal status of widowhood? Beyond these questions lie others even more basic. Who, in fact, were the widows? How old were they? A widow of thirty poses different challenges to a family and a community than does a widow of sixty. What were the frequency and duration of widowhood?

These questions, as well as the different models of family history, may be tested by examining, in detail, one local situation and associating it with other, broader data in the economic and social history of early America. Woburn, Massachusetts, during the first half of the eighteenth century, was an agricultural community, typical of many eastern Massachusetts towns which had been settled in the seventeenth century. Its population can be studied through surviving vital records, genealogies, tax lists, and probate records. The problems of and responses to widowhood cast a revealing light upon the history of women and upon the interactions of the individual family with population patterns, economic pressures, and legal structures.

II

The town of Woburn, in Middlesex County, is situated about twelve miles north and west of Boston. Incorporated in 1642, Woburn had sixty families and seventy-four church members within a decade.[7] Growing steadily and dividing its common lands with some rapidity, the town, by the turn of the century, had 187 taxpayers (thus a total population of roughly 800) and had abandoned the open-field system in favor of more dispersed but easily workable farms.[8] In the first decades of the eighteenth century, Woburn experienced the burst of population growth common to the area (by 1725, there were 305 taxpayers) and in 1730 spawned a second parish and the new township of Wilmington.[9] Located inland, the economy of Woburn was little affected by the fishing and shipping trades along the coast: its inhabitants were farmers, and their daily activities were those of the great bulk of the colonial population.

By 1700, Woburn's third generation was beginning to marry, establish households, and confront the pressures of an increasing population upon a fixed amount of land. According to the vital records, a total of sixty marriages, each involving at least one resident of Woburn, took place between 1701 and 1710. The demographic data on the lives of these sixty couples challenge the traditional models of marriage and widowhood in eighteenth-century Massachusetts.[10]

The average ages at marriage, for the men and women in the sample, agree closely with those found elsewhere, and affirm that images of youthful marriage in early Massachusetts have no statistical basis.[11] The average age at first marriage was 26.5 years for men and 23.6 years for women. For marriages where either party had been married previously (a sample of only fourteen, twelve men and two women), the average ages at marriage were 42.6 for men and 28.9 for women. Men, of course, were almost always older than the women they married; as might be expected, the gap between the ages of husband and wife was greater in marriages that ended in widowhood than it was for marriages which terminated in the death of a wife.[12]

It was possible to trace, with certainty, thirty-seven of the marriages until they were terminated by the death of one spouse. Twenty-two, or roughly sixty percent, ended with the death of the husband. Fifteen were broken by the wife's death.[13] The average duration of these marriages was the remarkably high total of 23.9 years. For marriages which ended with the death of the husband, thus leaving a widow, the average duration was 25.8 years; in those marriages where the wife died first, the duration, on the average, was 20.6 years. Table I presents the distribution of the duration of these marriages.

TABLE I

Duration of Marriages

Length of Marriage	Number of Marriages Where Husband Died First	Number of Marriages Where Wife Died First	Total
1–10 years	2	3	5
11–20 years	7	6	13
21–30 years	5	2	7
31–40 years	5	2	7
41–50 years	2	1	3
51– years	1	1	2
Total	22	15	37

These figures are simply not compatible with the traditional account of colonial family life. There were more widows than widowers in the Woburn sample, a situation which would not arise if the primary threat to the endurance of a marriage were the death of a woman in childbirth.[14] Only four women died before the age of forty, in illnesses associated with childbirth; indeed, as many men as women died in the first twenty years of marriage. More than half of the marriages lasted longer than twenty years; few were broken in less than ten. For better or worse, marriages in Woburn tended to be durable contracts.[15]

In consequence, these Woburn residents tended to be advanced in years when their households were disrupted by death: overall, men had lived 60.1 and women 50.6 years before the death of either spouse. In marriages where the husband died first, thus leaving a widow, the men were, on the average, 63.0 years old at death and their wives were 55.4 years old when they became widows. Table II, for an unfortunately small sample, presents a profile of those Woburn women whose precise ages at widowhood were determinable.

TABLE II

Age At Widowhood

Age	Number of Women
25–40 years	2
41–50 years	5
51–60 years	3
61– years	5
Total	15

The Woburn data strongly suggest that relatively few young women with young children, had to face the problems associated with the death of a husband. Most widows were mature in years: some, at least, of their children were adults. Widowhood, as a social issue, involved the accommodation of middle-aged or elderly women to a set of new roles in the family and society.

Remarriage, of course, was one possible accommodation: a widow who remarried would, at least, not have to support herself, head a household alone, or be an appendage to a younger family. Yet the Woburn sample indicates that the remarriage of a widow was not a frequent event. Only four of the twenty-two widows are known to have remarried, and only two of the sixty women who married between 1701 and 1710 were widows at that time. Thus, only ten percent of the women in the Woburn sample are known to have married more than once. Although there may be omissions from the vital records, if remarriage (especially rapid remarriage) were the *typical* pattern of behavior, one would expect to find a far greater number of recorded remarriages.

The data on remarriage of males lend support to these conclusions. Roughly between one-fourth and one-third of the men in the sample were known to have married more than once, and only one man more than twice. This proportion is only slightly lower than that found by Greven for third-generation Andover males and buttresses his conclusion that one marriage was the norm for early eighteenth-century colonists.[16] Moreover, it is entirely consistent that men would remarry with greater frequency and ease in a society which contained more widows than widowers.[17]

The extant tax lists of Woburn provide further information about the duration of widowhood and the remarriage of widows. These lists were examined for all of the even-numbered years between 1700 and 1750: the widows who appeared on the lists were then traced, through the vital records, until their remarriage or death. The data must be used with caution, but, nonetheless, this sample offers convincing evidence that widowhood, for most women, lasted for some years and was not terminated by remarriage.[18]

The names of seventy-six widows appeared on the tax lists which were examined.[19] Table III indicates the length of time during which these widows remained on the lists.

TABLE III

Length of Time on Tax Lists

Span of Years	Number of Widows
1	24
2	12
4	4
6	6
8	5
10	7
12	6
14	1
16	5
18	2
20	1
22	2
24	1

Total   76

Widowhood, clearly, was a social situation which often endured for a significant period of time. Forty women were on the tax lists for at least four years; twenty-five women, or a third of the total sample, were on the lists for ten years or more. The fifty-two women whose names appeared on the lists more than once averaged 9.2 years on the rolls. And these figures understate the time that women spent as widows since the span of years on the tax lists must, on the average, be shorter than the duration of widowhood. For instance, the vital records reveal that even those women whose names are inscribed only once on the tax rolls spent an average of four years as widows. The exact dates of death were determinable for twenty-three women who died as widows: their deaths occurred, on the average, 12.3 years from the time of their first appearance on the tax lists as widows. (See Table IV.) Although no precise figure can be calculated, the average duration of widowhood in Woburn was, apparently, between seven and ten years; the median would be slightly lower.[20] As Table IV indicates, some women, undoubtedly, would live large portions of their adult lives as widows.[21]

TABLE IV

Women Who Died as Widows

Years after First Appearance on Tax Lists	Number of Widows
0–5	7
6–10	5
11–15	2
16–20	4
21–25	1
26–	4
Total	23

The evidence from the tax lists also indicates that remarriage was not the norm for the widows of Woburn. Only eight women from the sample are known to have remarried: all remarried within five years of their first appearance on the lists and after an average of 2.5 years. An additional seven women probably remarried, after a somewhat longer period of time. It is notable that many more women are known to have died as widows than are known to have remarried.[22] Even with calculations to correct the bias in the sample, the total number of Woburn widows who remarried is extremely low.[23]

In sum, the traditional view that colonial widows remarried easily and rapidly does not conform with any of the data. In Woburn, during the first half of the eighteenth century, probably not more than a fourth of the women whose husbands died found new spouses. Moreover, after the first few years of widowhood had passed, their chances of remarrying were extremely slim. This was certainly due, in part, to the advanced age at which women generally became widows. Once widowed, a woman was far more likely to die a widow than to enter into a second marriage.

The residents of Woburn, during this period, married relatively late, married once, and married for a long time. However great the social and economic pressures to live in complete households, many women, in Woburn, would expect to live some part of their mature lives without a husband. The odds were that a Sarah Richardson, married in Woburn in the early eighteenth century, would outlive her husband and would pass some years in a different economic and social situation. The community would re-dub her "widow Richardson," and she, her family, and the community would face a new complex of problems.

III

Some of the questions raised by these basic facts about widowhood can be answered, at least in part, by relating the Woburn findings to the general population patterns of the colonies. The frequency and length of widowhood and the infrequency of remarriage are not isolated phenomena: they are integral parts of a broader demographic environment. That environment, for the towns of Massachusetts, was changing during this period: certain of these changes had a crucial impact upon widowhood.

The Massachusetts census of 1765 provides revealing data about the sex composition of the colonial population. In the seventeenth century, Massachusetts had had a decided surplus of males; by 1765, however, the ratio of white males to white females was 96.8 (to 100). Moreover, the ratio of adult white men to adult white women, in 1765, was 90.3, and one researcher has argued that Massachusetts probably had a surplus of adult women for most of the eighteenth century.[24] There were, however, significant variations in the sex composition of the population within Massachusetts: adult women outnumbered adult men most markedly in eastern towns like Woburn.

The ratio of adult white males to adult white females in Woburn in 1765 was 87.9. Virtually all of the towns in Suffolk, Middlesex, and Essex counties, the most settled areas in the province, had a comparable preponderance of adult women.[25] Neighboring Billerica had 360

TABLE V

Woburn In 1765

White males under 16	365
White females under 16	314
White males above 16	373
White females above 16	424
Negroes, male	20
Negroes, female	19
Total	1517

NOTE: I have kept the census figures intact although the correct total is 1515 not 1517.
SOURCE: Benton, *Census-Making;* the census facsimile itself is unpaginated.

females over sixteen and only 313 males; in Malden, the proportion was 289 to 230. Andover, in Essex County, had 700 adult women and only 565 adult men. Most, but not all, of these towns also recorded more males than females under the age of sixteen.[26]

The significant surplus of adult women in Woburn and towns like it unquestionably diminished the chances of a widow remarrying. Apparently, the first half of the eighteenth century, in Woburn, witnessed a steady shift in the sex ratio towards an excess of adult women; that shift was one cause of the lack of widow remarriage and the social patterns which ensued. Woburn's tax lists, once again, provide supporting evidence: decade by decade, from 1700 to 1750, the percentage of taxpayers who were widows increased from 2.5 to almost six percent. Moreover, the census data suggest that Woburn's pattern of widowhood was shared by other towns in eastern Massachusetts. Unless widows possessed greater wealth or some other advantage over younger, single women (a subject to be discussed in detail in section IV), the sheer numerical odds greatly restricted the possibility of remarriage.

However, the sex composition of the population changes as one moves further west, towards the frontier. Worcester County had seventeen towns with a surplus of women and sixteen with a surplus of men. In Hampshire County, fourteen towns had more men than women, and thirteen had more women than men: the margins are uniformly small. In sparsely settled Berkshire County, each town had a preponderance of men.[27] Massachusetts, as a whole, had more women than men within 145 years of its settlement largely because of the marked surplus of women in the more populated eastern regions.

An explanation of this surplus must account for the disappearance, from towns like Woburn, of a large number of males over the age of sixteen. Evidence from Andover indicates that, in the first half of the eighteenth century, the longevity of men declined while the longevity of women remained at or close to its remarkably high seventeenth-century level. In particular, there was a significant increase in the number of men who died between the ages of twenty and thirty-nine.[28] Although this phenomenon, if widespread, must have contributed to the altered sex ratio of eastern towns, it was apparently not the only factor. The contrast between western and eastern counties suggests that the pressures of population on the land in the older, settled towns produced a migration to the frontier which was sex-selective.[29] By the third and fourth generations, many young men would be unlikely to inherit a very large supply of land, and, whether they were married or not, they could leave the eastern agricultural communities and go west to claim new lands. The preponderance of men in western areas indicates that, in fact, a significant number of the migrants were unmarried. For single women, on the other hand, migration was not an easily available or acceptable option: because of the conditions of frontier life, unmarried women were far more likely than their male counterparts to remain in the east. The surplus of adult women in settled towns like Woburn, thus, was generated, in part, by the particular quality of emigration opportunities.

If this account of the population ratios is correct, one can construct a dynamic model of the effects upon widowhood of the growth and development of a town. In the early stages of a town's settlement, women would be scarce, and widows would find it relatively easy to remarry. As the town grew and expanded in population, however, the sex ratio would gradually balance and then shift towards a surplus of women when men headed off to the frontier. Widows would find it increasingly difficult to locate new spouses; unless they possessed considerable wealth, their families and the community would have to confront new problems and develop new ways of providing for widows. Ultimately, of course, emigration would diminish and the sex ratio would attain some kind of equilibrium. According to this model, Woburn's experience would be typical of agricultural towns in eastern Massachusetts in the eighteenth century. It might also represent a stage in the development of all such towns as the frontier pushed west. The problems of widowhood, then, were not static: they varied as a town grew and the structure of its population changed.

Yet not all New Englanders lived in farming communities, and residents of towns with different economies may have experienced different patterns of widowhood. Fishing towns along the coast, for instance, may well have had a continuously high proportion of widows. And there are indications that the number of widows in Boston was extraordinarily high. Cotton Mather, in a sermon in 1718, announced that "when I write up the People in the Church the Widows make up about a Fifth part of the communicants." [30] Mather's figure may reveal more about his church than about the composition of the population, but a census of Boston taken in 1742 reported that in a total population of 16,382 "souls" there were 1200 widows and "1000 of them poor." [31] To account for these statements with any certainty would require a much more detailed knowledge of Boston's population than any that is now available. Migration west, hazardous occupations such as fishing and shipping, a general decline in male longevity, and less pressure, both social and economic, towards living in complete households may all have contributed to this notable percentage of widows living in New England's largest town. In addition, it appears that the relatively urban areas may have offered widows chances of employment which did not exist elsewhere: this could, perhaps, have stimulated a migration of widows towards the city.[32] Such explanations are, however, speculative. What is important is simply to note that the patterns of widowhood in Woburn cannot be ascribed to all areas of colonial New England or even Massachusetts. Despite this qualification, they do appear to be representative of the widowhood patterns in a great many eastern New England towns in the first half of the eighteenth century. They may also be applicable, at one point in time or another, to the farming communities where the majority of Americans lived their lives well into the nineteenth century.

IV

A State of Widowhood is a state of Affliction: and very singularly so, if the widow is bereaved of the Main Support that after the Death of her Husband was left unto her ... when her Widowhood was yet more darkened by the Death of her Only Son who was now doubtless the Main Support of her Family. And how much are her Sorrows Embittered, by New Anxieties and Encumbrances coming upon her; Debts to be paid, and Mouths to be fed.

—Cotton Mather, 1728 [33]

The central problem of widowhood was the need for new sources of economic support for the widow and any young children living in the household. The death of a husband signified the loss of the labor and guidance of the legally recognized head of the household. If he had been a merchant, shopkeeper, or even perhaps an artisan, his widow might possibly earn a living by continuing the family business.[34] In towns like Woburn, however, the chances were great that the family occupation was farming and that a widow alone or a widow with small children would find it impossible or, at best, very difficult to continue operating the farm. The data on age at widowhood, however, indicate that most widows did have adult children, and, since the family was the basic institution of social welfare, these children were the most likely bearers of the responsibility of providing for the widow.[35] Yet the support of widows was not entirely a private matter. Widowhood was a problem that all families had to anticipate and many had to confront: the society had guidelines and rules for the care of widows. The laws pertaining to widowhood reveal some of the ways in which the government of the colony superintended the functioning of the family. Coupled with the probate records, they shed light on a variety of issues relating to widowhood, including the widespread failure of widows to remarry.

By the early eighteenth century the basic legal provisions for the care of widows in Massachusetts were firmly established. A detailed body of law referring to widowhood was legislated in 1647, and, after fifty years of minor vicissitudes, the principles of English common law dower were clearly expressed in colonial and provincial legislation.[36] Laws governing the distribution of the estates of intestates determined the methods of widow support in the large number of cases where a man died without leaving a will; they also served as guidelines for more private arrangements.

In brief, Massachusetts law provided that the widow of an intestate would receive one-third of her husband's personal property forever and one-third of his real property, lands and houses, as a life estate or dower.[37] If the real estate could not be divided, the widow would be endowed "in a special and certain manner, as of a third part of the rents, issues, or profits" of the estate.[38] Although a widow could dispose, as she wished, of the personal property that she inherited, no such freedom attached to her rights in the lands and houses. The widow had full right to the use, improvement, and profits of the real property, but she could not sell it, and, at her death, it reverted to the heirs of the estate. A widow, under common law, could not be an heir: unlike certain local English customs such as freebench, the common law gave to a widow no right of succession.[39] The widow's thirds in real property were a kind of trust fund, designed to give her support while protecting the estate and the line of succession.

A number of details of the law protected the widow from any encroachment upon her property rights. Dower rights attached upon marriage and could not be waived without her consent: to transfer clear title to land required the signatures of both parties in a marriage.[40] Furthermore, dower lands (but not personal property) were free from the claims of creditors. In the distribution of insolvent estates, the widow's portion was safeguarded: after her death, it would be distributed among her husband's creditors.[41] A later act, in 1710, ordered that "bedding, utensils, and implements of household" which a widow found "necessary for the upholding of life" were also not subject to creditors' claims: indeed, the act also instructed judges of probate to distribute such items to widows if a will existed and had made no mention of them.[42] Even the widow of a felon had her dower right reserved when her husband's crime resulted in the forfeiture of his estate.[43] Finally, the widow's interests were safeguarded by elaborate procedures for the administration of the estates of intestates, including the right to bring suit if her portion were not speedily assigned.[44]

Although these requirements, of course, did not technically apply to cases in which the husband had left a will, they were regarded as minimal standards for the support of widows. Early in the colony's history, the authorities of Massachusetts assumed the responsibility of insuring that families provide adequately for widows regardless of the precise stipulations contained in wills. The Body of Liberties of 1641 had two clauses entitled "Liberties of Women." One of them, Liberty 79, specified that "if any man at his death shall not leave his wife a competent portion of his estate, upon just complaint made to the Generall Court she shall be relieved." [45] Although legislation in later periods made no specific reference to supplementing the portions that widows received from wills, it was apparently an accepted practice that a widow could always choose her common law dower in place of her legacy.[46] Moreover, there is evidence that probate courts also exercised considerable discretion in determining the percentage of the estate allotted to widows. The seventeenth-century probate records from Essex County indicate that the size of the estate determined the proportion that a widow received: a widow from a poor household was likely to receive more than the thirds assigned to her by law.[47] Protecting the "best interests of the widow" meant that the courts could not be bound by the "rigid precedents" of English law.[48] The governmental authorities, by statute or by court action, could guarantee the use of family property for the satisfactory support of widows.

The laws of Massachusetts, thus, reflected a desire to protect both widows and landed estates. Implicitly, they recognized a social obligation to provide for widows, but, perhaps to limit the responsibility of the larger community, they sought to compel the family to fulfill that obligation. Closely following the English common law, the legal structure aimed at the sustenance, rather than the economic freedom, of widows. Women whose husbands had died could use but not dispose of the primary form of property and source of income that existed in Massachusetts. What this meant in practice for women in towns like Woburn is revealed by the probate records of Middlesex County.

The wills and administrations of the men in the Woburn marriage sample and some of their neighbors indicate that the problems of widow support were complex and were not entirely resolved by the statutory supervision of the family.[49] Approximately two-thirds of the men whose probate records were examined left widows: their wills or administrations contain provisions for widow support. Although there were potentially important differences between the terms of wills and the terms of administrations, there were no discernible social distinctions separating the men who wrote wills from those who died intestate.[50] Both forms of legal conveyance are rich in detail; indeed, the very fact that they are so detailed suggests some of the problems generated by the need for widow support in many colonial families.

The administrations of estates were fairly uniform in their provisions for widows: distributing the property, in general, among a widow and her children, the administrators (often the widow and the eldest son) closely followed the legal requirements. The widow received one-third of the lands and buildings for her natural life and a comparable portion of the personal property for ever. The most striking feature of the administrations is the detail of the real property provisions, the scrupulous reservation of the most minute rights. The administration of Joshua Sawyer, who died in Woburn in 1738, is typical. His widow was to receive, as her dower,

> the northwardly end of the new house with the whole of the cellar under the south end of said new house and the small chamber over the entry way with liberty of using the fore door and the entry way and the stairs up into the chambers and garrots, and of going out at the back door and liberty of using both the two wells belonging to said house.[51]

Clearly the legal division of rights to different parts of a single farm and farmhouse created, at least in theory, awkward problems of domestic travel. Joseph Hartwell's administration divided his entire large estate between his widow and his only son: their mutual rights of passage, outside the house, were spelled out in detail.

The said widow is to have liberty to pass and repass from the road through the two thirds to her part of the barn yard for driving carts and creatures as there shall be occasion. The barn floor is to be for the use of each. Joseph is to have liberty of passing and repassing from the road through the thirds to his part of the house the usual way for driving carts and creatures and other ways as there shall be occasion.[52]

According to the administrations, a widow usually lived with at least one of her children who was the legal owner of part of the family real estate. They shared the same dwelling house, but a specific part of the house was formally reserved for the widow's use. Precise stipulations guaranteed the widow's rights against unfair treatment by one of her own children.

In wills, Woburn men and their neighbors had more latitude in the distribution of their property. They could freely select the size and duration of grants, and they could bind their heirs to the fulfillment of specific obligations. The wills too display a remarkable quantity of detail; the widow's portion of the real and personal property was carefully described and safeguarded. Freed from the restraints of the common law, a man, in a will, could express his own desires and address directly the concrete problems of widowhood in eighteenth-century Massachusetts.

Often, wills granted to widows portions of the real and personal property larger than what they would have received under the rules for intestacy. Several poor men, like John Richardson, Jr., who died in 1745, left to their wives "the use and improvement" of their entire estates even though they had children.[53] Others, like Matthew Johnson, in 1740, who apparently had no living sons, left all of the personal property and the "use, profit, and improvement" of all real property to their widows.[54] In this way, a will could prevent the immediate distribution of parts of the estate to more distant heirs. A widow might also receive control of an entire estate if her children were all minors. Thus, James Converse, Jr., left the use of his real property to his widow until his son, Josiah, reached the age of twenty-one; she would then enjoy one-half of the housing and lands.[55] The precise configurations vary according to the size of the families and the estates, but many of the men in Woburn and surrounding areas clearly felt that a third of their real property would not satisfactorily support their widows. The widow's share was increased to prevent hardship or, in some cases, simply to provide more comfort.

Yet freedom from the laws governing intestacy also signified that a man could, in a will, regulate the length of time during which his widow would retain property rights. Moveable or personal property (generally of little value) was almost always granted "for ever," but a widow's portion of the real property, set out in a will, was not necessarily an estate for life. The writer of a will could lengthen or shorten that term, and this latitude did not generally redound to the widow's benefit. Only one man in the entire sample gave any significant amount of real property to his wife "for ever": in a document highlighted by what may be a revealing Freudian slip, Joseph Stevens, in 1721, left all of his lands (valued at £1000) "to dispose of and do with at her pleasure" to his "dearly beloved wife," Sarah.[56] On the other hand, a large number of wills reduced the widow's rights in real property to the "term of her widowhood." James Converse, for instance (the father of the James Converse, Jr., mentioned above), left his wife one-half of his real estate only as long as she remained his widow. Daniel Reed, in lieu of a dower, gave to his wife all of his personal property forever and all of his real estate "during her continuing my widow." [57] Apparently, men often concluded that a widow, if remarried, would have less need of real property than would the heirs to the estate. Whatever the motive behind limiting the duration of a grant, such restrictions could seriously influence the future prospects of a widow.

The wills also indicate that, in many cases, the legal right to the use of lands was not considered a sufficient source of support for widows. In part, no doubt, because a widow alone could not work a farm, men often demanded that their heirs and executors furnish the widow with annual supplies. These provisions, too, are remarkable for their detail; the will of John Lynde, who died in 1723, is representative.[58]

> And further I give to my said wife two cows to be maintained by my executors summer and winter as they do their own and to hasard the cows and said cows to be good cows. And my executors shall provide her a horse suitable for her to ride on during her widowhood. And further I give to my said wife yearly and every year eight bushels of indian meal, two bushels of rye meal, three bushels of malt and eighty pound of beef and fifty pound of pork. And all these before mentioned to be brought to her house. And further I give to my said wife five pounds of money to be paid the first year after my decease and five pounds the second year after my decease and after that three pounds a year yearly and every year of her life. And also ten cord of wood to be laid at her door every year for her own firing. . . . And further if my said wife Judith shall die my widow, she shall be decently buried by my executors out of my estate.[59]

Certain patterns of economic support for widows emerge from these documents. A widow with adult children would generally be allotted a specific "end" or room of the dwelling house, water and barn rights, the use of certain lands and orchards, a cow or two to be kept by the son ("as well as he keeps his own cow, or as a cow ought to be kept," one will specified [60]), and a variety of yearly provisions. The latter generally included significant quantities of meat, grains, and firewood and were to be supplied by the sons of the widow. The yearly portions were to be continued throughout the widow's natural life or widowhood. Moreover, a son could not afford to take his annual obligations lightly. Those sons responsible for the yearly supplies were, almost invariably, the executors of their fathers' estates. As such, they took out a bond to the judge of probate—a bond which generally was worth as much as the entire estate and which they would forfeit if they failed to carry out fully the terms of a will. John Lynde, Jr., stood to lose one thousand pounds if his mother did not receive her provisions.[61]

Although the scrupulous legal regulation of intra-family affairs may seem surprising, the detailed clauses of the wills and administrations were not simply repetitions of legal formulae. Their appearance in agreements less burdened by precedents of language and law affirms that these details were a response to the actual needs of the colonists. For instance, a marriage contract between a widow and her new husband, late in the seventeenth century, specifically guaranteed to the woman, in case she should be widowed again, "the new end of the dwelling house" and yearly supplies.[62] And the agreement of the heirs of John Richardson of Woburn, in 1715, is extremely revealing. Eschewing the formality of an administration, the widow and her adult children made a private settlement of the estate. Timothy Richardson, the eldest son, was to inherit the largest portion of the homestead.

> Also he the said Timothy Richardson ... is to provide and find for his honored mother, Susanna Richardson, widow of said deceased, in consideration of her right of dowry in the said estate, one good and convenient fire room in the said deceased's dwelling house and all other necessaries and conveniences ... And further the said Timothy Richardson ... is to provide for and keep two cows for his said mother both summer and winter free from charge to her from year to year, and to find and provide for her yearly, good convenient and sufficient firing wood. Also to allow and pay or cause to be well and truly paid five pounds money yearly. All which is to be paid, done and performed to and for her the said Susanna Richardson, widow, yearly and each year during the term of her widowhood.

A crucial clause was reserved until the end of the document.

> And the said Timothy Richardson to give, sign, and pass unto his
> mother, the widow of the said deceased, good and sufficient secu-
> rity for the faithful performance of his agreement and engage-
> ment to her during her widowhood.[63]

In a private agreement, too, the "honored" mother and widow could
not rely on familial bonds and affections: she demanded a security
deposit to guarantee that she would not be forsaken in her
widowhood.

These arrangements for the economic support of widows both reveal
and explain some of the problems of widowhood in towns like
Woburn. As noted earlier, for example, the infrequent incidence of
widow remarriage cannot be attributed entirely to the demographic
environment: if, as has been claimed, the wealth possessed by widows
made them particularly attractive marriage partners, the disadvantages
created by the surplus of adult women could have been at least partially overcome. But the probate records indicate that these women,
quite simply, did not possess forms of property which would be an
incentive to a potential new spouse. The bulk of a widow's wealth lay
in land which she could not sell, and the chances of renting the land
very profitably were extremely slim.[64] Moreover, the westerly end of a
small dwelling house, shared with another generation, would not necessarily be an alluring living arrangement for a new husband. On the
other hand, if a widow moved to the homestead of her new spouse
and he did not happen to be a nearby neighbor, her land would not
be accessible to be worked, and thus, given the labor-scarce conditions
of the economy, little or no income could be drawn from it. These
facts, coupled with the restriction of many widows' estates to the terms
of their widowhood, render untenable the theory that widows were in
high demand for remarriage because of their wealth.[65] Widow Denison may have held property that generated a considerable income, but
most widows, in Woburn and similar towns, did not. In fact, the
Woburn tax lists reveal only a slight correlation between wealth and
remarriage. It is true that the poorest widows did not remarry, and the
women who did remarry generally had average or better than average
holdings, for a widow. Nonetheless, some of the widows with the
largest estates lived for many years without remarrying. The limitations on a widow's property rights combined with the demographic
environment to make the remarriage of an early eighteenth-century
widow an unlikely event.

The juncture of the law with the peculiarities of the colonial economy enforced the dependence of widows on their children. Widows, in general, inherited little property which could be converted to their immediate support. Not only was a widow's estate usually far smaller than that of the average taxpayer,[66] but most of what widows received, land and housing, was capital in an economy where such capital was abundant and where labor was scarce. A widow could not work a farm alone, and finding tenants or farm workers was likely to be difficult and expensive. When land could readily be possessed in western areas of the state, men were unlikely to rent land or hire themselves out as laborers in Middlesex County. Widows, thus, possessed property which, without family labor, was difficult to utilize and which, because of legal restraints, they could not sell. Whatever the effects of dower law in England, where land was scarce and labor relatively abundant and cheap, widows in Massachusetts could not simply sit back and reap a steady, even if small, income from their property.[67] The provisions for yearly supplies in the wills were one result and resolution of this problem.

The economic dependence of widows, in turn, had significant effects on the lives of their children. The sharing of a house and the annual delivery of provisions resolved certain problems and generated others. In poorer families, no doubt, the care of a widow by a young household may have been an economic burden. More widespread, however, were the limits imposed on the mobility of the younger generation by the specifications for widow support. A widow possessed legal rights which could inhibit her children from selling the family estate and moving to a new area. In eastern Massachusetts, at a time when individual estates were growing smaller and the rate of mobility was high, these rights could have been of great consequence to many families.

Indeed, the presence of real or potential conflict between the dependence of a widow and the wishes of her children may explain some of the problematic features of the probate records. Why were the details of living arrangements for a family that had spent years together spelled out so precisely? Why could filial love or loyalty not be relied on as sufficient security for a widowed mother? Why was it not just assumed that a widow would be granted a room in the dwelling house? It appears that these details of the wills and administrations were explicitly designed to give the widow some control over the future actions and movements of her children. Unless a prospective purchaser were willing to live in a house whose "westerly end" was occupied by a widow (who also had claims to part of the lands and the barn), a son could not sell the family homestead against the wishes of his mother. Similarly, the legal obligation to deliver yearly supplies was an obstacle to emigration. Familial and generational tensions were reflected in the probate records: crucial clauses suggest the presence of anxieties about old age, about the fragmentation of the family due to mobility, and about the prospect of a newly dependent relationship between a mother and her children. Faced with these fears, the older generation sought security, in part, by imposing restraints upon the younger.

Most widows, then, did have adult children who would see that they did not become destitute. Such support was forthcoming, as one would expect, without resort to legal action. Neither the probate records nor the records of the Inferior Court of Pleas offer much evidence of disputes about dower or other rights of widows.[68] A widow, advanced in years and with a grown child, would expect to be cared for within the family; in case of difficulty or perhaps just to allay anxiety, she possessed a number of legal ways to fulfill that expectation. Relatively poor, dependent, and lacking in other options, she would at least be assured of a minimum level of sustenance until her death.

V

Yet not all widows had adult children who were able to support them. Although the evidence indicates that most widows did not face such a predicament, many women in the eighteenth century must have had to feed, clothe, and shelter themselves and perhaps their young children without the assistance of other adult members of the family. These widows probably possessed some real property, but they would find it difficult to convert that property into an annual income. Possibly it was these women, seeking employment in Boston, who provided that city with its disproportionate number of widows. Regardless, widows without families to support them became the concern of the larger community: the town records of Woburn and the private resolves of the General Court of Massachusetts offer some indication of the society's response to widows who could not fend for themselves.

The local community could subsidize the income of a widow in several different ways.[69] The widows of Woburn's ministers, for instance, continued to receive their husbands' salaries during the first period of their widowhood.[70] These grants, however, were in recognition of special, rather than typical, relationships between towns and widows. Others who possessed the requisite skills, like the widow Walker, could earn a small living by keeping school for the "lesser children." [71] In addition, some widows could put their dwelling houses to use by taking in boarders—often at the town's request and expense. In 1745, for instance, the town's debts included four payments to widows "for keeping" a presumably poor or helpless person.[72] The town, thus, could promote the welfare of a widow by engaging her to perform social welfare functions which the town required.

More direct methods could also be utilized. Tax exemptions recognized that widows might well possess property but have very little income. The town records of 1705 and 1749, for example, describe the town voting to pay a widow's rates out of the public treasury because she herself was unable to do so.[73] In cases of extreme need, the town would even assume the burden of supporting an indigent widow.

> The Selectmen being informed that the widow Hensher was in want, they ordered the Constable Holding to pay her five shillings for a present supply, out of the town rate committed to him to collect.
>
> (September 9, 1700)

> There was a contribution made for the widow Hensher: there was then gathered 3 = 5 = 3 and the Selectmen provided a cow for her supply with milk, and the cow cost 59 shillings and the cow remains the town's, only the said widow hath the use of the cow free; and the Selectmen laid out 7ˢ 6ᵈ for cloth to make her dumb child a coat, and 3ˢ 6ᵈ for a pair of shoes; and the remainder of the said contribution, being 6ˢ 3ᵈ it was delivered to the said widow by the Selectmen.
>
> (October 29, 1700) [74]

Although such relief was clearly administered on an *ad hoc* basis and its frequency and extent cannot be determined, these examples do indicate that local communities considered widows without grown children as legitimate recipients of town aid.

The General Court of Massachusetts also became involved in the problem of widow support. In addition to general laws granting tax exemptions to the widows of ministers and the payment of wages due to the widows of deceased soldiers, the General Court passed a large number of private resolves designed to remedy the plights of individual widows.[75] Many of these resolves concerned the payment of relief or expenses to the widows of soldiers, and they expressed the province's somewhat niggardly willingness to relieve out of public funds the widows of men who died in public service. In 1708–1709, 1712–1713, and again in the 1720s, the General Court received bursts of requests for small sums of money to be paid to the widows of soldiers and mariners who were killed in action. Most of the widows argued that they ought to receive money not simply because they were needy but because wages were due to their husbands, guns and clothing were lost in military operations, funeral and sickness expenses had to be met, or their husbands had spent considerable amounts to raise other volunteers.[76] In a few cases, the widow of a slain soldier would simply plead her "poor and distress'd condition." Such requests, for relatively small sums at least, were invariably granted although often the money was paid not directly to the widow but rather to a third party (such as the selectmen of her town) to be expended for her benefit.[77] The General Court thus made clear that provincial funds were not to be utilized for widow support without specific and rather extreme cause. These authorities, however, seem to have been less miserly when dealing with people of their own social class: in 1732, they granted one thousand acres of land to the widow and children of the late "Honorable William Tailer, Esq. as a testimony of gratitude of the court for his services to the country." [78]

The records of the General Court also contain numerous private resolves which aimed to alleviate a central economic problem of eighteenth-century widowhood. These were acts enabling widowed women to sell real property in order to support themselves. (A few additional resolves extended the right to sell dower lands to a son or son-in-law so that he could pay for widow support.[79]) Dozens of these petitions, involving exceptions to dower law or comparable stipulations in wills, were granted by the General Court in the first half of the eighteenth century; they suggest the ways in which widows' rights had to be expanded in order to meet the requirements of the provincial economy.

The petitions from the widows follow one distinct pattern: the widow requested the right to sell land or housing because "the income or profit thereof" was "of very little value." [80] One of the petitioners explained quite succinctly the economic reasoning behind the desire to sell land for cash. Abiel Metcalf, in 1725, argued that "Most of the personal estate is gone to pay the deceased's debts, and the real estate (though of considerable value if sold) will not support" by its rent the widow and her seven children.[81] Many cases simply pleaded that the land had to be sold for the "necessary relief and subsistence" of a widow.[82] These women possessed property, but the property did not yield a sufficient income, and only legal action could permit a widow to sell the estate.

This problem could affect the widows of Boston as well as those on farms in outlying districts: without the aid of adult children, elderly women often could not support themselves. The case of Katherine Nanny "alias Naylour" presented one extreme instance of need:

> Setting forth that she has been blind for near fifteen Years past and labours under the Infirmities of Old Age, and has been at great Expense for her necessary Support, and must now perish without some better Relief than is provided for her by her said Husband's Will who thereby gave her the Rents and Income of his Real Estate only during her Life, which consists of an old Dwelling House in Ann Street in Boston, now become ruinous and run to despair, the Charge of Repairing the same amounts to near as much as the yearly Profits. Her said Husband's Children being all dead without Leaving any known Relations in these Parts Praying she may be allowed to Make Sale of the said House and Land or to mortgage the same for a certain Term of Years to provide for her Support and Comfort.[83]

In this case, increased capital rather than labor could make the property profitable, and the court ordered the petitioner's nephew, who was willing to do so, to take possession of the estate, improve it, and use part of the income to support his widowed aunt. The General Court was willing to suspend the law to enable people to help themselves.

The case of Abiel Metcalf also suggests that the expanding, diversifying economy of eastern Massachusetts offered new means of widow support. The court ordered widow Metcalf to sell her land and invest whatever she received: a third of the interest or profits could be used for her support, and the remaining two-thirds would go towards the maintenance and education of her children.[84] There are numerous similar examples. Land values in the region increased substantially throughout the eighteenth century: in settled areas, a considerable cash price could be obtained for landed estates.[85] Equally important was the rise of investment opportunities. A widow could become self-supporting by selling her real property and investing her capital in some enterprise which did not require her own intensive labor.

Although the family had primary responsibility for the care of widows and the law sought to insure that families fulfilled that responsibility, indigent widows were not simply left to "perish." The town was the secondary agency of social welfare and was expected to intervene when family support was not available. In rare cases, when a destitute widow did not belong to "any town from whom she can have support," the General Court paid for her relief.[86] But outright poverty was not the only issue. Many widows possessed property but still found it difficult to live. The crucial economic need of an eighteenth-century widow was the possession of a form of property that could generate an adequate annual income without a great deal of labor. Thus, widows without adult children often confronted an economic problem caused by the bad fit between dower law and traditions and the labor-scarce conditions of the Massachusetts economy. The provincial authorities recognized that widows' lack of freedom to dispose of their real property could only increase the number of people who required public relief. The private resolves of the General Court implicitly acknowledge that stringent adherence to the law could undercut the ability of individuals to support themselves. Exceptions to the law could be made, and new economic opportunities rendered such exceptions quite promising. The private resolves, though affecting few people directly, were signals of the breakdown of an old system and harbingers of future changes in the modes of widow support.

VI

Population patterns, economic conditions, laws, and customs combine to determine the effects of the death of a married man upon family and society. The problems of widowhood, thus, are variable, and, contrary to the evidence of some literary sources, the eighteenth-century American family did not circumvent these problems by the widespread and rapid remarriage of widows. During the first half of the eighteenth century, in eastern Massachusetts, the longevity, structure, and mobility of the population produced a large number of widows, relatively advanced in age, whose chances for remarriage were notably slim. The economic support of widowed women, consequently, was a problem frequently confronted by colonial families. The limitations on widows' property rights and the particular conditions of the Massachusetts economy restricted the ability of widows to be self-supporting and made them more dependent upon aid from their children or, less commonly, from the town in which they lived. The province itself supervised and enforced the fulfillment of the individual family's responsibility to care for widows.

The particular form of widowhood in Massachusetts had an impact on various aspects of eighteenth-century life. What continuity there was in the population of eastern Massachusetts, for instance, may well have been affected by the need to provide for widows. Even the eldest sons of many third—and fourth—generation families did not inherit very large or productive estates. These sons, generally, were in their late twenties, at least, when their fathers died. Not yet burdened by a large number of young children, they would have been free to move elsewhere—except for the responsibility of supporting a widowed mother who could prevent any sale of the homestead. Ten or fifteen years later, they would be less likely to migrate. To be sure, there were many reasons for remaining in a town like Woburn, but the problems of widowhood were certainly an obstacle to geographic mobility. In this way, widowhood was not only influenced by but also could have influenced the population patterns of provincial Massachusetts.

The structure of families, too, was affected by widowhood, in particular by the existence of a significant number of widows who did not remarry. In eighteenth-century Woburn, most families, most of the time, were completely nuclear: households consisted of one couple and their children.[87] But categories of family structure should incorporate the different stages of development through which all families pass. Widows in eastern Massachusetts often lived in the households of their children, and consequently many families, perhaps a majority, lived for some period of time with three generations under the same roof. The frequency and duration of these somewhat "extended" households were, no doubt, increased by the prevailing pattern of widowhood. Family structure is not static, and widowhood is one of the determinants of its dynamic cycles.

Finally, the problems faced by widows reveal certain dimensions of the role and status of women in early Massachusetts: the solutions to these problems suggest ways in which widowhood affected the expansion of women's rights in the eighteenth century. Women were expected to marry, but women whose husbands had died occupied a legitimate station in society. Whether married or not, however, women were subject to restrictions that men would have found unacceptable. A widow did not acquire the property rights of the male head of the household: she was to be cared for, protected, and dependent. According to the terms of most wills and administrations, a widow's needs were to be met and conveniences provided, but there was little room for a widow to choose the kind of life she wanted to lead after her husband's death. The society sought to guarantee the sustenance of widows, but the statutes were also designed to protect landed estates, and this aim was not compatible with the economic independence of widows. An adult woman, whose husband had died, was constrained as well as sheltered.

Still, the rights of women, both married and single, were being enlarged in the eighteenth century, more rapidly in America than in England. In particular, women acquired greater legal rights to possess property and to make contracts. This expansion of proprietary and contractual rights has been attributed both to the importance of women as controllers of land and to the increasing significance of different types of property.[88] It appears, however, that the precise problems of widowhood in the colonies also contributed to this growth of women's rights. The frequency and duration of widowhood clearly augmented the number of women who had some control over real property. Moreover, Massachusetts society contained a significant percentage of adult women, without husbands, who lacked full proprietary and contractual rights to the property upon which they depended for a living. Since the traditional methods of satisfying a widow's economic needs—remarriage and dower lands—did not successfully apply to local conditions, widows, at times, had to seek new avenues of economic support. For some, this demanded taking over and running a husband's business.[89] For others, it meant eliminating restrictions on their property rights. Women's rights in Massachusetts, thus, were expanded at a time when a large number of widowed women stood in need of greater rights. The private resolves of the General Court, admitting exceptions to dower law, are a concrete indication that the widespread problems of widowhood created pressures towards the increased independence and equality of women.

Nonetheless, the family remained the primary agency of social welfare in Massachusetts, and the history of activities such as care for the aged or the widowed is one dimension of the history of the family. Shifts in the population, the economy, and the law converged upon the individual family: the particular, detailed problems of eighteenth-century widowhood affected the daily and yearly living patterns of innumerable households. The ability or inability of the family to respond effectively to these problems influenced, in turn, the social development of the colony. As the fundamental unit of economic and social organization, the family was a crucial participant in and indicator of the changes in America in the eighteenth century.

NOTES

1. Richard B. Morris, *Studies in the History of American Law,* 2d ed. (Philadelphia, 1959), pp. 128–30.
2. J. Potter, "The Growth of Population in America 1700–1860," in D.V. Glass and D.E.C. Eversley, eds., *Population in History: Essays in Historical Demography* (London, 1965), p. 647; Alice M. Earle, *Customs and Fashions in Old New England* (New York, 1894), p. 36; Arthur W. Cal-

houn, *A Social History of the American Family* (Cleveland, 1917), I, 69.

3. Edmund S. Morgan, *The Puritan Family,* 2d ed. (New York, 1966), pp. 55–59; Calhoun, *Social History,* I, 70.

4. Morgan, *The Puritan Family,* p. 58; Potter, "The Growth of Population," p. 647; Earle, *Customs and Fashions,* p. 47. Also see *Samuel Sewall's Diary,* ed. Mark Van Doren (New York City, 1927), pp. 242ff.

5. John Demos, *A Little Commonwealth* (New York, 1970) and "Families in Colonial Bristol, Rhode Island: An Exercise in Historical Demography," *William and Mary Quarterly,* 3rd. ser., 25 (1968), 40–57; Philip J. Greven, *Four Generations: Population, Land, and Family in Colonial Andover, Massachusetts* (Ithaca, 1970) and, for a bibliographic summary, "Historical Demography and Colonial America," *William and Mary Quarterly,* 3rd ser., 24 (1967), 438–54; also Kenneth Lockridge, "The Population of Dedham, Massachusetts, 1636–1736," *Economic History Review, 2nd ser.,* 19 (1966), 318–44, and *A New England Town: The First Hundred Years* (New York, 1970). A discussion of recent work is contained in Kenneth Lockridge, "Land, Population, and the Evolution of New England Society, 1630–1790; and an Afterthought," in Stanley Katz, ed., *Colonial America: Essays in Politics and Social Development* (Boston, 1971), pp. 466–91.

6. Greven, *Four Generations,* p. 29.

7. Samuel Sewall, *The History of Woburn* (Boston, 1868), p. 32.

8. Total population is approximated by multiplying the number of people on the tax lists times four, as suggested by Evarts B. Greene and Virginia D. Harrington, *American Population before the Federal Census of 1790* (New York, 1932), p. xxiii. On Woburn's open-field system, see Sewall, *Woburn,* pp. 39–40, 241.

9. Greven, *Four Generations,* pp. 103–04; Potter, "The Growth of Population," p. 648; Sewall, *Woburn,* p. 259.

10. The sample was derived from the *Woburn Records of Births, Deaths, and Marriages from 1640 to 1873,* arranged by Edward F. Johnson; I, Births (Woburn, 1890); II, Deaths (Woburn, 1890); III, Marriage (Boston, 1891). It was also necessary to use *Wilmington Records of Births, Marriages, and Deaths from 1730 to 1898,* arranged by James S. Kelly (Lowell, 1898). Although there is no way of ascertaining the completeness of the records, the sample of sixty couples represents an entirely plausible marriage rate of roughly 6.5–7.0 per thousand per year. This is almost identical to that found in Dedham for the period 1640–1690 by Lockridge, "The Population of Dedham," p. 330. Fewer marriages were recorded in Woburn in the sample decade than in either 1691–1700 or 1711–20, but this can be explained as a negative "echo" of the smallpox epidemic which struck the town in 1678–79. On echoes, see Lockridge, "The Population of Dedham," p. 341, and on the smallpox epidemic, see Sewall, *Woburn,* p. 122.

Genealogies also were used to determine or confirm the dates of birth and death of members of the sample. There is some genealogical data in Sewall's *History of Woburn.* Also consulted were William R. Cutter, *Historic Homes and Places and Genealogical and Personal Memoirs Relating to the Families of Middlesex County, Massachusetts,* 4 vols. (New York, 1908), and James Savage, *A Genealogical Dictionary of the First Settlers of New England,* 4 vols. (1860–1862; reprint ed., Baltimore, 1965). Because many citizens of Woburn possessed the same names, the probate records were invaluable for determining precise identities. For example, if three John Richardsons died in Woburn at different times, they could be identified by comparing the names of their children as they appeared in the vital records and the probate records. In some instances, the probate records revealed that a family had moved to another town whose vital records could then be examined. No questionable identifications are included, without mention, in the data.

The smallness of the sample is entirely the product of feasibility: tracing individuals through these records is a painstakingly slow process. The size of the sample would present problems if the data conflicted with the evidence from the tax lists, the probate records, or the early census records. But, as is demonstrated, all of these sources, as well as evidence from other studies, support the same conclusions. Moreover, the precise figures are not crucial to the argument of this study: whether the average age at widowhood was fifty-two or fifty-eight years rather than 55.4 years, as reported, is less important than the fact that widows were mature rather than young women. Finally, one should note that the average figures do not all fit with one another. For example, the average age at marriage plus the average duration of marriage will not exactly equal the average age at the rupture of the marriage. This is so because not all figures were available for all people, and I have calculated averages based on the largest possible sample. Again, the precise figures are not of great importance. In the one case where this discrepancy could make a difference, that fact is indicated in a footnote.

11. Lockridge, "The Population of Dedham," p. 330; Demos, *Little Commonwealth,* p. 151; Greven, *Four Generations,* pp. 119ff.

12. The age gap between husband and wife was four years greater in marriages that ended in widowhood. However, these figures should be regarded with caution. The size of the gaps, correlated with the data on age, indicates that this particular information was more available for older than for younger members of the sample, and that fact may bias the results considerably.

13. There are probable but not certain data for five marriages: two ended with death of the husband, three with the death of the wife.

14. Demos, in "Families in Colonial Bristol," p. 40, also claims that the frequency of deaths in childbirth has been exaggerated. Greven, *Four Generations,* pp. 192–94, notes that in Andover during this period, more men than women died before age forty. The theoretical point that in a society with a high rate of mortality in childbirth there ought to be more widowers than widows is also made in Jacques Henripin, *La Population Canadienne au Début du XVIII Siècle* (Paris, 1954), p. 95.

15. See Greven, *Four Generations,* p. 29.

16. Ibid., pp. 110–11. Also Demos, "Families in Colonial Bristol," p. 67, finds, for an earlier period, that sixty percent of the men married only once.

17. According to J. Hajnal, the remarriage of widowers works like polygamy in responding to a shortage of men. J. Hajnal, "European Marriage Patterns in Perspective," in D.V. Glass and D.E.C. Eversley, eds. *Population in History,* p. 128.

18. The tax lists for this period are in the Town Records of Woburn, Massachusetts, Volumes 4–8 (Office of the City Clerk, Woburn, Mass.). The tax records obviously do not include a complete tally of Woburn's widows, and there is no readily apparent principle governing the appearance and disappearance of names on the list. Moreover, using the lists for every other year introduces a definite bias into the sample: widows whose names appeared on the tax lists only once, during odd-numbered years, are omitted. Despite these qualifications, the sample does present important evidence. In judging the frequency of remarriage for the members of the sample, a calculation to allow for the bias has been used.

19. This includes only those widows who appeared on the lists for the first time after 1700.

20. This average duration of widowhood correlates well with the 55.4-year average of age at widowhood.

21. These figures reveal the importance, in studying the family, of tracing individual families through time as well as taking horizontal samples. If one examined, for instance, only the tax lists, one would find that the percentage of taxpayers who were widows, in any single year, was rarely higher than seven percent. Widowhood would not seem like a major problem although, in fact, it was. If sixty percent of the women in a society spend seven years (or roughly one-sixth) of their adult lives as widows, only ten percent of the adult women will be widows at any given time—and the proportion would be smaller in a society with a growing population. A horizontal sample could lead to ignoring an important family problem simply because few families face the problem simultaneously. For example, although changes in male and female longevity have led to an increasing widowhood problem in the United States, only 12.2 percent of all adult women were widows in 1960. See Felix M. Berardo, "Widowhood Status in the United States," in Benjamin Schlesinger, ed., *The One-Parent Family* (Toronto, 1969), pp. 29–30, 112.

22. It was possible to establish with certainty that twenty-three of these women died as widows: there is evidence that another five probably died as widows. These figures are considerably larger than the number of women known to have remarried. It is particularly notable because, in general, marriages were more frequently inscribed in the colonial records than either births or deaths.

23. The effect of the bias in the sample is to eliminate certain women who appeared on the tax lists only once, and it is among these women that a high rate of remarriage might be found. Twenty-four women from the actual sample of seventy-six did appear only once on the lists: of these, five definitely remarried and another may possibly have remarried. Nine definitely died as widows, and no information was available on the fate of the remaining nine women. Even if it is assumed that an additional twenty-four widows appeared on the tax records only once and during odd-numbered years and also that the rate of remarriage for those women for whom we have information applied to all women who did appear or might have appeared once on the lists (two generous assumptions), the remarriage rate of widows still is very low. If two-fifths (six out of fifteen) of the projected total of forty-eight women (who appeared only once on the lists) remarried, there would be twenty such remarriages. If all of the other definite and probable remarriages from elsewhere in the

sample are added in, there would be only twenty-nine remarriages in a total sample of one hundred widows.

24. Josiah H. Benton, Jr., *Early Census-Making in Massachusetts 1643–1765* (Boston, 1905); Herbert Moller, "Sex Composition and Correlated Culture Patterns of Colonial America," *William and Mary Quarterly*, 3rd ser., 2 (1945), 124-25.

25. Benton, *Census-Making,* unpaginated, and Demos, "Families in Colonial Bristol," p. 50.

26. Benton, *Census-Making.*

27. Ibid.

28. Greven, *Four Generations,* pp. 191–95.

29. Moller, "Sex Composition," p. 125. Data from other colonies indicate that the phenomenon was widespread. New Hampshire, which was still thinly settled in 1790, had a preponderance of men. The various censuses from New York also show, through the eighteenth century, the development of a surplus of women in the more settled areas and a surplus of men in outlying regions. Greene and Harrington, *American Population,* pp. 85, 95–102.

30. Cotton Mather, *Marah Spoken To* (Boston, 1718), p. 1.

31. *Collections of the Massachusetts Historical Society,* 3rd ser., I (1825), 158.

32. Elisabeth A. Dexter, *Colonial Women of Affairs* (Boston, 1924), pp. 2, 3, 44, 51, 53.

33. Cotton Mather, *The Widow of Nain* (Boston, 1728), pp. 10–11.

34. Dexter, *Colonial Women,* pp. 2, 3, 18–30, 44, 51, 53.

35. Indeed, the eighteenth-century breakdown of the geographically close-knit communities associated with the open-field system may have placed demands on the individual family that were greater than those existing fifty years earlier.

36. George L. Haskins, *Law and Authority in Early Massachusetts* (New York, 1960), p. 182; also George L. Haskins, "Reception of the Common Law in Seventeenth-Century Massachusetts: A Case Study," in George A. Billias, ed., *Law and Authority in Colonial America* (Barre, 1965), p. 23.

37. Haskins, *Law and Authority,* p. 180; also "An Act for the Settling and Distribution of the Estates of Intestates," in Abner C. Goodell, ed., *The Acts and Resolves Public and Private of the Province of Massachusetts Bay* (Boston, 1869), I, 43–45. (Hereafter cited as *Acts and Resolves.)*

38. "An Act for the Convenient and Speedy Assignment of Dower," *Acts and Resolves,* I, pp. 450–51.

39. Haskins, *Law and Authority,* p. 182.

40. Ibid., pp. 180–81.

41. "An Act for the Equal Distribution of Insolvent Estates," *Acts and Resolves,* I, p. 48. Also Haskins, *Law and Authority,* p. 181.

42. "An Act in Addition to, and For Explanation of the Act for the Settling and Distribtuion of the Estates of Intestates," *Acts and Resolves,* I, p. 652.

43. Morris, *American Law,* pp. 159–60.

44. *Acts and Resolves,* I, pp. 450–51. Although no systematic inquiry has been made, it appears that the laws of widow support in other colonies display a certain amount of variety. In Plymouth and in Connecticut the provisions closely resembled those of Massachusetts. A Dutch law in New

York, however, made a widow's property liable for her husband's debts. In Maryland, a widow received one-third of the land and a dower house which she occupied when the heir came of age. A Georgia law of 1739 gave a widow half of the property during her lifetime and, if there were no children, the entire estate—but this grant was voided if she remarried. Demos, *Little Commonwealth,* p. 85; Calhoun, *Social History,* I, 95, 176–77, 235–39.

45. W.H. Whitmore, *Bibliographical Sketch of the Laws of the Massachusetts Colony* (Boston, 1890), p. 51.

46. Morris, *American Law,* p. 157.

47. Haskins, *Law and Authority,* p. 215.

48. Morris, *American Law,* p. 156; also see Haskins, "Reception of the Common Law," pp. 24–26.

49. Middlesex County Probate Records, first series, individually filed original MSS, indexed (Middlesex County Registry of Probate, Cambridge, Mass.). All documents are from the first series and are on microfilm. (Hereafter cited as Middlesex Probate.) The probate records of approximately 100 men were examined. The core of the sample consisted of the members of the Woburn marriage sample (i.e., those men that married between 1701 and 1710), but the records of their relatives and namesakes were also, if sometimes inadvertently, explored.

50. To some extent, obviously, chance determined whether or not a man wrote a will: short illness and sudden death must, in some cases, have voided a man's intention to distribute property in a particular way. In addition, it should be noted that few men from the Woburn sample utilized restrictive deeds as a way of providing for their widows. One example where a deed had been used is discussed in Middlesex Probate, packet number 20837.

51. Ibid., packet number 19980.

52. Ibid., packet number 10570.

53. Ibid., packet number 18974.

54. Ibid., packet number 12728.

55. Ibid., packet number 4924.

56. Ibid., packet number 41410. The word "beloved" was added above the line with a caret.

57. Ibid., packet numbers 4925 and 18469.

58. Evidence of similarly detailed probate records can be found in Demos, *Little Commonwealth,* pp. 75, 99; Greven, *Four Generations,* pp. 84, 91ff.; and James T. Lemon, "Household Consumption in Eighteenth-Century America and Its Relationship to Production and Trade: The Situation among Farmers in Southeastern Pennsylvania," *Agricultural History,* 91 (1967), 59–68.

59. Middlesex Probate, packet number 14415.

60. Ibid., packet number 9436.

61. Ibid., packet number 14415.

62. *The New England Historical and Genealogical Register,* XII (1858), 353.

63. Middlesex Probate, packet number 18972.

64. Percy W. Bidwell and John I. Falconer, *History of Agriculture in the Northern United States 1620–1860* (1925; reprint ed., New York, 1941), pp. 116–17.

65. See above, p. 84, and cf. Morgan, *Puritan Family,* pp. 55–59.

66. For a sample tax list which illustrates the small holdings of widows relative to most other taxpayers, see Woburn Town Records, Volume 4, pp. 161ff.

67. Bidwell and Falconer, *History of Agriculture,* pp. 116–18; Robert E. Brown, *Middle-Class Democracy and the Revolution in Massachusetts* (Ithaca, 1955), pp. 12–13; Jackson T. Main, *The Social Structure of Revolutionary America* (Princeton, 1965), p. 70.

68. There is not a single case of dispute over widows' rights in the Records of the Inferior Court of Pleas of Middlesex County (Third District Court, Cambridge, Mass.) for the period March 1722-March 1727. In addition, only one instance of such a dispute is listed in the *Abstract and Index of the Records of the Inferior Court of Pleas (Suffolk County Court) Held at Boston 1680-1698,* prepared by the Historical Records Survey of the Work Projects Administration (Boston, 1940). Dale Rosen, in unpublished research, has examined the records of the Middlesex County Inferior Court of Pleas for the years 1725, 1735, 1745, and 1755, and she reports a similar paucity of such cases.

69. This section is based upon an examination of selected portions of the thousands of pages of Woburn town records.

70. Sewall, *Woburn,* p. 66.

71. Ibid., pp. 209–10.

72. Woburn Town Records, Volume 6, unnumbered page.

73. Ibid., Volume 5, meeting of March 5, 1704/5, and Volume 8, p. 39.

74. Cited in Sewall, *Woburn,* p. 59.

75. *Acts and Resolves,* II (1874), 167, and IV (1890), 197.

76. *Acts and Resolves,* IX, ed. Melville M. Bigelow (1902), 13, 63, 85, 178, 252, 261, 303; and XI, ed. Melville M. Bigelow (1903), 17.

77. *Acts and Resolves,* X, ed. Melville M. Bigelow (1902), 239.

78. Ibid., XI, 655.

79. Ibid., IX, 64, 209, 221, 286.

80. Ibid., p. 175.

81. Ibid., X, 619.

82. Ibid., IX, 15, 199, 311.

83. Ibid., p. 338.

84. Ibid., X, 619.

85. William B. Weeden, *Economic and Social History of New England 1620-1789* (1890; reprint ed., New York, 1963), I, 335, 492; also Lockridge, "Land, Population, and the Evolution of New England," p. 474; Bidwell and Falconer, *History of Agriculture,* pp. 70–71.

86. *Acts and Resolves,* IX, 577.

87. See Greven, *Four Generations,* p. 15.

88. Morris, *American Law,* pp. 128–30, 135ff., 173ff.

89. There are many examples in Dexter, *Colonial Women,* pp. 1–60.

WOMEN IN
NINETEENTH-CENTURY
SOCIETY

The forces of industrialization and urbanization in nineteenth-century America transformed the roles of women. During the early colonial period, most income-producing activities were integrated into family life. But in the eighteenth century, as the economy expanded and towns grew into cities, home and workplace became separated. As women were gradually isolated from these economic activities, their work became limited to domestic responsibilities. The role of nineteenth-century women, then, became increasingly one of service.

The occupational options for the small number of women who worked outside the home also decreased. Women were driven out of some areas, such as medicine, by the process of professionalization. Likewise, the proportion of women in the crafts declined. Though negative attitudes toward women working at nondomestic jobs predominated in nineteenth-century American society, women did respond to the opportunities offered in the early stages of industrial development. They were the main source of labor in the infant textile factories in New England, primarily because of the shortage of male workers. Men had ready access to land and considered agriculture a more important occupation. Furthermore, women had been responsible for home textile production; therefore, work in textile factories was acceptable for them because they were still engaged in the manufacture of products traditionally associated with female labor. Finally, women were expected to work only temporarily in order to supplement family income and would therefore not become a demanding labor force. The article by Gerda Lerner discusses the implications of these changes in female domestic functions and occupational patterns on both the status of women in society and status differentiation among women.

While the entrance of women into factory work was an important step, it affected only a small number of women; most were still limited to domestic responsibilities. However, many women were drawn into new roles by the evangelical enthusiasm of the Second Great Awakening, which provided them with expanded opportunities for involvement in religious life. Keith Melder describes the growing participation of women in a variety of religious organizational activities and their incorporation of the notion of voluntarism into the sphere of female life. He argues that these activities laid the groundwork for the predominance of women in a wide variety of nineteenth-century charitable and reform causes, eventually leading some into the woman's rights movement.

The chaos of war allowed women to transform a voluntary role into a legitimate female profession. Ann Doublas Wood argues that, during the Civil War, women aggressively asserted their right to care for the sick and wounded, thereby creating the foundations of the nursing profession. In order to do so, they justified the particular suitability of women for nursing care on the basis of their instinctively warm and nurturing character. Wood suggests that they succeeded in legitimizing this profession because it did not conflict with contemporary notions of appropriate female behavior, but rather broadened them.

Other occupations identified with women also drew on the cultural construct of femininity upon which women's domestic and maternal roles were based. Professions such as teaching, librarianship and social work were rationalized through expanded concepts of women's roles as homemaker, mother and moral guardian. Other occupations dominated by women drew on the more vulnerable feminine characteristics. R. Laurence Moore analyzes nineteenth-century spiritualism as a dramatic example of an occupation stemming directly from contemporary definitions of the female personality. He shows that the ideal medium was highly emotional, sensitive, passive and self-effacing—qualities associated with the ideal woman.

The earliest educational institutions developed for women were also geared toward their maternal and domestic roles. The female seminaries and the early experiments in coeducational colleges reflected this orientation. It was not until after the Civil War, when several colleges for women opened in the East, that women were able to pursue an education that stressed intellectual achievement. However, these new educational opportunities were not paralleled by opportunities in the male-dominated professions. The selection by John Rousmaniere focuses on the difficulties faced by the graduates of these colleges in adapting their intellectual training to their limited role options. He posits that the solution for one early group of graduates was to recreate the close-knit intellectual environment of college life in the structure of the settlement house.

The patterns of women's nondomestic roles in the nineteenth century reflected the contemporary ideology of womanhood. New emphasis was placed on those characteristics thought to differentiate women from men, which justified the more rigid separation of sex roles. The selection by Barbara Welter traces the development of this new cultural definition of women in the popular literature of the early nineteenth century. This ideal of womanhood dictated four essential qualities of femininity—purity, piety, submissiveness and domesticity. Though this ideology supported the limitation of women's roles outside the home, its emphasis on the uniqueness of female virtues was also a source for increasing their authority.

One of the ways in which women expanded their societal roles was by asserting control over family life. As Joan Burstyn demonstrates, Catharine Beecher strove to transform women's domestic work from an instinctive function to a science by establishing educational programs to train women in household management and childrearing. Through these efforts to systematize and professionalize the role of homemaker, Beecher sought to increase the authority of women in the home. Daniel Scott Smith argues that women did in fact increase their power and autonomy in the family. He interprets the decline in fertility rates and the change in birth patterns as indications that women gained control over reproduction. By relating these changes to women's activities in reform movements and to Victorian sexual ideology, Smith concludes that the status of women improved significantly in the nineteenth century.

Within the domestic sphere, women evolved a culture from which men were, for the most part, excluded. Carroll Smith-Rosenberg illustrates that, bound together by the biological cycle of menstruation, pregnancy, childbirth and menopause, women developed a complex network of intimate, emotionally rich relationships. She suggests that these supportive female friendships and the rituals associated with the various stages of female life, constituted a cultural framework that provided continuity in a rapidly changing society. Since their lives were structured by this female culture, women often did not respond to social change in the same way as men. Johnny Faragher and Christine Stansell find, for example, that many women experienced the movement West as one of loss or exile, not of opportunity. The letters and diaries of women on the Overland Trail reveal their struggle to re-establish the female culture from which they had been uprooted.

Though this female sphere provided women with comfort and satisfaction, there were nevertheless problems inherent in the roles ascribed to them. In another article, Carroll Smith-Rosenberg examines hysteria, a common female disorder in the nineteenth century, as an available role option for women unable to cope with the demands of their housekeeping and childrearing duties. She suggests that this extreme reaction stemmed from basic inconsistencies between the socialization process for girls and their adult roles.

The experience of women in nineteenth-century America cannot be viewed simply in terms of isolation and loss. While their societal roles were in some respects confined, they were able, nevertheless, to forge new avenues of social participation. Within the sex role separation that characterized nineteenth-century society, women were able to develop a richly textured female culture. By the end of the century, however, with the emergence of a modern industrial society, women's roles were once again redefined.

SELECTED READINGS

Abbott, Edith. *Women in Industry.* New York and London: D. Appleton and Co., 1928.

Barker-Benfield, G.J. *The Horrors of the Half-Known Life: Male Attitudes Toward Women and Sexuality in Nineteenth-Century America.* New York: Harper and Row, 1976.

Berg, Barbara J. *The Remembered Gate: Origins of American Feminism.* New York: Oxford University Press, 1978.

Conway, Jill. "Perspectives on the History of Women's Education in the United States," *History of Education Quarterly* 14 (Spring 1974): 1–12.

Conway, Jill. "Women Reformers and American Culture, 1870–1930," *Journal of Social History* 5 (Winter 1971–72): 164–77.

Cott, Nancy F. *The Bonds of Womanhood: "Woman's Sphere" in New England 1780–1835.* New Haven: Yale University Press, 1977.

Cott, Nancy F. "Young Women in the Second Great Awakening in New England," *Feminist Studies* 3 (Fall 1975): 15–30.

Degler, Carl N. "What Ought to Be and What Was: Women's Sexuality in the Nineteenth Century," *American Historical Review* 79 (Dec. 1974): 1467–90.

Dexter, Elisabeth A. *Career Women of America 1776–1840.* Francestown, N.H.: Marshall Jones Company, 1950.

Douglas, Ann. *The Feminization of American Culture.* New York: Alfred A. Knopf, 1977.

Douglas, Ann. "The 'Scribbling Women' and Fanny Fern: Why Women Wrote." *American Quarterly* 23 (Spring 1971): 3–24.

Dublin, Thomas. "Women, Work, and the Family: Female Operatives in the Lowell Mills, 1830–1860." *Feminist Studies* 3 (Fall 1975): 30–39.

Flexner, Eleanor. *Century of Struggle: The Woman's Rights Movement in the United States.* Cambridge, Mass.: Harvard University Press, 1959.

Garrison, Dee. "The Tender Technicians: The Feminization of Public Librarianship, 1876–1905," in *Clio's Consciousness Raised,* ed. Mary Hartman and Lois Banner. New York: Harper Torchbooks, 1974, pp. 158–78.

Haller, John S., Jr., and Robin M. Haller. *The Physician and Sexuality in Victorian America.* Urbana: University of Illinois Press, 1974.

Hogeland, Ronald W. "Coeducation of the Sexes at Oberlin College: A Study of Social Ideas in Mid-Nineteenth Century America." *Journal of Social History* 6 (Winter 1972/73): 160–73.

Melder, Keith. *Beginnings of Sisterhood: The American Woman's Rights Movement,* 1800–1850. New York: Schocken Books, 1977.

Melder, Keith. "Mask of Oppression: The Female Seminary Movement in the United States," *New York History* LV (July 1974): 260–79.

Rosenberg, Charles E. "Sexuality, Class, and Role in Nineteenth-Century America," *American Quarterly* 25 (May 1973): 131–53.

Scott, Anne Firor. *The Southern Lady: From Pedestal to Politics 1830–1930.* Chicago: University of Chicago Press, 1970.

Sklar, Kathryn Kish. *Catharine Beecher: A Study in American Domesticity.* New Haven: Yale University Press, 1973.

Smith-Rosenberg, Carroll. "Beauty, the Beast and the Militant Woman: A Case Study in Sex Roles and Social Stress in Jacksonian America." *American Quarterly* 23 (October 1971): 562–84.

Smith-Rosenberg, Carroll and Charles Rosenberg. "The Female Animal: Medical and Biological Views of Woman and Her Role in Nineteenth-Century America," *Journal of American History* 60 (Sept. 1973): 332–56.

Smith-Rosenberg, Carroll. "Puberty to Menopause: The Cycle of Femininity in Nineteenth-Century America," in *Clio's Consciousness Raised* eds. Mary Hartman and Lois Banner. New York: Harper Torchbooks, 1974, pp. 23–37.

Trecker, Janice Law. "Sex, Science and Education." *American Quarterly* 26 (Oct. 1974): 352–66.

Walsh, Mary Roth. *"Doctors Wanted: No Women Need Apply," Sexual Barriers in the Medical Profession, 1835-1975.* New Haven: Yale University Press, 1977.

Welter, Barbara. *Dimity Convictions: The American Woman in the Nineteenth Century.* Athens: Ohio University Press, 1976.

The Lady and the Mill Girl:
Changes in the Status of Women
in the Age of Jackson

Gerda Lerner

The period 1800–1840 is one in which decisive changes occurred in the status of American women. It has remained surprisingly unexplored. With the exception of a recent, unpublished dissertation by Keith Melder and the distinctive work of Elisabeth Dexter, there is a dearth of descriptive material and an almost total absence of interpretation.[1] Yet the period offers essential clues to an understanding of later institutional developments, particularly the shape and nature of the women's rights movement. This analysis will consider the economic, political and social status of women and examine the changes in each area. It will also attempt an interpretation of the ideological shifts which occurred in American society concerning the "proper" role for women.

Periodization always offers difficulties. It seemed useful here, for purposes of comparison, to group women's status before 1800 roughly under the "colonial" heading and ignore the transitional and possibly atypical shifts which occurred during the American Revolution and the early period of nationhood. Also, regional differences were largely ignored. The South was left out of consideration entirely because its industrial development occurred later.

The status of colonial women has been well studied and described and can briefly be summarized for comparison with the later period. Throughout the colonial period there was a marked shortage of women, which varied with the regions and always was greatest in the frontier areas.[2] This (from the point of view of women) favorable sex ratio enhanced their status and position. The Puritan world view regarded idleness as sin; life in an underdeveloped country made it absolutely necessary that each member of the community perform an economic function. Thus work for women, married or single, was not only approved, it was regarded as a civic duty. Puritan town councils expected single girls, widows and unattached women to be self-supporting and for a long time provided needy spinsters with parcels of land. There was no social sanction against married women working; on the contrary, wives were expected to help their husbands in their trade and won social approval for doing extra work in or out of the home. Needy children, girls as well as boys, were indentured or apprenticed and were expected to work for their keep.

The vast majority of women worked within their homes, where their labor produced most articles needed for the family. The entire colonial production of cloth and clothing and partially that of shoes was in the hands of women. In addition to these occupations, women were found in many different kinds of employment. They were butchers, silversmiths, gunsmiths, upholsterers. They ran mills, plantations, tan yards, shipyards and every kind of shop, tavern and boarding house. They were gate keepers, jail keepers, sextons, journalists, printers, "doctoresses," apothecaries, midwives, nurses and teachers. Women acquired their skills the same way as did the men, through apprenticeship training, frequently within their own families.[3]

Absence of a dowry, ease of marriage and remarriage and a more lenient attitude of the law with regard to woman's property rights were manifestations of the improved position of wives in the colonies. Under British common law, marriage destroyed a woman's contractual capacity; she could not sign a contract even with the consent of her husband. But colonial authorities were more lenient toward the wife's property rights by protecting her dower rights in her husband's property, granting her personal clothing and upholding pre-nuptial contracts between husband and wife. In the absence of the husband, colonial courts granted women "femme sole" rights, which enabled them to conduct their husband's business, sign contracts and sue. The relative social freedom of women and the esteem in which they were held was commented upon by most early foreign travelers in America.[4]

But economic, legal and social status tell only part of the story.

Colonial society as a whole was hierarchical, and rank and standing in society depended on the position of the men. Women did not play a determining role in the ranking pattern; they took their position in society through the men of their own family or the men they married. In other words, they participated in the hierarchy only as daughters and wives, not as individuals. Similarly, their occupations were, by and large, merely auxiliary, designed to contribute to family income, enhance their husbands' business or continue it in case of widowhood. The self-supporting spinsters were certainly the exception. The underlying assumption of colonial society was that women ought to occupy an inferior and subordinate position. The settlers had brought this assumption with them from Europe; it was reflected in their legal concepts, their willingness to exclude women from political life, their discriminatory educational practices. What is remarkable is the extent to which this felt inferiority of women was constantly challenged and modified under the impact of environment, frontier conditions and a favorable sex ratio.

By 1840 all of American society had changed. The Revolution had substituted an egalitarian ideology for the hierarchical concepts of colonial life. Privilege based on ability rather than inherited status, upward mobility for all groups of society and unlimited opportunities for individual self-fulfillment had become ideological goals, if not always realities. For men, that is; women were, by tacit consensus, excluded from the new democracy. Indeed their actual situation had in many respects deteriorated. While, as wives, they had benefitted from increasing wealth, urbanization and industrialization, their role as economic producers and as political members of society differed sharply from that of men. Women's work outside of the home no longer met with social approval; on the contrary, with two notable exceptions, it was condemned. Many business and professional occupations formerly open to women were now closed, many others restricted as to training and advancement. The entry of large numbers of women into low status, low pay and low skill industrial work had fixed such work by definition as "woman's work." Women's political status, while legally unchanged, had deteriorated relative to the advances made by men. At the same time the genteel lady of fashion had become a model of American femininity and the definition of "woman's proper sphere" seemed narrower and more confined than ever.

Within the scope of this article only a few of these changes can be more fully explained. The professionalization of medicine and its impact on women may serve as a typical example of what occurred in all the professions.

In colonial America there were no medical schools, no medical journals, few hospitals and few laws pertaining to the practice of the healing arts. Clergymen and governors, barbers, quacks, apprentices and women practiced medicine. Most practitioners acquired their credentials by reading Paracelsus and Galen and serving an apprenticeship with an established practitioner. Among the semi-trained "physics," surgeons and healers the occasional "doctoress" was fully accepted and frequently well rewarded. County records of all the colonies contain references to the work of the female physicians. There was even a female Army surgeon, a Mrs. Allyn, who served during King Philip's war. Plantation records mention by name several slave women who were granted special privileges because of their useful service as midwives and "doctoresses." [5]

The period of the professionalization of American medicine dates from 1765, when Dr. William Shippen began his lectures on midwifery in Philadelphia. The founding of medical faculties in several colleges, the standardization of training requirements and the proliferation of medical societies intensified during the last quarter of the eighteenth century. The American Revolution dramatized the need for trained medical personnel, afforded first hand battlefield experience to a number of surgeons and brought increasing numbers of semi-trained practitioners in contact with the handful of European-trained surgeons working in the military hospitals. This was an experience from which women were excluded. The resulting interest in improved medical training, the gradual appearance of graduates of medical colleges and the efforts of medical societies led to licensing legislation. In 1801 Maryland required all medical practitioners to be licensed; in 1806 New York enacted a similar law, providing for an examination before a commission. By the late 1820s all states except three had set up licensing requirements. Since most of these laws stipulated attendance at a medical college as one of the prerequisites for licensing, women were automatically excluded. [6] By the 1830s the few established female practitioners who might have continud their practice in the old ways had probably died out. Whatever vested interest they had had was too weak to assert itself against the new profession.

This process of pre-emption of knowledge, institutionalization of the profession and legitimation of its claims by law and public acceptance is standard for the professionalization of the sciences, as George Daniels has pointed out. [7] It inevitably results in the elimination of fringe elements from the profession. It is interesting to note that women had been pushed out of the medical profession in sixteenth-century Europe by a similar process. [8] Once the public had come to accept licensing and college training as guarantees of up-to-date practice the outsider, no matter how well qualified by years of experience, stood no chance in the competition. Women were the casualties of medical professionalization.

In the field of midwifery the results were similar, but the process was more complicated. Women had held a virtual monopoly in the profession in colonial America. In 1646 a man was prosecuted in Maine for practicing as a midwife.[9] There are many records of well trained midwives with diplomas from European institutions working in the colonies. In most of the colonies midwives were licensed, registered and required to pass an examination before a board. When Dr. Shippen announced his pioneering lectures on midwifery, he did it to "combat the widespread popular prejudice against the man-midwife" and because he considered most midwives ignorant and improperly trained.[10]

Yet he invited "those women who love virtue enough, to own their Ignorance, and apply for instruction" to attend his lectures, offering as an inducement the assurance that female pupils would be taught privately. It is not known if any midwives availed themselves of the opportunity.[11]

Technological advances, as well as scientific, worked against the interests of female midwives. In sixteenth-century Europe the invention and use of the obstetrical forceps had for three generations been the well-kept secret of the Chamberlen family and had greatly enhanced their medical practice. Hugh Chamberlen was forced by circumstances to sell the secret to the Medical College in Amsterdam, which in turn transmitted the precious knowledge to licensed physicians only. By the time the use of the instrument became widespread it had become associated with male physicians and midwives. Similarly in America, introduction of the obstetrical forceps was associated with the practice of male midwives and served to their advantage. By the end of the eighteenth century a number of male physicians advertised their practice of midwifery. Shortly thereafter female midwives also resorted to advertising, probably in an effort to meet the competition. By the early nineteenth century male physicians had virtually monopolized the practice of midwifery on the Eastern seaboard. True to the generally delayed economic development in the Western frontier regions, female midwives continued to work on the frontier until a much later period. It is interesting to note that the concepts of "propriety" shifted with the prevalent practice. In seventeenth-century Maine the attempt of a man to act as a midwife was considered outrageous and illegal; in mid-nineteenth-century America the suggestion that women should train as midwives and physicians was considered equally outrageous and improper.[12]

Professionalization, similar to that in medicine with the elimination of women from the upgraded profession, occurred in the field of law. Before 1750, when law suits were commonly brought to the courts by the plaintiffs themselves or by deputies without specialized legal training, women as well as men could and did act as "attorneys-in-fact." When the law became a paid profession and trained lawyers took over litigation, women disappeared from the court scene for over a century.[13]

A similar process of shrinking opportunities for women developed in business and in the retail trades. There were fewer female storekeepers and business women in the 1830s than there had been in colonial days. There was also a noticeable shift in the kind of merchandise handled by them. Where previously women could be found running almost every kind of retail shop, after 1830 they were mostly found in businesses which served women only.[14]

The only fields in which professionalization did not result in the elimination of women from the upgraded profession were nursing and teaching. Both were characterized by a severe shortage of labor. Nursing lies outside the field of this inquiry since it did not become an organized profession until after the Civil War. Before then it was regarded peculiarly as a woman's occupation, although some of the hospitals and the Army during wars employed male nurses. These bore the stigma of low skill, low status and low pay. Generally, nursing was regarded as simply an extension of the unpaid services performed by the housewife—a characteristic attitude that haunts the profession to this day.

Education seems, at first glance, to offer an entirely opposite pattern from that of the other professions. In colonial days women had taught "Dame schools" and grade schools during summer sessions. Gradually, as educational opportunities for girls expanded, they advanced just a step ahead of their students. Professionalization of teaching occurred between 1820–1860, a period marked by a sharp increase in the number of women teachers. The spread of female seminaries, academies and normal schools provided new opportunities for the training and employment of female teachers.

This trend which runs counter to that found in the other professions can be accounted for by the fact that women filled a desperate need created by the challenge of the common schools, the ever-increasing size of the student body and the westward growth of the nation. America was committed to educating its children in public schools, but it was insistent on doing so as cheaply as possible. Women were available in great numbers and they were willing to work cheaply. The result was another ideological adaptation: in the very period when the gospel of the home as woman's only proper sphere was preached most loudly, it was discovered that women were the natural teachers of youth, could do the job better than men and were to be preferred for such employment. This was always provided, of course, that they would work at the proper wage differential—thirty to fifty percent of the wages paid male teachers was considered appropriate. The result was that in 1888 in the country as a whole sixty-three percent of all teachers were women, while the figure for the cities only was 90.04 percent.[15]

It appeared in the teaching field, as it would in industry, that role expectations were adaptable provided the inferior status group filled a social need. The inconsistent and peculiar patterns of employment of black labor in the present-day market bear out the validity of this generalization.

There was another field in which the labor of women was appreciated and which they were urged to enter—industry. From Alexander Hamilton to Matthew Carey and Tench Coxe, advocates of industrialization sang the praises of the working girl and advanced arguments in favor of her employment. The social benefits of female labor particularly stressed were those bestowed upon her family, who now no longer had to support her. Working girls were "thus happily preserved from idleness and its attendant vices and crimes" and the whole community benefitted from their increased purchasing power.[16]

American industrialization, which occurred in an underdeveloped economy with a shortage of labor, depended on the labor of women and children. Men were occupied with agricultural work and were not available or willing to enter the factories. This accounts for the special features of the early development of the New England textile industry: the relatively high wages, the respectability of the job and relatively high status of the mill girls, the patriarchal character of the model factory towns and the temporary mobility of women workers from farm to factory and back again to farm. All this was characteristic only of a limited area and of a period of about two decades. By the late 1830s the romance had worn off; immigration had supplied a strongly competitive, permanent work force willing to work for subsistence wages; early efforts at trade union organization had been shattered and mechanization had turned semiskilled factory labor into unskilled labor. The process led to the replacement of the New England-born farm girls by immigrants in the mills and was accompanied by a loss of status and respectability for female workers.

The lack of organized social services during periods of depression drove ever greater numbers of women into the labor market. At first, inside the factories distinctions between men's and women's jobs were blurred. Men and women were assigned to machinery on the basis of local need. But as more women entered industry the limited number of occupations open to them tended to increase competition among them, thus lowering pay standards. Generally, women regarded their work as temporary and hesitated to invest in apprenticeship training, because they expected to marry and raise families. Thus they remained untrained, casual labor and were soon, by custom, relegated to the lowest paid, least skilled jobs. Long hours, overwork and poor working conditions would characterize women's work in industry for almost a century.[17]

Another result of industrialization was in increasing differences in life styles between women of different classes. When female occupations, such as carding, spinning and weaving, were transferred from home to factory, the poorer women followed their traditional work and became industrial workers. The women of the middle and upper classes could use their newly gained time for leisure pursuits: they became ladies. And a small but significant group among them chose to prepare themselves for professional careers by advanced education. This group would prove to be the most vocal and troublesome in the near future.

As class distinctions sharpened, social attitudes toward women became polarized. The image of "the lady" was elevated to the accepted ideal of femininity toward which all women would strive. In this formulation of values lower class women were simply ignored. The actual lady was, of course, nothing new on the American scene; she had been present ever since colonial days. What was new in the 1830s was the cult of the lady, her elevation to a status symbol. The advancing prosperity of the early nineteenth century made it possible for middle class women to aspire to the status formerly reserved for upper class women. The "cult of true womanhood" of the 1830s became a vehicle for such aspirations. Mass circulation newspapers and magazines made it possible to teach every woman how to elevate the status of her family by setting "proper" standards of behavior, dress and literary tastes. *Godey's Lady's Book* and innumerable gift books and tracts of the period all preach the same gospel of "true womanhood"—piety, purity, domesticity.[18] Those unable to reach the goal of becoming ladies were to be satisfied with the lesser goal—acceptance of their "proper place" in the home.

It is no accident that the slogan "woman's place is in the home" took on a certain aggressiveness and shrillness precisely at the time when increasing numbers of poorer women *left* their homes to become factory workers. Working women were not a fit subject for the concern of publishers and mass media writers. Idleness, once a disgrace in the eyes of society, had become a status symbol. Thorstein Veblen, one of the earliest and sharpest commentators on the subject, observed that it had become almost the sole social function of the lady "to put in evidence her economic unit's ability to pay." She was "a means of conspicuously unproductive expenditure," devoted to displaying her husband's wealth.[19] Just as the cult of white womanhood in the South served to preserve a labor and social system based on race distinctions, so did the cult of the lady in an egalitarian society serve as a means of preserving class distinctions. Where class distinction were not so great, as on the frontier, the position of women was closer to what it had been in colonial days; their economic contribution was more highly valued, their opportunities were less restricted and their positive participation in community life was taken for granted.

In the urbanized and industrialized Northeast the life experience of middle class women was different in almost every respect from that of the lower class women. But there was one thing the society lady and the mill girl had in common—they were equally disfranchised and isolated from the vital centers of power. Yet the political status of women had not actually deteriorated. With very few exceptions women had neither voted nor stood for office during the colonial period. Yet the spread of the franchise to ever wider groups of white males during the Jacksonian age, the removal of property restrictions, the increasing numbers of immigrants who acquired access to the franchise, made the gap between these new enfranchised voters and the disfranchised women more obvious. Quite naturally, educated and propertied women felt this deprivation more keenly. Their own career expectations had been encouraged by widening educational opportunities; their consciousness of their own abilities and of their potential for power had been enhanced by their activities in the reform movements of the 1830s; the general spirit of upward mobility and venturesome entrepreneurship that pervaded the Jacksonian era was infectious. But in the late 1840s a sense of acute frustration enveloped these educated and highly spirited women. Their rising expectations had met with frustration, their hopes had been shattered; they were bitterly conscious of a relative lowering of status and a loss of position. This sense of frustration led them to action; it was one of the main factors in the rise of the woman's rights movement.[20]

The women, who in 1848 declared boldly and with considerable exaggeration that "the history of mankind is a history of repeated injuries and usurpations on the part of man toward woman, having in direct object the establishment of an absolute tyranny over her," did not speak for the truly exploited and abused working woman.[21] As a matter of fact, they were largely ignorant of her condition and, with the notable exception of Susan B. Anthony, indifferent to her fate. But they judged from the realities of their own life experience. Like most revolutionaries, they were not the most downtrodden but rather the most status-deprived group. Their frustrations and traditional isolation from political power funneled their discontent into fairly utopian declarations and immature organizational means. They would learn better in the long, hard decades of practical struggle. Yet it is their initial emphasis on the legal and political "disabilities" of women which has provided the framework for most of the historical work on women. For almost a hundred years sympathetic historians have told the story of women in America from the feminist viewpoint. Their tendency has been to reason from the position of middle class women to a generalization concerning all American women. This distortion has obscured the actual and continuous contributions of women to American life.[22] To avoid such a distortion, any valid generalization concerning American women after the 1830s should reflect a recognition of class stratification.

For lower class women the changes brought by industrialization were actually advantageous, offering income and advancement opportunities, however limited, and a chance for participation in the ranks of organized labor. They, by and large, tended to join men in their struggle for economic advancement and became increasingly concerned with economic gains and protective labor legislation. Middle and upper class women, on the other hand, reacted to actual and fancied status deprivation by increasing militancy and the formation of organizations for women's rights, by which they meant especially legal and property rights.

The four decades preceding the Seneca Falls Convention were decisive in the history of American women. They brought an actual deterioration in the economic opportunities open to women, a relative deterioration in their political status and a rising level of expectation and subsequent frustration in a privileged elite group of educated women. The ideology still pervasive in our present-day society regarding woman's "proper" role was formed in those decades. Later, under the impact of feminist attacks this ideology would grow defensive and attempt to bolster its claims by appeals to universality and pretentions to a history dating back to antiquity or, at least, to *The Mayflower*. Women, we are told, have always played a restricted and subordinate role in American life. In fact, however, it was in mid-nineteenth-century America that the ideology of "woman's place is in the home" changed from being an accurate description of existing reality into a myth. It became the "feminine mystique"—a longing for a lost, archaic world of agrarian family self-sufficiency, updated by woman's consumer function and the misunderstood dicta of Freudian psychology.

The decades 1800–1840 also provide the clues to an understanding of the institutional shape of the later women's organizations. These would be led by middle class women whose self-image, life experience and ideology had largely been fashioned and influenced by these early, transitional years. The concerns of middle class women—property rights, the franchise and moral uplift—would dominate the women's rights movement. But side by side with it, and at times cooperating with it, would grow a number of organizations serving the needs of working women.

American women were the largest disfranchised group in the nation's history, and they retained this position longer than any other group. Although they found ways of making their influence felt continuously, not only as individuals but as organized groups, power eluded them. The mill girl and the lady, both born in the age of Jackson, would not gain access to power until they learned to cooperate, each for her own separate interests. It would take almost six decades before they would find common ground. The issue around which they finally would unite and push their movement to victory was the "impractical and utopian" demand raised at Seneca Falls—the means to power in American society—female suffrage.

NOTES

The generalizations in this article are based on extensive research in primary sources, including letters and manuscripts of the following women: Elizabeth Cady Stanton, Susan B. Anthony, Abby Kelley, Lucretia Mott, Lucy Stone, Sarah and Angelina Grimke, Maria Weston Chapman, Lydia Maria Child and Betsey Cowles. Among the organizational records consulted were those of the Boston Female Anti-Slavery Society, the Philadelphia Female Anti-Slavery Society, Anti-Slavery Conventions of American Women, all the Woman's Rights Conventions prior to 1870 and the records of various female charitable organizations.

   1. Keith E. Melder, "The Beginnings of the Women's Rights Movement in the United States: 1800–1840," (Unpublished dissertation, Yale University, 1964); Elisabeth A. Dexter, *Colonial Women of Affairs: Women in Business and Professions in America before 1776* (Boston, 1931); Dexter, *Career Women of America: 1776–1840* (Francestown, N.H., 1950).

2. Herbert Moller, "Sex Composition and Corresponding Culture Patterns of Colonial America," *William and Mary Quarterly,* Ser. 3, II (April, 1945): 113–53.

3. The summary of the status of colonial women is based on the following sources: Mary Benson, *Women in 18th Century America: A Study of Opinion and Social Usage* (New York, 1935); Arthur Calhoun, *A Social History of the American Family,* 3 vols. (Cleveland, 1918); Dexter, *Colonial Women;* Dexter, *Career Women;* Edmund S. Morgan, *Virginians at Home: Family Life in the 18th Century* (Williamsburg, 1952); Julia C. Spruill, *Women's Life and Work in the Southern Colonies* (Chapel Hill, 1938).

4. E.M. Boatwright, "The political and legal status of women in Georgia: 1783–1860," *Georgia Historical Quarterly,* 25 (April, 1941); Richard B. Morris, *Studies in the History of American Law* (New York, 1930), Chap. 3. A summary of travelers' comments on American women may be found in: Jane Mesick, *The English Traveler in America: 1785–1835* (New York, 1922), pp. 83–99.

5. For facts on colonial medicine the following sources were consulted: Wyndham B. Blanton, *Medicine in Virginia,* 3 vols. (Richmond, 1930); N.S. Davis, M.D., *History of Medical Education and Institutions in the United States. . . .* (Chicago, 1851); Dexter, *Career Women;* K.C. Hurd-Mead, M.D., *A History of Women in Medicine: from the Earliest Times to the Beginning of the 19th Century* (Haddam, Conn., 1938); Geo. W. Norris, *The Early History of Medicine in Philadelphia* (Philadelphia, 1886); Joseph M. Toner, *Contributions to the Annals of Medical Progress in the United States before and during the War of Independence* (Washington, D.C., 1874). The citation regarding Mrs. Allyn is from Hurd-Mead, *Women in Medicine,* p. 487.

6. Fielding H. Garrison, M.D., *An Introduction to the History of Medicine* (Philadelphia, 1929). For licensing legislation: Davis, pp. 88–103.

7. George Daniels, "The Professionalization of American Science: the emergent period, 1820–1860," paper delivered at the joint session of the History of Science Society and the Society of the History of Technology, San Francisco, December 28, 1965.

8. Hurd-Mead, *Women in Medicine,* p. 391.

9. Ibid., p. 486.

10. Betsy E. Corner, *William Shippen Jr.: Pioneer in American Medical Education* (Philadelphia, 1951), p. 103.

11. Ibid.

12. Benjamin Lee Gordon, *Medieval and Renaissance Medicine* (New York, 1959), pp. 689–91; Blanton, *Medicine,* II, 23–24; Hurd-Mead, *Women in Medicine,* pp. 487-88; Annie Nathan Meyer, *Woman's Work in America* (New York, 1891); Harriot K. Hunt, M.D., *Glances and Glimpses or Fifty Years Social including Twenty Years Professional Life* (Boston, 1856), pp. 127–40; Eleanor Flexner, *Century of Struggle: The Woman's Rights Movement in the United States* (Cambridge, Mass., 1959), pp. 115–19.

13. Sophie H. Drinker, "Women Attorneys of Colonial Times," *Maryland Historical Society Bulletin,* LVI, No. 4 (Dec., 1961).

14. Dexter, *Colonial Women,* pp. 34–35, 162–65.

15. Harriet W. Marr, *The Old New England Academies* (New York, 1959),

Chap. 8; Thomas Woody, *A History of Women's Education in the United States*, 2 vols. (New York, 1929) II, 100–09, 458–60, 492–93.

16. Matthew Carey, *Essays on Political Economy*. (Philadelphia, 1822), p. 459.

17. The statements on women industrial workers are based on the following sources: Edith Abbott, *Women in Industry* (New York, 1910), pp. 66–80; Edith Abbott, "Harriet Martineau and the Employment of Women in 1836," *Journal of Political Economy*, XIV (Dec., 1906), 614–26; Matthew Carey, *Miscellaneous Essays* (Philadelphia, 1830), pp. 153–203; Helen L. Sumner, *History of Women in Industry in the United States*, in *Report on Conditions of Woman and Child Wage-Earners in the United States*, 19 vols. (Washington, D.C., 1910), IX. Also: Elizabeth F. Baker, *Technology and Woman's Work* (New York, 1964), Chaps. 1–5.

18. Emily Putnam, *The Lady: Studies of Certain Significant Phases of Her History* (New York, 1910), pp. 319–20; Barbara Welter, "The Cult of True Womanhood: 1820–1860," *American Quarterly*, XVIII, No. 2, Part 1 (Summer, 1966): 151–74.

19. Veblen generalized from his observations of the society of the Gilded Age and fell into the usual error of simply ignoring the lower class women, whom he dismissed as "drudges . . . fairly content with their lot," but his analysis of women's role in "conspicuous consumption" and of the function of women's fashions is unsurpassed. For references see: Thorstein Veblen, *The Theory of the Leisure Class* (New York, 1962, first ptg, 1899), pp. 70–71, 231–32. Thorstein Veblen, "The Economic Theory of Woman's Dress," *Essays in Our Changing Order* (New York, 1934), pp. 65–77.

20. Like most groups fighting status oppression women formulated a compensatory ideology of female superiority. Norton Mezvinsky has postulated that this was clearly expressed only in 1874; in fact this formulation appeared in the earliest speeches of Elizabeth Cady Stanton and in the speeches and resolutions of the Seneca Falls Conventions and other pre-Civil War woman's rights conventions. Rather than a main motivating force, the idea was a tactical formulation, designed to take advantage of the popularly held male belief in woman's "moral" superiority and to convince reformers that they needed the votes of women. Those middle class feminists who believed in woman's "moral" superiority exploited the concept in order to win their major goal—female equality. For references see: Norton Mezvinsky, "An Idea of Female Superiority," *Midcontinent American Studies Journal*, II (Spring, 1961): 17–26; E.D. Stanton, S.B. Anthony and M.J. Gage, eds., *A History of Woman Suffrage*, 6 vols. (New York, 1881–1922), I, 72, 479, 522, 529 and *passim;* Alan P. Grimes, *The Puritan Ethic and Woman Suffrage* (New York, 1967), Chaps. 2 and 3.

21. Stanton *et al, History of Woman Suffrage*, I, 70.

22. Mary R. Beard, *Woman as Force in History: A Study of Traditions and Realities* (New York, 1946).

Ladies Bountiful:
Organized Women's Benevolence in Early Nineteenth-Century America

Keith Melder

Observers of American society have long been impressed by the inclinations of United States citizens for "joining" countless societies for fraternal, social, intellectual, and religious purposes. Observing the nation during the 1830s, Alexis de Tocqueville made much of the "principle of association," as he called it, which drove Americans to establish voluntary organizations of all sorts:

> The Americans make associations to give entertainments, to found seminaries, to build inns, to construct churches, to diffuse books, to send missionaries to the antipodes; in this manner they found hospitals, prisons, and schools. If it is proposed to inculcate some truth or to foster some feeling by the encouragement of a great example, they form a society.[1]

Tocqueville perceived that voluntary organizations substituted in a democracy for the stable institutions and status relationships of Europe: "Feelings and opinions are recruited, the heart is enlarged, and the human mind is developed only by the reciprocal influence of men upon one another. I have shown that these influences are almost null in democratic countries; they must therefore be artificially created, and this can only be accomplished by associations." [2]

Other writers have remarked upon the proliferation of organized voluntary societies in the United States. Robin M. Williams, Jr., comments on the great numbers and variety of voluntary organizations and argues that historically such groupings have filled an institutional and power vacuum and have functioned as major integrating forces in an individualistic, equalitarian, and permissive society.[3] Most recently, T. Scott Miyakawa in his study of the dissenting sects on the American frontier, *Protestants and Pioneers,* finds that the voluntary organizations fostered by pioneering Methodist and Baptist congregations had a profound impact upon frontier development. These voluntary groups exercised a controlling influence on individual behavior, fostered practical grass-roots democracy, functioned as educational institutions, encouraged mutual assistance and group activities, and helped to produce a relatively integrated society.[4]

Most commentators on American voluntarism have dealt with societies founded and conducted by men, but far less attention has been paid to the growth and influence of organizations of women.[5] The present narrative will consider the background, the general pattern of development, and some of the consequences of voluntary women's organizations, during the first forty years of the nineteenth century.

Rudimentary organizations of women sprang up during the Revolutionary era. Anti-tea leagues, temporary consumers' organizations, scattered associations for the provision of clothing to the ragged army, and similar groups represented this earliest organizing tendency.[6] But the pattern does not seem to have survived the war. The movement for women's organizations appeared as a religious impulse in about 1800. Dedicated to pious and charitable ends, these ladies' societies had consequences reaching far beyond the worthy aims of their founders.

The background of American humanitarian organizations may be traced to the eighteenth-century evangelical revival in England. Motivated by an aggressive, emotional piety, English religious leaders sponsored various forms of active benevolence—reaching out to the poor and suffering with a message of love and a program of charitable enterprises.[7] Religious benevolence created a vocation for converts, enabling them to exhibit their Christian spirit. During the second half of the eighteenth century English evangelicals engaged in several significant benevolent efforts—prison reform, abolition of the African slave trade, Sunday schools for poor children, and other causes. A number of important charitable institutions were founded during this period.

The evangelical emphasis on sentiment and righteous conduct attracted to the benevolent movement a number of notable English women. Mrs. Sarah Trimmer, one of the leaders of the English movement, summarized the appeal of humanitarianism to women:

> Can ladies view these noble exertions of the other sex, and not be inspired with emulation to join with equal ardour in an undertaking which has as its object the reformation of so considerable a part of the kingdom; and which, in the end, may lead to a general reformation? Can a woman, accustomed to the exercise of maternal affection towards her own beloved offspring, be indifferent to the happiness of poor children who have no means of learning their duty but what these [Sunday] schools afford?

> Working for the poor is a species of charity which forms a part of the prerogative of our sex, and gives to those who have leisure for it an opportunity of doing much good with very little trouble or expense.[8]

Yet Mrs. Trimmer feared that opposition to women's benevolence and "the natural diffidence of our sex," would hinder this great work for which women were, "in some respects preeminently qualified." [9] The themes stressed in these appeals—the sincere faith in woman's power to do good, the natural maternal aspect of charity, the need to convert the poor to evangelical religion, and the benefits deriving, "with little trouble or expense," from the reformation of vicious and sinful mankind—were typical of the later appeals made to American women.

Probably no single individual was more influential in spreading the benevolent message to America than the eminent Englishwoman, Hannah More. "A fitter example could not easily be proposed . . . than that of this virtuous lady," her biographer wrote. Her pious battles with worldly impulses had "brought her safe out of the conflict, into that humble path of moderation, circumspection, and trust, which made her example so profitable, and her teaching so efficacious." [10] After a precocious childhood, Miss More entered into fashionable society where she scored successes as a woman of wit and brilliance. In time, however, she forsook her fashionable associates and turned toward Christian benevolence and writing. She participated in the Sunday-school and tract-distribution movements and contributed substantial amounts of her own funds to these causes. She also wrote voluminously and piously—sacred dramas, moralistic tales and essays, and many simple but powerful religious tracts. In the late eighteenth and early nineteenth centuries American publishers found a ready market for these works. As late as 1835 Harriet Martineau was impressed by the number of American women who read and were influenced by Hannah More.[11] Her life and works were the embodiment of Christian vocation at a time when American women were being urged to seek such a vocation for themselves. Thus the English evangelical movement crossed the Atlantic.[12]

In addition to the energetic examples set by British reformers, American women were affected by a domestic situation which challenged their piety and their patriotism. During the eighteenth century the Great Awakening quickened religious impulses among women but did not lead to a dramatic growth in organized benevolence. At the close of the century, however, new threats from at home and abroad seemed to make organization imperative. No doubt the fears of clergymen and conservative laymen were exaggerated, but they were real nevertheless. Respectable people feared the mob, the "lower orders," who seemed irresponsible, immoral, and uncontrolled. Deism and ir-religion also appeared as dangers, and the French Revolution threatened to undermine the established classes. The growing complexity of American society menaced the social order: religious denominations and congregations were separating, the west attracted restless families, upsetting settled communities and threatening orthodox denominations; and cities with their diverse and disorderly populations opened additional avenues for the spread of infidelity. Disturbed and even fearful, respectable church-going people saw the ideal of religious and social unity—embodied in the New England town—endangered by rapid social change. The militant evangelical movement appeared to such people as a potent weapon in their battle for stability and order.[13] And by participating in religious benevolence, women might be enlisted in the energetic Protestant struggle for supremacy.

The precise beginnings of organized benevolence are not easy to chart. Numerous individual ministers and religious organizations had been interested in missions to the American Indians. Some benevolent institutions were founded during the eighteenth century—a Bethesda Society and orphan asylum at Savannah, Georgia; prison reform, poor relief, and anti-slavery societies among the Philadelphia Quakers.[14] Women became involved in religious causes at the end of the century after a strong sense of mission had infected American denominations. Following examples set by British and Scottish missionary organizations, the pious set out to exert their utmost efforts in converting their neighbors and maintaining the faith in unchurched areas of the nation.[15] The Boston Female Society for Missionary Purposes, one of the earliest women's organizations, resolved in 1800 to raise funds for Congregational missions in the west. A Female Mite Society, formed at Providence in 1806, supported Baptist missions through penny-a-week contributions.[16] Other scattered societies began operation during the decade.

The missionary movement expanded rapidly after 1810. To cite one example, the Massachusetts Society for Promoting Christian Knowledge—founded in 1811 to support missionaries in upper New England and New York state—solicited the support of female auxiliaries, receiving funds from twelve women's groups in 1813 and from thirty in 1817.[17] In cities the "domestic missionary" program inaugurated a vigorous evangelical effort to protect and extend religious influence. Formed in 1816, the Female Domestic Missionary Society for the Poor of the City of New York and its Vicinity promoted Sabbath schools, distributed Bibles and other religious publications, and aided churches in the needy sections of the city. The ladies were urged to form associations in every ward and neighborhood for observing and reforming the religion and morals of the inhabitants.[18] Philadelphia women also supported domestic missions, believing that they would instill in the poor "the principle of Religion which cannot fail to convince them, that industry brings its own reward; that idleness is the root from which great evils spring. . . ." Working with other religious crusaders, the city missionaries might reclaim the vicious; "harmony and order would then be cherished. . . ." [19] Thus the new associations might serve as agents of social control.

The missionary cause developed a wide following in rural areas and in small towns. The New Hampshire Missionary Society depended principally upon more than fifty local female organizations for the support of its program of local preaching, foreign missions, education, Bible and tract distribution.[20] Between 1810 and 1815 female "cent a week" societies became common in New Hampshire and other states. Having been urged "that if people would retrench a little of their expenses, a revenue might easily be saved, which might do considerable toward extending the means of salvation," thousands of women joined "cent" societies and saved their pennies and mites for the extension of religion.[21] The missionary impulse spread quickly into New York state where the Female Missionary Society of the Western District, organized in 1816, maintained six missionaries and raised more than $2,000 in the year 1818 from forty-six towns and villages in ten counties.[22] The religious crusade stimulated the growth of centralized, nonsectarian, national organizations dedicated to the circulation of Bibles and tracts, and many women's societies became affiliates of the national groups.[23] New Hampshire's female Bible societies numbered 138 local groups at the height of their activities in 1828.[24] In 1817 the managers of the American Bible Society paid tribute to their lady assistants:

> It would be an act of injustice to that sex who contribute so essentially to the relief of our cares, whilst they heighten our purest pleasures, not to notice, in a prominent manner, their active benevolence in aid of the Society not only in forming Auxiliaries, but also in constituting, in so many places, their Pastors Members for life. They thus manifest the sense which they cherish of their obligations to that holy volume, whose truths have elevated them in Christian lands to their just and all-important station in society, and qualified them to perform the duties of that station with honour and success.[25]

The day-to-day activities of the female Bible societies represented those of most women's organizations. Local societies, such as that of Middlebury, Vermont, "associated together once a week for the purpose of sewing and knitting; thus by their own industry, accumulating a small fund, which, together with a few subscriptions from married ladies, was to be annually transmitted to the Parent Society." [26] Facing somewhat different problems, urban female Bible societies carried out aggressive programs to distribute the Scriptures among the poor and degraded in order to reform them.[27] Other causes engaged the interests of pious women. Between 1815 and 1835 hundreds of women's societies were formed to promote the distribution of tracts.[28] Women responded to the call to alleviate the shortage of clergymen by helping indigent but pious young men to study for the gospel ministry.[29] The professors at Princeton University were grateful for feminine assistance as they wrote: "The institution of Cent Societies in aid of the indigent students in the Theological Seminary at this place we acknowledge as a remarkable interposition of Divine Providence. . . ." [30] Other female societies organized Sabbath schools to teach reading and religion to poor and unconverted children. For more than twenty years respectable people fought for the "moral and religious improvement of seamen," and as the task of reformation proved difficult, women were called upon to pay for Bibles, tracts, and "suitable books," and to contribute toward the support of mariners' churches.[31]

In addition to their work in spreading the Gospel and their support of strictly religious causes, many women's organizations became involved in assistance to the poor and suffering. At Baltimore in 1798 a Female Humane Association was founded to help indigent women. Similar organizations appeared in New York City and Philadelphia.[32] These early charitable efforts appealed to women's maternal feelings by offering assistance to orphan girls and distressed widows. The ladies met periodically to discuss the unfortunate objects of their charity, they accumulated small sums of money, made clothing, and occasionally brought food to the sufferers. Charity spread quickly to smaller communities. At the Massachusetts seaports of Newburyport and Salem, female societies were chartered to assist orphans and aged widows.[33] A Salem minister noted with satisfaction the formation of "Female associations for the benefit of the female children" in his own and other communities.[34] Annual lectures or sermons were given to raise money for the deserving poor, and a woman was engaged to care for orphan girls by the Female Charitable Society of Salem.[35]

From the beginning these organizations were concerned about the elimination, as well as the amelioration, of poverty through education. The Female Humane Association of Baltimore opened a charity school in 1800, "to remedy the evil at its source, to snatch the child from a fate similar to that of its mother...." [36] In the same year the ladies of New York founded a school which filled them with hope: "The youthful mind is rescued from the dominion of idleness and ignorance; it is prepared for reflection; and for the performance of its active duties in the business of life." [37] Charity schools taught basic skills—the 3 r's, needlework, good conduct, and morals, and they attempted to inculcate habits of religion and industry. Although the poor would not be encouraged to ascend the economic and social ladder, they might aspire to industrious and fruitful lives.

The years between 1800 and 1830 witnessed a remarkable expansion of women's charitable activities: a quantitative growth of organizations, an impressive geographical expansion, and a great diversification in the kinds of work supported. In New York City the charity school for girls grew steadily until it had an annual attendance of more than 500 pupils.[38] In Boston the Fragment Society was established among respectable ladies of several congregations in 1812 "to alleviate the distress of the indigent...." According to its records the Society assisted 10,275 families, distributed 38,876 pieces of clothing, and spent $22,298.05 during the course of thirty years.[39] Not content merely to provide relief, the ladies of the Fragment Society were eager to carry a message to the poor: "Let us penetrate the lanes and by-ways of the city, enter the abodes of poverty and distress, and show to the destitute inmates that we sympathize in their sufferings and commiserate with them in their losses. Let us secure their confidence, and then, by kind advice, suggest a way to their self-maintenance and support." Just how the ladies would eliminate the "dejection and despondency" of the poor was not clear, but they would be rewarded in their efforts by "That solid satisfaction, which results from the consciousness of having done right. . . ." [40] Philadelphia had a most ambitious system of voluntary relief organizations. As early as 1793 members of the Society of Friends formed a women's society for the relief and employment of the poor, and additional organizations were begun in 1800 and 1808. In the latter year, the Female Hospitable Society began distributing spinning to needy women, providing work instead of charity to the destitute. [41]

Although women's relief work was concentrated in cities where the greatest need existed, long-lived societies operated in many smaller communities. For more than forty years, the Concord, New Hampshire, Female Charitable Society was concerned with the "spiritual and temporal wants" of their fellow creatures. [42] In the village of Bedford, Westchester County, New York, a Female Charitable Society existed for over fifty years "for the purpose of affording advice, assistance and relief to distressed and indigent women and children." Organized in 1816 on an interdenominational basis, the Bedford society distributed raw wool to the "industrious poor" for spinning and weaving. Several hundred children received some education from the proceeds of this enterprise, and many articles of clothing were donated to the poor. [43] In at least two cities, Philadelphia and Boston, organizations for voluntary relief became so numerous as to require a central administrative structure. Philadelphia's Union Benevolent Association was formed in 1831 during a particularly hard winter "to absorb the several other charity organizations . . . and so prevent the injurious repetitions in alms. . . ." [44] The Associations had a gentlemen's and ladies' branch. The latter embodied a notable innovation in providing lady visitors who circulated among the poor, performing a primitive species of social work and impressing the subjects of their charity with the "advantages of temperance, economy, cleanliness, order, regularity, and unwearied industry. . . ." [45] Recognizing the female aptitude for this work the Association

> Resolved: that women by their constitution and habits are more suitable for the work; that they are the best judges of the wants of women, whose sex is necessarily the greatest charge on charity; that they possess superior intuitions, are more sympathetic, more self-denying, gentler, and that their time as a rule is more generally at their command. [46]

The Ladies' Branch of the Union Benevolent Association operated five provision rooms in different sections of Philadelphia for distribution of relief and several hundred lady visitors covered the city in a carefully organized pattern.[47] In Boston representatives of twelve benevolent societies, most of them operated by women, attempted in 1834 to organize a city-wide relief program by dividing the city into districts and assigning a member of each society to every district. In this way they hoped to prevent the undeserving poor from exploiting the various societies in order to avoid working.[48] Although their manners were always patronizing, and although they did not begin to supply relief to all needy families, the women's benevolent societies contributed substantially to the support of the destitute. In some of their practices— counseling and visiting among the slum dwellers—they anticipated modern welfare techniques. Their activities represented the pattern of voluntary, private assistance that has been characteristic of much American philanthropy and relief.

The spread of women's benevolence was affected by several factors. As they became aware of the immediate earthly satisfactions and the more-distant heavenly rewards for their work, pious ladies with substantial social positions, leisure time, and a sense of responsibility answered clerical appeals for their assistance. The religious revival, in particular, offered strong inducements to women's benevolence and helped to carry the benevolent system into the west. Migrating from New England through New York state into the Western Reserve of Ohio, and the Middle West, Yankee settlers carried, along with their household goods, a great amount of evangelical enthusiasm and the memories of strong religious institutions.[49] Utica in the "burned-over" district of New York, was the center of a vigorous women's benevolent movement before 1820. Farther west, the town of Rochester had a female missionary society, organized in 1818 "to assist in supporting the preaching of the gospel in feeble and destitute churches in the new settlements."[50] At Cleveland, Ohio, several women's benevolent societies were established during the 1830s, and at Oberlin College, another center of New England influence, the young lady students were active in the benevolent movement after 1835.[51] As far west as Jacksonville, Illinois, where New England influence was strong, women's benevolence spread. A few early urban centers in the west developed networks of worthy organizations. By 1829 Cincinnati had a small network of women's organizations devoted to religious purposes.[52]

The clergy and their pious lay assistants were impressed and grateful for the contributions made by female benevolence. After all, the benefits of thousands of ladies' societies throughout the country could be measured on an economic as well as a spiritual scale. Ministers everywhere encouraged the women to undertake good works, and countless sermons and "discourses" were preached on the subject. According to the conventional view, women were more pious than men; wrote one observer: "The fact that there are twice as many female as male professors in every denomination of Christianity is unquestionable." [53] Their superior religious feelings constituted a natural endowment of the sex: "Women are happily formed for religion. Their sensibility, their vivacity, and sprightly imagination, their sympathy or tenderness toward the distressed and those in imminent danger of distress, as natural endowments, qualify them, with the grace of God added, to make Christians of the first cast." [54] A clergyman in Philadelphia was confident of the response of "Christian females" to his appeal for the support of missions: "The heart of *man* may be avaricious, and cold and unmoved. . . . But never—never did we meet with such a repulse from lovely women!" [55] Thus the argument went: religious benevolence naturally suited women, hence they should be glad to assist in almost every charitable task. Women also owed a special obligation to religion, for their condition in life had been greatly elevated by Christianity. One Doctor of Divinity confidently and somewhat patronizingly asserted: "Christianity has restored you to your true rank in society; and it gives you the honour and privilege—in grateful return, of taking the lead in charitable and missionary enterprizes." [56] Women were urged to support Bible societies because the Scriptures established a "charter of the female sex against degradation and oppression." [57] Another minister appealed to women's sense of sin and responsibility to mankind: "Women appear to be under a special obligation to embrace and promote Christianity, as our common original mother proved a tempter to her husband, and instigated him to the crime, which brought ruin on them both, and on all the human race." [58] Women had proven to be efficient, willing, and pliable laborers in the Lord's vineyard, and no appeal for their efforts, however flattering or threatening it might be, was too strong.

Despite their urgency in promoting women's benevolence, the ministers were anxious to maintain the correct principles of modesty and decorum. Addressing a "Plea for the Orphan" to members of the Female Charitable Society of Newburyport, Massachusetts, the Reverend S. P. Williams declared:

> Christianity, alone, has marked with precision, the official boundaries between the two great divisions of mankind; clearly defined the duties of their several relations, and wisely assigned the stations which they may occupy with appropriate dignity. It is from

this we learn, that the modesty which gives a polish to the sternest virtues of our sex, is essential to the very nature of virtue in woman. It is this, which while it prescribes a silent and gentle manner, allows, and commands in her, a powerful and extensive influence.[59]

Another minister attributed great influence to woman's sphere: "Though a wise Providence has much circumscribed for females their sphere of public action; yet the same wise Providence has permitted their influence in society to be very great and powerful." [60] Female power was intended to be subtle, and "the pious female" was "satisfied in being an *assistant* of man." [61] Yet although her behavior had to be modest and subordinate, woman had new opportunities to do good in a direct fashion. A New England minister described the altered conditions of female benevolence:

But Charity makes its appearance with us now, in a manner to which we have hitherto been unaccustomed. Until of late years, females have encouraged charitable associations by their persuasive efforts to soften the harder hearts of men, and to inspire them with so lively a sensibility of the sufferings and woes of those around them ... They at the present time, *associate themselves*, for the purpose. Who will say charity the most distinct and active doth not become them.[62]

Whereas in earlier years women had urged their husbands and brothers to relieve the suffering poor, now they formed their own societies to engage in good works, content in the knowledge that *"female charities for moral and religious purposes,* however small, will not fail to meet the divine approbation...." [63] When their timidity threatened the progress of their good deeds or the fullness of their purses, they were reassured that woman's action in "certain official characters necessary for the conducting of business ..." was no more reprehensible than "presiding at a dinner, or at a tea table." [64] The clergy had been thoroughly convinced of the practicality and utility of women's participation in voluntary benevolent organizations. They were prepared to defend the most energetic moral enterprises, but they emphasized over and over again the need for "Christian modesty, meekness, submission, wisdom, and fortitude" among the ladies.[65]

The sermons preached about women's benevolence indicate an ambiguity and a questioning of attitudes toward the sex. By encouraging voluntary societies, the clergy unintentionally enlarged woman's sphere, establishing the "right" of women to work for the public good.

Early in the nineteenth century a minister asserted that woman's efforts to promote religion, her assistance in educating future generations, and her aid to the poor represented "not the fancied, but the real 'Rights of Women'. They give them an extensive power over the fortunes of Man in every generation. They can never be exercised by them with too much constancy and zeal. . . ." [66] Of the implications or consequences of these rights, little concern or fear was expressed. But in encouraging women's benevolence the clergy recognized a "right" of women which had not been urged previously, for except in the Society of Friends and other unorthodox sects, no formal recognition was given to women's special religious duties. Perhaps in their newly emerging attitudes toward women, the ministers were rationalizing an unprecedented situation from which they derived great advantage, but rationalization or not, the new attitudes represented a break with the past. The praise which ministers heaped upon their feminine assistants and the comparisons with men which demonstrated the superior female moral sense added immeasurably to woman's stature. They served as building blocks and mortar for woman's moral pedestal, preparing the way for the Victorian ideal of the lady during the three decades before Victoria's ascension to the throne.

The benevolent movement stimulated concern for the status of women, emphasizing the powers and obligations of the sex. Women formed organizations, they collected and disbursed funds, they conducted promotional campaigns, they participated in and presided over business meetings. Genteel, pious ladies of high social standing engaged, perhaps for the first time, in organizational pursuits. Although they insisted that female activities be modest and unobtrusive, the ministers could not in fact sustain the myth of woman's complete subordination. Benevolence necessarily became a semi-public activity. Women went into the world to raise funds, they visited the poor or taught in charity schools, and their work attracted notice. No longer was woman's sphere defined strictly by the hearthstone, the parlor door, and the nursery.

By 1830 a great network of women's voluntary organizations flourished in settled portions of the United States, contributing thousands of dollars annually for the advancement of evangelical religion and the regeneration of the needy. Operating by Tocqueville's "principle of association," these women's societies were typical, in many respects, of the emerging pattern of voluntary collective action which characterized American society during this period. But as the system of organizations developed, its emphasis shifted in several respects. During the second and third decades of the century the conversion of souls and resulting reformation of behavior were the primary goals of missionary, Bible, and tract societies. The next evolutionary step was a more concerted effort to change personal attitudes and conduct; reform became equally important with or took precedence over conversion. Two significant reform movements attracted women during the 1830s: moral reform—the campaign against prostitution and the double moral standard—and the antislavery agitation. Both of these crusades had immense implications and important direct influence on the development of American feminism.

Moral reform was assuredly a radical movement. The moral reformers proposed to do no less than abolish prostitution and revolutionize relations between the sexes. The cause was not entirely new. Asylums for penitent females had been established in several American cities between 1810 and 1830. In Boston domestic missionaries hoped to change the conduct of "Females, given up to the practice of every enormity," by offering the wretched creatures a home where they might be taught religion and habits of industry. Delicate and sensitive ladies were not expected to make public acknowledgement of the evil, yet they might discreetly give financial aid to the movement.[67] The radical moral reform movement began in 1830 with the appearance of John R. McDowall, a pious young Presbyterian minister, who "with a thrill of horror" discovered Five Points, a notorious center of vice in New York City. The young reformer began to publish detailed accounts of his discoveries in two lurid periodicals, *McDowall's Journal* and *Magdalen Facts*. He estimated that 10,000 loose women swarmed the streets of New York and concluded that these females constituted a great danger to the social order:

> But it is clearly ascertained that bad women multiply the seduction of heedless youth, more rapidly than bad men seduce modest women. A few of these courtesans suffice to corrupt whole cities, and there can be no doubt that some insinuating prostitutes have initiated more young men into these destructive ways, than the most abandoned rakes have debauched virgins during their whole lives.[68]

McDowall's disclosure created a public uproar and efforts were made to suppress his publications. One of his supporters later admitted that "Mr. McDowall was not always so prudent and discreet as he should have been, and . . . his zeal and courage were greater than his judgement. He was also more gifted in searching out and exposing iniquities than in suggesting remedies. It was a subject of great delicacy . . ."[69]

Despite the public outrage at McDowall's work, his movement became popular with women, and during the 1830s hundreds of female moral reform societies were formed throughout the country. But as leadership passed into female hands the movement's emphasis changed from the protection of young men to a bold defense of women. Ladies of the female Moral Reform Society in Boston resolved not to "turn aside to contend with obstacles or opposition. . . . The cause of moral reform involves principles which, if fully and perseveringly applied, will elevate woman to her proper standing in society, without moving her from her 'appropriate sphere'. . . ." [70] Women were urged to protect one another as they "Resolved, that in maintaining the *rights* of women, we will not neglect her appropriate duties, one of the principal of which duties is to guard our daughters, sisters, and female acquaintances from the delusive arts of corrupt and unprincipled men." [71] The reformers would "elevate" the character of woman in order to protect her against "the various allurements by which the evil and designing would entangle her." [72] Essentially the reformers demanded a single moral standard applying to men and women alike: "Would men but treat their own sex, when convicted of disgraceful crime, as we treat ours under similar circumstances, the work of reformation would be comparatively easy." [73]

Moral reform struck at fundamental human attitudes and relationships, threatening one of the most important traditions of feminine inferiority. Advocates of the new cause attempted to prove that because she was pure and innocent, woman was morally superior to base, animalistic man. As a consequence of her purity, woman occupied a moral pedestal that permitted her to judge the behavior of others. The moral reformers carried to an extreme the earlier assertions of feminine power and influence made by clergymen to gain women's support for religious benevolence. The new movement provoked further questioning of the status and duties of women, it contributed substantially to the feminist spirit, and it opened the long women in the campaign and they pointed with pride to the vigorous antislavery efforts of English women. At the first meeting the founders of the American Anti-Slavery Society "Resolved, that all the ladies of and many hundreds of local societies were founded to realize the goal of equal sexual relations.

The antislavery movement was more radical in certain respects than the crusade for moral reform, and its consequences for women were more dramatic. Opposition to slavery began long before 1830, but abolitionism, with its sectional character and its radical, divisive techniques, appeared in 1831 with William Lloyd Garrison's paper the *Liberator*. Garrison and other abolitionists were delighted to enlist women in the campaign and they pointed with pride to the vigorous antislavery efforts of English women. At the first meeting the founders of the American Anti-Slavery Society "Resolved, that all the ladies of the land are respectfully and earnestly invited by this Convention to form Anti-Slavery Societies in every State, County, and town in the Union; and that we recommend them to publish tracts and addresses calculated to wake up the slumbering nation." [74] Between 1833 and 1838 more than 100 female antislavery societies were established in northeastern cities and towns.[75] The movement was centered in New England, but numerous organizations appeared in other states. Some were inspired by Yankee immigrants but others were not of New England origin. A leading Ohio abolitionist welcomed the formation of an Ashtabula County female antislavery society in that state:

> I hail you as dear sisters and coworkers in the most glorious cause that has ever claimed the attention of the philanthropist and christian. And what agent is so powerful in correcting public sentiment as woman? Wherever the light of revelation shines woman's influence is great and it is our glory that in this above any other land her rights are acknowledged and her power felt. In what way can that power be so appropriately put forth as in rescuing a portion of the sex from deep and perpetual degredation.[76]

Another male abolitionist supported women's antislavery work: " 'In Christ Jesus there is neither male nor female.' That is, in moral enterprises, moral worth and intellect are the standard. A mind whether deposited in a male or female body is equally valuable for all moral and intellectual purposes." [77]

Women entered into abolitionism as they had joined other benevolent movements. It seemed only natural that they should agitate and raise money for the cause. Leading abolitionists discovered that they were valuable allies in circulating and signing antislavery petitions to Congress and state legislatures. Petitioning was a quasi-political activity, however, far beyond the traditional limitations on feminine decorum. Women's petitions were denounced by politicians, clergymen, and leading citizens as unfeminine and positively immoral. In other respects, too, the female antislavery movement carried women further along toward political action. The ladies held three national conventions to discuss the slavery question, to consider their responsibilities at this critical time, and to organize and coordinate female activities. These conventions were milestones in the developing self-consciousness and the changing status of American women. When they spoke in public, organizing and conducting their own conventions, women moved into roles never before anticipated in connection with benevolent work. Abolitionism brought women into a public sphere, an arena of controversy, setting precedents for additional public reform work. (For example, in the field of temperance and prohibition agitation.) The slavery issue raised questions about the status of women in a more direct manner than earlier benevolent and charitable work had done. In discussing slavery, women dealt with basic questions of human rights and freedom, principles which could apply to the condition of women as well as that of the slaves. These principles were soon made relevant to women, and it was not long before the "woman question" became a major public issue.[78]

Between 1800 and 1840 the women's benevolent movement had evolved from minute beginnings in a few American cities and towns into a great body of organizations numbering well into the thousands. The impulse to voluntary, collective action had affected all Americans, and women had been motivated by a tremendous sense of optimism, a faith in their moral influence and their united power, to undertake campaigns that would alter American society in certain significant ways. To some extent the women's benevolent movement in the United States was derivative from England. Whatever they did, whether it involved Sunday schools, tract and Bible distribution, or abolition, American women followed precedents set by their English sisters. But women in this country seem to have carried their activities further than their counterparts in England. Proportionately more persons were involved in the American movements and the women became more independent of male authority in their activities. Certainly they went further than English women in dealing with the implications which their efforts had for the rights and duties of woman.

Beginning as a moderate endeavor with conservative aims, carried out by women with relatively high social standing, the female benevolent movement developed in the course of twenty years more radical principles in both its ideology and its techniques. Veering away from religious efforts and moving toward reformist goals, militant women became disenchanted with moderation, for the millenium did not materialize. Goals were sharpened: relief for the poor developed into efforts to convert the poor and reform their habits of living. Finally the reformers began attacking specific evils—prostitution, the double standard, and slavery. Techniques, too, became less orthodox: sewing for the poor, fund raising through genteel, discreet means were recognized by many persons to be inadequate, and women became more active, less traditionally domestic in their good works. In some cities they organized visiting teams to work with the poor, and they became more and more active in carrying on organizational business. As abolitionists, women were called upon to circulate petitions and submit them to the state and national legislatures, they began speaking in public, and they held the earliest women's conventions.

Other features of the women's benevolent movement deserve brief attention. A certain regionalism is evident in its growth. The Yankee influence was primary, not only in New England itself, but in other parts of the country settled by New Englanders. Particularly in rural areas and in small towns, evangelical Yankee enthusiasm and moralism produced much interest in benevolence and reforms. Following a "psychic highway" through New York state and Ohio into Michigan, Illinois, Wisconsin, and Kansas, New England women carried their moralistic yearnings and their attachment to collective action. New England was not the *only* center or influence on reform, however. In Philadelphia the Quakers and members of orthodox denominations maintained a vigorous benevolent effort, probably not approached by any other city in the United States. Other cities had their women's charitable societies to provide relief and religious comfort to the poor. In the South, where Yankee influence was not great, there were many women's benevolent organizations. Nevertheless, the New England mind had an affinity for reform, often reform of the more radical and exotic sort. Men were extremely influential, and few women's benevolent organizations flourished without encouragement from the other sex. Especially during its formative years the movement received potent support from clergymen and from leading respectable citizens.

Organized women's benevolence made a number of significant contributions to American society during the first half of the nineteenth century. Women served at the right hand of the clergy in seeking to maintain and expand the nation's allegiance to evangelical religion. Women's organizations contributed substantially to American philanthropy at this time. In their day the funds raised through the pennies and "mites" collected by these forgotten ladies were prodigious. Like the voluntary organizations of men, women's societies had a significant role in spreading democratic values and techniques. To some extent these societies were equalizing influences, bringing their members together on an equal basis and seeking to "uplift" the poor. They served also as forces of social integration in a nation which had relatively few integrating institutions.[79] With their typical characteristics of constitution-making, elective offices, and "political" action, these organizations were miniature democratic laboratories. They made it possible for later generations of female reformers and social workers to serve the poor and the needy. Dorothea Dix, Clara Barton, Jane Addams, and many other leaders may be considered as the direct descendants of the early nineteenth century benevolent movement. The benevolent societies were predecessors of thousands of modern organizations—women's clubs, Leagues of Women Voters, church sewing circles, and countless others.[80]

The benevolent movement reflected subtle changes in attitudes toward the status of women and aided in establishing a basis for further changes in these attitudes. Because of their charitable and reformist efforts, questions were raised concerning women's rights and duties. More specifically, women began to assert their "rights" in a general sense when their immediate "right" to engage in social reform was challenged. A line of evolution may be discerned from female Bible, tract, and missionary work, to ladies' aid to their sisters in distress and to moral reform and abolition. Women's cent societies, poor schools, and charitable associations provided examples, patterns of organization, and even members for the later, more radical reformist crusades. And further, such associations had similar consequences for societies dedicated to temperance and feminism. Having learned that women had a responsibility to defend the friendless and work for the regeneration of humankind, the women reformers defended their "right" to agitate in their own behalf. Although only a minority of women ever asserted this "right," those who did so had been educated in the women's benevolent movement. Lydia Maria Child, author, reformer, and intellectual, summed up the impact of women's organized, voluntary efforts in an editorial written after many years of observation. A keen observer, she wrote with authority:

> In modern times, the evangelical sects have highly approved of female prayer meetings. In the cause of missions and the dissemination of tracts, they have eloquently urged upon women their prodigious influence and consequent responsibility, in the great work of regenerating a world lying in wickedness. Thus it is with those who urged women to become missionaries, and form tract societies. They have changed the household utensil into a living, energetic being; and they have no spell to turn it into a broom again.[81]

There is little doubt that the "principle of association" which Alexis de Tocqueville observed in the 1830s has been a key factor in the development of American society. The consequences of voluntary organizations deserve far more scholarly attention than they had received. And when the interpretation of American voluntarism comes to be written, it should include some consideration of the way in which women learned to be "living, energetic beings" through their participation in charitable and religious organizations.

NOTES

1. Alexis de Tocqueville, *Democracy in America*, the Henry Reeve text as revised by Francis Bowen, ed. by Phillips Bradley (New York, 1960), II, 106.
2. Ibid., pp. 108–09.
3. Robin M. Williams, Jr., *American Society: A Sociological Interpretation* (New York, 1960), pp. 494–500.
4. T. Scott Miyakawa, *Protestants and Pioneers: Individualism and Conformity on the American Frontier* (Chicago, 1964), pp. 3–9, 199–201, 213–16, 229–32.
5. Exceptions to this neglect may be found; see for example Whitney R. Cross, *The Burned-Over District* (Ithaca, 1950), pp. 38, 237; Charles R. Keller, *The Second Great Awakening in Connecticut* (New Haven, 1942), pp. 233–35.
6. Eleanor Flexner, *Century of Struggle: The Woman's Rights Movement in the United States* (Cambridge, 1959), pp. 12–14.
7. The secondary literature concerning the eighteenth-century evangelical revival and the benevolent movement is considerable. The English background is covered in Edward P. Cheyney, *Modern English Reform: From Individualism to Socialism* (Philadelphia, 1931), pp. 37–69; Frank J. Klingberg, "The Evolution of the Humanitarian Spirit in Eighteenth-Century England," *The Pennsylvania Magazine of History and Biography* LXVI (July, 1942), 260–78; Betsey Rodgers, *The Cloak of Charity* (London, 1949).
8. Mrs. [Sarah] Trimmer, *The Oeconomy of Charity, or, An Address to the Ladies Concerning Sunday Schools, etc.* (London, 1787), pp. 19, 48.
9. Mrs. Trimmer, *The Oeconomy of Charity; or an Address to the Ladies; Adapted to the Present State of Charitable Institutions in England, etc.* (London, 1801), I, 3–4.
10. William Roberts, Esq., *Memoirs of the Life and Correspondence of Mrs. Hannah More* (New York, 1835), I, 14.
11. Harriet Martineau, *Society in America* (2nd. edition, London, 1837), III, 219. Miss More's influence was not confined to women. The Rev. Henry C. Wright, an evangelical minister and reformer, soon to become a radical nonresistant and a Garrisonian abolitionist, was deeply impressed by Hannah More. See his Commonplace Book and Journal (Boston), Ms., Henry C. Wright Papers, Boston Public Library, entry for February 4, 1835.
12. Charles I. Foster, *An Errand of Mercy: The Evangelical United Front, 1790–1837* (Chapel Hill, 1960), p. 10.
13. Ibid., pp. 23–27. For comments on the dangers of Deism and infidelity, see Merle E. Curti, *The Growth of American Thought* (2nd ed., New

York, 1952), ch. 8, and Clifford S. Griffin, *Their Brothers' Keepers: Moral Stewardship in the United States, 1800, 1865* (New Brunswick, N.J., 1960), chs. 1–2. Denominational changes, especially the rise of Baptists and Methodists in the late 18th century, are discussed in Miyakawa, *Protestants and Pioneers*, ch. 2. This breakdown of unity and its influence on revivalism is the subject of a chapter by Perry Miller, "Covenant to Revival," pp. 322–68, in James Ward Smith and A. Leland Jamison, *The Shaping of American Religion*, vol. I, Religion in American Life series (Princeton, 1961).

14. Quaker benevolence flowered during the second half of the eighteenth century; it is well described in Sydney V. James, *A People Among Peoples: Quaker Benevolence in Eighteenth-Century America* (Cambridge, Mass., 1963).

15. *An Address of the General Association of Connecticut, to the District Associations on the Subject of A Missionary Society.* . . . (Norwich, 1797); Oliver W. Elsbree, *The Rise of the Missionary Spirit in America* (Williamsport, Penna., 1928).

16. *A Brief Account of the Origin and Progress of the Boston Female Society for Missionary Purposes* (Boston, 1818); Henry Jackson, *A Discourse in Commemoration of the Fifty-sixth Anniversary of the Mite Society.* . . . (Providence, 1854).

17. Massachusetts Society for Promoting Christian Knowledge, *Annual Reports, 1813, 1817* (Andover, Mass., 1813, 1817).

18. Ward Stafford, *New Missionary Field; A Report to the Female Missionary Society for the Poor of the City of New-York and its Vicinity.* . . . (New York, 1817).

19. *The Second Annual Report of the Managers of the Female Domestic Missionary Society of Philadelphia* (Philadelphia, 1818).

20. *Report on the Concerns of the New-Hampshire Cent Institution, for September, 1816 by the Committee of the Missionary Society* (Concord, 1816).

21. Ethan Smith, *A Sermon Preached to the Ladies of the Cent Institution, in Hopkinton, New Hampshire, August 18, 1814* (Concord, 1814), p. 8.

22. *The Third Annual Report of the Trustees of the Female Missionary Society of the Western District of New York, Presented Sept. 7, 1819* (Utica, 1819).

23. *The Constitution of the Female Bible Society of Philadelphia. Instituted the Sixteenth of March, 1814* (Philadelphia, 1814); *The First Report of the Female Bible Society of Philadelphia* (Philadelphia, 1815); *Second Annual Report of the New York Female Auxiliary Bible Society.* (New York, 1818).

24. Edwin J. Aiken, *The First Hundred Years of the New Hampshire Bible Society, 1812–1912* (Concord, 1912), pp. 66–67.

25. *The First Annual Report of the Board of Managers of the American Bible Society, Presented May 8, 1817* (New York, 1817), pp. 16–18; see also *The Second Annual Report . . . 1818*, pp. 37–42; *The Third Annual Report . . . 1819*, pp. 41–53.

26. *The Fourth Annual Report of the . . . American Bible Society.* . . . (New York, 1820), pp. 97–98.

27. *Ninth Annual Report of the Female Auxiliary Bible Society of Boston and its Vicinity* (Boston, 1823), pp. 3–4.

28. *The First Annual Report of the Philadelphia Female Tract Society, for the year 1816....* (Philadelphia, 1816); *First Annual Report of the American Tract Society,...* (New York, 1826), pp. 16, 40–44; *Second Annual Report of the American Tract Society* (New York, 1827), pp. 18, 49–55; *Eighth Annual Report of the American Tract Society* (New York, 1833), pp. 22*ff.*

29. Education Society of Connecticut, and Female Education Society of New Haven *Annual Reports, 1816–1826* (New Haven).

30. *The First Annual Report of the Directors of the Female Society of the Presbyterian Congregation in Cedar-Street for the Support of Theological Students* (New York, 1814), pp. 4–5. See also, for example, the "Fourth Annual Report of the Western Education Society," in the Utica, N.Y., *Christian Repository* I, 383 (December, 1822).

31. *Eleventh Annual Report of the Female Seamen's Friend Society of Philadelphia* (Philadelphia, 1843); *Twentieth Annual Report of the Seamen's Union Bethel Society of Baltimore* (Baltimore, 1843); *Second Annual Report of the Board of Directors of the Boston Seamen's Friend Society* (Boston, 1830); *First Annual Report of the Seamen's Aid Society of the City of Boston* (Boston, 1834).

32. *A Brief Account of the Female Association Charity School of the City of Baltimore* (Baltimore, 1803); Charles Varle, *A Complete View of Baltimore, with a Statistical Sketch....* (Baltimore, 1833), pp. 43–45; *An Account of the Female Association for the Relief of the Sick Poor....* (New York, 1814); *The Constitution of the Female Association of Philadelphia, for the Relief of Women and Children in Reduced Circumstances* (Philadelphia, 1803).

33. Thomas Barnard, *A Sermon Preached Before the Salem Female Charitable Society, ...* July 6th, 1803 (Salem, 1803); S.P. Williams, *A Plea for the Orphan, Delivered on the Anniversary of the Female Charitable Society, of Newburyport, May 21, 1822* (Boston, 1822).

34. *The Diary of William Bentley, D.D. Pastor of the East Church Salem, Massachusetts* (Salem, 1907), II, 408–09.

35. Ibid., III, 31, 299.

36. *A Brief Account of the ... Charity School of ... Baltimore,* p. 3.

37. *An Account of the Female Association for the Relief of the Sick Poor,...* p. 6.

38. *Annual Report of the Female Association in the City of New York* (New York, 1815, 1824).

39. *Thirty-First Annual Report of the Fragment Society in the City of Boston* (Boston, 1843).

40. Ibid., see also the *Constitution and Bye-Laws of the Fragment Society....* (Boston, 1825); *Twenty-Second Annual Report of the Fragment Society* (Boston, 1834); and *Constitution of the Female Samaritan Society. Instituted in Boston November 29th 1817....* (Boston, 1825).

41. *Articles of Association, Act of Incorporation, and Reports of the Transactions of the Female Hospitable Society of Philadelphia, Since its Commencement* (Philadelphia, 1831); *Philadelphia in 1824; or, a Brief Account of the Various Institutions and Public Objects in this Metropolis....* (Philadelphia, 1824); Matthew Carey, *Essays on the Public Charities of Philadelphia....* (Philadelphia, 1830); C.A. Pendleton, "Poor Relief in

Philadelphia, 1790–1840," *Pennsylvania Magazine of History and Biography* LXX, April, 1946, 161–72.

42. *Synopsis of the Concord Female Charitable Society, 1812–1856* (Concord, N.H., 1857).

43. Records of the Bedford, N.Y., Female Charitable Society, Mss., New-York Historical Society.

44. *Historical Sketch of the First Half Century of the Union Benevolent Association. . . .* (Philadelphia, 1881), p. 10.

45. *Reflections on the System of the Union Benevolent Association, Stating its Beneficent Effect. . . . by a Citizen of Philadelphia* (Philadelphia, 1837), p. 3.

46. *Historical Sketch of the . . . Union Benevolent Association. . . .* p. 11.

47. Minute Book, Constitution, Records of the Ladies Branch of the Union Benevolent Association of Philadelphia, 1831–1845, Mss., Historical Society of Pennsylvania.

48. *Report of the Committee of Delegates from the Benevolent Societies of Boston* (Boston, 1834).

49. Cross, *Burned-Over District, passim.*, discusses the transmission of Yankee benevolence into the "burned-over" section of New York. Much of his analysis could be applied to migrations of Yankee enthusiasm further west. See also, Foster, *Errand of Mercy*, chs. 8–11.

50. Elisha Ely, *A Directory for the Village of Rochester. . . .* (Rochester, 1827), p. 107, pp. 101–10.

51. Mrs. W.A. Ingham, *Women of Cleveland and their Work, . . . A History. . . .* (Cleveland, 1893), pp. 17–19, 53, 76, 77; Julius B. MacCabe, *Directory of Cleveland and Ohio City, For the Years 1837–38* (Cleveland, 1837), pp. 105–09; Robert S. Fletcher, *History of Oberlin College From its Founding to the Civil War*, 2 vols., (Oberlin, 1943).

52. *Cincinnati Directory for 1829* (Cincinnati, 1829), pp. 190–95; Richard C. Wade, *The Urban Frontier: The Rise of Western Cities, 1790–1830* (Cambridge, 1959), pp. 106, 120–24, 135.

53. Utica (N.Y.) *Christian Repository* II, 156 (May 1823).

54. Daniel Chaplin, *A Discourse Delivered Before the Charitable Female Society in Groton, October 19, 1814* (Andover, 1814), pp. 8–9. Similar sentiments are expressed in Benjamin Wadsworth, *A Sermon Delivered. . . . at the Request of the Charitable Female Cent Society in Danvers and Middleton, for Promoting Christian Knowledge, Nov. 7, 1816* (Andover, 1817), p. 26.

55. William Craig Brownlee, D.D., *For Christian Missions. An Oration, Delivered by Appointment of the Board of Missions, in the First Presbyterian Church of Philadelphia, . . . May 23, 1825* (Philadelphia, 1825), pp. 21–22.

56. Ibid., p. 22.

57. Address by the Right Rev. Bishop White in *The Constitution of the Female Bible Society of Philadelphia. . . .* (Philadelphia, 1814), p. 6. Similar arguments are urged in W.R. DeWitt, *Woman: Her Excellence and Usefulness* (Harrisburg, Pa., 1841), p. 11.

58. Chaplin, *Discourse*, p. 8.

59. S.P. Williams, *Plea for the Orphan, Delivered on the Anniversity of the Female Charitable Society, of Newburyport, May 21, 1822* (Newburyport, 1822), p. 4.

60. *Report on the Concerns of the New-Hampshire Cent Institution, for September, 1816, by the Committee of the Missionary Society* (Concord, 1816), p. 12.
61. Matthew laRue Perrine, *Women Have a Work to do in the House of God: A Discourse Delivered at the First Annual Meeting of the Female Missionary Society for the Poor of the City of New-York and its Vicinity. . . .* (New York, 1817), p. 11.
62. Thomas Barnard, *A Sermon Preached Before the Salem Female Charitable Society. . . .* (Salem, 1803), p. 17.
63. Wadsworth, *Sermon*, p. 6.
64. *Constitution of the Female Bible Society of Philadelphia, . . .* p. 6.
65. Perrine, *Discourse*, p. 26.
66. Barnard, *Sermon*, p. 14.
67. *Sixth Report of the Directors of the Penitent Females' Refuge, December, 1824* (Boston, 1825).
68. *First Annual Report of the Executive Committee of the New York Magdalen Society, Instituted, January 1, 1830* (New York, 1831), p. 12.
69. Lewis Tappan, *The Life of Arthur Tappan* (New York, 1870), p. 114; ch. 7 of this work includes an account of McDowall's work. See also Robert McDowall, *Memoir of Rev. John R. M'Dowall, by his Father* (New York, 1838).
70. *Second Annual Report of the Boston Female Moral Reform Society* (Boston, 1837), pp. 10–11.
71. *Third Annual Report of the Boston Female Moral Reform Society* (Boston, 1838), p. 7.
72. New England Golden Rule Association, *Prospectus for Publishing a New Periodical, to be Called the Golden Rule* (Boston, 1839).
73. Ibid.
74. *Liberator* III, no. 51 (December 21, 1833).
75. American Anti-Slavery Society, *Annual Reports*, 1836–1838.
76. A.A. Guthrie to Betsey M. Cowles, Secretary of Ashtabula County Female Anti-Slavery Society, October 29, 1835, Ms., Betsey Cowles Papers, in possession of Mrs. Robert Ticknor, Austinburg, Ohio.
77. Augustus Wattles to Betsey M. Cowles, April 9, 1836, Ms., Cowles Papers.
78. See chs. 4–5 of my dissertation, *The Beginnings of the Women's Rights Movement in the United States, 1800–1850* (Ann Arbor: University Microfilms, 1965), for details on the development of the "woman question" and the slavery controversy between 1837 and 1840.
79. Louis B. Wright has pointed out the influence of women's organizations as bearers of culture and civilization on the frontier in his *Culture on the Moving Frontier* (New York, 1961), pp. 193–94, 224–30.
80. The historian of the woman's club movement, Mrs. Jane C. Croly, in *The History of the Woman's Club Movement in America* (New York, 1898), recognized the importance of early nineteenth-century women's benevolence in setting the pattern for later work. See especially pp. 1, 8–9.
81. New York *National Anti-Slavery Standard* II, 22 (July 15, 1841).

The War Within a War:
Women Nurses in the Union Army

Ann Douglas Wood

Dr. A. Curtis, President of the Botanico-Medical College of Ohio and author of *Lectures on Midwifery* published in 1836, lamented the passing of women midwives, and the take-over of their occupation by men. "The destruction of scores of modern women and infants, and the miserable condition of multitudes that escape immediate death" testified all too clearly, he believed, that the change was "not made for the better." [1] For better or worse, the change was very real. In 1646, as Gerda Lerner tells us, a man had been prosecuted in Maine for practicing as a midwife. One hundred and thirty years later, Dr. William Shippen started to lecture on midwifery in Philadelphia. In the next half century, medical schools proliferated, and state after state legislated that a physician had to be licensed to practice. [2] Professionalization served to drive women from medicine as it automatically excluded them from formal training, licenses, and hence practice. As Victor Robinson, the historian of nursing in America, sums it up, "in the change from colonial to national medicine, the casualty was woman: woman was not ignored, she was expelled." [3] This expulsion was hardly an unforeseen result of professionalization; rather, it was a desired and sought-after end. One Boston doctor boasted in 1820:

It was one of the first and happiest fruits of improved medical education in America that females were excluded from practice, and this has only been effected by the united and persevering efforts of some of the most distinguished individuals of the profession.[4]

Women continued to play a role in the healing process, but it was a totally unprofessional one. Any sister, daughter or mother was expected to be able to nurse the sick of her household; indeed, she was idealized and glorified as a bedside watcher. Catharine Beecher's comparison of woman's role as healer to that of Jesus Christ was a commonplace.[5] Woman's silent, long-suffering ministry was the subject of countless poems and tales, but it was to hold sway principally in the home, usually her own, and never in any circumstance to come into competition with the professional doctor's role. William A. Alcott, a Boston physician and author of many books on women's health, proposed that all women should be trained to care for the sick at home. Women needed a little occupation to save them from "ennui," "disgust," and even "suicide," and they were by nature better qualified as nurses than men: self-sacrificing and self-forgetful, "they are formed for days and nights and months and years of watchfulness." Not only capable of such marathons of selflessness, women also "more readily anticipate our wants." Naturally, given such altruistic natures, the women nurses who are to be employed officially outside of their homes, "can be employed much cheaper" than men.[6] The essence of professionalism in nineteenth-century America was competition, and competition should clearly be anathema to the womanly watcher Alcott paints.

A rough bargain was being struck here as in so many other occupational fields at the turn of the nineteenth century. Women were exchanging some kind of professional expertise and official recognition for a domesticated version of the occupation in question, a version fed by official veneration but sapped by its distance from technological, scientific advance and its closeness to the hearth.[7] In other words, women, told that they had been third-rate professional doctors, were promised that they could be first-rate amateur nurses. They could no longer be midwives, but they could be madonnas. One can even speculate that the sentimental adulation granted the mother watching at the sickbed was a kind of guilty, if unconscious compensation for the hostility which drove the female doctor from her paying patient. Be that as it may, it is clear that in the mid-nineteenth century, American women were to use this new mystique as an important weapon in an attack against the very professionalism which had exiled them to a domestic shrine, and as the basis for a renewed claim on their own part to active professional life.

Lerner and other historians who have treated the subject agree that the American Revolution hastened the professionalization of medicine by vastly increasing the need for medical skill and providing a battlefield on which to gain it.[8] Hence, the Revolution was the death-knell of the woman physician. The Civil War, almost a hundred years later, also dramatically changed the medical picture. The study of gun-shot wounds led to important discoveries, anesthetics were developed, and the basic principles of sanitation slowly became apparent if only because they were so terribly violated. But as important as any of these was the opportunity this war offered women to return to the medical ranks from which they had been ejected at the time of the Revolution.

Wartime nursing, newly elevated and glamorized in the 1850s by the work of Florence Nightingale in the Crimea, not only provided wider outlets for feminine skills, but afforded women a way to debunk the officialdom which had been their enemy. In coming on to the battlefield, they brought with them the myth of the bedside Madonna, still resplendent with her healing maternal power, and pitted its potency against masculine authority. As northerners, the nurses who followed the Union Army reckoned the Confederacy to be the enemy, but in daily practice their battles were more often with the ponderous war machine of their own menfolk and with the bureaucratic professionals—military and medical—who struggled to maintain it.

Of course, the majority of American women, as contemporary feminine observers delighted to stress, stayed home during the war and suffered. Mary Livermore, a leader in the Sanitary Commission, pointed out rather proudly that the pain of men in battle, inspired by martial enthusiasm or at least distracted by military necessities, was as nothing next to the agony that women feel sending forth their loved ones to war, "knowing full well the risks they run—this involves exquisite suffering, and calls for another kind of heroism." [9] Elizabeth Stuart Phelps, author of the best-selling novel *Gates Ajar*, designed to comfort the thousands of mourning women left in the war's wake, almost seemed to see the war as an act of hostility committed by men against the all-too-delicate sensibilities of their women-folk. She never worried greatly about the men who lost loved ones in the war, for the war, she implied, was their choice, their doing. It was rather "the women,—the helpless, outnumbering, unconsulted women; they whom war trampled down, without a choice at protest" [10] who were her concern. These anxious, grieving women were very much performing their madonna-function, the selfless sickbed watchers, taking all the suffering of their ill husbands and brothers on their slender shoulders.

But the efforts of the women at home to aid their men were not all so passive. They formed some ten thousand Soldier's Aid Societies, they made countless bandages, they held huge Sanitary Fairs that together netted three million dollars.[11] And not all of them confined their labors to the home-front. George A. Sale, a British journalist, wrote with some wonder that no conflict in history was so much "a woman's war" as the Civil War.[12] These ladies would not let go. Mary Livermore proudly advertised their indomitability as they "refused to release their hold upon the men of their households although the government had taken them out of the home and organized them into an army." [13] Waging their own war on military professionalism and on the masculine establishment that tried to exclude them, they simply refused to let this be the old kind of war, fought by men, with the wounded tended by men.[14] They came along in a multitude, some on a single trip to care for a wounded or dying son or husband, but thousands "enlisted for the war" as volunteer nurses.

Their backgrounds ranged from blue-blood society to poor white communities, but they all had one thing in common. Whether they worked under Dorothea Dix, appointed by the government as Superintendent of Nurses, or later for the Sanitary Commission, or appeared, as many did, sent by themselves and God, they were all without formal training. No schools for nurses opened until after the Civil War,[15] and so these volunteers had no experience beyond caring for the sick at home. Their ideal was, consequently, not the hospital, and certainly not the barracks, but the home. Indeed, many of them apparently were determined to turn the army camp with its masculine military code into the home, dominated by the maternal creed. This was a way of keeping their hold on the men who had just left the fireside for the campfire, but it was also a dramatic claim for greatly extended power. Woman's "influence," the genteel word favored by *Godey's Lady's Book,* was recognized as supreme within the sacred realm of home and family: [16] not surprising, then, that these women seemed bent, with Clara Barton, in making the "mother earth" of the battlefield into their "kitchen hearth" [17] and the soldiers into their sons. If the world was a home, where would their "influence" end? This subtle, yet sweeping question was posed by the actions of a minority. Most northern women, as we have seen, suffered patiently at home, sending only prayers, letters or bandages to wounded soldiers; but some moved to participate more directly in the Union effort, refusing to let sympathetic healing be outdistanced by destructive conflict. The progression from feminine self-abnegation to competitive involvement is clear, and it was all done under the maternal banner and the flags of the home fireside.

Many of the boys in blue were just that—boys, and they missed their homes and sang their songs not about their sweethearts, but about their mothers.[18] The women who came to nurse them kept voicing a sense, however, that *all* these men, young and old, playing at war with such terrible earnestness, were just children, children, moreover, who had not quite known what they were doing when they put themselves so far from home. Sophronia Bucklin, a talented volunteer nurse explained sagely:

> Woman's help had not been counted upon, when, in the first tremultuous rush of excited feeling, the citizen enlisted to serve under the banner of the soldier. And when her hand with its softer touch pressed on the aching forehead, and bathed the fevered face, words failed in the attempt to express the gratitude of a full heart.

Miss Bucklin clearly had a sense that these men, whose "universal childishness" she stressed, were like little boys who had run away from home, heedless of the consequences, and were only too grateful when mother appeared.[19] There is pity, but there is an undernote of I-told-you-so in the tone of these nurses when they describe, as Mary Livermore did, mutilated men, deliriously screaming, "Mother! Mother!" [20] Intent on rescuing such orphans, Clara Barton called the soldiers her "boys," and Emily E. Parsons, a handicapped but courageous nurse, wrote about the patients in her ward as her "forty-five children." [21]

Re-establishing the rule of mother on the battlefield meant fighting loose military morals with hometown ethics. As Mary Elizabeth Massey has noted, "stories of drinking, gambling, and immorality in camp spread like wildfire," [22] and they were not without foundation. E. W. Locke, the popular song-writer and temperance reformer who was constantly with the Union troops, devoted his chapter on "Women in the Army" in his war memoirs not just to the mothers and nurses, but also to "the Delilahs and Magdalenes" who followed the soldiers everywhere.[23] When duty called, the nurses could act like fierce watchdogs for the domestic virtues. " 'What, my boy, playing checkers on Sunday?' " one nurse reproved a wounded patient, offering him a New Testament.[24] But the real guardian was the legendary Dorothea Dix herself, pioneer in insane asylum and prison reform, now official Superintendent of Nurses, and determined to clean up the army as she had cleaned up the jails and asylums. Backed by her troops of nurses (by her own absolute requirement "plain-looking women," over thirty, dressed in black or brown, "with no bows, no curls, no jewelry, and no hoop-skirts"), she was a vigilance committee in herself. She did not take one day off in the entire course of the war.[25]

Opening a branch of the American Home at the front was not the only way these women found to extend their power. Coupled with their maternal lust to care for the soldier was a desire to compete with him, even to outdo him. Historians now estimate that approximately four hundred women joined the ranks disguised as men.[26] One, unmasked before Annie Wittenmeyer, a temperance leader prominent in the Sanitary Commission, when asked why she had done it, replied succinctly, " 'I thought I'd like camp-life, and I did.' "[27] The adventures of Pauline Cushman, actress and Federal spy, who disguised herself as a man, became the subject of two popular biographies.[28] These pretenders to masculinity occasionally came rather frighteningly close to the real thing. Emma Edmonds, another spy and male impersonator, who wrote up her wartime adventures under the catchy title of *The Female Spy of the Union Army,* narrated with relish shooting a southern woman, and then, Achilles-like, dragging her prey behind her horse.[29] Even some of the women at home waxed warrior-like, and one member of the fair sex complained that "the gentle-hearted ladies [were] admiring swords, guns, and pistols." [30]

The actual Amazons were few, but many of the volunteer nurses showed sparks of the same martial fire. Katharine Wormeley, a nurse working for the Sanitary Commission, wrote a letter on board a hospital ship describing the chaos and confusion and activity around her and closed it, "Good-bye! *This is life."* [31] These women were getting a taste of a larger life; they were entering the masculine world of hard work and struggle, and many of them loved it. "I am in the army just as Chauncey [her brother] is, and I must be held to work just as he is," Emily Parsons explained proudly to her anxious parents. For the first time in her sheltered life, she senses she has become a participant in American history:

> I feel now as if I had really entered into the inner spirit of the times,—the feeling which counts danger as nothing, but works straight on as our Puritan forefathers worked before us.[32]

Even though she knows her parents will worry, she cannot refrain from telling them how hard her bed is, how she is rained on at night, how poor the food is: these hardships are her badge of honor.

Many of the women leaders in the war were fighters from birth. A contemporary described Dix as "a general on a battlefield" long before the Civil War, and she herself knew that "the tonic I need is the tonic of opposition." [33] But her best battles had already been fought elsewhere. Not so with Clara Barton. Forty when the war began, after two decades of teaching and civil service work, she was inwardly restless and deeply melancholy. Raised by a "soldier-father" as she loved to call him, she had grown up riding fast horses and listening "breathlessly to his war stories." [34] When Fort Sumter was fired on, she went out to a rifle-range and shot at a target, "putting nine balls successively within the space of six inches at a distance of fifty feet." [35] She obtained her father's blessing, and then promptly went to war. Only Dr. Mary Walker, surgeon and suffragist, outdid her: she joined the ranks in pants,—but *not* disguised as a man—shot at the first soldier who was insolent with her, and retired from action dressed in an officer's uniform.[36]

Such strongly aggressive, not to say belligerent gestures, conspicuous in the careers of not a few of the most famous nurses during the war, seem to unmask the element of competitive attack in their volunteer crusade. They said they wanted to take care of the men: but did not they also want to take them over? Onlookers may have wondered. This unspoken anxiety perhaps accounts for the ambivalent feelings expressed by American men about the invasion within an invasion taking place before their eyes. Despite popular tributes from the troops, the nurses received little monetary compensation and less government recognition. Compilations of laudatory sketches like Frank Moore's *Women of the War: Their Heroism and Sacrifice* (1866) sold immensely,[37] but unpublished criticism of the women nurses was also current. Dr. Samuel Howe, although himself one of the original leaders of the Sanitary Commission, forbade his restless and patriotic wife, Julia Ward Howe, to be a nurse during the war. "If he had been engaged to Florence Nightingale," he explained, "and had loved her ever so dearly, he would have given her up as soon as she commenced her career as a public woman." [38] No wonder that women like Mary Livermore felt compelled to stress how reluctant they were to leave cherished home duties even for the pressing obligations that wartime presented.[39]

The hostility towards the female ranks was strongest, however, not at home, but in the army and at the front. Effort after effort was made by various officials to drive women out of the army,[40] and even the most powerful of the nurses had to deal with constant challenges to their presence and their authority. Once, when Clara Barton was in the midst of heroic labors after a terrible battle, an officer remarked to her. " 'Miss Barton, this is a rough and unseemly position for you, a woman to occupy.' " She quickly and unanswerably retorted, " 'Is it not as rough and unseemly for these pain-racked men?' " But she did not always come off as easily. In 1863, she was rudely ousted from her post by the officials, and spent the winter in depressed inactivity before she was again allowed to return to the troops.[41] At the same time Dorothea Dix, originally given complete control over the appointment of nurses, was gently pushed aside, and her authority became permanently subordinate to that of the Surgeon-General's.

This resistance to the women volunteers was apparently not shared by the men in the ranks, as the nurses typically got plenty of unofficial appreciation. The problem centered on their official professional status, and their opponents were principally, and predictably, the army officials and doctors. In Nurse Bucklin's opinion, these two groups were "determined by a systemmatic course of ill-treatment ... to drive women from the service." [42] Of course, some of the women volunteers were undoubtedly incompetent, ineffectual, and even harmful, but the skillful ones, as we have seen, had almost equal trouble establishing their position. They aroused official hostility precisely because they were challenging the male authorities directing the war, calling for credentials from men who thought they had left such tests decades of professional life behind, and then implicitly comparing the worth of such testimonies with that of the sources of their own vaunted authority as women and as mothers. Naturally the military officials were antagonized and threatened by this challenge, but the medical officials, directly dealing with these nurses in the wards, and supposedly having double authority over them as officers and as doctors, were especially threatened. And contemporary evidence suggests that they were especially antagonistic.

Indeed, many of these doctors apparently took an attitude of no-holds-barred in their resistance. Mary Phinney von Olnhausen, a protégé of Dorothea Dix's, summed up her impression of her male colleagues simply if sharply: surgeons were "the most brutal men I ever saw." [43] Another nurse, Georgeanna Woolsey, bore eloquent witness to the sufferings inflicted by doctors on nurses. Explaining that the surgeons "determined to make their [the nurses'] lives so unbearable that they should be forced in self-defense to leave," she elaborates:

> [no-one knows] how much opposition, how much ill-will, how much unfeeling want of thought these women nurses endured. Hardly a surgeon of whom I can think, received or treated them with even common courtesy.... I have known women, delicately

cared for at home, half fed in hospitals, hard worked day and night, and given, when sleep must be had, a ... closet, just large enough for a camp bed to stand in.

Only the knowledge that they were "pioneers," blazing a trail for those to come, sustained the first volunteers.[44]

Perhaps the doctors so fiercely defended their position because it was a particularly vulnerable one. The Medical Department of the Army consisted of the Surgeon General, an Assistant Surgeon General, and a number of short-term "contract surgeons." It was this latter group who received most criticism. They deserved it, but it is hardly surprising that they should have done a bad job. One of their more sympathetic critics, Jane Woolsey, a war-time nurse, explained their dilemma:

> Contract surgeons were more or less victims of a system which made them an anomalous civil element in a military establishment, with but little military restrictions, and no military incentive in the shape of promotion. They had no position, small pay, and mere nominal rank. They were a temporary expedient in the first place.... They served their little term, made their little experiments, and disappeared. The class was bad; it was under no obligations to be anything else.[45]

As a result of this incentive problem, the men who became surgeons in the army were either talented physicians, patriotically donating their talents to the war effort at considerable loss to themselves, or men who had failed in their home practice, "to whose care," as one commentator ruefully noted, "we would not be willing to intrust a sick or disabled horse." [46] Not surprisingly, *medical*—not war—casualties were such that one historian has calculated that a soldier's safety was more imperiled if he had to undergo medical treatment in an army hospital for an injury than if he fought all three days at Gettysburg.[47]

Of this rather mixed crew of doctors, moreover, complicated demands were made. As E. W. Locke remarked, their medical knowledge, while absolutely necessary, was not all-sufficient as it might be in peacetime. In an age when few people, no matter how sick, went to hospitals, the doctor customarily drew for his nursing help chiefly on the amateur feminine nurses in his patients' homes. Now on the front, dealing with wounded or sick men who were far from their homes, he was asked to supply not only his professional skill, but this almost familial care as well. He must, in Locke's words, "stand in the place of parent, wife, or sister." As a result, Locke concludes, the best doctors were those with "heart-power," which goes far "deeper" than medicine, and they were "almost like mothers." [48] Maternity had nearly become a professional requirement.

Locke's analysis, backed up by the motherly role a man like Walt Whitman chose to assume at the bedside of the wounded, casts the doctors and volunteer nurses in a competitive double contest for maternal and medical pre-eminence, a contest whose potential the women were quick to grasp. They were not officials of any kind. Poorly paid volunteers attached to various military hospitals, they had no regular professional status. But they *were* mothers or potential ones, and this apparently could now provide the basis for a professional claim. Not surprisingly, they proceeded to attack the errors and false professionalism of the surgeons and of the military authorities who backed them up with all the dignity and force lent them by their consecrated maternal natures.

Basic to these women's complicated urge to make the front truly a home-front, to replace the captain with the mother, the doctor with the nurse, and even to out-soldier the soldiers, was their sense that they were being kept out, of medicine, of war, of *life itself,* by a complicated professional code that simply boiled down to men's unwillingness to let anyone—including themselves—know what a mess they had made. And the first thing the volunteers wanted to reveal was the mess in all its enormity. Eliza Howland, an energetic nurse, wrote her husband about her herculean labors in a veritable Augean stable of a hospital. She and her fellow nurses cleaned the floors, covered with dust, nails, and shavings, taking up the "rubbish" with shovels and putting it in barrels. But the plight of the patients, "crowded in upon us" was less easily rectified: they were "soaked with malignant malarial fever, from exposure night after night, to drenching rain." She could only damn the prevalent "murderous, blundering want of prevision and provision" which caused their plight.[49]

These women had little hesitation in calling a spade a spade and in marshalling their forces against the (in their view) heedless men in local positions of command. Annie Wittenmeyer was shocked to find an acting medical director of a military hospital on the job "reeling drunk." No wonder he ordered such a right-minded and astute woman off the premises, drunkenly insisting, " 'I'm boss here.' " Calmly but grimly thinking, " 'One or the other of us must certainly leave that hospital,' " she arranged for his dismissal. When she found another surgeon putting logwood in the coffee intended for the wounded, a "righteous indignation" burned in her heart, and another head rolled.[50] Dorothea Dix, astonished by the laxities and lapses perhaps inevitable in the early stages of an unforeseen war, irritated military authorities by being in a perpetual state of "breathless excitement," as one exasperated official called it. Cynically, George Templeton Strong, a Sanitary Commissioner, could seize on the absurd and hysterical aspects of her over-concern:

> She is disgusted with us because we do not leave everything else and rush off the instant she tells us of something that needs attention. The last time we were in Washington she came upon us in breathless excitement to say that a cow in the Smithsonian grounds was dying of sunstroke, and she took it very ill that we did not adjourn instantly to look after the case.[51]

What Strong understandably failed to note was that her anxiety, like Annie Wittenmeyer's strong-minded indignation, rose from her horror, here focused on a petty detail, that all these *men,* not just professing Christians (women were that, after all), but wage-earners and professionally trained, might be incompetent—incompetent despite the reassuring tokens of self-confidence, responsibility, training, in sum, of masculinity, which she and all her world were accustomed to accept as some kind of seal of approval. After she had opened the first door of her first state-run jail and seen the enormities of neglect and maltreatment there, she *doubted.* She enjoyed the doubts, because they implied that if men were apparently not helped, were even *disabled* by their training for the task of running the world right, the burden fell on her, and her apparent (and feminine) lack of qualifications became a positive asset for the task. Yet the intense reactions and distorted, but oppressive sense of responsibility which resulted from her frightening conclusion that she was the only wakeful passenger on a ship headed for certain wreck,[52] were real too. When the Civil War came, thousands of other American women put themselves in a position to open the same door (or raise the equivalent tent-flap), and they saw similar sights and felt the same complex mingling of hysterical fear and righteous elation.

If this nightmare of untended men, dirty wards, overworked and sometimes incompetent doctors was military professional medicine, there was only one resource for these ladies: opposition. The necessary force and authority came from many different sources, as did the women volunteers themselves; some had or made friends in power, some had the backing of Dix's organization, some were acting for the increasingly powerful Sanitary Commission, some used personal

charm. In the more belligerent line, Dix, who demanded no professional training of her nurses (she had seen enough to know what good
that did!), simply told them to disregard the surgeons and obey her.[53]
In a different fashion, young and delicate Mary Safford, finding all
"surgeons and authorities everywhere" opposed to her presence, dis-
armed the opposition by "her sweetness and grace and beauty."
Hailed like Clara Barton as an "angel," she was also "the most indomitable little creature living." According to a contemporary report, *"She
did just what she pleased."* [54]

And what these women wanted to do was to cut through the "red
tape,"—a phrase they used over and over again to signify what they
were fighting against. They wanted to destroy the professionalism, the
bureaucracy that was keeping them out and keeping the wounded
uncared for, and they hoped to replace it by the new and better
professionalism at their command. Georgeanna Woolsey, in a witty
mood, characterized "that sublime, unfathomed mystery—'Professional
Etiquette' " as an "absolute Bogie," a Bogie "which puts its cold paw
on private benevolence ... which kept shirts from ragged men, and
broth from hungry ones." [55]

The past-mistress of the art of defying and outwitting this omnipres-
ent Bogie was a little-educated but superbly shrewd Illinois woman in
her forties named Mary Ann Bickerdyke. She was soon called
"Mother" Bickerdyke by the troops, and became the heroine of
women like Annie Wittenmeyer and Mary Livermore. Both devote
more space to her in their war memoirs than to any other single
person, and their adoration is extremely significant. Leaders in the
male-dominated, highly organized Sanitary Commission with its
quickly developing professional code, Wittenmeyer and Livermore
showed their true colors in their adulation of such a maverick as
Bickerdyke. Totally unprofessional by any conventional standard, she
made a profession of the calling both these women also exploited:
motherhood. Wittenmeyer, who set up special sanitary diet kitchens in
military hospitals was cooking for a vastly extended family. "Mother"
Bickerdyke, who had practiced before the war informally as a botanic
doctor, was doing home nursing on an equally vast scale. The fact that
all three women left families behind them to join the war effort indicates that they went to war not so much to satisfy their maternal urges
as to use their maternal status as the basis for a play for a professional
one. But the profession (nursing) they evolved was intended to share
none of the weaknesses of its masculine rival. "Mother" Bickerdyke's
work in the war represents the clearest example of this effort on the
part of the volunteer nurses to put to shame the male bureaucratic

professional organization behind the military hospitals by the shining example of a militant motherhood, which outdid its rival in efficiency but showed the heart its competitor so conspicuously lacked.

Bickerdyke's husband, whom, she privately stated, would have lived twenty years longer "had he not worn himself into the grave trying to boss her," [56] was dead when she agreed in 1861 to accompany medical supplies for the boys to Cairo, Illinois. Her words on that occasion were a battle cry:

> I'll go to Cairo, and I'll clean things up there [she promised]. You don't need to worry about that, neither. Them generals and all ain't going to stop me. This is the Lord's work you're calling me to do.[57]

She kept her pledge. The Lord's was the only authority she ever did accept, and He generally sounded a good deal like Mother Bickerdyke. Even General Sherman toed her line. An admirer of Bickerdyke's, he told one furious officer that he could not help him against this formidable foe: " 'She ranks me,' " he explained.[58] She brought in countless supplies, she nursed thousands, and, as Annie Wittenmeyer said, she "cut red tape." She explained to one of many irate doctors as she calmly sidestepped medical protocol in her customary fashion: " 'It's of no use for you to try to tie me up with your red tape. There's too much to be done down here to stop for that.' " [59] The underlying reproach to the dangerously silly men in command around her, unwilling to stop playing the games they have been trained to play even when life and death are at stake, is clear. Men can be allowed to play at authority in peacetime, she implies, but when a war comes, it's time to obey the women. In such a crisis, Mother Bickerdyke, an Admirable Crichton in the Union army, simply must assume her natural place of leadership. Bringing the primitive justice of the frontier and the ready kindness of what her biographers liked to call her "great maternal heart" to the front, she moved always to the point. When she discovered that an officer was stealing clothes reserved for sick soldiers, she stripped him publicly, "leaving him nude save his pantaloons." [60]

Clara Barton too had a way of kicking over regulations to get to the men and their needs. Working alone, outside the Sanitary Commission and Dix's organization, she was the first woman, and one of very few, to take the actual front as her territory, turning up during battles with medical supplies and her own considerable nursing skill before any organized help could arrive. This was the absolute essence of her tactics: not to cut through red tape so much as to anticipate, and hence to forestall it, to appear at the actual moment of crisis when officialdom is always irrelevant. Many of the most prominent nurses saw their role in similar terms and loved to tell stories of how they provided some desperate or dying soldier, not with the standard treatment, so little susceptible of being bent to individual needs, but with precisely that thing which they, with lightning quick feminine intuition, knew he needed most.[61]

Clara Barton's mission was to bring this instinct to a kind of perfection on the battlefield itself. She knew when to obey the doctors, but she had feuds with certain military medics and distrusted medicine to the point of being a near Christian Scientist in later life. At the core of her being was a profound suspicion of all organizations, and it seems significant that the great organization she helped to found, the Red Cross, was in key ways an anti-institution, at least as she ran it. Like the special kitchens run by Wittenmeyer, it was an effort which drew complex and double strength from implicitly attacking existing professional efforts in the same field even while endowing its own anti-institutional unprofessionalism with the forces of a profession—money, publicity and organized labor.[62] The Red Cross was, in other words, an extension of the principles behind Barton's and Bickerdyke's work in the Civil War. As she explained it, its purpose was to deal with the damage wrecked by the forces "that red tape is not strong enough to hold ... in check." [63] It was "unlike any other organization in the country" because, in her words,

> It is an organization of physical action, of instantaneous action, at the spur of the moment; it cannot await the ordinary deliberations of organized bodies if it would be of any use to suffering humanity; ... it has by its nature a field of its own.[64]

The Red Cross as it began in America was organized feminine intuition, anti-professional and anti-institutional in nature, the logical culmination of the spirit of woman's efforts in the Civil War.

Clara Barton, with Mother Bickerdyke and many others, felt that she had the right to break through official medical protocol because she had the healing touch. Her thinking, like that of Dorothea Dix, in many ways paralleled that of Mary Baker Eddy. Dix had tremendous faith in what her first biographer called "the renovating power over bodily infirmity of a great purpose": [65] it was this which gave her her fabled "divine magnetism," as Horace Mann reverently called it. In her work with the insane, she was given to rather expansive, not to say Messianic, statements about her power. Considering herself "the

Hope" of all "poor, crazed beings" and "the Revelation" to them,[66] she promised, "I shall see their chains off, I shall take them into the green fields ... and a little child shall lead them."[67] One of Barton's early biographers felt compelled to make similar claims for her: she had "magnetic power," the "magnetism of mercy."[68] It is not far from here to the primitive healing power, originally allied to "animal magnetism," which Mary Baker Eddy advertised as her own.[69]

At the start of the twentieth century, Robert Herrick would write a novel called *The Healer* (1911) about a brilliant young doctor who possessed this almost magical gift, but could keep it only if he disavowed totally the corrupt professionalism of modern medicine. The women nurses of the Civil War were believers in this creed: *because* they had been excluded from the ranks of the official medical world, they had found the healing power which their male colleagues had perhaps forever lost. Time after time, the diaries, letters and biographies of wartime nurses assert that what the wounded men need is not just medicine and food (which the nurses of course bring), but the *presence* of a woman, the touch of her hand. They seem to insinuate that if manhood brought on a war, womanhood was in itself healing. E. H. Locke makes clear the tremendous regenerating effect the simple appearance of two women actually had on a group of sick men in an army hospital: "Their very few words were woman's words, but they had a power man's do not." Unwilling or unable to explain this effect, Locke can only say that they seemed like beings from "another sphere," "representative" of all the women "at home."[70] The magical perfume they exude is clearly the aura of home, and this aura was the secret weapon all the volunteer nurses possessed, a weapon both powerful in its effects and safe for its user.

Women had been told that the precincts of home were sacred and assured by men desirous of keeping them there that *they* were sacred because they stayed at home. Barred from professional medical ranks, they were encouraged to believe they could be healers by the hearth. Who could argue, then, when, at the imperious call of a land battling with itself, of a country engaged in *family* strife, some women charitably shared with the nation the precious powers they had lavished on their kin—the maternal gifts of protection and healing? And in doing so, they accomplished a great deal. Their work in improving sanitary conditions in Civil War hospitals has never been questioned, but they did more. In bringing home virtues to witness against "professional" methods, they did not so much make the world a home, as they helped to make themselves at home *in the world.* Nursing the troops in the Civil War had not only offered them a chance to criticize the imprisoning professional code of the military medical corps from the perspective of their maternal natures; it had also given them the opportunity to make a profession, and a competitive one, out of their maternity. Significantly, after the war accredited schools for nurses opened their doors and women doctors began to appear in small but increasing numbers.[71] The wartime nurses, it seems, had joined a bigger army than they knew.

NOTES

1. A. Curtis, *Lectures on Midwifery and the Forms of Disease Peculiar to Women and Children* (Columbus, 1841), p. 9.

2. Gerda Lerner, "The Lady and the Mill Girl: Changes in the Status of Women in the Age of Jackson," *Midcontinent American Studies Journal* X (1969): 7–8.

3. Victor Robinson, *White Caps: The Story of Nursing* (Philadelphia and New York, 1946), p. 139.

4. Ibid.

5. See Catharine Esther Beecher and Harriet Beecher Stowe, *The American Home: or Principles of Domestic Science* (New York, 1869), pp. 335–47. This attitude and the related practice were so prevalent throughout the nineteenth century that the famous Philadelphian physician S. Weir Mitchell attacked prolonged familial nursing as in itself a prominent source of ill-health in women. See his *Doctor and Patient* (Philadelphia and London, 1888), pp. 125–27 and *Fat and Blood and How to Make Them* (Philadelphia, 1877), pp. 29–30.

6. W.A. Alcott, "Female Attendance on the Sick," *Ladies' Magazine* 7 (1834): 303–04.

7. This applies to all kinds of industrial occupations (see Lerner, "Lady and the Mill Girl," 6, 9) and, in a different but related way, to the writing profession, see Ann D. Wood, "The 'Scribbling Women' and Fanny Fern: Why Women Wrote," *American Quarterly* XXIII(1971): 3–24.

8. See Lerner, "Lady and the Mill Girl," 8.

9. Mary A. Livermore, *My Story of the War* (Hartford, Conn., 1889), p. 110.

10. Elizabeth Stuart Phelps, *Chapters from a Life* (Boston and New York, 1897), p. 98.

11. Agatha Young, *The Women and the Crisis: Women of the North in the Civil War* (New York, 1959), pp. 67, 312. Another, although less good, book on the same subject is Marjorie Barstow Greenbie, *Lincoln's Daughters of Mercy* (New York, 1944).

12. Quoted in Mary Elizabeth Massey, *Bonnet Brigades* (New York, 1966), p. 25.

13. Livermore, *My Story of the War,* p. 470.

14. In the War of 1812 most of the nursing had been done by men. See Robinson, *White Caps,* pp. 140–42.

15. On the history of nursing and its organization, see Mary M. Roberts, *American Nursing: History and Interpretation* (New York, 1955), Robin-

son, *White Caps,* and Lucy Ridgely Seyner, *A General History of Nursing* (New York, 1949). For a detailed and valuable discussion of Florence Nightingale's role, see Cecil Woodham-Smith, *Florence Nightingale 1820–1910* (New York, 1951). On the Sanitary Commission, see *The United States Sanitary Commission: A Sketch of Its Purposes and Its Work* (Boston, 1863); George Fredrickson, *The Inner Civil War: Northern Intellectuals and the Crisis of the Union* (New York, 1965), pp. 98–113; William Quentin Maxwell, *Lincoln's Fifth Wheel: The Political History of the United States Sanitary Commission* (New York, London, and Toronto, 1956).

16. To understand fully the doctrine of female "influence," one must look through the ten volumes of the *Ladies' Magazine* (1828–1837) edited and largely written by Sarah J. Hale, who later edited *Godey's Lady's Book.*
17. Percy H. Epler, *The Life of Clara Barton* (New York, 1917), p. 352.
18. Emily Elizabeth Parsons notes this allegiance in the *Memoir of Emily Elizabeth Parsons* (Boston, 1880), p. 68, published by her family.
19. Sophronia E. Bucklin, *In Hospital and Camp: A Woman's Record of Thrilling Incidents Among the Wounded in the Late War* (Philadelphia, 1869), pp. 32–33.
20. Livermore, *My Story of the War,* pp. 188–89.
21. Parsons, *Memoir,* pp. 19, 21, 27, 52, 79.
22. Massey, *Bonnet Brigades,* p. 213.
23. E.H. Locke, *Three Years in Camp and Hospital* (Boston, 1870), p. 195.
24. Young, *Women and the Crisis,* p. 227.
25. Helen E. Marshall, *Dorothea Dix: Forgotten Samaritan* (Chapel Hill, 1937), pp. 206, 210. Young, *Women and the Crisis,* pp. 62–63, 75–76, 98–104, 193–96, 308–09, also covers Dix's war efforts skillfully.
26. Young, *Women and the Crisis,* p. 43.
27. Annie Wittenmeyer, *Under the Guns: A Woman's Reminiscences of the Civil War* (Boston, 1895), p. 18.
28. See V.L. Sarmiento, *Life of Pauline Cushman the Celebrated Union Spy and Scout* (Philadelphia, 1865).
29. S. Emma E. Edmonds, *The Female Spy of the Union Army: the Thrilling Adventures, Experiences and Escapes of a Woman, a Nurse, Spy, and Scout in Hospitals, Camps and Battlefields* (Boston, 1864), p. 94. Interestingly enough, the book was also published as *Nurse and Spy: or Unsexed, the Female Soldier.* It had tremendous popularity.
30. Quoted in Massey, *Bonnet Brigades,* p. 259.
31. Quoted in Young, *Women and the Crisis,* p. 177.
32. Parsons, *Memoir,* pp. 44, 54. Barton felt this sense of expanded activity strongly and wrote a poem about it. See "The Women Who Went to the Field," in Epler, *Clara Barton,* pp. 399–401.
33. Francis Tiffany, *Life of Dorothea Lynde Dix* (Boston and New York, 1890), pp. 163, 161.
34. Epler, *Clara Barton,* p. 6.
35. Young, *Women and the Crisis,* p. 45.
36. For an account of Dr. Walker's rather amazing career, see Charles McCool Snyder, *Mary Walker: the Little Lady in Pants* (New York, Washington, and Hollywood, 1962).
37. For the nurses' poor pay, see Massey, *Bonnet Brigades,* pp. 63–64. Other

popular tributes to the volunteers were L. P. Brockett and Mary C. Vaughan, *Woman's Work in the Civil War: A Record of Heroism, Patriotism, and Patience* (Philadelphia, Chicago, St. Louis, and Boston, 1867), and Mary A. Gardner Holland, *Our Army Nurses: Interesting Sketches and Photographs of Over One Hundred of the Noble Women Who Served in Hospitals and on Battlefields During Our Late Civil War 1861–1865* (Boston, 1897).

38. Quoted in Young, *Women and the Crisis,* p. 61.
39. Mary Livermore, *The Story of My Life: or, the Sunshine and Shadows of Seventy Years* (Hartford, Conn., 1898), p. 471.
40. See Young, *Women and the Crisis,* pp. 120–21, 319–20.
41. Ishbel Ross, *Angel of the Battlefield: The Life of Clara Barton* (New York, 1956), pp. 35, 61ff.
42. Bucklin, *In Hospital and Camp,* pp. 124–25.
43. Sylvia G.L. Dannett, ed., *Noble Women of the North* (New York and London, 1959), p. 95. It should be remembered that these women were coming in contact principally with surgeons, rather than doctors, and were horrified by the sights of the amputation-table. See ibid., pp. 99–104.
44. Ibid., pp. 88–89.
45. Ibid., p. 98.
46. Locke, *Three Years in Camp and Hospital,* p. 73. For a recent account of doctors in the Civil War, see George Worthington Adams, *Doctors in Blue* (New York, 1952).
47. Robinson, *White Cap,* p. 153.
48. Locke, *Three Years in Camp and Hospital,* pp. 71–72.
49. Dannett, *Noble Women,* p. 82.
50. Wittenmeyer, *Under the Guns,* pp. 75, 193ff.
51. Young, *Women and the Crisis,* p. 104.
52. It seems no chance similarity that both she and Clara Barton were chronic insomniacs. Barton in fact slept with a lighted candle and pen and pad by her bed, ready to write down any important thoughts that occurred to her in the night.
53. Young, *Women and the Crisis,* p. 134.
54. Brockett and Vaughan, *Women's Work in the Civil War,* pp. 359–60.
55. Dannett, *Noble Women,* p. 89.
56. Livermore, *My Story of the War,* p. 479.
57. Quoted in Nina Brown Baker, *Cyclone in Calico: the Story of Mary Ann Bickerdyke* (Boston, 1952), p. 11.
58. Young, *Women and the Crisis,* p. 266. General Butler was reported to have used the same phrase about Clara Barton in a similar situation (see Ross, *Angel of the Battlefield,* p. 78). Clearly the line had a significance which made it dwelt upon and even transferable.
59. Livermore, *My Story of the War,* p. 509.
60. Ibid., p. 481.
61. Adelaide Smith, another nurse, is very explicit on this point. See Robinson, *White Caps,* p. 162.
62. Epler, *Clara Barton,* p. 204. Epler also charts the course of her struggle to retain power over the Red Cross and to prevent it from becoming the kind of bureaucratic organization it became after her forced retirement.

For her own account of the Red Cross, see Clara Barton, *The Red Cross: A History of This Remarkable International Movement in the Interest of Humanity* (Albany, N.Y., 1898). Note how even in her title she avoids calling it an organization or an institution. For an unfavorable view of her connection with the Red Cross, see Robinson, *White Caps*, pp. 219ff.

63. Quoted in Epler, *Clara Barton*, p. 235.
64. Quoted in Ross, *Angel of the Battlefield*, p. 239.
65. Tiffany, *Dorothea Lynde Dix*, p. 262.
66. Marshall, *Dorothea Dix*, pp. 140–215.
67. Tiffany, *Dorothea Lynde Dix*, p. 266.
68. Epler, *Clara Barton*, p. 381.
69. For an account of Mrs. Eddy, see Edwin Franden Dakin, *Mrs. Eddy: The Biography of a Virginal Mind* (New York and London, 1929).
70. Locke, *Three Years in Camp and Hospital*, p. 184.
71. On the progress of nursing, see Roberts, *American Nursing*, and Robinson, *White Caps*. On women doctors, see Kate Campbell-Hurd, *Medical Women in America: A Short History of the Pioneer Medical Women of America and of a Few of Their Colleagues in England* (Fort Pierce Beach, Fla., 1933), and Esther Pohl Lovejoy, *Women Doctors of the World* (New York, 1957). The women pioneers of medicine in America appeared in the decade before the Civil War, most notably the Blackwell sisters in New York and Marie Zakrewska in Boston, but their numbers did not reach any significant count until after the war.

The Spiritualist Medium:
A Study of Female
Professionalism in
Victorian America

R. Laurence Moore

In his journal Emerson included the spiritualist medium among the new professions that he believed had emerged in America in the 1850s. It was not a happy admission for him. The sudden and rapid proliferation of men and women who (for a fee) claimed to provide scientific evidence of an afterlife was in his mind anything but a sign of a spiritual awakening in the United States.[1] His listing of the medium along with the daguerreotypist, the railroad man and the landscape gardener represented a troubled concession to the realities of a country that already had more than its share of hucksters and humbugs. The leveling ethos of Jacksonian America encouraged all kinds of "unlearned" people to aspire to professional status. None pressed the claim more vociferously than those who presumed to act as channels of communication with the spirit world. Spiritualism grew into a strong cultural force in nineteenth-century America. Once the Fox sisters, with the aid of Horace Greeley and the publicity of the New York *Tribune,* had proved that people would pay to witness spirit manifestations, mediums appeared in almost every city and town in the country.[2]

Not all of them demanded remuneration (most of them would take it), and those who did, even in the age of the common man, encountered a host of difficulties in carving out their claim to professionalism. A medium first of all faced the difficult task of establishing a reputation for honesty. After that, an inevitable ambiguity clouded the issue of whether he or she possessed a trained skill or was tastelessly exploiting a divine gift. If what mediums did required no education and no planned effort, then what right did they have to ask for a professional fee? In fact, was it not a denigration of their spiritual gift to set a price on it?

Believers in the reality of spirit communication advanced various and conflicting answers to these questions.[3] A majority of leading spokesmen of the spiritualist movement, however, eventually joined in a defense of the professional nature of mediumship. Whatever the source of inspiration, they said, mediums had expenses, their work was tiring, and they performed a service that not everyone could render. One medium who originally had worked for free changed her mind and said to her critics: "If my mediumistic gift is the one most in requisition, it is no less worthy of being exchanged for bread than any other." [4] The most successful mediums who in the last half of the nineteenth century advertised in the press, hung out shingles and roamed all over the country meant to earn a living while giving something beneficial to their "clients." Professional jealousy ran high, and they were never very successful in building organizations to protect professional standards and interest. However, the Mediums Mutual Aid Association, which was founded in Boston in 1860, and a few similiar short-lived groups, did what they could "to secure favorable conditions for the development and instruction of those who use mediumistic powers professionally as a business or means of support." [5]

Mediumship became a professional role identified primarily with women, even though many of the practitioners of the mediums' art were men. One census of spirit mediums which was conducted in 1859 showed a fairly even balance between the sexes—121 women as against 110 men.[6] The men even accounted for some of the most famous of the nineteenth-century spirit communicators. For example, no female medium in Victorian America ever quite captured the attention accorded over many years to Daniel Dunglas Home. Home's admirers in a dozen countries claimed not only that he put his sitters in contact with the dead, but also that he levitated his own body and floated horizontally above their heads. In his most celebrated exhibition he reportedly floated out of a window seventy feet above a London street and came in through another window seven and a half feet away.[7]

Despite Home, however, and despite other men allegedly adept at invoking spirits, the popular impression persisted that mediumship was female. Newspapers hostile to the vogue of spiritualism, and there were many of them, characterized male mediums as "addle-headed feminine men." [8] For, according to unfriendly accounts, mediumship represented above all else the corruption of feminity. A medium was a person whose generalized female traits had developed in perverse and bizarre ways. Spiritualists themselves, while they rejected the notion that mediumship involved any corruption of womanly qualities, at least agreed with critics that mediumship was an occupation suited especially for women. It was in any case one of the few career opportunities open to women in the nineteenth century. The females who tool advantage of it did nothing to discourage the notion that successful mediumship grew from the cultivation of specific traits that in the nineteenth century defined feminity.[9]

A search through nineteenth-century spiritualist literature readily reveals what those traits were considered to be. Phrenological studies, which figured in many essays about mediumistic powers, reported the same thing. Mediums were weak in the masculine qualities of will and reason and strong in the female qualities of intuition and nervousness. They were impressionable (i.e., responsive to outside influences) and extremely sensitive. Above all they were passive. After all, it was queried, what spirit could manifest anything through a medium whose own personality was strongly assertive? The success of spirit communication depended on the ability of mediums to give up their own identity to become the instruments of others.[10]

Self-sacrifice and passiveness were among the things that, in the nineteenth-century understanding, made for the moral superiority of women over men. Those were the qualities that women used in the home to promote domestic felicity.[11] The uses to which female mediums put those same qualities in areas outside the home appeared dangerously inappropriate to many people, even rebellious. But if putting female traits to professional uses was rebellious, the conservative aspects of the rebellion, at least in the case of mediumship, need to be kept in mind. Female mediums did not reject the concept of Victorian womanhood in its entirety. To an amazing degree they accepted sickness, suffering and self-sacrifice as part of the natural lot of women. Those ills in fact served to justify the importance of their profession. Their everlasting willingness to give of themselves for the spiritual benefit of others—even to the point of their own physical impairment—

made mediumship in their eyes a dignified calling. The medium could not boast of a college degree to justify professional status. A long illness preceding and accompanying the career of a successful medium served as a common substitute.

The female medium's acceptance of the feminine definition of her profession was not merely a ploy contrived to gain a place in a man's world that she was determined to have anyway. She took her womanhood seriously, and her concept of femininity affected her professional behavior in a variety of ways. For one thing she was extremely reluctant to accept personal responsibility for her vocational choice. She blamed her course of action on the spirits that controlled her. The story is the same in all autobiographies of female mediums. They were, they reported, frightened by their powers and reluctant to develop and demonstrate them. However, the spirit controls insisted and forced their wills into compliance. Emma Hardinge came from England to America as a young person, and, after failing as an actress, she became one of the most successful public mediums of the late nineteenth century. However, when she first learned of her professional destiny at a spirit circle, she rushed out of the room with horror and tumbled down the stairs.[12] Miss Ellen D. Starkweather, when initially confronted with the news that she was to become a medium, also tried a dash from the room. She luckily was saved a similar crash in the stairwell when a table mysteriously slid across the room to block her exit and seal her fate.[13]

Female mediums almost always went on the stage as "trance" mediums. In this respect they differed significantly from their male counterparts. Male mediums needed their own rationalizations to take up work in so highly controversial a field as mediumship. But at least, once set upon their course, they did not have to overcome additional scruples about the appropriateness of their sex appearing before a public audience. In contrast, the female medium who gave public performances stood in defiance of St. Paul's admonition against women preaching in public—an admonition that most American churches still heeded in the nineteenth century. Speaking in trance was good theater. It was also a way to blunt the defiance. The words of the female medium, delivered while she was in a deep state of somnambulism, were supposedly not her own but those of her spirit control. In the campaign to make the truths of spiritualism known to the world, female mediums left what was termed "normal speaking" to the men.[14] In many of their activities, and certainly in private sittings, male and female mediums did much the same sorts of things. But the women, in contrast to the men, generally mounted the public stage as passively as possible.

One must ask, of course, in view of the deference that many female mediums paid to social conventions, why they bothered with a professional role at all. The deference was certainly not sufficient to placate critics. In many instances they faced the scorn of friends and family who disapproved generally of women who worked, and especially of women who worked in so public and controversial an enterprise. The use of the trance and the shifting of the blame to spirit controls did not make the work more palatable to those who thought that either trickery or the Devil was behind spiritualist performances.

If the money had been better, the motives of the female medium would pose less of a problem. Wealth overcame as many principles in the nineteenth century as it does in our own and provided compensation for the friends one had lost in the process of acquiring it. Yet mediumship, contrary to the charges frequently made by the enemies of spiritualism, was not usually a way to get rich. Sometimes a wealthy benefactor would act as a patron of mediums. For example, Horace Day used some of the profits from the manufacture of rubber products to house Kate Fox in comfortable circumstances in New York City. In the mid-1850s he paid her a $1,200 annual salary to give free sittings for all interested investigators. Cornelius Vanderbilt, Charles Partridge, Henry Seybert, Henry J. Newton and David Underhill were others who at one time or another rendered financial aid to various mediums. Luther Marsh, an aging New York attorney, went so far as to turn over his handsome private residence to Madame Diss Debar, one of the most notorious charlatans of the 1880s.[15] A few American mediums also managed to move in European aristocratic circles, for spiritualism became an entertainment demanded by the crowned heads of England and the Continent. D. D. Home, surely the most successful in this respect, levitated tables for Napoleon III, Czar Alexander II and Queen Sophia of Holland. In addition he married a Russian noble lady, whose estate unfortunately did not pass to him after her death, and almost succeeded in getting a seventy-five-year-old English widow worth 140,000 pounds to adopt him as her son and legal heir.[16]

Normal earnings, however, for both male and female mediums were modest. The average medium, and the available evidence indicates that the sex of the medium was not important with respect to fees, got five dollars for an evening's work away from home in the last half of the nineteenth century. Private home sittings brought in one dollar per hour.[17] Income was irregular because mediums normally could not depend on a regular clientele—at least for extended periods of time in any one place. When a medium traveled, the financial returns were even more undependable. Warren Chase, who was a well-known spiritualist lecturer for over forty years, reported a typical year's earnings as $425, a sum derived from 121 lectures. He paid for his own travel arrangements and a good share of the cost of food and lodging.[18] Through their letters to the spiritualist press, female mediums complained bitterly of low compensation.[19] Of course, such complaints do not suggest that mediums could have done better in any other line of work. Nor is there much evidence to suggest that mediums typically ended their careers as paupers. On the other hand, the monetary returns from the professional practice of mediumship do not by themselves provide an explanation for the willingness of people to endure the very real hardships of the work. While the self-conscious frauds who entered the field cared nothing about social ostracism, there were many others who did believe in the worth and dignity of what they were doing. For them social ostracism was not a pleasant thing. Yet they persisted in their calling, some for amazingly long periods of time.

Personal conviction drove mediums on in their calling. And so did the attention which they received. The women who gravitated toward mediumship had rarely received public attention, first because they were women, and second because they came from a level on the social scale where the men they knew reflected little glory on them. The vicarious sense of fame that came from being wives of respected husbands was by and large unknown to them. Some had lost their fathers early in life and had not been doted on in childhood. Many had had unfortunate experiences with male suitors and husbands. There was no consistent marital pattern among mediums. Many married. Many divorced and remarried. Many remained single. But almost all of them who began their careers as adults felt neglected and useless before undertaking professional life.

The most successful mediums in the nineteenth century derived enormous satisfaction from public acclaim. In their autobiographies they made no effort to conceal that fact.[20] Acclaim made up for any public abuse, which was itself better than no notice at all. Even imagined applause can bring genuine pleasure. Confined to a sickbed in her last years, Cora Maynard recalled her days of glory when as a young girl she had been Mrs. Lincoln's favorite medium. However flawed her memory of specific events, her professional life had most certainly brought her into contact with important Washington officials, including the President. While Lincoln had not issued the Emancipation Proclamation at the command of her spirits, her conviction that he had goes a long way toward accounting for her behavior. In her memory, she, "an unlettered girl," had been led "to become the honored guest of the Ruler of our Great Nation, during the most memora-

ble events in its histories." Those present at her séances, when her
spirits had counseled on important affairs of state, "had lost sight of
the timid girl in the majesty of the utterance, the strength and force of
the language, and the importance of that which was conveyed, and
seemed to realize that some masculine spirit force was giving speech to
almost divine commands."[21] Perhaps from a logical point of view,
Mrs. Maynard had no reason to take personal pride in what her spirit
controls accomplished through her when she was unconscious. A considerable ambiguity attached to the question of just what personal
credit mediums could claim for their work. But it did not detract from
the immediate satisfaction they felt in knowing that they had impressed an audience.

Mrs. Maynard's seizure by a "masculine spirit force" suggests that
part of the satisfaction felt by female mediums derived from their
assumption of an otherwise forbidden male social role during the
trance state. Time and again female mediums under the influence of
their spirit controls turned into swearing sailors, strong Indian braves
or oversexed male suitors. The best of them displayed an impressive
talent for acting. Many in fact had worked at one time in the theater.[22] The cast of spirit characters who performed through them could
assume a staggering variety. At one typical "materializing séance" in
the 1880s, thirty-one spirits paraded out of the medium's cabinet. Captain Hodges, a "firm erect military man," was followed by Alice, "a
tall queenly soprano." Further down the line came Helen, who sang
"Sweet Beulahland," Little Wolf, "a perfect Indian brave," and Mrs.
McCarthy, an Irish lady whose vocabulary amused without offending
genteel taste.[23] Allowing for the deliberate fraud in many of these
performances (the incidence of fraud was especially high among materializing mediums), one may still suggest that trance mediums found
outlets for unexpressed and unexpressible desires in the personalities
of the spirits. If a spirit control kept throwing the medium's wedding
ring away, the medium could with all sincerity disclaim responsibility.[24]

The possession trance has served similar functions in cultures very
different from nineteenth-century America. For example, Judith Gussler, in a study of the Nguni in South Africa, has argued that trance
behavior in that society provided compensation for its hardest pressed
members, most notably the women and children.[25] Similar to what has
been noted in studies of hypnotized subjects, the trance personality
showed none of the signs of subservience of the normal personality
and was universally acclaimed as evincing more brilliance than the
normal personality.[26] Moreover, according to Lenora Greenbaum, in

an analysis of various cultures of Sub-Saharan Africa, possession trance was more common in rigid societies where simple decision making was fraught with danger from internal and external social controls.[27] While nineteenth-century America was by comparison to traditional African societies a flexible rather than a rigid society, women enjoyed the advantage of its egalitarian and democratic features far less than men.[28] The trance condition relieved individual women of personal responsibility for decisions by temporarily changing their identity into a spirit. At least one American medium tried (unsuccessfully) to plead irresponsibility as a legal defense against charges of fraud.[29] The medium and the petitioner seeking the medium's services could, under the cover of the séance, solve problems in making crucial life decisions without personally challenging the established order of society. Not insignificantly, one of the most serviceable functions of nineteenth-century spirits was the sanction that they so freely issued to American wives to divorce their husbands.

The envy of male and more powerful social roles discernible in the utterances and behavior of female mediums assumed some interesting variations. For one thing, female mediums took obvious joy in conquering male adversaries. Emma Hardinge and her equally famous rival, Cora Richmond, both wrote autobiographies that recorded scores of such triumphs. In one of Hardinge's first public lectures at Rondout, New York, she encountered an entire audience of "rough-looking" men who refused to take their hats off. Coming to scoff, they stayed to cheer. She remembered those hats when later in her career she overwhelmed a similar audience in Glasgow, Scotland. The baring of heads was the signal of her victory, just as it had been earlier.[30] Richmond, unlike Hardinge, never subdued a band of armed robbers in Nevada, but she had the satisfaction of reducing Isaiah Rynders to tears. Rynders was a Tammany Hall ruffian whom the New York machine had used on one occasion to disrupt a rally of William Lloyd Garrison. The spirit voices of Richmond were more than his match, and at the end of her address, which he had come to heckle, he cried with conviction.[31]

Both Hardinge and Richmond were "trance lecturers" and followed a similar routine in their public performances. They invited the audience to choose a jury from among themselves that would in turn select a topic of discourse for the medium. Announcing the subject to the medium, the audience then gave her a few moments to enter a trance. Once in trance, she proceeded to talk, usually in excess of an hour. The address constituted the test of her powers. Delivered on subjects chosen almost always by male juries and usually concerning "manly" scientific questions, the subject was presumably something that the uneducated medium could not tackle unless spirits came to her aid. As even hostile newspaper accounts admitted, the discourses, whatever their deficiencies in scientific accuracy, usually left the audience, at the very least, with a healthy respect for the extemporaneous logic of the medium. Hardinge may or may not have known more Hebrew than a Canadian rabbi who tried to challenge her explication of a Jewish text, but the majority of those present took her side.[32] According to Richmond, Lincoln and the Joint Congressional Committee on Reconstruction sought her advice because she could answer "questions that involved a practical knowledge of finance, history, political economy, jurisprudence, and the science of government." [33] Her memory of events is more important here than the actual facts. Just like Cora Maynard, Richmond recalled her days in Washington as a time when she had met men on their own turf and bested them all. For her, those occasions were the best times in the life of a medium.

When Hardinge and Richmond and their co-laborers were not out subduing hostile male audiences, they were busy conquering communities where male spiritualist lecturers had previously met with dismal failure. Hardinge journeyed to Indian Valley, Nevada, to help out a local spiritualist preacher who just happened to be a male and a cripple. Whereas he had never drawn much of an audience on the arid western deserts, her own Fourth of July address made believers of everyone. Of the crowd reaction to her speech she wrote: "The cheers grew into shouts; the clapping of hands into perfect leaps and yells of applause; and at the end of about an hour's address ... I was literally pelted with flowers. The women kissed my dress, and held up their dear little children for me to kiss also, whilst the men almost wrung my arm out, and my hand off, with grips and shaking." [34]

Not all the adulation that mediums received from males in their audience proved equally welcome. Hardinge was thoroughly indignant over the attention of one young man who wrote love letters to her and followed her (in his "astral body") everywhere she spoke. She finally had the satisfaction of seeing him confined in an insane asylum.[35] But an admiring note from afar could be flattering so long as it did not threaten professional independence. Richmond could not resist recording the text of one such letter: "To possess such a lovely, fairy mortal—for her intellectual genius—I would have given a kingdom, or braved a world of dangers." [36] She did not in this case even bother to remind her readers that the intellectual genius ascribed to the medium belonged rather to the spirits.

Aside from the acclain that went with it, the professional life of public mediums gave many women an opportunity for travel and sexual adventure far beyond the lot of the average American woman. The travel is easier to document. Mediums of both sexes were an itinerant bunch. The many advertisements that spiritualist speakers placed in the *Banner of Light* and other spiritualist publications provide abundant testimony to their continuous movement. While some women restricted the engagements they would accept to specific localities, most of them thought little of long absences from home on trips covering many miles. K. Graves traveled through the subzero weather of the Midwest, constantly losing her health and staying in the homes of strangers, in order to carry out her professional duties. Operating along the Pacific coast, Miss Jennie Leys regularly trekked from San Francisco down through San Jose, Stockton, Santa Barbara and Los Angeles to San Bernardino. Many advertised a route in advance and offered to accept engagements along the way. For example, Mrs. Laura Gordon announced that she would start west on April 1 to "receive calls to lecture during the month of April on the route from Boston to Quincy, Ill., via Buffalo, Cleveland and Chicago." Laura Cuppy and Lizzie Doten turned up everywhere. Perhaps none outdid Mrs. C. M. Stowe, a "devoted wife and mother," who "traveled unaccompanied, by steamboat, railroad and stage, day and night, and the latter over roads that would appall many a man who has never traveled over these mountains." In an average trip of five weeks, she covered eight hundred miles, entering towns she had never seen, hiring her own hall, doing her own advertising and entertaining her own audience.[37]

In any line of work traveling is not always viewed as an advantage by the person forced on the road. Many mediums kept on the move not because they cared for a life of wandering, but because their displays bore only limited repetition in any one locale. Complaining endlessly about the hardships of travel and the lack of hospitality they received en route, some of them longed for the security of a settled parish that ministers in many other churches enjoyed.[38] Since spiritualist believers in the nineteenth century who cared to form churches at all generally lacked the funds to provide long-range and regular support to a permanent minister, perpetual motion presented itself to most public mediums in the form of a forced option.

Nonetheless, there are many examples of female lecturers who traveled by choice and rejected offers of permanent settlement when they were made. When she finally married, Emma Hardinge briefly advertised herself as a healing medium with the specific intention of setting up an office in Boston. But she grew restless and resumed her lecture tours. Cora Richmond did accept a permanent position that a spiritualist congregation in Chicago offered to her—but only on the condition that she could take long leaves of absence to continue her routine of travels to England, across America and to Australia. In addition to the gratification of seeing the world, travel provided mediums, just as it did other Americans in the nineteenth century, an opportunity to escape something. Husbands and domestic life often. Unhappy love affairs occasionally. Routine always. In the act of escape mediums proved something to society. They were tough, albeit gentle. They were resourceful, albeit mild. And they had a service to offer that was too important to be confined within narrow geographic boundaries.[39]

The efforts of some feminist leaders after the American Civil War to liberate women from "the narrow limits of the domestic circle" received strong vocal support at nearly every spiritualist convention held in the latter part of the century.[40] Mediums of course had a vested interest in battling the opponents of the feminist movement who charged that women, once removed from the constant surveillance of their male spouses, would fall victim to every sensual temptation lying in their paths. But the intent of some of the resolutions adopted by spiritualists was not entirely clear. For example, in saying that "a female whose talents are valuable to the public ... should not be tongue-tied and pen-tied by the ceremony of marriage," were spiritualists joining Victoria Woodhull (who was three times the president of a national spiritualist association) in attacking the institution of marriage?[41] Or were they, in milder tones, only suggesting the compatibility of marriage with a career other than household management? Most spiritualist publications supported the latter interpretation and defended "the exclusive conjugal love between one man and one woman."[42] But both points of view were represented among spiritualists, and those of them who declared in favor of both marriage and female professionalism had to worry about all the evidence linking mediumship to marital inconstancy.

In his novel *The Bostonians,* Henry James linked feminism to the cause of spiritualism and damned them both. It was a common attitude. Spiritualism, it was charged time and again, inevitably led to free love. By approving of women who operated independently of men, spritualism was ipso facto a free love movement. The *Los Angeles Times* complained of a woman who, after hearing several spiritualist lectures, divorced her husband to run "around the country playing doctor." In prompting five or six other ladies in the area to do the same thing, her contagious example, in the opinion of the *Times,* posed a serious threat to sexual morality in Southern California.[43]

In the early years of the spiritualist movement, Dr. Benjamin Hatch, the first husband of Cora Richmond, published a sensational pamphlet that described mediumistic practices as "shameless goings on that vie with the secret Saturnalia of the Romans." Divorced by his wife, who then went on to become Cora Daniels and Cora Tappan before assuming her final matrimonial surname, the aggrieved Hatch charged that of three hundred married mediums he had surveyed in the Northern states, half had dissolved their conjugal relations. A large proportion of the remainder had abandoned the bed of their partners to cohabit "with their 'affinities' by the mutual consent of their husband or wife." Apparently the problem went beyond spiritualism's tolerance of a public sphere for women because male mediums were as guilty as female mediums in forming these "promiscuous" marriages. Thus, Hatch's sinners included John Murphy Spear, a Universalist clergyman turned spiritualist. He had forsaken his wife to travel with his paramour who "last Fall, bore to him what they call a spiritual baby." Also S. C. Hewitt, who had left his invalid wife in a water cure to go off lecturing with his "spiritual affinity." And Warren Chase who harbored a wife "in every Spiritualist port." [44] However, male promiscuity was nothing new. What most bothered the critics of feminism and spiritualism was the encouragement they saw both movements giving to women's desertion of the home and family.

Many spiritualist spokesmen accepted the accuracy of some of the reports of sexual misbehavior. Lamentably, they said, the discordant relations reported among spiritualist mediums had a basis in fact. "We are compelled," one unusually honest source wrote, "to admit that more than half of our traveling media, speakers and prominent spiritualists, are guilty of immoral and licentious practices, that have justly provoked the abhorrence of all right thinking people." [45] Purity was the one assumed trait of Victorian womanhood that did not seem at all necessary to the practice of good mediumship. On the other hand, the *Banner of Light* insisted that actual promiscuity was not to be confused with the advocacy of promiscuity. Moreoever, there were social and economic reasons for the moral lapses. Its editorials usually blamed low wages for whatever deficiencies could be charged against the morality of mediums. When mediums were paid better, the *Banner of Light* argued, mediums, especially female mediums, would no longer have to seek favors from people of questionable character.[46]

While it is hard to fault the logic of the editorialists writing for the *Banner of Light,* their arguments remind us that the professional life of a medium was not all bliss. There was a vast difference between feminist leaders, spiritualist or otherwise, who spoke against marriage as a form of chattel slavery and underpaid female mediums who in their travels spent the night with any man who would buy their whiskey. In part the problem goes back to the underlying assumptions about the nature of the medium's professional skills. It was difficult at best to maintain a professional status on traits universally recognized as qualities of physical and intellectual weakness, even if they did imply moral superiority. Female mediums risked a serious confusion about their identity when they described themselves as passive agents controlled by outside intelligences. In their professional roles, by their own repeated admissions, they were "obedient instruments" or "humble followers." As we have seen, such self-definitions justified the medium's sense of self-importance. At the same time they undermined it. They had the same effect on the way that others viewed the importance of the medium. Séance-goers often treated a private medium as an unimportant (because passive) intermediary, to be praised if things went well, but only for her strange gifts rather than for her trained skill. A good sitting might save the medium a scolding, but not necessarily the humiliating posture of being bound, gagged and searched to insure proper "test conditions." [47]

The public trance lecturer enjoyed higher professional status and escaped some of the pettier trials of the private "test" medium. So long as she confined her activities to speaking, and did not try to lift tables or materialize grandmothers, her audience had no occasion to strip and search her. But the trance speaker, perhaps to a greater degree than other types of mediums, viewed herself as "a negative passive instrument." She worried about falling under the influence of "inharmonious, impure" spirits and the unwholesome thoughts of people in her audience.[48] Mediums of all types emphasized the danger of their calling in hopes that the hazards would increase its prestige. Thus, they reported without embarrassment an instance when a crew of spirit pirates took over the "organism" of the medium and almost strangled her.[49] In another case reported in spiritualist literature, two leading trance speakers tore at each other like cats and dogs only to find, after being forcibly parted and restored to consciousness, that their spirit controls were bitter enemies.[50]

Unfortunately, critics of professional mediums saw no heroism in the "particular susceptibility to surrounding influences" which they manifested.[51] On this point opponents of spiritualism made clear why they regarded mediumship as a corruption of womanhood. Whenever women voluntarily relinquished whatever will, reason, and self-assertion they had in the first place, and did so in an unprotected environment, they were asking for trouble. Passiveness was not a professional virtue. It was a good reason for women to stay at home and perfect the arts of domestic science.

In addition to accepting a stereotyped version of themselves as passive creatures, female mediums also believed that they were of necessity frail. By all accounts, vigorous and healthy people did not become mediums. To convey their messages, spirits needed a person of a "nervous temperament." Cold hands and a light complexion, accompanied by a long record of sickness and physical suffering, gave the best possible signs of budding mediumship. Mrs. Marietta Munson, born with a "peculiarly delicate" constitution, developed her mediumistic powers after a severe attack of lung fever. Another talented medium, Mrs. J. S. Adams, suffered from a "general weakness of her whole physical being," and was often confined to bed suffering constant pain "almost beyond endurance." Two other mediums, who were sisters, were "very slight frail persons, suffering under the most pitiable condition of ill-health." Mollie Fancher, the "Brooklyn Enigma," became clairvoyant after landing on her head in a fall from a horse. A series of incredibly painful illnesses ensued. "Confined to her bed, subject to tortures, from the contemplation of which the mind will naturally recoil," she made her living promoting articles for invalids manufactured by the George F. Sargent Company. "We have no faith," the *Banner of Light* wrote, "that the 'nature of things' permits high mediumship unaccompanied by intense suffering." [52]

Female mediums tried in the only possible ways open to them to reconcile conflicting impulses. In become professional, they did not want to cease being feminine. Cora Richmond's emphasis on her own "etherial, virgin beauty" and "her gentle and mild saintliness" justified to herself her entrance into a man's world. But her own early career gave eloquent testimony to the difficulties of combining the qualities of feminity (she described herself as a "frail bark") with professional independence.[53] Dr. Hatch, her first husband, had lived off her earnings. His bitter narrative of the marriage, which he published in the same pamphlet containing his exposé of the sexual lives of mediums, was extremely flattering to himself. By his account, when he discovered Cora, she was an indigent teenaged girl. She had an undeniable gift, but no sense of how to use it to elevate herself. Having married her, Hatch began, with "untiring toil," to take his wife on the lecture circuit. He attended to all the business details, did all the promotion and finally managed to lay some money aside above expenses. Hatch kept, he admitted, firm control over the profits, but he was, he said, extremely generous in the outlays for his wife. "My rule was to anticipate her wants as far as possible, and thus supply them before requested to do so." Meanwhile, while Hatch performed all this hard work, Cora lay around lazily with not even the need to prepare speeches between her appearances.[54]

Understandably, the wife recalled this epoch in her life differently. Her version of the story, which was supported by an investigation of several prominent spiritualist gentlemen, accused Hatch of seeking an unfair advantage from her immaturity. Lying to her about his social position and financial ability, he completely stopped his own dentistry practice after the wedding. His income thereafter came strictly from what she earned. As sole manager of the finances, he was stingy both with her and her mother. He let her wear her few decent clothes only during performances. Moreover, Hatch boasted to his new wife of his infidelity to his old one and made sexual demands upon her that Cora claimed damaged her "health and delicacy." He forced on her the company of a woman of "abandoned character," whose miniature he kept, and gave her the distinct feeling that it was not "safe to cohabit with him." [55]

Undoubtedly, neither husband nor wife gave an entirely accurate account of the marriage. Only shortly before the divorce, one spiritualist leader had seen nothing wrong in the conduct of Dr. Hatch. In fact, he had viewed the mixture of Hatch's masculine qualities with Cora's feminine qualities as perfect complements: "His strong will and determined purpose and powers of mind, acting with her passive and feminine mildness, are doubtlessly well-calculated to bring out and present her medium excellences in a way to affect the greatest amount of good for the people." [56] However, given the wide range of possibilities for male abuse of his female partner in the nineteenth century, one's instinctive sympathy lies with the young Mrs. Hatch. The husband's outraged reaction to his wife's charges against him gave a sufficient idea of what she was up against. "No right minded woman," he wrote, "would ever leave her husband on such a basis, were the complaint true." [57]

Cora Richmond left her husband and learned enough from the experience of matrimony to retain the control of her earnings through a succession of husbands. Not every female medium who traveled with a male manager suffered callous exploitation. Emma Hardinge married only after her career had been successfully established, and at that point in her life she was happy enough to turn over the promotional and financial details of her tours to her husband. She remained the star of the show, and her willingness to surrender the management of the practical matters of life served her no better or no worse than it did leisured ladies in any time and place. Men could be useful protectors as well as business partners. In addition to her husband, Hardinge had the comfort of an Indian spirit named Arrowhead who stood over her in times of danger brandishing a war hatchet.[58]

The dangers of exploitation may have been greatest when the medium was young, for many female mediums made their professional debut when their fathers started dragging them around the countryside. Cora Richmond's father, not Benjamin Hatch, first put her on a public platform. The father of Laura Ellis advertised her presentations of spirit wonders when she was thirteen. Bound and gagged by audiences along the East Coast, she somehow managed to get spirits to play musical instruments which had been laid beside her in a darkened room.[59] Laura and others like her did not feel abused. Children enjoyed the attention they got and were glad in any case when the spirits ordered them to quit school. There were cases of fathers who became obsessed with the spirits and turned the whole family's attention totally away from other things. In these instances, the obsession could destroy the family's fortunes.[60] More normally, however, the child medium became a modest and welcome source of supplemental family income. The only question was whether the young medium thereafter ever achieved a healthy psychological independence both from the flattering encouragement of her manager or the expectations of her audience.

Potentially the most crippling damage that accompanied the practice of mediumship was not exploitation but serious self-deception. Of course, as has already been suggested, a fantasy which was taken seriously by the medium had its uses and comforts. Mediums who in trance acted out forbidden desires or expressed repressed aspects of their personality were often making the only approach to reality which their society and culture allowed them. Much evidence suggests that mediumship got many women off their sickbeds. Whatever the throat and chest afflictions, the lung hemorrhages and the rheumatic aches, mediums traveled long distances with little rest and somehow felt a renewed burst of health when they mounted the speaker's platform. Miss A. W. Sprague lay for two years, utterly prostrate, in a sick room where no sunlight intruded. Medical doctors ministered to her in vain. Then, from spirits speaking through her sister, she learned that she was to become a great medium. She recovered sufficiently to begin a career as a trance speaker, and as the career advanced, her health improved.[61] As we all know, Mary Baker Eddy's miraculous recovery of health was not a unique story in the nineteenth century. What we may not yet realize is the extent to which such recoveries were commonplace.

On the other hand, self-delusion put as many people into sickbeds as it put on their feet. Unless we assume that mediumistic phenomena were genuine (i.e., produced with the aid of spirits) or, alternatively, that they were all the contrivances of conscious fraud, then we must suppose that honest mediums on some psychic level were kidding themselves. And if something damaged the medium's imagined image of herself and forced her to recognize herself as an impostor, the result could be tragic. It was safer to be a fraud from the beginning.

Biographies of spiritualist mediums contain many puzzles that defy explanation. One particular pattern, however, does seem to fit many of their lives. They associated their first awareness of spirit company with the early years of lonely childhoods and dated their actual mediumship from adolescence. In other words a belief in their spiritual powers began with childhood reveries and received reinforcement in a period of life when they desperately wanted to impress adults. They did believe in the specialness of their gift even if later they also came to believe that the gift needed the gilding of trickery to render it truly impressive. Mediumship was a competitive business. Practitioners all too commonly found that a reliance on one dishonest prop forced them to keep seeking for others.[62] After all, the medium who failed to produce spirits on any given occasion and made excuses about bad conditions lost her reputation and her audience. As professionals, they had a mystique of infallibility to worry about. Similar (they thought) to the lawyer caught with a bad case or a doctor who did not recognize the disease, they proceeded to do their best in unfavorable circumstances. Average séance-goers had no knowledge of professional secrets. Their ignorance in that respect coupled with their predisposition to accept any sign that a spirit relative was near made it easy to cheat. And what was a poor medium to do when her overeager clients claimed to see more spirits than she herself believed to be present in the room? Mediums faced as many moral dilemmas from too much success as from too little.

When conscious deception, by degrees, became the normal practice of the medium rather than the exception, she was forced to wonder whether she had ever been anything other than a willful deceiver. The reckoning could be a hard one. When Margaret Fox tried to reclaim her dignity by publicly confessing in 1888 to her fraudulent methods, she had long before turned to the comfort of drink. Her almost instant retraction of her confession raises a suspicion that she never knew exactly what she was up to. Willed deceit may or may not explain the first raps that Kate and Margaret Fox heard in the cottage of their parents in Hydesville. It may or may not explain their first successes in

New York City and their ability to attract attention from the educated and the well-born. But in the long run, it certainly explains their wrecked lives. At the time of their deaths even spiritualists refused to honor them. A general appeal in 1892 asking spiritualists to contribute money for an ailing Margaret Fox netted $86.80.[63]

In their pursuit of self-respect, mediums got very little support from the society around them. Increasingly in the nineteenth century they found themselves the objects of legal restrictions. As early as 1865, Charles Colchester, one of the several mediums reputed to have conducted séances for Lincoln, was arrested in Buffalo for failing to purchase a license as a juggler. Although Colchester defended himself by citing his right to pursue whatever religion he chose, a jury found him guilty and fined him forty dollars plus $743 in court costs.[64] Legislative bodies continued to levy heavy fines on the activities of mediums or banned them altogether. In the 1890s the city of Philadelphia made a wholesale roundup of spiritualist mediums, mostly women, and jailed them for violating a city ordinance against fortunetelling.[65] The raising of state medical standards put spiritualist healers out of business. Courts threw out wills because the deceased author had been a spiritualist and obviously mentally incompetent. Spiritualists even ran the risk of being committed to asylums by their unsympathetic families.

Confronted with legal restrictions that defined them as deviant, dangerous and insane, the professional mediums took what comfort they could in viewing themselves as martyrs. It was not always very much. Their egos took a beating from psychologists as well as lawyers. To George Beard, an important neurologist who wrote a book about American nervousness, mediumship was a disabling malady. Writing in the *North American Review* in 1879, he said: "Trance is a very frequently occurring functional disease of the nervous system, in which cerebral activity is concentrated in some limited region of the brain, the activity of the rest of the brain being for the time suspended." [66] Particularly in the last quarter of the nineteenth century, with the emergence of a psychology of the unconscious, mediumship became the subject of lively commentary in the journals of abnormal psychology. Psychologists pored over the life history of mediums for information about hysterical behavior. The medium became a key figure in the development of the concept of split and multiple personality.[67]

There is no question that the behavior of mediums sometimes gave occasion for serious alarm. For every one of them who found new strength and happiness in her work, others by their own account threw convulsions and regularly succumbed to hysterical sobbing. Many mediums at the conclusion of a séance showed almost no pulse and remained for hours, or in extreme cases for weeks, rigid and cold.[68] Even Emma Hardinge, a rock of stability among mediums, did some peculiar things. The "snapping doctor" of St. Louis, a man celebrated for the "unwashed filth" on his hair and body, once kept her rolling on the dirt floor of his office for over two hours, at one moment worshiping the sun, at the next rattling and hissing like a snake.[69]

Still, the historian may wonder whether much of this behavior would have suggested the need for medical treatment if certain elements in the culture had not seen it as socially disruptive. Rachel Baker was a trance speaker who was cured of her disease. According to William Hammond, a nineteenth-century American neurologist who told her tale, she had drawn large crowds to her performances. And though Hammond was intent on linking mediumship to mental derangement, he admitted that her "discourses were highly respectable in point of style and arrangement, and were interspersed with Scripture quotations." Not Rachel, but her parents who were unhappy which such an odd daughter, sought out the doctors who "restored her health." Rachel Baker lost her faculty of trance preaching and never regained it.[70] A happy ending? Undoubtedly for the parents and for Hammond. But nothing in the story indicated that the girl was any happier for her cure. As a matter of fact, it never occurred to Hammond to ask.

If a belief that one had spiritualist powers was a malady, a lot of nineteenth-century American women suffered from it. And if a conviction that spirit phenomena were real constituted a dangerous delusion, many of America's most talented women were led astray by it throughout their adult life. Whatever the clinical conclusion, mediumship and a belief in spirit voices had their uses for those who accepted them.[71] They offered relief from boredom, routine and responsibility. They provided consolation in the face of family deaths, marital abuse and loneliness. And of course in many cases they helped to launch successful professional careers. Amanda Jones in fact used her mediumship, which was discovered during several periods of protracted illness, to futher other careers as poet and inventor. Believing her actions to be governed by spiritual guardians, she shared credit with her spirits in securing patents for an oil burner and a vacuum process for preserving food. The spirits gave her less useful advice about business practices, for her enterprises usually failed financially. But her autobiography, written with the strong encouragement of William James, gave every indication that she had lived a satisfying life. She died, unmarried and self-supporting, at the age of seventy-nine.[72]

Mediums bore the double stigma of doing something most women did not do in the service of a cause that many people laughed at. Yet they persisted, many of them for decades. Mediumship was not an occupation pursued by women of social standing and of education. But for other women, further down the social scale, mediumship, whatever the seamy sides of its practice, offered the possibility of transforming a miserable life into one that brought happiness for oneself and not infrequently for others. The frail sensitiveness that characterized nineteenth-century womanhood was put to far worse uses. To be sure a medium's career could also end in unfortunate ways. But if we can cite examples of mediums who in the last half of the nineteenth century led degenerate and unhappy lives, we should understand that the profession was not the most important cause of the degeneracy or the unhappiness.

NOTES

1. Emerson, *Journals* (Boston: Houghton Mifflin, 1912), 8:574. John B. Wilson, "Emerson and the 'Rochester Rappings,'" *New England Quarterly*, 41 (June 1968), 248–58.
2. The number of historical studies of nineteenth-century spiritualism has increased in recent years. Among scholarly works, see Geoffrey K. Nelson, *Spiritualism and Society* (London: Routledge and Kegan Paul, 1969); Howard Kerr, *Mediums and Spirit Rappers and Roaring Radicals. Spiritualism in American Literature, 1850–1900* (Urbana: Univ. of Illinois Press, 1972); Burton Gates Brown, "Spiritualism in Nineteenth Century America" (Diss. Boston Univ., 1973); Mary Farrell Bednarowski, "Nineteenth Century American Spiritualism: An Attempt at Scientific Religion" (Diss. Univ. of Minnesota, 1973). Katherine H. Porter, *Through a Glass Darkly: Spiritualism in the Browning Circle* (Lawrence, Kan.: Univ. of Kansas Press, 1958), remains in many ways the best book on the subject. Anyone interested in the historical origins of spiritualism in America should consult Ernest Isaacs, "A History of American Spiritualism: The Beginnings, 1845–1855" (M.A. thesis, Univ. of Wisconsin, 1957). Also R. Laurence Moore, "Spiritualism and Science: Reflections on the First Decade of the Spirit Rappings," *American Quarterly*, 24 (Oct. 1972), 474–500; "American Spiritualism and American Religion in the Nineteenth Century," in Edwin Gaustad, ed., *The Rise of Adventism* (New York: Harper, 1974).
3. For a summary of the issues and two opposite points of view, see Emma Hardinge, "Compensation of Mediums," *Banner of Light* (hereafter *BL*), Oct. 22, 1859, and the letter from A.C. Robinson, *BL*, May 5, 1866. The *BL*, a weekly spiritualist newspaper that lasted through the nineteenth century, is the richest single printed source on all aspects of the movement. Despite its wide circulation, complete runs are rare (to my knowledge the American Antiquarian Society has the most complete set) and historians have made very little use of it.
4. Letter from Emma Hardinge to *BL*, July 27, 1861.

5. Quote in Isaaces, "A History of Spiritualism," p. 180.
6. Uriah Clark, ed., *The Spiritual Register for 1859—Facts, Philosphy, Statistics of Spiritualism.*
7. Slater Brown, *The Heyday of Spiritualism* (New York: Hawthorn Books, 1970), pp. 243–45.
8. Mortimer Thomson, *Doesticks What He Says* (New York, 1855), quoted in Kerr, *Mediums and Spirit Rappers and Roaring Radicals,* p. 40.
9. For an analysis of another professional role identified with women, see Dee Garrison, "The Tender Technicians: The Feminization of Public Librarianship, 1876-1905," *Journal of Social History* 6 (Winter 1972-73), 131–59. Other professional roles for women included nursing and teaching. Also on the problem of professional women, see Ann Douglas Wood, "The 'Scribbling Women' and Fanny Fern: Why Women Wrote," *American Quarterly,* 23 (Spring 1971), 3–24.
10. For nineteenth-century images of women, see Carroll Smith-Rosenberg and Charles Rosenberg, "The Female Animal: Medical and Biological Views of Woman and Her Role in Nineteenth-Century America," *Journal of American History,* 60 (Sept. 1973), 332–56; Carroll Smith-Rosenberg, "The Hysterical Woman: Sex Roles and Role Conflict in 19th Century America," *Social Research,* 39 (Winter 1972), 652–78; Ann Douglas Wood, "The Fashionable Diseases: Women's Complaints and Their Treatment in Nineteenth-Century America," *Journal of Interdisciplinary History,* 4 (Summer 1973), 25–52.
11. The theme of self-sacrifice is a central concern in Kathryn Kish Sklar, *Catharine Beecher: A Study in American Domesticity* (New Haven: Yale University Press, 1973). See also Barbara Welter, "The Cult of True Womanhood, 1820-1860," *American Quarterly,* 18 (Summer 1966), 151–74, and Carroll Smith-Rosenberg, "Beauty, the Beast and the Militant Woman: A Case Study in Sex Roles and Social Stress in Jacksonian America," *American Quarterly,* 23 (Oct. 1971), 562–84.
12. *Autobiography of Emma Hardinge Britten,* Mrs. Margaret Wilkinson, ed. (London: John Heywood, 1900), 22–26. Because she married late in her professional career, I have retained the maiden name of Hardinge throughout the text.
13. "Biography of Miss Ellen D. Starkweather," *BL,* Nov. 27, 1858.
14. "Normal speaking" meant that one spoke from one's own prepared text. In one count most of the men listed as spiritual orators fell into the category "normal speakers." However, 100 of the 121 listed women were "trance speakers." Clark, *The Spiritual Register for 1859.*
15. *New York Times,* March 29, 30, 31, April 1, 2, 3, 1888.
16. D.D. Home, *Incidents in My Life,* Vol. I (New York: Carleton, 1863), Vol. II (New York: Holt and Williams, 1872); Jean Burton, *Heyday of a Wizard: Daniel Home, the Medium* (New York: Knopf, 1944).
17. Letter of A.B. Child to *BL,* July 31, 1868. A wealth of other material in the *BL* and other spiritualist publications, including advertisements, gives general support to the modest level of fees.
18. Emma Hardinge Britten, *Modern American Spiritualism: A Twenty Years' Record of the Communion Between Earth and the World of Spirits* (New York: published by the author, 1870), p. 273.
19. For example, Augusta A. Currier wrote to the *BL,* Dec. 23, 1865, that

she had yet to see "the first medium who has been able to earn a decent competency by the exercise of his or her spiritual gifts." The level of fees became a matter of professional jealousy. Lita H. Barney charged that famous mediums set too high a fee, leaving nothing for the rest of them whose spiritual gifts were just as great. *BL,* Sept. 21, 1861.

20. Autobiographical and semiautobiographical accounts of nineteenth-century female mediums include Amanda T. Jones, *A Psychic Autobiography* (New York: Graves Pub. Co., 1910); Reuben Briggs Davenport, *The Death Blow to Spiritualism: Being the True Story of the Fox Sisters* (New York: G.W. Dillingham, 1888); Margaret Wilkinson, ed., *Autobiography of Emma Hardinge Britten* (London: John Heywood, 1900); Harrison D. Barrett, *Life Work of Cora L.V. Richmond* (Chicago: Hack and Anderson, 1895); Mrs. Nettie Colburn Maynard, *Was Abraham Lincoln a Spiritualist? or, Curious Revelations from the Life of a Trance Medium* (Philadelphia: Rufus C. Hartranft, 1891); Abram H. Dailey, *Mollie Fancher, The Brooklyn Enigma* (Brooklyn: Press of Eagle Book Printing Dept., 1894); Anne Manning Robbins, *Past and Present with Mrs. Piper* (New York: Henry Holt, 1921). These should be compared to the memoirs of twentieth-century female mediums; for example, Mrs. Cecil M. Cook, *The Voice Triumphant: The Revelations of a Medium* (New York: Knopf, 1931); Eileen J. Garrett, *Many Voices: The Autobiography of a Medium* (New York: Putnams, 1968); Gladys Osborne Leonard, *Brief Darkness* (London: Cassell and Co., 1942); Estelle Roberts, *Fifty Years a Medium* (New York: Avon, 1972). There is also a long list of autobiographical material concerning male mediums.

21. Maynard, *Was Abraham Lincoln a Spiritualist,* pp. 4, 72.

22. Emma Hardinge is the most obvious nineteenth-century example. The theater background is more common in the twentieth century. Note, for example, the lives of Eileen Garrett, Hester Dowden, Gladys Leonard and Jeane Dixon.

23. Report of a séance conducted by Mrs. James A. Bliss, *BL,* July 26, 1884.

24. Suzy Smith, *The Mediumship of Mrs. Leonard* (Hyde Park: University Books, 1964), p. 48.

25. Judith Gussler, "Social Change, Ecology, and Spirit Possession Among the South African Nguni," in *Religion, Altered States of Consciousness and Social Change,* ed. by Erika Bourguignon (Columbus: Ohio State Univ. Press, 1973).

26. Henri Ellenberger, *The Discovery of the Unconscious* (New York: Basic Books, 1970), pp. 173-74.

27. Lenora Greenbaum, "Possession Trance in Sub-Saharan Africa: A Descriptive Analysis of Fourteen Societies," in *Religion ... and Social Change,* ed. Bourguignon. Also see Keith Thomas, *Religion and the Decline of Magic* (New York: Scribner's, 1971), p. 48; Vieda Skultans, *Intimacy and Ritual: A Study of Spiritualism, Mediums and Groups* (London: Routledge and Kegan Paul, 1974); Gail Parker, "Mary Baker Eddy and Sentimental Womanhood," *New England Quarterly,* 43 (March 1970), 13-24.

28. See, for example, David Potter, "American Women and American Character," in *History and American Society* (New York: Oxford, 1973), pp. 278-303.

29. Brown, "Spiritualism in Nineteenth Century America," p. 218.
30. *Autobiography of Emma Britten*, pp. 77, 217.
31. *Life Work of Cora Richmond*, pp. 106ff. Walter M. Merrill, *Against Wind and Tide: A Biography of William Lloyd Garrison* (Cambridge, Mass.: Harvard Univ. Press, 1963), pp. 257-60.
32. *Autobiography of Emma Britten*, p. 88.
33. *Life Work of Cora Richmond*, p. 225.
34. *Autobiography of Emma Britten*, p. 198.
35. Ibid., p. 170.
36. *Life Work of Cora Richmond*, p. 183.
37. One of the best sources for information about itinerancy are the advertisements placed by mediums in the *BL*. On Mrs. Stowe, see *BL*, April 14, 1866.
38. For conflicting opinion on the wisdom of settling speakers, see editorial on "Itinerancy," *BL*, April 28, 1866, and D.W. Hull, "Settled Speakers," *BL*, March 4, 1871.
39. For the impact of mobility on various types of Americans I am indebted to George Wilson Pierson, *The Moving American* (New York: Knopf, 1973).
40. Most spiritualist conventions in the nineteenth century were local and regional rather than national, but they were frequent and well-attended. The declarations in favor of women received strong support from the spirits. See, for example, *Twelve Messages from the Spirit of John Quincy Adams Through Joseph D. Stiles, Medium, to Josiah Brigham* (Boston: Bella Marsh, 1859), pp. 348-49.
41. Letter from Warren Chase, *BL*, May 7, 1862. Chase may have had himself in mind as much as any of the oppressed women. His wife very much disapproved of his travels in behalf of spiritualism, and he responded to her nagging by breaking off sexual relations. Gossip linked Chase to many women, but he denied any illicit sexual activity. See his autobiography, *The Life Line of the Lone One, Or, Autobiography of the World's Child* (Boston: Bella Marsh, 1858).
42. The language is drawn from a resolution of a spiritualist convention in Rutland, Vermont, in the summer of 1858, reported in *BL*, July 10, 1858.
43. *Los Angeles Times*, Aug. 17, 1888. For literary works other than *The Bostonians* that drew connections between spiritualism, femininism, and/or free love, see Kerr, *Mediums and Spirit Rappers*.
44. Benjamin F. Hatch, *Spiritualists' Iniquities Unmasked, and the Hatch Divorce Case* (New York, 1859), pp. 5-6, 13-15 and passim.
45. Wm. Bailey Porter, *Spiritualism as It Is: Or the Results of a Scientific Investigation of Spirit Manifestations* (New York, 1865), p. 20. Also Warren Chase, "Spiritualism and Social Discord," *BL*, May 12, 1860.
46. Lizzie Doten, "A Plea for Working Women," *BL*, May 10, 1862; "Lottie Fowler," *BL*, April 22, 1899; Letter from Augusta Currier, *BL*, Dec. 23, 1865.
47. *Life Work of Cora Richmond*, p. 725. Kathryn Sklar in her biography of Catharine Beecher has written in a very illuminating way about the efforts by women to shift what were arguably stereotyped weaknesses (submission, self-sacrifice) to their advantage. Those efforts, as Sklar notes, had mixed results.

48. *BL*, June 23, 1866; "Mediumship and Morality," *BL*, June 22, 1878.
49. Thomas R. Hazard, "Mediums and Mediumship," *BL*, Dec. 9, 1871.
50. Biography of Mrs. J.H. Conant, *BL*, May 22, 1875.
51. "Mediumship and Morality," *BL*, June 22, 1878. Reverend William H. Ferris, a harsh critic of spiritualism, listened to a doctor describe the traits of a medium in the following way: "I never knew a vigorous and strong-minded person who was a medium. I do not believe that such a one can ever become one. It requires a person of light complexion, one in a negative passive condition, of a nervous temperament with cold hands, of a mild, impressible, and gentle disposition. Hence girls and females make the best mediums." Such persons, Ferris thought, had no business casting themselves unprotected into new environments. "Review of Modern Spiritualism," *Ladies Repository*, 16 (Feb. 1856), 92.
52. *BL*, Sept. 25, 1858; *BL*, May 29, 1858; Britten, *Modern American Spiritualism*, p. 201; Dailey, *Mollie Fancher*, p. 2; *BL*, Feb. 12, 1870.
53. *Life Work of Cora Richmond*, p. 471.
54. Hatch, *Spiritualists' Iniquities Unmasked*, pp. 32–41.
55. Ibid.
56. A.B. Child, "Cora L.V. Hatch," *BL*, July 17, 1858.
57. Hatch, *Spiritualists' Iniquities Unmasked*, p. 36.
58. *Autobiography of Emma Britten*, pp. 218–19.
59. Reports in *BL*, April 7, April 21, 1866.
60. Britten, *Modern American Spiritualism*, p. 319.
61. *BL*, Feb. 9, 1861.
62. For a biased but interesting account of the network of fraud that grew up among professional mediums (a network complete with a supporting industry manufacturing props), see David P. Abbott, *Behind the Scenes With the Mediums* (Chicago: Open Court Publishing Co., 1908), pp. 270–73 and passim.
63. *BL*, Jan. 9, 1892.
64. Brown, "Spiritualism in Nineteenth Century America," p. 147.
65. *Proceedings of the Third Annual Convention of the National Spiritualists' Association*, p. 16.
66. George Beard, "The Psychology of Spiritism," *North American Review*, 129 (July 1879), 67. One twentieth-century commentator, who has subjected mediums to Freudian scrutiny, has concluded, among other things, that normal sexual activity is extremely rare among them. See George Lawton, *The Drama of Life After Death: A Study of the Spiritualist Religion* (New York: Henry Holt, 1932), pp. 480ff.
67. The interest of depth psychologists in the life histories of mediums is a subject requiring extensive treatment elsewhere. Janet, James, Jung, Freud and Hall all studied mediumship.
68. "Mrs. R.I. Hull," *BL*, June 10, 1882.
69. Britten, *Modern American Spiritualism*, p. 371.
70. William Hammond, "The Physics and the Physiology of Spiritualism," *North American Review*, 110 (April 1870), 257.
71. Carroll Smith-Rosenberg in "The Hysterical Woman" provides an excellent discussion of a related historical problem.
72. Jones, *A Psychic Autobiography*.

Cultural Hybrid in the Slums: The College Woman and the Settlement House, 1889–1894

John P. Rousmaniere

Students of American culture have, since Tocqueville, celebrated this country's voluntary associations. We have long praised the large numbers, active programs and enthusiasm of political parties and pressure groups, philanthropies and professional organizations, athletic and alumni clubs. But the student concerned with social history rather than historial sociology, with change and process rather than statics, must admit that his fellows rarely consider the key question of origins with the same care they use in their descriptions of the activities of mature associations. Certainly, this student exclaims, the latter is important, but is it not at least equally valuable for an understanding of changing norms and values to understand why an organization was founded at a precise moment in American cultural development?

This study of the origins of the first women's (and first successful) settlement organization in the United States was stimulated by just that question, rephrased in this manner: Why did a *particular* group of women found a strikingly *unique* philanthropic organization *in 1889?*

The answer has important implications, specifically about the impact of changes in women's higher education in the Gilded Age and, more generally, about the link between social marginality and organizational structure.[1]

Emily Greene Balch, reformer, teacher and peace agitator, once wrote, apparently in criticism of neo-Freudian attacks on spinsterhood: "If the educated unmarried woman of the period between the Civil War and the [First] World War represent an unique phase, it is one that has important implications which have not yet been adequately recognized by those who insist upon the imperious claims of sex." A popular and influential activity of educated women in the later years of this period was residency in settlement houses. Three-fifths of all settlement residents between 1889 and 1914 were women and, of these, almost nine-tenths had been to college.[2]

Several writers have claimed idealism as the main stimulus to settlement residency for both men and women. To Allen F. Davis, the settlement movement was engined by "a broadly religious humanitarian urge to help solve the problems of urban industrial America." A historian of higher education has viewed the settlement as an outgrowth of the introduction of courses in "social harmony" into the college curriculum. Settlement activity, this historian has argued, provided "an exciting release to the feelings of purposelessness" for students whose learned idealism had no extracurricular outlet. On the other hand, Staughton Lynd has claimed that middle-class young people joined the settlements on a "radical impulse" to ease the guilt occasioned by the period's discovery of poverty.[3]

Other writers have traced more unconscious factors. Richard Hofstadter argued in *The Age of Reform* that the settlement was an outlet of tensions created by the breakdown of religious institutions through which middle-class Protestants had traditionally articulated their strong sense of responsibility for social order. Jane Addams saw societal hypocrisy as a major cause of the settlement movement. The young woman returns home from college, Addams wrote in 1892, and "begins to recognize her social claim to the 'submerged tenth.'" But society, which has heretofore pressed "altruistic instincts" upon her, now asserts the "family claim" and tells the young woman that she is ill-advised in her desire to share the "race life" with the poor. Thus the settlement was the product both of the altruistic desire to fulfill the social claim and of the alienation that came in reaction to society's hypocritical assertion of the family claim. Christopher Lasch has generalized from Addams' argument to argue that this clash between the social and the family claims took on the proportions of a cultural crisis, generating a revolution of the young. The educated young of the 1880s and 1890s suddenly found themselves unable "to pursue the goals their parents held up before them and also unable to explain why they felt themselves [in Addams' words] 'simply smothered and sickened with advantages.'" They moved into the slums to actualize their renunciation of middle-class values.[4]

An analysis more subtle than any of the above has traced a complex social dynamic spawning the women's settlement. College women of the eighties and nineties, Jill Conway has written, shared a sense of mission as pioneers on an educational frontier. And, as educated individuals, they were strongly in need of a challenging activity, so they took as their model the active man. But these women were trapped by accepted norms in their role of inactive woman. By defining a new role for themselves in the settlement house, college women were able to satisfy the demands of their sense of mission and of their need for activity.[5]

There are many problems with each of these explanations, but I shall start and end my discussion of them with a question that none satisfactorily answers: Why did college women express their ideals, guilt or frustration through the novel *structure* of the settlement house? Unlike all preceding charitable institutions, the settlement was a "colony": it was a home as well as a philanthropy. Why, we must ask, was it necessary to merge these two characteristics? This close study of the first five years of the College Settlement Association is addressed to this and the other questions I have posed.[6]

The College Settlement Association's (CSA) residents were not all college women. Three-fifths of the ninety-two residents who spent any time in the houses between 1889 and 1894 had been to some college. College women, however, were more committed to settlement work, judging by their tendency to stay longer than noncollege women. The college-educated residents represented twelve schools, three of which— Vassar, Smith and Wellesley—provided all of the sixteen first-year residents, almost half of the 1889–94 residents and a majority of the long-term residents.[7]

Close analysis of CSA annual reports reveals an interesting recruitment pattern (see Tables I and II). One half of the Vassar women and the great majority of the Smith and Wellesley women joined the settlement in a total of eight groups composed of two or more actual or near peers. Over three-fourths of these and the Bryn Mawr women (in some, more than three-fifths of all college-educated CSA residents)

TABLE I

CSA Peer Group Recruitment by College Class and Year of Entry, by Percentage

Peer Group	College Vassar	Smith	Wellesley	Bryn Mawr	TOTAL	Others	TOTAL
Primary [a]	20%	83%	50%	67%	58%	0%	46%
Secondary [b]	30	0	42	0	19	0	15
Primary & Secondary	50	83	92	67	77	0	61
Non-Peers [c]	50	17	8	33	23	100	39
TOTAL	100%	100%	100%	100%	100%	100%	100%
N	(10)	(18)	(12)	(3)	(43)	(11)	(54)

[a] Women from the same or successive college classes entering the settlement in the same year.

[b] Women from the same or successive college classes entering the settlement in successive years.

[c] Women not qualified for primary or secondary peer groups.

TABLE II

Summary: Number of Primary and Secondary Peer Groups, by College

College	Groups Primary & Secondary Groups
Vassar	2
Smith	4
Wellesley	2
Bryn Mawr	1
TOTAL	9

had the opportunity of knowing well at school at least one other woman who was also to become a resident. And over two-thirds of all college-educated residents who remained longer than the requested three months were members of actual or near peer groups.

These figures reveal only a statistical correlation between residency and college peer groupings; they do not tell us who knew whom, although evidence in college records, memoirs and autobiographies reveals close friendships among many founders. The correlation strongly indicates, however, that the settlements were not the outlets for the spontaneously expressed ideals or frustrations of Gilded Age college women that several historians would like us to see. Instead, these figures stimulate two interesting questions: Why were the three colleges so heavily represented? And why was there so much variation in patterns of representation? We should start our inquiry by coming to an understanding of the state of women's higher education in the late nineteenth century.

The founder of Wells College nicely summarized the educational philosophy of pre-1875 women's colleges and seminaries when he pictured the ideal college as

> a "Home" in which, surrounded with appliances and advantages beyond the reach of separate families, however wealthy, young ladies may assemble to receive that education which shall qualify them to fulfil their duties as women, daughters, wives, and mothers, to practice that pleasant demeanor, to cultivate those womanly graces, to exercise that winning courtesy, which so befit those whom our mother tongue characterizes as "the gentler sex." [8]

Wells, Mount Holyoke, Elmira and Vassar were the more established of the early seminaries and "female colleges" in New England and upstate New York. These schools accommodated girls in their mid-teens to early twenties whose parents demanded little more than a couple of years of training in the feminine "accomplishments"—sewing, music, art and "moral philosophy," or elementary religion. The degree was worth so little at Wells that in 1883, for example, there were twenty freshmen, fourteen sophomores, nine juniors and only two seniors. The authoritarian "lady principal" controlled social life and the students were crammed into large, stuffy dormitories or rooming houses. Prevailing medical opinion held outdoors activity to be unhealthy for young women, so the students' extracurricular life was limited to chapel, sewing and discussions of religion. All involved, from the trustees and the distant president down to the lowly student, were single-minded in their devotion to what a Mount Holyoke teacher called "that highest conception of the nineteenth century—a complete and consecrated womanhood." Following Barbara Welter, I shall call this all-important ideal "true womanhood." It was a cult on whose altar were displayed the icons of purity, innocence, virtue, affection, service and devotion to duty.[9]

Vassar was the most famous of the early women's colleges. Matthew Vassar, a Poughkeepsie brewer, founded the school in 1860 firmly believing in the intellectual equality of men and women. Although the emphasis at the school rapidly changed from the intellect to true womanhood, Vassar differed from other women's colleges and seminaries in picturing its alumnae serving in places other than the home. College women, President John H. Raymond said in 1871, would be lifted above "the average level" by their education to become "wiser, truer, purer, nobler women" whose mission would be to commend high culture to the less fortunate by exemplifying its beneficial effects.[10]

By the mid-seventies a competing philosophy of education for women emerged. In two new colleges, Smith and Wellesley, intellectual discipline received more emphasis than the accomplishments. The founding trustees of Smith College first preached the gospel of discipline in their announcement in 1872. The school's main purpose, they wrote, was to produce disciplined women who would be influences "in forming manners and morals, moulding society, and shaping public sentiment" as teachers, missionaries and writers.[11] Smith opened in 1875 to fourteen students carefully chosen by the first president, the Rev. Lawrence Clarke Seelye.

Seelye, who was to remain at the college's head until 1910, was no less devoted to the ideal of true womanhood than were his peers at older schools, but he was careful to mix disciplined intelligence with purity in his pedagogical brew. He felt that college aided women in two ways. It increased their efficiency, making them more valuable to society. But, more importantly, as he once told his students, education forced women "to enlarge [their] capacities, that [they might] receive more of God's fullness and to quicken [their] apprehension of those eternal verities out of which right affection springs.[12] Smith's original motto well summarized Seelye's educational philosphy: "Add to your virtue, knowledge."

Wellesley College was founded in 1875 by Henry Fowle Durant, a colorful pietistic Boston philanthropist who tried to inspire moral purity, religious commitment and feminine militancy in his students. "Moral strength" best summarizes his educational philosophy, passed on after his death in 1880 through Wellesley's presidents and trustees. Everything he did—from making rowing mandatory to checking, like a nineteenth-century Cotton Mather, on the state of his students' souls—testified to his sense of mission. Durant firmly believed that God was calling woman "to come up higher, to prepare herself for great conflicts, for vast reforms in social life, for noble usefulness." Higher education was "but putting on God's armor for the contest," he wrote; and he once addressed an inspirational poem to his ideal female:

> A perfect woman, nobly planned
> To warn, to comfort and command;
> And yet a spirit still, and bright
> With something of an angel light.[13]

Durant's choice of a motto reveals in a sentence his commitment: from Dante he selected *"Incipit vita nuova"*—the new life begins. Although he differed with the heads of the other two colleges on the precise role of the educated woman, Durant shared with them a strong faith in her high status. The college-educated woman was now privy to an exclusive, extra-familial calling.

As the emphasis in female higher education changed to the uniqueness of college women, such relatively unimportant details as curriculum and social arrangements came to be considered vital to proper schooling. The reforms of Charles W. Eliot at Harvard in the elective system and of Herbert Baxter Adams at Johns Hopkins in the teaching of the social sciences first began making their impact at the three colleges in the early 1880s. In Vassar's early years, "the discipline of the faculties" and "the furnishing of the mind" were not, as we have seen, of the highest priority. Eventually faculty and alumnae pressure brought improvement in admissions and academic standards. By the mid-eighties all three of the new colleges required laboratory science courses of their students. Smith and Wellesley offered multi-course programs in political science and political economy by the late eighties. These were taught by such reformers as the Christian Socialist John Bates Clark, who was writing the essays that were to make up *The Philosophy of Wealth,* and Katherine Coman, an activist who was to help found the College Settlement Association.

Clark, who taught at Smith, fully agreed with President Seelye's conception of the active woman. He felt that the importance of his courses lay in "the direction that is given to the life studies that are to follow." At Wellesley Katherine Coman gave courses that included discussion of the competitive system, of poverty and relief, of "the uses and abuses of public charity," and of anarchism and Christian Socialism. Wellesley, she once wrote, aimed to prepare women for active lives in a variety of fields. In a sentence highly revealing of her moderation as well as of her commitment, she voiced the hope that her courses would enable her students "to be tolerant and just in their action on the temperance question or on the textbook question, or the servant question. ...." [14]

A college does not manifest an educational philosophy through its curriculum alone; it also works through such social arrangements as regulations, social activities and housing—what Cotton Mather long ago called "The Collegiate Way." A Smith alumna recognized the value of the Way in 1886.

> ... I got something at Smith, in the way of class-feeling and college pride, which I value as much as anything I learned out of books there. There is a kind of discipline in the community of interests which a number of persons living together necessarily have. ...

In the same vein the editors of the 1891 Wellesley yearbook wrote of the typical student club that "by its work, its influence, its results, may be measured with considerable accuracy the conditions and value of the college education." [15]

At Vassar the students slept, ate, studied and prayed together in the huge main hall. Their few clubs were class-centered, to the extent that a girl with friends in classes other than her own was thought unusual. These large organizations gathered periodically to discuss religion, to sing or to put on plays. If anyone cut across class lines it was the suffragette Quaker astronomy teacher, Maria Mitchell. An annual party in the college observatory for "her" girls saw her lauding the students as persons who,

> lifting their hearts to the heavenly blue
> Will do women's work for the good and the true
> And as sisters and daughters, or mothers or wives
> Will take the star-sight into their lives! [16]

Though a suffragette, Mitchell had a limited vision of the capabilities of college women.

The circumscribed group life of women's college came under attack in the mid-seventies. As *Scribner's Monthly* suggestively put it, the women's college was a breeder of "diseases of body, diseases of imagination, vices of body and imagination—everything we would save our children from. ...." These unnamed evils surely included neurasthenia and nervous breakdowns and might have included homosexual behavior. *Scribner's* felt that their origin lay in the strains of crowded living and the magazine urged that students be housed in small cottages so that "*there shall be a real family in every house,* and it shall not be hard for every woman to feel that, for the time, she is a member of it." [17]

From their founding years, Smith and Wellesley honored this ideal. Privacy was as respected in social life as independence was eventually to be in intellectual activity. Most students occupied not large dormitories but single rooms in twenty-five resident cottages, each watched over by a housemother who, an alumna once wrote, was more "a counsellor and friend than a supervisor." [18] Academic life was bounded by the class, but unlike Vassar, in social activities groups were small and independent. Each cottage had its own club, common room and dining facilities. The two newer schools had one or two college-wide organizations to which all students belonged, but the focus of attention was on the small cottage clubs, some of which even sponsored newspapers and literary journals.

The faculty were influential at each of the three colleges and, in those pre-AAUP days, echoed their presidents' and founders' educational philosophies. Maria Mitchell's moderate feminism reflected Vassar's conception of the young lady and she touched many of her students, judging from alumnae comments. At Smith, John Bates Clark's ideal of the active, constantly learning young woman matched that of President Seelye. But it is at Wellesley where we best see how the founder manifested his educational goals. The militant Durant established a policy of hiring only female instructors. He felt that strong, active women set the best example for their students. By the late eighties the Wellesley faculty included Katherine Coman, Vida Scudder and Katherine Lee Bates, all founders of the College Settlement Association, and Ellen Hayes, who later, as Emily Greene Balch put it, dragged the Communist Manifesto into her astronomy lectures. Durant succeeded; the editors of the 1890 yearbook urged the freshmen to take "the noble faculty" for their model.[19]

To summarize this discussion about life at the three schools, I should emphasize five elements differentiating it from that at older and more traditional colleges and seminaries. First, more emphasis was placed on student freedom and initiative, in social life as well as studies. Second, the schools encouraged the students to be well-rounded, to balance their studies with participation in extracurricular activities. Third, many of the students came into contact with what was for the period moderately advanced social thought, stressing women's activities outside the home. Fourth, the value of small independent peer groups came to be emphasized, especially at Smith and

Wellesley in the cottage system. And fifth and most important, the newer schools constantly impressed on the students their uniqueness and superiority to other young women. In a while we will trace how the students bloomed in the hothouses of a new conception of womanhood. But first we should see how two later colleges, founded in the eighties, differed from the three just described.

The Harvard Annex, soon to become Radcliffe College, was little more than an extension school where most students took but one or three courses taught by Harvard instructors. Students lived in boarding houses or in their own homes and met for classes and tea in a small Cambridge house. Consequently there was nothing approaching the intense community life institutionalized at Vassar, Smith and Wellesley. There was not even a degree to identify the school—something a visiting Smith student found inconceivable.[20]

The other new school was Bryn Mawr, certainly the most radical woman's college before the founding of Bennington in 1932. The educational philosophy of Bryn Mawr and of its determined dean, M. Cary Thomas, assumed a revolutionary conception of the role of the educated woman in America. Like the three colleges on which I have focused, the new college promised an education equal to that offered men. But Cary Thomas carried this promise to its logical conclusion. The older schools worked for a modified true womanhood; their alumnae would be educated, certainly, but they would be educated *women,* superior to their less disciplined sisters because they were hybrids of intellect and virtue. Thomas argued that the world of the intellect existed above considerations of sex. Only marriage and sexual needs—which the truly disciplined woman could control—stood between the educated female and high achievement.[21] The Bryn Mawr woman's uniqueness was defined by her isolation from considerations of true womanhood. Her model of behavior was the male; the model of the Vassar, Smith and Wellesley woman was the disciplined yet noble female.

Judging from undergraduate literature, the students at the three colleges shared their institutions' faith in their uniqueness. Vassar's class of 1878 floridly articulated this belief in its senior ode:

> The pioneers have bravely cleared the way.
> And claimed for us a better, broader life,
> A richer future, and they cannot pour
> The ripe fruits in our laps: 't is for us
> Which they so boldly claim for womanhood.

At first they expressed this sense of mission in competitiveness with men. The motto of Smith's first student society (self-consciously called the Alpha) was *"Cur Non"*—why not, if such societies existed at men's colleges. President Seelye thought this fighting spirit unfeminine but by 1884 he was able to note happily that "the young ladies have ceased to fear that the intellectual character of the college will suffer by developing the utmost womanly traits." [22]

The hybridization of discipline and womanliness was a constant theme in undergraduate essays, though the authors were more concerned with domesticity than with social activism. "Has the educated woman a duty towards the kitchen?" a Vassar student asked. Her answer was that the kitchen is exactly where the college woman belongs: the orderly, disciplined, independent graduate is the woman best prepared to manage the home, in which lies the salvation of the world. A Smith alumna argued that "the breadth of college culture" reveals to the young woman "the necessities and duties of a practical and useful life," among them housekeeping. "We are making experiments here on a small scale in our miniature households, clubs, and societies," a Smith student confidently noted. "We are gaining in experience, self-confidence and readiness of resource. . . . We are acquiring the prudential virtues of social life." And a Vassar undergraduate challenged her classmates to "do our part royally, then, as becomes daughters of our Alma Mater, thinking no work too humble for our hands, no ideal too lofty for our lives." [23]

Thus it was that the college woman's values, expectations, norms and self-perceived status were defined by her college experience. Her referent was not solely that of the sexless college graduate, as symbolized by the intellect alone, or purely that of the true woman, as symbolized by the accomplishments alone. Rather it was that of a new hybrid of these two cultures—an individual with a responsibility to the union of disciplined intellect and home. Secure in her status, this young woman left the college and "returned" to late nineteenth century society. She had her hopes of what to expect of middle-class America, but what was middle-class America to expect of her?

Like her less well-educated sister, the female college graduate of the eighties was meant to serve society in one of three socially-approved activities: marriage, charity work or teaching. The highest calling was marriage and child-rearing. "The true profession of every woman is that of Queen," went a typical comment. "For this she was created, to rule wisely and well over 'A Woman's Kingdom,' a well-ordered home." It is well worth noting that this quotation comes from an educational journal that closely followed the continuing development of women's higher education. The single woman did volunteer charity work, if she had an independent income. But if she lacked for money she was left with but one approved occupation: "How much," a wail went up in 1885, "How much is the time to be desired when so many avenues of useful and honorable work shall be open to women that teaching will no longer be regarded as the one available resource of the cultivated but impecunious lady." [24]

The iron hand of the service norm policed Vassar, Smith and Wellesley graduates as strictly as it did other young middle-class women in the Gilded Age. The popular image of the college woman— both then and now—is that of a liberated spirit. But close study of the postgraduate lives of some five hundred Smith and Vassar alumnae leads one to agree with a contemporary observer who described college women as "conservative, retiring, and more apt to disappoint expectation by differing too little than too much from other respectable, conventional folk—exactly as college men do." Only four of these women, from ten classes between 1868 and 1891, never married or taught school. The majority of the thirty-seven women who went to graduate school became college teachers or doctors, and most of the doctors married.[25]

The standard voluntary way to satisfy the service norm was activity in organized charity, imported from England in the seventies to replace the old relief societies. With their faith in the economic benefits of moral purity, their emphasis on record-keeping and "friendly visiting," and their terror of the consequences of class antagonism, the Charity Organization Society activists set two goals for themselves. They were to get the jobless off the relief rolls and they were to bring to the workers something a mere job could not provide: culture, which, Josephine Shaw Lowell believed, would "make their lives not only easier, but richer and nobler, and more what a human life should be." [26]

The founders of the first social settlements shared in organized charity's faith in the moral causes of poverty. The first one, Toynbee Hall, was formed in East London in 1884 by a group of Oxford students inspired by Matthew Arnold's faith in the redeeming influence of culture. They wanted the poor to come into contact with "the best thoughts and aspirations of the age" through knowing university men. The residents would themselves gain from their experience, which would "react most practically upon the thought of the educated classes upon whom, in a democratic country, falls so deep a responsibility for local and central good government. . . ." [27]

In the fall of 1887, when Stanton Coit formed America's first settlement, the short-lived Neighborhood Guild, and two years before Jane Addams was to decide to move into the slums of Chicago, a group of Smith alumnae visiting their alma mater got to talking about charitable institutions. One of these young women was Vida Dutton Scudder, of the class of 1884, an Episcopalian disciple of that Gilded Age religious phenomenon, Phillips Brooks, and a Christian Socialist like her teacher John Bates Clark. She had spent half a year at Oxford and told her companions of her work with the Salvation Army in London and of Toynbee Hall, which she knew only by reputation. [28] The settlement idea immediately appealed to the young women, but their attempts to raise funds for such a project met with parental fears about their safety. Unlike the wealthy orphan Jane Addams, they had parents who asserted control through the pocketbook.

An article Scudder wrote at the time for an Episcopalian weekly indicates how openly college women received the settlement idea. She most admired Toynbee Hall for its realism, for, unlike organized charity, the settlement did not waste its energies on the jobless—the most helpless of the poor. Rather, it wisely focused its attention on "the most-valuable and self-respecting of the working class," whose greatest needs were for beauty, brightness and culture. Why, Scudder asked, should not women take part in this kind of work, in which "the most effective instruments are usually supposed to be womanly tact, sympathy, and devotion"? Volunteers, "united and sympathetic in tastes, ideals, desires," would live together in a boardinghouse, where they would teach their neighbors "a few of the practical things which the better classes of the poor in our great cities so desperately need to know," especially housekeeping. In addition to teaching these skills, the settlement residents would work to instill in their neighbors, "the spiritual and hidden wealth of a sensitive nature attuned to beauty, a mind rejoicing in its own fair powers, a soul rejoicing in the unseen." And the residents would also benefit, Scudder continued. Their confrontation with the basic facts of life would be educational and the resulting "hearty, mutual comprehension and friendship between classes" would help society to "avert our social dangers." [29]

Vida Scudder joined the Wellesley faculty as an English instructor in the fall of 1888. Her enthusiasm for the settlement was contagious and soon two colleagues, Katherine Coman and Katherine Lee Bates, and a young trustee, Cornelia Warren, were helping her to raise funds from a variety of college women, philanthropists and clergymen. They bought a house—"one of the wonderful old survivals of a formerly aristocratic quarter"—on Rivington Street on New York's Lower East Side and appointed as paid head resident Jean Fine, a member of the group that first discussed settlements at Smith two years earlier.[30] Five other Smith and Wellesley women, paying six dollars a week for room and board, moved in with her in September 1889.

What were their intentions? We can summarize the founders' conception of the needs of their neighbors in four words: virtue, entertainment, work and home. The first would be satisfied by constant contact with the noble residents—women, a visitor reported, honest, truthful, gentle, kind, unselfish and helpful. But, Jean Fine told the visitor, only the younger children could possibly benefit from the residents' example; it was too late for their elders to unlearn their bad habits.[31]

Children's clubs would satisfy the second need with constructive entertainment. The girls could join the Good Seed Club to learn about flowers; the boys had the Hero Club, which revealed the "elements of success," and the Knights of the Round Table, where they learned how to be "chivalrous and true." Dues were charged to inculcate self-respect, to encourage self-government and, probably, to exclude the offspring of the "helpless" and "useless." [32]

The founders shared a Puritan's faith in the redeeming nature of work, especially for children. "It is not the lack of money which is the poverty we most deplore," wrote the head resident of the Philadelphia settlement, "but lack of self-hood, that self-hood that comes from work and makes it a blessing even though it is a bitter struggle for existence." The settlement, she continued, should urge work on the young jobless, "happy in an idleness that means soul-stagnation." [33]

For us, the most interesting of the needs of the poor as seen by the founding settlement residents was that for a proper home life. As William E. Bridges has documented, Americans at this time saw the home, the family and true womanhood united in defense of traditional morality against the encroachments of materialism. The popular preacher and writer Edward Everett Hale could define "home" not in social or economic terms but as a collection of feminine virtues: "With this word always comes the idea of family, of feminine presence, of woman's patient sympathy and tender care. . . ." The settlement was to exemplify to neighborhood women the virtues of "pure, true, simple living," with the residents recreating the genteel atmosphere of their own upbringing. Settlement life, wrote a founder years later, "was all very satisfying and natural." [34]

Her pleasant memory gives us a clue to the expressive value of the settlement house for its residents: perhaps the life was so satisfying *because it was so familiar.* We might now take a look at the self-conceptions of the early settlement residents to see what they reveal about the attractiveness of the settlement as home, as "colony." The self-image of the founders breaks up into three general attitudes, each reflecting a self-consciousness about being well-educated women living together among the poor. One was a strong sense of adventure, "an abandonment," a founder wrote, "of ourselves to the life and to whatever might come along that charmed us all." They were inspired by the British Christian Socialists and Tolstoy to embrace "Lady Poverty" and lead a simple life. Abandonment also took form in claims of brotherhood with the poor, which the "Return to the People" movement of the young Russian aristocrats and Walter Besant's novels about peasant hospitality served to inspire. To the founders, brotherhood precluded charity; this was not a relationship between donor and receiver but one between equals, and the founders were sensitive about being labeled philanthropists.[35]

But beneath these claims of equality lay a second attitude, a sense of *noblesse oblige.* Tolstoy did, after all, have his work shirts tailored in silk. For example, residents contrasted the simple beauty of the settlement house—its paintings showing "refinement, taste, travel, culture"— with the dirty children playing within. One founder emphasized this vivid contrast in picturesquely describing an encounter between a resident and a neighborhood boy:

> She met him in the hall [of the settlement house], as she came home from church, and with the street door wide open, she stooped and kissed him, as she would have her own small brother, making quite unconsciously a beautiful picture for the stunned inhabitants of Rivington Street.[36]

Clearly, then, for all the claims of equality and brotherhood, there was a gulf between the residents and their neighbors.

The founding residents also saw a gulf between themselves and other women. They thought of themselves as unique not because they were the first settlement residents but because they were members of the first generation of college women. Ascribing to themselves a new and special status—" a new factor in the social order," Vida Scudder said of them in the late eighties—the settlement founders saw college women acting as mediators between the idle rich and the working poor. These new women had the best of two virtues, true womanhood and discipline. They were, Scudder boasted, "women of the new order" no longer willing "to be put in niches and worshipped as saints ... nor to be put in the chimney-corner and relegated to stockings." Instead, through such institutions as the settlement, they were able to join in doing the world's work.[37]

These feelings of uniqueness and mission were formalized in the founding of the College Settlement Association in 1890. The CSA would "unite all college women, and all who would count themselves our friends, in the trend of a great modern movement; would touch them with a common sympathy and inspire them with a common ideal." The CSA, then, was *a voluntary association of college women rather than an association of settlement residents.* On this basis the founders emphasized the benefits of the settlement and the settlement movement for themselves, as college women. "Many of us feel that the new conceptions of life we have gained are of far more worth than anything we have been able to give our neighbors," a resident wrote. "We feel that we know life for the first time." They used academic terminology: the settlement was "a graduate school in life" for women "whose university is the outer world." And they used academic institutions: a resident drew up a syllabus of suggested readings; fellowships were awarded one or two recent college graduates to pay residency expenses.[38]

The family and home aspects of settlement life received even more attention than the academic. A critic once accused the house of being little more than a women's club. Vida Scudder angrily responded that only men instinctively form clubs: women form homes. The self-contained, independent settlement "family" consisted of a paid head resident, who was more advisor than supervisor; her assistant; a resident doctor; one or two fellowship residents; a half dozen or so paying residents who were expected to stay at least three months and a few visitors who could stay for several weeks at a time. Each resident had her own room on an upper floor. Claims about the moral benefits of work notwithstanding, the residents hired a cook and a maid for heavy housework.[39]

The head resident and the nonresident Association secretary jointly selected residents from among the many applicants. Judging from the backgrounds of thirty-six of the 188 CSA residents in the first ten years, the typical worker was small-town born and college-educated. She was likely to have taught in a private secondary school immediately after graduation, although several taught in public schools and colleges, became librarians and went to graduate school, in declining order of preference. Graduate students studied medicine and nursing in the United States and academic subjects in Europe. The typical settlement resident was active and had traveled, if only to get to her college. She seems to have been uninterested in organized charitable work.[40]

Having come to an understanding of the goals of the settlement founders, of the self-conceptions and recruitment patterns of the early residents and of their backgrounds in the women's colleges of the Gilded Age, we can begin to develop answers to the questions stimulated by the statistics at the opening of this essay, which can be summarized: Why was the settlement house so attractive to college women and especially to groups of women from three colleges? This summary analysis will take the form of a discussion of the four ascriptive characteristics of the CSA settlements: as charity, as social movement, as "colony" and as voluntary association.

Although its founders were repelled by the word, most Americans would regard the settlement as a charity. As such, residency satisfied what I have called the service norm and thus made the settlement a socially approved institution, a functional alternative to marriage, teaching and organized charity. However, this characterization only tells us why the settlement was a charity; it does not indicate why it took the form it did.

The CSA shared another characteristic with organized charity, since they were both social movements. But where the National Conference of Charities and Correction unified supporters of a value—the merits of organized, "scientific" charity—the CSA brought together women of a common status—"all college women, and all who would count themselves our friends. . . ." Social movements centering, like the CSA, around a group norm and expectation are generally fostered by strains creating "demands for readjustment in the social situation." These strains result when a subsystem of society changes more rapidly than other subsystems and its members experience an alteration of expectations. As we have seen, with the development of the disciplined true woman hybrid at Smith, Wellesley and, to a lesser extent, Vassar, a rather sizable number of college women assumed a new self-image and, simultaneously, a group norm centering around their uniqueness and felt superiority. As Katherine Coman put it, these women were "particularly sensitive to the principles of *noblesse oblige.* So much has been given them of intellectual and spiritual treasure that they feel under heavy obligation to the world." [41]

Yet when these women, overflowing with confidence and optimism, left the closed group of their college years, they entered a culture not only unused to well-educated females but, more importantly, also utterly unfamiliar with women so self-conscious about their uniqueness vis-à-vis other women. They felt scorned, rejected. Emily Greene Balch was annoyed that going to college in the eighties "was to feel oneself a marked character in the neighborhood, when returning as a college graduate meant to be constantly met with the would-be amusing protest that people were afraid to talk with me, I was so learned." College *men* encouraged no such cynical honor. A *Nation* parody of how an older woman of the period felt about college women was probably not too much of an exaggeration. The educated female, this lady would think,

> is undomestic in her habits and unfeminine in her tastes . . . [,] takes the initiative in conversation, is perpetually agitating for some "cause," or "reform," is ill-dressed and untidy, in fact regards dress as an unimportant matter, and the desire to attract the attention and interest of men as "frivolous." [42]

The point here is not that this description was true. In some cases it must have been, in most cases it probably was not. Rather, this quotation is valuable because it reveals, even as a parody, a widely-believed myth articulated in type-casting.

Facing such antagonism, some young college graduates, like Marion Talbott of Boston University's class of 1880, were forced to doubt the value of their education because it provided neither friends nor a niche in their communities. In 1882 Talbott helped found the Association of Collegiate Alumnae, which was "to unite alumnae of different institutions for practical educational work"—mainly, it appears, by encouraging girls to go to college and helping to resocialize them into middle-class America when they graduated.[43]

Other college women, however, were more convinced of the worth of their education, however unsure they were of America's ability to agree. The problem was not simply one of fitting in; rather, as one CSA founder put it, "Some of us were not yet sure that the world needed us—in any case it was not evident where, or for what. . . ." They required, Jean Fine wrote, "a place in the world where we may *help* and be helped." So convinced were they of their own uniqueness and talents and so set were they in their mission that they could not simply retire into the inward-looking Associate of Collegiate Alumnae and lick their wounds. "We were looking," Vida Scudder proudly wrote, "to wide horizons beyond our own borders." [44]

So these young women needed an institution and an activity that would, first, satisfy the service norm as well as their sense of mission and that, second, would support their vulnerable status so that they might regain the equilibrium they had been secure in at college. The seminary woman had no such need, for her education had but socialized her into the traditional female role. Likewise, the Bryn Mawr graduate had few of these problems, since her expectations had not been raised by a faith in the ultimate compatibility of true woman-hood and sexless intellect. The problem was unique for the cultural hybrid—the Vassar, Smith and Wellesley woman.

To solve the problem, she innovated by constructing a new institu-tion and a new role out of bits and pieces of the most familiar institu-tions and roles. Thus it was that the third of the settlement's ascriptive characteristics, its "colony" structure, was a reproduction. The found-ers appropriated the most indelible institutions of their alma maters, which had literally fostered and mothered the self-conceptions whose clash with dominant standards made these women so ill at ease. We have already seen how they borrowed academic jargon. Even more interestingly, they imitated the Smith and Wellesley cottage. Both the settlement and the cottage were "homes" for "families" of women "with congenial tastes, common interests, and independent convic-tions." Both were self-sufficient and self-contained institutions serving as moral and social centers for the occupants and the immediate community. In each "home" the emphasis was on individual privacy alongside group activity overseen by older and more experienced women, more friendly advisors than supervisors.

In addition, the settlement's recruitment patterns clearly reflect the cottage system's emphasis on small peer groups. The high proportion of Smith and Wellesley women who entered the College Settlements at the same time as classmates and near-classmates indicates that peer group influence was an important factor behind their decision to be-come settlement residents. Vassar, where there was relatively less em-phasis on small student groups, was represented in the CSA settlements by fewer and smaller peer groups. The prevalence and patterning of peer and near-peer groups among residents was not acci-dental and neither was the structural similarity between the settlement and the cottage. Both represented the need of certain college women for a familiar and stable "home" in a hostile world. Through its social arrangements and "family" and academic rhetoric alone, the settle-ment as colony was functional.

Its geographical location was also functional. These young women felt a uniqueness that society did not recognize as constructive. In their attempt to define and institutionalize a unique, but socially approved, role, the founders constructed a social class that was above, yet part of, all other classes—a kind of superclass characterized by living a genteel middle-class home life in the midst of poverty. The doctrine of the settlement as home, not charity, supported this uniqueness. Since the poor were not clients but guests invited to share the benefits of "respectable" home life, the hostesses could restrict the right of entry to those most appreciative of the values within. Not only could a resident kiss a poverty-stricken boy in the doorway of a middle-class home, but she could also choose which boy to kiss.

But the self-image of these women was not limited to uniqueness, for the hybrids saw themselves as superior women of rare ability and dedication. To defend this high status against the ravages of an un-believing society, they isolated themselves through the mechanism of an exclusive voluntary association. By tightly restricting membership, such organizations served a vital function for members of felt and actual high-status groups by reaffirming hierarchy. In the CSA settle-ments noncollege women desiring admission as residents had to swear fealty to values asserting the special mission of college women. The former thus made the latter group their referent even though they were not natural members.[45] In this way, the settlement's founders asserted their felt superiority as college women by asserting an aristoc-racy of merit that was identical with a defense of a vulnerable status.

The settlement, then, was functional for our college women in four interconnected ways. As a philanthropy it was a socially-approved al-ternative to a very few service activities. As a "colony" the institution was dually functional: it was a reconstruction of a familiar ideological and social "home" for young college women confused by a hostile world; and it was a middle-class outpost that concretized an otherwise abstract sense of uniqueness. Finally, as an exclusive voluntary asso-ciation it articulated—as no other institution could—the college woman's sense of superiority over other young women.

My analysis of the settlement as the product of a cultural rather than of a purely moral or ideological conflict is not an attempt to denigrate it as an institution that was eventually to play an instrumen-tal role in social and political reform. Neither am I arguing that all Vassar, Smith and Wellesley women were even to be attracted to settlement residency. As a student of English Puritanism has written in a somewhat similar analysis, "None of these group experiences make individual conversion predictable, each of them makes it comprehensi-ble." [46] To view the settlement as I have is to see it as a child—a rather gangling child—of a period of painful cultural transition and not sim-ply as an impulsive, institutionalized Topsy.

NOTES

1. This is the first of several case studies I am preparing of representative voluntary associations formed in the closing years of the nineteenth cen-

tury. The paradigm for a functional analysis presented by Robert K. Merton in his *Social Theory and Social Structure* (rev. ed.: Glencoe, 1957) has greatly influenced my approach to the solution of the problem described in the first part of this essay. I am also indebted to Walter P. Metzger for his criticism and guidance.

2. Quotation in Ray Ginger, *Altgeld's America* (New York, 1958), p. 191; statistics from Allen F. Davis, "Spearheads for Reform: The Social Settlements and the Progressive Movement, 1890–1914" (Ph.D. diss, University of Wisconsin, 1959), pp. 3, 373. (This is a more detailed and more clear exposition than Davis' recent book of the same title.)

3. Ibid., p. 18; George E. Peterson, *The New England College in the Age of the University* (Amherst, Mass., 1964), p. 179; Staughton Lynd, "Jane Addams and the Radical Impulse," *Commentary* XXXII (July 1961): 54.

4. Richard Hofstadter, *The Age of Reform* (New York, 1955), pp. 204–14; Jane Addams, *Twenty Years at Hull-House* (New York, 1960 [first pub. 1910]), pp. 94, 96; Christopher Lasch, *The New Radicalism in America, 1889–1963* (New York, 1965), p. 36.

5. Jill Conway, "Jane Addams: An American Heroine," in *The Woman in America*, ed. Robert J. Lifton (Boston, 1965), p. 248.

6. The first women's college settlement was founded in New York in 1889. Its founders formed the College Settlement Association a year later. After CSA houses were opened in Boston and Philadephia in the early 1890s, the parent organization's name was changed to College Settlements Association. I will use the singular form in this essay. The year 1894 is a good termination point, since it marks a rising interest among settlements residents in relief programs.

7. Residents are listed with college years in CSA, *Annual Report* (1890–1895). Over two-thirds of all residents who managed to stay the three months requested by the Association were college women, as were three-fourths of those who stayed over three years. The following colleges were represented: Smith, eighteen; Wellesley, fifteen; Vassar, ten; Bryn Mawr, three; University of California and Barnard, two each; Boston University, Cornell, Mt. Holyoke, Syracuse, Wells and uncertain, one each. Over one-half of the college women who stayed at least three months were from Vassar, Smith and Wellesley, as were more than four-fifths of those remaining over three years. The vast majority of these women were from classes in the 1880s.

8. Henry Wells, in Wells College *Catalogue* (1883), p. 29.

9. Julia H. May, "Mount Holyoke College," *Education* VIII (1888): 488; Barbara Welter, "The Cult of True Womanhood, 1820–1860," *American Quarterly* XVIII (1966): 151–74.

10. John H. Raymond, "Mission of Educated Women," Vassar College, *Baccalaureate Sermon* (1871), p. 6. Pamphlet in Vassar College Special Collections (hereafter VCSC).

11. Smith College Trustees, *Higher Education for Women* (1872), n.p. Pamphlet in Smith College Archives (hereafter SCA).

12. Smith College, *President's Report* (1890), p. 2, typescript in SCA.

13. In Florence Morse Kingsley, *Life of Henry Fowle Durant, Founder of Wellesley College* (New York, 1924), pp. 239–41.

14. J. B. Clark, "Preparation for Citizenship, III: At Smith College," *Education* IX (1889): 404; Katherine Coman, "Preparation for Citizenship, V:

At Wellesley College," *Education* X (1890): 347.

15. Minna Caroline Smith, "The Harvard Annex," *Education* VI (1886): 572; *Legenda* (1891), p. 64. Yearbook in Wellesley College Archives (hereafter WCA).

16. For an example of the effect of this class-centeredness, see Jane Addams, *My Friend Julia Lathrop* (New York, 1935), p. 42; poem in Helen Wright, *Sweeper of the Sky* (New York, 1949), p. 229.

17. "A New Woman's College," *Scribner's Monthly* VI (Oct. 1873): 749. Italics in original.

18. Caroline E. Hilliard, "Smith College: An Historical Sketch," *Education* VIII (1887): 16.

19. Balch quoted in Mercedes M. Randall, *Improper Bostonian: Emily Greene Balch* (New York, 1964), p. 106; *Legenda* (1890), p. 61, WCA.

20. Minna Caroline Smith, "Harvard Annex," pp. 572–73.

21. For a concise summary of Cary Thomas' views on education, see Barbara M. Cross, "Introduction," *The Educated Woman in America* (New York, 1965), pp. 30–47.

22. Vassar College, *Class Day Exercises, June 25, 1878*, p. 26. Pamphlet in VCSC; for Smith's clubs, see Elizabeth Lawrence Clarke, "Student Life," in L. Clark Seelye, *The Early History of Smith College, 1871–1910* (Boston, 1923), pp. 170–220; Smith College, *President's Report* (1884), p. 15, typescript in SCA.

23. L.A.S., "Has the Educated Woman a Duty towards the Kitchen?" *Vassar Miscellany* VIII (Nov. 1878): 12–15, periodical in VCSC; Anon., "The College and the Kitchen," *Chip Basket* I (May 15, 1880): 61–65, periodical in SCA; Anon., "The Value of College Training," *Alpha* XI (Nov. 15, 1890); 2–3, periodical in SCA; L.A.S., "Has the Educated Woman?" p. 15.

24. Marriage quotation in Julia S. Tutweiler, "The Technical Education of Women," *Education* III (1882): 201; Jane M. Bancroft, "Occupations and Professions for College Bred Women," *Education* V (1885): 490. A 1959 study of occupations open to women since 1890 supports my analysis. See Robert W. Smuts, *Women and Work in America* (New York, 1959), pp. 19–21.

25. From my analysis of the *Smith College Alumnae Biographical Register, 1871-1935* (Northampton, 1935) and the *Vassar College Alumnae Biographical Register* (Poughkeepsie, 1939). Interestingly enough, there was no great difference in patterns of postgraduate activities between that of alumnae of the early seventies and that of those of the "more liberated" late eighties and early nineties; quotation in Milicent Washburn Shinn, "The Marriage Rate of College Women," *Century* L (Oct. 1895): 948.

26. Lowell, "Charity," in *Woman's Work in America*, ed. Annie Nathan Meyer (New York, 1891), pp. 333, 335.

27. From the first annual report of the Toynbee Hall Association, in Arthur C. Holden, *The Settlement Idea* (New York, 1922), pp. 13–14.

28. For descriptions of this gathering, see Vida Scudder, *On Journey* (New York, 1937), pp. 107, 109–10, and Helen Rand Thayer, "Blazing the Settlement Trail," *Smith Alumnae Quarterly* II (1911): 130.

29. "A New Departure in Philanthropy, I," *Christian Union* XXXVII (May 10, 1888): 588; ibid., II (May 17, 1888): 620.

30. In Thayer, "Blazing," p. 130.

31. H. F. Freeman, "University Settlement," *Lend a Hand* V (Mar. 1890): 158.

32. CSA, *Annual Report* (1890), p.4

33. CSA, *Annual Report* (1892), pp. 17–19.

34. William E. Bridges, "Family Patterns and Social Values in America, 1825–1875," *American Quarterly* XVII (1965): 3–11; [Edward Everett Hale], "Woman's Work in Philanthropy," *Lend A Hand* II (Feb. 1887): 94; "virtues" quotation in Anon., "A 'Toynbee Hall' Enterprise in New York," *Churchman* LXI (June 8, 1889): 727; "satisfying" quotation in Jane Robbins, "The First Year at the College Settlement," *Survey* XXVII (Feb. 24, 1912): 1801.

35. "Abandonment" quotation in Robbins, "First Year . . . .," p. 1802; "Lady Poverty" in Scudder, *On Journey,* p. 112; prospective CSA residents were urged to read works of "two or three Social Radicals Inspired by Religion," including Charles Kingsley and Tolstoy. See Caroline Williamson, *Syllabi for the Study of Social Questions* (n.p., n.d.). Pamphlet in Sophia Smith Collection, Smith College; for the influence of the Russian Populists and Walter Besant, see Robbins, "First Year," p. 1800; for an example of CSA distaste for "charity," see CSA, *Annual Report* (1890), p.8.

36. For the description of the house, see Caroline Williamson, "Sketches Involving Problems: A Settlement Study," *Wellesley Magazine* I (Jan. 1893): 198, periodical in WCA; for the kissing incident, see Robbins, "First Year . . . ," p. 1801.

37. Vida Scudder, *The Relation of College Women to Social Need* (1890), pp. 2, 3, 5. Pamphlet in Rare Book Room, Boston Public Library. Scudder was "perpetually" speaking on this subject before religious, alumnae and academic groups in the late eighties. See *On Journey*, p. 135.

38. CSA, *Annual Report* (1891), pp. 7–8; ibid., (1893), p. 9.

39. Scudder, "The Place of College Settlements," *Andover Review* XVIII (Oct. 1892): 341; description of settlement life in Caroline Williamson, "Six Months at Denison House," *Wellesley Magazine* III (Feb 9, 1895): 237, periodical in WCA. Denison House was the Boston CSA settlement.

40. In 1890–91 there were over eighty applicants for six positions in the New York settlement. The biographical data was culled from the Smith and Vassar alumnae registers (ftn. 25), from clippings in college alumnae files and, especially, from the *Woman's Who's Who of America, 1914–15* (New York, 1914).

41. Social movement quotation in Neil J. Smelser, *Theory of Collective Behavior* (New York, 1963), pp. 290–91; Coman, "The Wellesley Alumnae as Social Servants," *Wellesley Magazine* XIII (Nov. 1904): 47, 48.

42. Balch quoted in Mercedes Randall, *Improper Bostonian,* p. 51; *Nation* XXXVI (Feb 8, 1883): 118–19.

43. Marion Talbott and Lois Kimball Matthews Rosenberry, *History of the American Association of University Women, 1881–1931* (Boston and New York, 1931), pp. 4–12.

44. Thayer, "Blazing," p. 133; Fine in CSA, *Annual Report* (1891), p. 14. Italics in original; Scudder, *On Journey,* pp. 136–37.

45. For voluntary associations, see Joan W. Moore, "Patterns of Women's

Participation in Voluntary Associations," *American Journal of Sociology* LXVI (1961): 598, and David L. Sills, "Voluntary Associations: Sociological Aspects," *International Encyclopedia of the Social Sciences* (n.p., 1968), v. 16, 362–79; for nonmembership reference groups, see Merton, *Social Theory and Social Structure,* pp. 288–97.

46. Michael Walzer, *The Revolution of the Saints* (Cambridge, Mass., 1965), p. 308.

The Cult of True Womanhood: 1820-1860

Barbara Welter

The nineteenth-century American man was a busy builder of bridges and railroads, at work long hours in a materialistic society. The religious values of his forebears were neglected in practice if not in intent, and he occasionally felt some guilt that he had turned this new land, this temple of the chosen people, into one vast counting-house. But he could salve his conscience by reflecting that he had left behind a hostage, not only to fortune, but to all the values which he held so dear and treated so lightly. Woman, in the cult of True Womanhood [1] presented by the women's magazines, gift annuals and religious literature of the nineteenth century, was the hostage in the home. [2] In a society where values changed frequently, where fortunes rose and fell with frightening rapidity, where social and economic mobility provided instability as well as hope, one thing at least remained the same—a true woman was a true woman, wherever she was found. If anyone, male or female, dared to tamper with the complex of virtues which made up True Womanhood, he was damned immediately as an enemy of God, of civilization and of the Republic. It was a fearful obligation, a solemn responsibility, which the nineteenth-century American woman had—to uphold the pillars of the temple with her frail white hand.

The attributes of True Womanhood, by which a woman judged herself and was judged by her husband, her neighbors and society could be divided into four cardinal virtues—piety, purity, submissiveness and domesticity. Put them all together and they spelled mother, daughter, sister, wife—woman. Without them, no matter whether there was fame, achievement or wealth, all was ashes. With them she was promised happiness and power.

Religion or piety was the core of woman's virtue, the source of her strength. Young men looking for a mate were cautioned to search first for piety, for if that were there, all else would follow.[3] Religion belonged to woman by divine right, a gift of God and nature. This "peculiar susceptibility" to religion was given her for a reason: "the vestal flame of piety, lighted up by Heaven in the breast of woman" would throw its beams into the naughty world of men.[4] So far would its candle power reach that the "Universe might be Enlightened, Improved, and Harmonized by WOMAN!!"[5] She would be another, better Eve, working in cooperation with the Redeemer, bringing the world back "from its revolt and sin."[6] The world would be reclaimed for God through her suffering, for "God increased the cares and sorrows of woman, that she might be sooner constrained to accept the terms of salvation."[7] A popular poem by Mrs. Frances Osgood, "The Triumph of the Spiritual Over the Sensual" expressed just this sentiment, woman's purifying passionless love bringing an erring man back to Christ.[8]

Dr. Charles Meigs, explaining to a graduating class of medical students why women were naturally religious, said that "hers is a pious mind. Her confiding nature leads her more readily than men to accept the proffered grace of the Gospel."[9] Caleb Atwater, Esq., writing in *The Ladies' Repository,* saw the hand of the Lord in female piety: "Religion is exactly what a woman needs, for it gives her that dignity that best suits her dependence."[10] And Mrs. John Sandford, who had no very high opinion of her sex, agreed thoroughly: "Religion is just what woman needs. Without it she is ever restless or unhappy. . . . "[11] Mrs. Sandford and the others did not speak only of that restlessness of the human heart, which St. Augustine notes, that can only find its peace in God. They spoke rather of religion as a kind of tranquilizer for the many undefined longings which swept even the most pious young girl, and about which it was better to pray than to think.

One reason religion was valued was that it did not take a woman away from her "proper sphere," her home. Unlike participation in other societies or movements, church work would not make her less domestic or submissive, less a True Woman. In religious vineyards, said the *Young Ladies' Literary and Missionary Report,* "you may labor without the apprehension of detracting from the charms of feminine delicacy." Mrs. S. L. Dagg, writing from her chapter of the Society in Tuscaloosa, Alabama, was equally reassuring: "As no sensible woman will suffer her intellectual pursuits to clash with her domestic duties" she should concentrate on religious work "which promotes these very duties." [12]

The women's seminaries aimed at aiding women to be religious, as well as accomplished. Mt. Holyoke's catalogue promised to make female education "a handmaid to the Gospel and an efficient auxiliary in the great task of renovating the world." [13] The Young Ladies' Seminary at Bordentown, New Jersey, declared its most important function to be "the forming of a sound and virtuous character." [14] In Keene, New Hampshire, the Seminary tried to instill a "consistent and useful character" in its students, to enable them in this life to be "a good friend, wife and mother" but more important, to qualify them for "the enjoyment, of Celestial Happiness in the life to come." [15] And Joseph M' D. Mathews, Principal of Oakland Female Seminary in Hillsborough, Ohio, believed that "female education should be preeminently religious." [16]

If religion was so vital to a woman, irreligion was almost too awful to contemplate. Women were warned not to let their literary or intellectual pursuits take them away from God. Sarah Josepha Hale spoke darkly of those who, like Margaret Fuller, threw away the "One True Book" for others, open to error. Mrs. Hale used the unfortunate Miss Fuller as fateful proof that "the greater the intellectual force, the greater and more fatal the errors into which women fall who wander from the Rock of Salvation, Christ the Saviour. . . . " [17]

One gentlemen, writing on "Female Irreligion" reminded his readers that "Man may make himself a brute, and does so very often, but can woman brutify herself to his level—the lowest level of human nature—without exerting special wonder?" Fanny Wright, because she was godless, "was no woman, mother though she be." A few years ago, he recalls, such women would have been whipped. In any case, "woman never looks lovelier than in her reverence for religion" and, conversely, "female irreligion is the most revolting feature in human character." [18]

Purity was as essential as piety to a young woman, its absence as unnatural and unfeminine. Without it she was, in fact, no woman at all, but a member of some lower order. A "fallen woman" was a "fallen angel," unworthy of the celestial company of her sex. To contemplate the loss of purity brought tears; to be guilty of such a crime, in the women's magazines at least, brought madness or death. Even the language of the flowers had bitter words for it: a dried white rose symbolized "Death Preferable to Loss of Innocence." [19] The marriage night was the single great event of a woman's life, when she bestowed her greatest treasure upon her husband, and from that time on was completely dependent upon him, an empty vessel,[20] without legal or emotional existence of her own.[21]

Therefore all True Women were urged, in the strongest possible terms, to maintain their virtue, although men, being by nature more sensual than they, would try to assault it. Thomas Branagan admitted in *The Excellency of the Female Character Vindicated* that his sex would sin and sin again, they could not help it, but woman, stronger and purer, must not give in and let man "take liberties incompatible with her delicacy." "If you do," Branagan addressed his gentle reader, "You will be left in silent sadness to bewail your credulity, imbecility, duplicity, and premature prostitution." [22]

Mrs. Eliza Farrar, in *The Young Lady's Friend*, gave practical logistics to avoid trouble: "Sit not with another in a place that is too narrow; read not out of the same book; let not your eagerness to see anything induce you to place your head close to another person's." [23]

If such good advice was ignored the consequences were terrible and inexorable. In *Girlhood and Womanhood: Or Sketches of My Schoolmates,* By Mrs. A. J. Graves (a kind of mid-nineteenth-century *The Group),* the bad ends of a boarding school class of girls are scrupulously recorded. The worst end of all is reserved for "Amelia Dorrington: The Lost One." Amelia died in the almshouse "the wretched victim of depravity and intemperance" and all because her mother had let her be "high-spirited not prudent." These girlish high spirits had been misinterpreted by a young man, with disastrous results. Amelia's "thoughtless levity" was "followed by a total loss of virtuous principle" and Mrs. Graves editorializes that "the coldest reserve is more admirable in a woman a man wishes to make his wife, than the least approach to undue familiarity." [24]

A popular and often-reprinted story by Fanny Forester told the sad tale of "Lucy Dutton." Lucy "with the seal of innocence upon her heart, and a rose-leaf on her cheek" came out of her vine-covered cottage and ran into a city slicker. "And Lucy was beautiful and trusting, and thoughtless: and he was gay, selfish and profligate. Needs the story to be told? ... Nay, censor, Lucy was a child—consider how young, how very untaught—oh! her innocence was no match for the sophistry of a gay, city youth! Spring came and shame was stamped upon the cottage at the foot of the hill." The baby died; Lucy went mad at the funeral and finally died herself. "Poor, poor Lucy Dutton! The grave is a blessed couch and pillow to the wretched. Rest thee there, poor Lucy!" [25] The frequency with which derangement follows loss of virtue suggests the exquisite sensibility of woman, and the possibility that, in the women's magazines at least, her intellect was geared to her hymen, not her brain.

If, however, a woman managed to withstand man's assaults on her virtue, she demonstrated her superiority and her power over him. Eliza Farnham, trying to prove this female superiority, concluded smugly that "the purity of women is the everlasting barrier against which the tides of man's sensual nature surge." [26]

A story in *The Lady's Amaranth* illustrates this dominance. It is set, improbably, in Sicily, where two lovers, Bianca and Tebaldo, have been separated because her family insisted she marry a rich old man. By some strange circumstance the two are in a shipwreck and cast on a desert island, the only surviors. Even here, however, the rigid standards of True Womanhood prevail. Tebaldo unfortunately forgets himself slightly, so that Bianca must warn him: "We may not indeed gratify our fondness by caresses, but it is still something to bestow our kindest language, and looks and prayers, and all lawful and honest attentions on each other." Something, perhaps, but not enough, and Bianca must further remonstrate: "It is true that another man is my husband, but you are my guardian angel." When even that does not work she says in a voice of sweet reason, passive and proper to the end, that she wishes he wouldn't but "still, if you insist, I will become what you wish; but I beseech you to consider, ere the decision, that debasement which I must suffer in your esteem." This appeal to his own double standards holds the beast in him at bay. They are rescued, discover that the old husband is dead, and after "mourning a decent season" Bianca finally gives in, legally.[27]

Men could be counted on to be grateful when women thus saved them from themselves. William Alcott, guiding young men in their relations with the opposite sex, told them that "Nothing is better calculated to preserve a young man from contamination of low pleasures and pursuits than frequent intercourse with the more refined and virtuous of the other sex." And he added, one assumes in equal innocence, that youths should "observe and learn to admire, that purity and ignorance of evil which is the characteristic of well-educated young ladies, and which, when we are near them, raises us above those sordid and sensual considerations which hold such sway over men in their intercourse with each other." [28]

The Rev. Jonathan F. Stearns was also impressed by female chastity in the face of male passion, and warned woman never to compromise the source of her power: "Let her lay aside delicacy, and her influence over our sex is gone." [29]

Women themselves accepted, with pride but suitable modesty, this priceless virtue. *The Ladies' Wreath,* in "Woman the Creature of God and the Manufacturer of Society" saw purity as her greatest gift and chief means of discharging her duty to save the world: "Purity is the highest beauty—the true pole-star which is to guide humanity aright in its long, varied, and perilous voyage." [30]

Sometimes, however, a woman did not see the dangers to her treasure. In that case, they must be pointed out to her, usually by a male. In the nineteenth century any form of social change was tantamount to an attack on woman's virtue, if only it was correctly understood. For example, dress reform seemed innocuous enough and the bloomers worn by the lady of that name and her followers were certainly modest attire. Such was the reasoning only of the ignorant. In another issue of *The Ladies' Wreath* a young lady is represented in dialogue with her "Professor." The girl expresses admiration for the bloomer costume—it gives freedom of motion, is healthful and attractive. The "Professor" sets her straight. Trousers, he explains, are "only one of the many manifestations of that wild spirit of socialism and agrarian radicalism which is at present so rife in our land." The young lady recants immediately: "If this dress has any connexion with Fourierism or Socialism, or fanaticism in any shape whatever, I have no disposition to wear it at all ... no true woman would so far compromise her delicacy as to espouse, however unwittingly, such a cause." [31]

America could boast that her daughters were particularly innocent. In a poem on "The American Girl" the author wrote proudly:

> Her eye of light is the diamond bright,
> Her innocence the pearl,
> And these are ever the bridal gems
> That are worn by the American girl. [32]

Lydia Maria Child, giving advice to mothers, aimed at preserving that spirit of innocence. She regretted that "want of confidence between mothers and daughters on delicate subjects" and suggested a woman tell her daughter a few facts when she reached the age of twelve to "set her mind at rest." Then Mrs. Child confidently hoped that a young lady's "instinctive modesty" would "prevent her from dwelling on the information until she was called upon to use it." [33] In the same vein, a book of advice to the newly-married was titled *Whis-*

per to a Bride.[34] As far as intimate information was concerned, there was no need to whisper, since the book contained none at all.

A masculine summary of this virtue was expressed in a poem, "Female Charms":

> I would have her as pure as the snow on the mount—
>> As true as the smile that to infamy's given—
> As pure as the wave of the crystalline fount,
>> Yet as warm in the heart as the sunlight of heaven.
> With a mind cultivated, not boastingly wise,
>> I could gaze on such beauty, with exquisite bliss;
> With her heart on her lips and her soul in her eyes—
>> What more could I wish in dear woman than this.[35]

Man might, in fact, ask no more than this in woman, but she was beginning to ask more of herself, and in the asking was threatening the third powerful and necessary virtue, submission. Purity, considered as a moral imperative, set up a dilemma which was hard to resolve. Woman must preserve her virtue until marriage and marriage was necessary for her happiness. Yet marriage was, literally, an end to innocence. She was told not to question this dilemma, but simply to accept it.

Submission was perhaps the most feminine virtue expected of women. Men were supposed to be religious, although they rarely had time for it, and supposed to be pure, although it came awfully hard to them, but men were the movers, the doers, the actors. Women were the passive, submissive responders. The order of dialogue was, of course, fixed in Heaven. Man was "woman's superior by God's appointment, if not in intellectual dowry, at least by official decree." Therefore, as Charles Elliott argued in *The Ladies' Repository,* she should submit to him "for the sake of good order at least." [36] In *The Ladies Companion* a young wife was quoted approvingly as saying that she did not think woman should "feel and act for herself" because "When, next to God, her husband is not the tribunal to which her heart and intellect appeals—the golden bowl of affection is broken." [37] Women were warned that if they tampered with this quality they tampered with the order of the Universe.

The Young Lady's Book summarized the necessity of the passive virtues in its readers' lives: "It is, however, certain, that in whatever situation of life a woman is placed from her cradle to her grave, a spirit of obedience and submission, pliability of temper, and humility of mind, are required from her." [38]

Woman understood her position if she was the right kind of woman, a true woman. "She feels herself weak and timid. She needs a protector," declared George Burnap, in his lectures on *The Sphere and Duties of Woman.* "She is in a measure dependent. She asks for wisdom, constancy, firmness, perseverance, and she is willing to repay it all by the surrender of the full treasure of her affections. Woman despises in man every thing like herself except a tender heart. It is enough that she is effeminate and weak; she does not want another like herself." [39] Or put even more strongly by Mrs. Sandford: "A really sensible woman feels her dependence. She does what she can, but she is conscious of inferiority, and therefore grateful for support." [40]

Mrs. Sigourney, however, assured young ladies that although they were separate, they were equal. This difference of the sexes did not imply inferiority, for it was part of that same order of Nature established by Him "who bids the oak brave the fury of the tempest, and the alpine flower lean its cheek on the bosom of eternal snows." [41] Dr. Meigs had a different analogy to make the same point, contrasting the anatomy of the Apollo of the Belvedere (illustrating the male principle) with the Venus de Medici (illustrating the female principle). "Woman," said the physician, with a kind of clinical gallantry, "has a head almost too small for intellect but just big enough for love." [42]

This love itself was to be passive and responsive. "Love, in the heart of a woman," wrote Mrs. Farrar, "should partake largely of the nature of gratitude. She should love, because she is already loved by one deserving her regard." [43]

Woman was to work in silence, unseen, like Wordsworth's Lucy. Yet, "working like nature, in secret" her love goes forth to the world "to regulate its pulsation, and send forth from its heart, in pure and temperate flow, the life-giving current." [44] She was to work only for pure affection, without thought of money or ambition. A poem, "Woman and Fame," by Felicia Hemans, widely quoted in many of the gift books, concludes with a spirited renunciation of the gift of fame:

> Away! to me, a woman, bring
> Sweet flowers from affection's spring.[45]

"True feminine genius," said Grace Greenwood (Sara Jane Clarke) "is ever timid, doubtful, and clingingly dependent; a perpetual childhood." And she advised literary ladies in an essay on "The Intellectual Woman"—"Don't trample on the flowers while longing for the stars." [46] A wife who submerged her own talents to work for her husband was extolled as an example of a true woman. In *Women of Worth: A Book for Girls,* Mrs. Ann Flaxman, an artist of promise herself, was praised because she "devoted herself to sustain her husband's genius and aid him in his arduous career." [47]

Caroline Gilman's advice to the bride aimed at establishing this proper order from the beginning of a marriage: "Oh, young and lovely bride, watch well the first moments when your will conflicts with his to whom God and society have given the control. Reverence his *wishes* even when you do not his *opinions.*" [48]

Mrs. Gilman's perfect wife in *Recollections of a Southern Matron* realizes that "the three golden threads with which domestic happiness is woven" are "to repress a harsh answer, to confess a fault, and to stop (right or wrong) in the midst of self-defense, in gentle submission." Woman could do this, hard though it was, because in her heart she knew she was right and so could afford to be forgiving, even a trifle condescending. "Men are not unreasonable," averred Mrs. Gilman. "Their difficulties lie in not understanding the moral and physical nature of our sex. They often wound through ignorance, and are surprised at having offended." Wives were advised to do their best to reform men, but if they couldn't, to give up gracefully. "If any habit of his annoyed me, I spoke of it once or twice, calmly, then bore it quietly." [49]

A wife should occupy herself "only with domestic affairs—wait till your husband confides to you those of a high importance—and do not give your advice until he asks for it," advised the *Lady's Token.* At all times she should behave in a manner becoming a woman, who had "no arms other than gentleness." Thus "if he is abusive, never retort." [50] *A Young Lady's Guide to the Harmonious Development of a Christian Character* suggested that females should "become as little children" and "avoid a controversial spirit." [51] *The Mother's Assistant and Young Lady's Friend* listed "Always Conciliate" as its first commandment in "Rules for Conjugal and Domestic Happiness." Small wonder that these same rules ended with the succinct maxim: "Do not expect too much." [52]

As mother, as well as wife, woman was required to submit to fortune. In *Letters to Mothers,* Mrs. Sigourney sighed: "To bear the evils and sorrows which may be appointed us, with a patient mind, should be the continual effort of our sex. ... It seems, indeed, to be expected of us; since the passive and enduring virtues are more immediately within our province." Of these trials "the hardest was to bear the loss of children with submission" but the indomitable Mrs. Sigourney found strength to murmur to the bereaved mother: "The Lord loveth a cheerful giver." [53] *The Ladies' Parlor Companion* agreed thoroughly in "A Submissive Mother," in which a mother who had already buried two children and was nursing a dying baby saw her sole remaining child "probably scalded to death. Handing over the infant to die in the arms of a friend, she bowed in sweet submission to the double stroke." But the child "through the goodness of God survived, and the mother learned to say 'Thy will be done.' " [54]

Woman then, in all her roles, accepted submission as her lot. It was a lot she had not chosen or deserved. As *Godey's* said, "the lesson of submission is forced upon woman." Without comment or criticism the writer affirms that "To suffer and to be silent under suffering seems the great command she has to obey." [55] George Burnap referred to a woman's life as "a series of suppressed emotions." [56] She was, as Emerson said, "more vulnerable, more infirm, more mortal than man." [57] The death of a beautiful woman, cherished in fiction, represented woman as the innocent victim, suffering without sin, too pure and good for this world but too weak and passive to resist its evil forces.[58] The best refuge for such a delicate creature was the warmth and safety of her home.

The true woman's place was unquestionably by her own fireside—as daughter, sister, but most of all as wife and mother. Therefore domesticity was among the virtues most prized by the women's magazines. "As society is constituted," wrote Mrs. S. E. Farley, on the "Domestic and Social Claims on Woman," "the true dignity and beauty of the female character seem to consist in a right understanding and faithful and cheerful performance of social and family duties." [59] Sacred Scripture re-enforced social pressure: "St. Paul knew what was best for women when he advised them to be domestic," said Mrs. Sandford. "There is composure at home; there is something sedative in the duties which home involves. It affords security not only from the world, but from delusions and errors of every kind." [60]

From her home woman performed her great task of bringing men back to God. *The Young Ladies' Class Book* was sure that "the domestic fireside is the great guardian of society against the excesses of human passions." [61] *The Lady at Home* expressed its convictions in its very title and concluded that "even if we cannot reform the world in a moment, we can begin the work by reforming ourselves and our households—It is woman's mission. Let her not look away from her own little family circle for the means of producing moral and social reforms, but begin at home." [62]

Home was supposed to be a cheerful place, so that brothers, husbands and sons would not go elsewhere in search of a good time.

Woman was expected to dispense comfort and cheer. In writing the biography of Margaret Mercer (every inch a true woman) her biographer (male) notes: "She never forgot that it is the peculiar province of woman to minister to the comfort, and promote the happiness, first, of those most nearly allied to her, and then of those, who by the Providence of God are placed in a state of dependence upon her." [63] Many other essays in the women's journals showed woman as comforter: "Woman, Man's Best Friend," "Woman, the Greatest Social Benefit," "Woman, A Being to Come Home To," "The Wife: Source of Comfort and the Spring of Joy." [64]

One of the most important functions of woman as comforter was her role as nurse. Her own health was probably, although regrettably, delicate.[65] Many homes had "little sufferers," those pale children who wasted away to saintly deaths. And there were enough other illnesses of youth and age, major and minor, to give the nineteenth-century American woman nursing experience. The sickroom called for the exercise of her higher qualities of patience, mercy and gentleness as well as for her housewifely arts. She could thus fulfill her dual feminine function—beauty and usefulness.

The cookbooks of the period offer formulas for gout cordials, ointment for sore nipples, hiccough and cough remedies, opening pills and refreshing drinks for fever, along with recipes for pound cake, jumbles, stewed calves head and currant wine.[66] The Ladies' New Book of Cookery believed that "food prepared by the kind hand of a wife, mother, sister, friend" tasted better and had a "restorative power which money cannot purchase." [67]

A chapter of The Young Lady's Friend was devoted to woman's privilege as "ministering spirit at the couch of the sick." Mrs. Farrar advised a soft voice, gentle and clean hands, and a cheerful smile. She also cautioned against an excess of female delicacy. That was all right for a young lady in the parlor, but not for bedside manners. Leeches, for example, were to be regarded as "a curious piece of mechanism . . . their ornamental stripes should recommend them even to the eye, and their valuable services to our feelings." And she went on calmly to discuss their use. Nor were woman to shrink from medical terminology, since "If you cultivate right views of the wonderful structure of the body, you will be as willing to speak to a physician of the bowels as the brains of your patient." [68]

Nursing the sick, particularly sick males, not only made a woman feel useful and accomplished, but increased her influence. In a piece of heavy-handed humor in Godey's, a man confessed that some women were only happy when their husbands were ailing that they might have the joy of nursing him to recovery, "thus gratifying their medical vanity and their love of power by making him more dependent upon them." [69] In a similar vein a husband sometimes suspected his wife "almost wishes me dead—for the pleasure of being utterly inconsolable." [70]

In the home women were not only the highest adornment of civilization, but they were supposed to keep busy at morally uplifting tasks. Fortunately most of housework, if looked at in true womanly fashion, could be regarded as uplifting. Mrs. Sigourney extolled its virtues: "The science of housekeeping affords exercise for the judgment and energy, ready recollection, and patient self-possession, that are the characteristics of a superior mind." [71] According to Mrs. Farrar, making beds was good exercise, the repetitiveness of routine tasks inculcated patience and perseverance, and proper management of the home was a surprisingly complex art: "There is more to be learned about pouring out tea and coffee, than most young ladies are willing to believe." [72] *Godey's* went so far as to suggest coyly, in "Learning vs. Housewifery" that the two were complementary, not opposed: chemistry could be utilized in cooking, geometry in dividing cloth, and phrenology in discovering talent in children.[73]

Women were to master every variety of needlework, for, as Mrs. Sigourney pointed out, "Needle-work, in all its forms of use, elegance, and ornament, has ever been the appropriate occupation of woman." [74] Embroidery improved taste; knitting promoted serenity and economy.[75] Other forms of artsy-craftsy activity for her leisure moments included painting on glass or velvet, Poonah work, tussymussy frames for her own needlepoint or water colors, stands for hyacinths, hair bracelets or baskets of feathers.[76]

She was expected to have a special affinity for flowers. To the editors of *The Lady's Token* "A Woman never appears more truly in her sphere, than when she divides her time between her domestic avocations and the culture of flowers." [77] She could write letters, an activity particularly feminine since it had to do with the outpourings of the heart,[78] or practice her drawingroom skills of singing and playing an instrument. She might even read.

Here she faced a bewildering array of advice. The female was dangerously addicted to novels, according to the literature of the period. She should avoid them, since they interfered with "serious piety." If she simply couldn't help herself and read them anyway, she should choose edifying ones from lists of morally acceptable authors. She should study history since it "showed the depravity of the human heart and the evil nature of sin." On the whole, "religious biography was best." [79]

The women's magazines themselves could be read without any loss of concern for the home. *Godey's* promised the husband that he would find his wife "no less assiduous for his reception, or less sincere in welcoming his return" as a result of reading their magazine.[80] *The Lily of the Valley* won its right to be admitted to the boudoir by confessing that it was "like its namesake humble and unostentatious, but it is yet pure, and, we trust, free from moral imperfections." [81]

No matter what later authorities claimed, the nineteenth century knew that girls *could* be ruined by a book. The seduction stories regard "exciting and dangerous books" as contributory causes of disaster. The man without honorable intentions always provides the innocent maiden with such books as a prelude to his assault on her virtue.[82] Books which attacked or seemed to attack woman's accepted place in society were regarded as equally dangerous. A reviewer of Harriet Martineau's *Society in America* wanted it kept out of the hands of American women. They were so susceptible to persuasion, with their "gentle yielding natures" that they might listen to "the bold ravings of the hard-featured of their own sex." The frightening result: "such reading will unsettle them for their true station and pursuits, and they will throw the world back again into confusion." [83]

The debate over women's education posed the question of whether a "finished" education detracted from the practice of housewifely arts. Again it proved to be a case of semantics, for a true woman's education was never "finished" until she was instructed in the gentle science of homemaking.[84] Helen Irving, writing on "Literary Women," made it very clear that if women invoked the muse, it was as a genie of the household lamp. "If the necessities of her position require these duties at her hands, she will perform them nonetheless cheerfully, that she knows herself capable of higher things." The literary woman must conform to the same standards as any other woman: "That her home shall be made a loving place of rest and joy and comfort for those who are dear to her, will be the first wish of every true woman's heart." [85] Mrs. Ann Stephens told women who wrote to make sure they did not sacrifice one domestic duty. "As for genius, make it a domestic plant. Let its roots strike deep in your house...." [86]

The fear of "blue stockings" (the eighteenth-century male's term of derision for educated or literary women) need not persist for nineteenth-century American men. The magazines presented spurious dialogues in which bachelors were convinced of their fallacy in fearing educated wives. One such dialogue took place between a young man and his female cousin. Ernest deprecates learned ladies *("A Woman* is far more lovable than a *philosopher"),* but Alice refutes him with the beautiful example of their Aunt Barbara who "although she *has* perpetrated the heinous crime of writing some half dozen folios" is still a model of "the spirit of feminine gentleness." His memory prodded, Ernest concedes that, by George, there was a woman: "When I last had a cold she not only made me a bottle of cough syrup, but when I complained of nothing new to read, set to work and wrote some twenty stanzas on consumption." [87]

The magazines were filled with domestic tragedies in which spoiled young girls learned that when there was a hungry man to feed French and china painting were not helpful. According to these stories many a marriage is jeopardized because the wife has not learned to keep house. Harriet Beecher Stowe wrote a sprightly piece of personal experience for *Godey's,* ridiculing her own bad housekeeping as a bride. She used the same theme in a story "The Only Daughter," in which the pampered beauty learns the facts of domestic life from a rather difficult source, her mother-in-law. Mrs. Hamilton tells Caroline in the sweetest way possible to shape up in the kitchen, reserving her rebuke for her son: "You are her husband—her guide—her protector—now see what you can do," she admonishes him. "Give her credit for every effort: treat her faults with tenderness; encourage and praise whenever you can, and depend upon it, you will see another woman in her." He is properly masterful, she properly domestic and in a few months Caroline is making lumpless gravy and keeping up with the darning. Domestic tranquillity has been restored and the young wife moralizes: "Bring up a girl to feel that she has a responsible part to bear in promoting the happiness of the family, and you make a reflecting being of her at once, and remove that lightness and frivolity of character which makes her shrink from graver studies." [88] These stories end with the heroine drying her hands on her apron and vowing that *her* daughter will be properly educated, in piecrust as well as Poonah work.

The female seminaries were quick to defend themselves against any suspicion of interfering with the role which nature's God had assigned to women. They hoped to enlarge and deepen that role, but not to change its setting. At the Young Ladies' Seminary and Collegiate Institute in Monroe City, Michigan, the catalogue admitted few of its graduates would be likely "to fill the learned professions." Still, they were called to "other scenes of usefulness and honor." The average woman is to be "the presiding genius of love" in the home, where she is to "give a correct and elevated literary taste to her children, and to assume that influential station that she ought to possess as the companion of an educated man." [89]

At Miss Pierce's famous school in Litchfield, the students were taught that they had "attained the perfection of their characters when they could combine their elegant accomplishments with a turn for solid domestic virtues." [90] Mt. Holyoke paid pious tribute to domestic skills: "Let a young lady despise this branch of the duties of woman, and she despises the appointments of her existence." God, nature and the Bible "enjoin these duties on the sex, and she cannot violate them with impunity." Thus warned, the young lady would have to seek knowledge of these duties elsewhere, since it was not in the curriculum at Mt. Holyoke. "We would not take this privilege from the mother." [91]

One reason for knowing her way around a kitchen was that America was "a land of precarious fortunes," as Lydia Maria Child pointed out in her book *The Frugal Housewife: Dedicated to Those Who Are Not Ashamed of Economy.* Mrs. Child's chapter "How To Endure Poverty" prescribed a combination of piety and knowledge—the kind of knowledge found in a true woman's education, "a thorough religious *useful* education." [92] The woman who had servants today, might tomorrow, because of a depression or panic, be forced to do her own work. If that happened she knew how to act, for she was to be the same cheerful consoler of her husband in their cottage as in their mansion.

An essay by Washington Irving, much quoted in the gift annuals, discussed the value of a wife in case of business reverses: "I have observed that a married man falling into misfortune is more apt to achieve his situation in the world than a single one ... it is beautifully ordained by Providence that woman, who is the ornament of man in his happier hours, should be his stay and solace when smitten with sudden calamity." [93]

A story titled simply but eloquently "The Wife" dealt with the quiet heroism of Ellen Graham during her husband's plunge from fortune to poverty. Ned Graham said of her: "Words are too poor to tell you what I owe to that noble woman. In our darkest seasons of adversity, she has been an angel of consolation—utterly forgetful of self and anxious only to comfort and sustain me." Of course she had a little help from "Faithful Dinah who absolutely refused to leave her beloved mistress," but even so Ellen did no more than would be expected of any true woman.[94]

Most of this advice was directed to woman as wife. Marriage was the proper state for the exercise of the domestic virtues. "True Love and a Happy Home," an essay in *The Young Ladies' Oasis,* might have been carved on every girl's hope chest.[95] But although marriage was best, it was not absolutely necessary. The women's magazines tried to remove the stigma from being an "Old Maid." They advised no marriage at all rather than an unhappy one contracted out of selfish motives.[96] Their stories showed maiden ladies as unselfish ministers to the sick, teachers of the young, or moral preceptors with their pens, beloved of the entire village. Usually the life of single blessedness resulted from the premature death of a fiancé, or was chosen through fidelity to some high mission. For example, in "Two Sisters," Mary devotes herself to Ellen and her abandoned children, giving up her own chance for marriage. "Her devotion to her sister's happiness has met its reward in the consciousness of having fulfilled a sacred duty." [97] Very rarely, a "woman of genius" was absolved from the necessity of marriage, being so extraordinary that she did not need the security or status of being a wife.[98] Most often, however, if girls proved "difficult," marriage and a family were regarded as a cure.[99] The "sedative quality" of a home could be counted on to subdue even the most restless spirits.

George Burnap saw marriage as "that sphere for which woman was originally intended, and to which she is so exactly fitted to adorn and bless, as the wife, the mistress of a home, the solace, the aid, and the counsellor of that ONE, for whose sake alone the world is of any consequence to her." [100] Samuel Miller preached a sermon on women: "How interesting and important are the duties devolved on females as WIVES . . . the counsellor and friend of the husband; who makes it her daily study to lighten his cares, to soothe his sorrows, and to augment his joys; who, like a guardian angel, watches over his interests, warns him against dangers, comforts him under trials; and by her pious, assiduous, and attractive deportment, constantly endeavors to render him more virtuous, more useful, more honourable, and more happy." [101] A woman's whole interest should be focused on her husband, paying him "those numberless attentions to which the French give the title of *petits soins* and which the woman who loves knows so well how to pay . . . she should consider nothing as trivial which could win a smile of approbation from him." [102]

Marriage was seen not only in terms of service but as an increase in authority for woman. Burnap concluded that marriage improves the female character "not only because it puts her under the best possible tuition, that of the affections, and affords scope to her active energies, but because it gives her higher aims, and a more dignified position." [103] *The Lady's Amaranth* saw it as a balance of power: "The man bears rule over his wife's person and conduct. She bears rule over his inclinations: he governs by law; she by persuasion. . . . The empire of the woman is an empire of softness . . . her commands are caresses, her menaces are tears." [104]

Woman should marry, but not for money. She should choose only the high road of true love and not truckle to the values of a materialistic society. A story "Marrying for Money" (subtlety was not the strong point of the ladies' magazines) depicts Gertrude, the heroine, rueing the day she made her crass choice: "It is a terrible thing to live without love. . . . A woman who dares marry for aught but the purest affection, calls down the just judgments of heaven upon her head." [105]

The corollary to marriage, with or without true love, was motherhood, which added another dimension to her usefulness and her prestige. It also anchored her even more firmly to the home. "My Friend," wrote Mrs. Sigourney, "If in becoming a mother, you have reached the climax of your happiness, you have also taken a higher place in the scale of being . . . you have gained an increase of power." [106] The Rev. J. N. Danforth pleaded in *The Ladies' Casket*, "Oh, mother, acquit thyself well in thy humble sphere, for thou mayest affect the world." [107] A true woman naturally loved her children; to suggest otherwise was monstrous.[108]

America depended upon her mothers to raise up a whole generation of Christian statesmen who could say "all that I am I owe to my angel mother." [109] The mothers must do the inculcating of virtue since the fathers, alas, were too busy chasing the dollar. Or as *The Ladies' Companion* put it more effusively, the father "weary with the heat and burden of life's summer day, or trampling with unwilling foot the decaying leaves of life's autumn, has forgotten the sympathies of life's joyous springtime. . . . The acquisition of wealth, the advancement of his children in worldly honor—these are his self-imposed tasks." It was his wife who formed "the infant mind as yet untainted by contact with evil . . . like wax beneath the plastic hand of the mother." [110]

The Ladies' Wreath offered a fifty-dollar prize to the woman who submitted the most convincing essay on "How May An American Woman Best Show Her Patriotism." The winner was Miss Elizabeth Wetherell who provided herself with a husband in her answer. The wife in the essay of course asked her husband's opinion. He tried a few jokes first—"Call her eldest son George Washington," "Don't speak French, speak American"—but then got down to telling her in sober prize-winning truth what women could do for their country. Voting was no asset, since that would result only in "a vast increase of confusion and expense without in the smallest degree affecting the result." Besides, continued this oracle, "looking down at their child," if "we were to go a step further and let the children vote, their first act would be to vote their mothers at home." There is no comment on this devastating male logic and he continues: "Most women would follow the lead of their fathers and husbands," and the few who would "fly off on a tangent from the circle of home influence would cancel each other out."

The wife responds dutifully: "I see all that. I never understood so well before." Encouraged by her quick womanly perception, the master of the house resolves the question—an American woman best shows her patriotism by staying at home, where she brings her influence to bear "upon the right side for the country's weal." That woman will instinctively choose the side of right he has no doubt. Besides her "natural refinement and closeness to God" she has the "blessed advantage of a quiet life" while man is exposed to conflict and evil. She stays home with "her Bible and a well-balanced mind" and raises her sons to be good Americans. The judges rejoiced in his conclusion and paid the prize money cheerfully, remarking "they deemed it cheap at the price." [111]

If any woman asked for greater scope for her gifts the magazines were sharply critical. Such women were tampering with society, undermining civilization. Mary Wollstonecraft, Frances Wright and Harriet Martineau were condemned in the strongest possible language—they were read out of the sex. "They are only semi-women, mental hermaphrodites." The Rev. Harrington knew the women of America could not possibly approve of such perversions and went to some wives and mothers to ask if they did want a "wider sphere of interest" as these nonwomen claimed. The answer was reassuring. " 'NO!' they cried simultaneously, 'Let the men take care of politics, *we will take care of the children!'* " "Again female discontent resulted only from a lack of understanding: women were not subservient, they were rather "chosen vessels." Looked at in this light the conclusion was inescapable: "Noble, sublime is the task of the American mother." [112]

"Women's Rights" meant one thing to reformers, but quite another to the True Woman. She knew her rights,

> The right to love whom others scorn,
> The right to comfort and to mourn,
> The right to shed new joy on earth,
> The right to feel the soul's high worth ...
> Such women's rights, and God will bless
> And crown their champions with success.[113]

The American woman had her choice—she could define her rights in the way of the women's magazines and insure them by the practice of the requisite virtues, or she could go outside the home, seeking other rewards than love. It was a decision on which, she was told, everything in her world depended. "Yours it is to determine," the Rev. Mr. Stearns solemnly warned from the pulpit, "whether the beautiful order of society . . . shall continue as it has been" or whether "society shall break up and become a chaos of disjointed and unsightly elements." [114] If she chose to listen to other voices than those of her proper mentors, sought other rooms than those of her home, she lost both her happiness and her power—"that almost magic power, which, in her proper sphere, she now wields over the destinies of the world." [115]

But even while the women's magazines and related literature encouraged this ideal of the perfect woman, forces were at work in the nineteenth century which impelled woman herself to change, to play a more creative role in society. The movements for social reform, westward migration, missionary activity, utopian communities, industrialism, the Civil War—all called forth responses from woman which differed from those she was trained to believe were hers by nature and divine decree. The very perfection of True Womanhood, moreover, carried within itself the seeds of its own destruction. For if woman was so very little less than the angels, she should surely take a more active part in running the world, especially since men were making such a hash of things.

Real woman often felt they did not live up to the ideal of True Womanhood: some of them blamed themselves, some challenged the standard, some tried to keep the virtues and enlarge the scope of womanhood.[116] Somehow through this mixture of challenge and acceptance, of change and continuity, the True Woman evolved into the New Woman—a transformation as startling in its way as the abolition of slavery or the coming of the machine age. And yet the stereotype, the "mystique" if you will, of what woman was and ought to be persisted, bringing guilt and confusion in the midst of opportunity.[117]

The women's magazines and related literature had feared this very dislocation of values and blurring of roles. By careful manipulation and interpretation they sought to convince woman that she had the best of both worlds—power and virtue—and that a stable order of society depended upon her maintaining her traditional place in it. To that end she was identified with everything that was beautiful and holy.

"Who Can Find a Valiant Woman?" was asked frequently from the pulpit and the editorial pages. There was only one place to look for her—at home. Clearly and confidently these authorities proclaimed the True Woman of the nineteenth century to be the Valiant Woman of the Bible, in whom the heart of her husband rejoiced and whose price was above rubies.

NOTES

1. Authors who addressed themselves to the subject of women in the mid-nineteenth century used this phrase as frequently as writers on religion mentioned God. Neither group felt it necessary to define their favorite terms; they simply assumed—with some justification—that readers would intuitively understand exactly what they meant. Frequently what people of one era take for granted is most striking and revealing to the student from another. In a sense this analysis of the ideal woman of the mid-nineteenth century is an examination of what writers of that period actually meant when they used so confidently the vague phrase True Womanhood.

2. The conclusions reached in this article are based on a survey of almost all of the women's magazines published for more than three years during the period 1820–60 and a sampling of those published for less than three years; all the gift books cited in Ralph Thompson, *American Literary Annuals and Gift Books, 1825–1865* (New York, 1936) deposited in the Library of Congress, the New York Public Library, the New-York Historical Society, Columbia University Special Collections, Library of the City College of the University of New York, Pennsylvania Historical Society, Massachusetts Historical Society, Boston Public Library, Fruitlands Museum Library, the Smithsonian Institution and the Wisconsin Historical Society; hundreds of religious tracts and sermons in the American Unitarian Society and the Galatea Collection of the Boston Public Library; and the large collection of nineteenth-century cookbooks in the New York Public Library and the Academy of Medicine of New York. Corroborative evidence not cited in this article was found in women's diaries, memoirs, autobiographies and personal papers, as well as in all the novels by women which sold over 75,000 copies during this period, as cited in Frank Luther Mott, *Golden Multitudes: The Story of Best Sellers in the United States* (New York, 1947) and H. R. Brown, *The Sentimental Novel in America, 1789–1860* (Durham, N.C., 1940). This latter information also indicated the effect of the cult of True Womanhood on those most directly concerned.

3. As in "The Bachelor's Dream," in *The Lady's Gift: Souvenir for All Seasons* (Nashua, N.H., 1849), p. 37.

4. *The Young Ladies' Class Book: A Selection of Lessons for Reading in Prose and Verse,* ed. Ebenezer Bailey, Principal of Young Ladies' High School, Boston (Boston, 1831), p. 168.

5. A Lady of Philadelphia, *The World Enlightened, Improved, and Harmonized by WOMAN!!!* A lecture, delivered in the City of New York, before the Young Ladies' Society for Mutual Improvement, on the following question, proposed by the society, with the offer of $100 for the

best lecture that should be read before them on the subject proposed;— What is the power and influence of woman in moulding the manners, morals and habits of civil society? (Philadelphia, 1840), p. 1.

6. *The Young Lady's Book: A Manual of Elegant Recreations, Exercises, and Pursuits* (Boston, 1830), p. 29.

7. *Woman As She Was, Is, and Should Be* (New York, 1849), p. 206.

8. "The Triumph of the Spiritual Over the Sensual: An Allegory," in *Ladies' Companion: A Monthly Magazine Embracing Every Department of Literature, Embellished With Original Engravings and Music,* XVII (New York) (1842), 67.

9. *Lecture on Some of the Distinctive Characteristics of the Female,* delivered before the class of the Jefferson Medical College, Jan. 1847 (Philadelphia, 1847), p. 13.

10. "Female Education," *Ladies' Repository and Gatherings of the West: A Monthly Periodical Devoted to Literature and Religion, I* (Cincinnati), 12.

11. *Woman, in Her Social and Domestic Character* (Boston, 1842), pp. 41–42.

12. *Second Annual Report of the Young Ladies' Literary and Missionary Association of the Philadelphia Collegiate Institution* (Philadelphia, 1840), pp. 20, 26.

13. *Mt. Holyoke Female Seminary: Female Education. Tendencies of the Principles Enbraced, and the System Adopted in the Mt. Holyoke Female Seminary* (Boston, 1839), p. 3.

14. *Prospectus of the Young Ladies' Seminary at Bordentown, New Jersey* (Bordentown, 1836), p. 7.

15. *Catalogue of the Young Ladies' Seminary in Keene, New Hampshire* (n.p., 1832), p. 20.

16. "Report to the College of Teachers, Cincinnati, October, 1840," in *Ladies' Repository,* I (1841), 50.

17. *Woman's Record: or Sketches of All Distinguished Women from 'The Beginning' Till A.D. 1850* (New York, 1853), pp. 665, 669.

18. "Female Irreligion," *Ladies' Companion,* XIII (May-Oct. 1840), 111.

19. *The Lady's Book of Flowers and Poetry,* ed. Lucy Hooper (New York, 1842), has a "Floral Dictionary" giving the symbolic meaning of floral tributes.

20. See, for example, Nathaniel Hawthorne, *The Blithedale Romance* (Boston, 1852), p. 71, in which Zenobia says: "How can she be happy, after discovering that fate has assigned her but one single event, which she must contrive to make the substance of her whole life? A man has his choice of innumerable events."

21. Mary R. Beard, *Woman as Force in History* (New York, 1946) makes this point at some length. According to common law, a woman had no legal existence once she was married and therefore could not manage property, sue in court, etc. In the 1840s and 1850s laws were passed in several states to remedy this condition.

22. *Excellency of the Female Character Vindicated: Being an Investigation Relative to the Cause and Effects on the Encroachments of Men Upon the Rights of Women, and the Too Frequent Degradation and Consequent Misfortunes of The Fair Sex* (New York, 1807), pp. 227, 278.

23. By a Lady (Eliza Ware Rotch Farrar), *The Young Lady's Friend* (Boston, 1837), p. 293.

24. *Girlhood and Womanhood: or Sketches of My Schoolmates* (Boston, 1844), p. 140.
25. Emily Chubbuck, *Alderbrook* (Boston, 1847), 2nd. ed., II, 121, 127.
26. *Woman and Her Era* (New York, 1864), p. 95.
27. "The Two Lovers of Sicily," *The Lady's Amaranth: A Journal of Tales, Essays, Excerpts—Historical and Biographical Sketches, Poetry and Literature in General* (Philadelphia), II (Jan 1839), 17.
28. *The Young Man's Guide* (Boston, 1833), pp. 229, 231.
29. *Female Influence: and the True Christian Mode of Its Exercise, a Discourse Delivered in the First Presbyterian Church in Newburyport, July 30, 1837* (Newburyport, 1837), p. 18.
30. W. Tolles, "Woman The Creature of God and the Manufacturer of Society," *Ladies' Wreath* (New York), III (1852), 205.
31. Prof. William M. Heim, "The Bloomer Dress," *Ladies' Wreath,* III (1852), 247.
32. *The Young Lady's Offering: or Gems of Prose and Poetry* (Boston, 1853), p. 283. The American girl, whose innocence was often connected with ignorance, was the spiritual ancestress of the Henry James heroine. Daisy Miller, like Lucy Dutton, saw innocence lead to tragedy.
33. *The Mother's Book* (Boston, 1831), pp. 151, 152.
34. Mrs. L. H. Sigourney, *Whisper to a Bride* (Hartford, 1851), in which Mrs. Sigourney's approach is summed up in this quotation: "Home! Blessed bride, thou art about to enter this sanctuary, and to become a priestess at its altar!," p. 44.
35. S.R.R., "Female Charms," *Godey's Magazine and Lady's Book* (Philadelphia), XXXIII (1846), 52.
36. Charles Elliott, "Arguing With Females," *Ladies' Repository,* I (1841), 25.
37. *Ladies' Companion,* VII (Jan. 1838), 147.
38. *The Young Lady's Book* (New York, 1830), American edition, p. 28. (This is a different book than the one of the same title and date of publication cited in note 6.)
39. *Sphere and Duties of Woman* (5th ed., Baltimore, 1854), p. 47.
40. *Woman,* p. 15.
41. *Letters to Young Ladies* (Hartford, 1835), p. 179.
42. *Lecture, p. 17.*
43. *The Young Lady's Friend,* p. 313.
44. Maria J. McIntosh, *Woman in America: Her Work and Her Reward* (New York, 1850), p. 25.
45. *Poems and a Memoir of the Life of Mrs. Felicia Hemans* (London, 1860), p. 16.
46. Letter "To an Unrecognized Poetess, June, 1846" (Sara Jane Clarke), *Greenwood Leaves* (2nd ed.; Boston, 1850), p. 311.
47. "The Sculptor's Assistant: Ann Flaxman," in *Women of Worth: A Book for Girls* (New York, 1860), p. 263.
48. Mrs. Clarissa Packard (Mrs. Caroline Howard Gilman), *Recollections of a Housekeeper* (New York, 1834), p. 122.
49. *Recollections of a Southern Matron* (New York, 1838), pp. 256, 257.
50. *The Lady's Token: or Gift of Friendship,* ed. Colesworth Pinckney (Nashua, N.H., 1848), p. 119.

51. Harvey Newcomb, *Young Lady's Guide to the Harmonious Development of Christian Character* (Boston, 1846), p. 10.

52. "Rules for Conjugal and Domestic Happiness," *Mother's Assistant and Young Lady's Friend*, III (Boston), (April 1843), 115.

53. *Letters to Mothers* (Hartford, 1838), p. 199. In the diaries and letters of women who lived during this period the death of a child seemed consistently to be the hardest thing for them to bear and to occasion more anguish and rebellion, as well as eventual submission, than any other event in their lives.

54. "A Submissive Mother," *The Ladies' Parlor Companion: A Collection of Scattered Fragments and Literary Gems* (New York, 1852), p. 358.

55. "Woman," *Godey's Lady's Book*, II (Aug. 1831), 110.

56. *Sphere and Duties of Woman*, p. 172.

57. Ralph Waldo Emerson, "Woman," *Complete Writings of Ralph Waldo Emerson* (New York, 1875), p. 1180.

58. As in Donald Fraser, *The Mental Flower Garden* (New York, 1857). Perhaps the most famous exponent of this theory is Edgar Allan Poe who affirms in "The Philosophy of Composition: that "the death of a beautiful woman is unquestionably the most poetical topic in the world. . . ."

59. "Domestic and Social Claims on Woman," *Mother's Magazine*, VI (1846), 21.

60. *Woman*, p. 173.

61. *The Young Ladies' Class Book*, p. 166.

62. T.S. Arthur, *The Lady at Home: or, Leaves from the Every-Day Book of an American Woman* (Philadelphia, 1847), pp. 177, 178.

63. Caspar Morris, *Margaret Mercer* (Boston, 1840), quoted in *Woman's Record*, p. 425.

64. These particular titles come from: *The Young Ladies' Oasis: or Gems of Prose and Poetry*, ed. N.L. Ferguson (Lowell, 1851), pp. 14, 16; *The Genteel School Reader* (Philadelphia, 1849), p. 271; and *Magnolia*, I (1842), 4. A popular poem in book form, published in England, expressed very fully this concept of woman as comforter: Coventry Patmore, *The Angel in the Home* (Boston, 1856 and 1857). Patmore expressed his devotion to True Womanhood in such lines as:

> The gentle wife, who decks his board
> And makes his day to have no night,
> Whose wishes wait upon her Lord,
> Who finds her own in his delight. (p. 94)

65. The women's magazines carried on a crusade against tight lacing and regretted, rather than encouraged, the prevalent ill health of the American woman. See, for example, *An American Mother, Hints and Sketches* (New York, 1839), pp. 28ff. for an essay on the need for a healthy mind in a healthy body in order to better be a good example for children.

66. The best single collection of nineteenth-century cookbooks is in the Academy of Medicine of New York Library, although some of the most interesting cures were in hand-written cookbooks found among the papers of women who lived during the period.

67. Sarah Josepha Hale, *The Ladies' New Book of Cookery: A Practical System for Private Families in Town and Country* (5th ed.; New York, 1852), p. 409. Similar evidence on the importance of nursing skills to every female is found in such books of advice as William A. Alcott, *The Young Housekeeper* (Boston, 1838), in which, along with a plea for apples and cold baths, Alcott says "Every female should be trained to the angelic art of managing properly the sick," p. 47.

68. *The Young Lady's Friend*, pp. 75–77, 79.

69. "A Tender Wife," *Godey's*, II (July 1831), 28.

70. "MY WIFE! A Whisper," *Godey's*, II (Oct. 1831), 231.

71. Letters to Young Ladies, p. 27. The greatest exponent of the mental and moral joys of housekeeping was the *Lady's Annual Register and Housewife's Memorandum Book* (Boston, 1838), which gave practical advice on ironing, hair curling, budgeting and marketing, and turning cuffs—all activities which contributed to the "beauty of usefulness" and "joy of accomplishment" which a woman desired (I, 23).

72. *The Young Lady's Friend*, p. 230.

73. "Learning vs. Housewifery," *Godey's*, X (Aug. 1839), 95.

74. Letters to Young Ladies, p. 25. W. Thayer, *Life at the Fireside* (Boston, 1857), has an idyllic picture of the woman of the house mending her children's garments, the grandmother knitting and the little girl taking her first stitches, all in the light of the domestic hearth.

75. "The Mirror's Advice," *Young Maiden's Mirror* (Boston, 1858), p. 263.

76. Mrs. L. Maria Child, *The Girl's Own Book* (New York, 1833).

77. P. 44.

78. T.S. Arthur, *Advice to Young Ladies* (Boston, 1850), p. 45.

79. R.C. Waterston, *Thoughts on Moral and Spiritual Culture* (Boston, 1842), p. 101. Newcomb's *Young Lady's Guide* also advised religious biography as the best reading for women (p. 111).

80. Godey's, I (1828), 1. (Repeated often in *Godey's* editorials.)

81. *The Lily of the Valley*, n.v. (1851), p. 2.

82. For example, "The Fatalist," *Godey's*, IV (Jan. 1834), 10, in which Somers Dudley has Catherine reading these dangerous books until life becomes "a bewildered dream.... O passion, what a shocking perverter of reason thou art!"

83. Review of *Society in America* (New York, 1837) in *American Quarterly Review* (Philadelphia), XXII (Sept. 1837), 38.

84. "A Finished Education," *Ladies' Museum* (Providence), I (1825), 42.

85. Helen Irving, "Literary Women," *Ladies' Wreath*, III (1850), 93.

86. "Women of Genius," *Ladies' Companion*, XI (1839), 89.

87. Intellect vs. Affection in Woman," *Godey's*, XVI (1846), 86.

88. "The Only Daughter," *Godey's*, X (Mar. 1839), 122.

89. *The Annual Catalogue of the Officers and Pupils of the Young Ladies' Seminary and Collegiate Institute* (Monroe City, 1855), pp. 18, 19.

90. *Chronicles of a Pioneer School from 1792 to 1833: Being the History of Miss Sarah Pierce and Her Litchfield School, Compiled by Emily Noyes Vanderpoel;* ed. Elizabeth C. Barney Buel (Cambridge, 1903), p. 74.

91. *Mt. Holyoke Female Seminary*, p. 13.

92. *The American Frugal Housewife* (New York, 1838), p. 111.

93. "Female Influence," in *The Ladies' Pearl and Literary Gleaner: A Collec-*

tion of Tales, Sketches, Essays, Anecdotes, and Historical Incidents (Lowell), I (1841), 10.

94. Mrs. S. T. Martyn, "The Wife," *Ladies' Wreath*, II (1848–49), 171.
95. *The Young Ladies' Oasis*, p. 26.
96. "On Marriage," *Ladies' Repository*, I (1841), 133; "Old Maids," *Ladies' Literary Cabinet* (Newburyport), II (1822) (Microfilm), 141; "Matrimony," *Godey's*, II (Sept. 1831), 174; and "Married or Single," *Peterson's Magazine* (Philadelphia) IX (1859), 36, all express the belief that while marriage is desirable for a woman, it is not essential. This attempt to reclaim the status of the unmarried woman is an example of the kind of mild crusade which the women's magazines sometimes carried on. Other examples were their strictures against an overly-genteel education and against the affectation and aggravation of ill health. In this sense the magazines were truly conservative, for they did not oppose all change but only that which did violence to some cherished tradition. The reforms they advocated would, if put into effect, make woman even more the perfect female, and enhance the ideal of True Womanhood.
97. *Girlhood and Womanhood*, p. 100. Mrs. Graves tells the stories in the book in the person of an "Old Maid" and her conclusions are that "single life has its happiness too" for the single woman "can enjoy all the pleasures of maternity without its pains and trials" (p. 140). In another one of her books, *Woman in America* (New York, 1843), Mrs. Graves speaks out even more strongly in favor of "single blessedness" rather than "a loveless or unhappy marriage" (p. 130).
98. A very unusual story is Lela Linwood, "A Chapter in the History of a Free Heart," *Ladies' Wreath*, III (1853), 349. The heroine, Grace Arland, is "sublime" and dwells "in perfect light while we others struggle yet with the shadows." She refuses marriage and her friends regret this but are told her heart "is rejoicing in its *freedom.*" The story ends with the plaintive refrain:

> But it is not a happy thing,
> All fetterless and free,
> Like any wild bird, on the wing,
> To carol merrily?

But even in this tale the unusual, almost unearthly rarity of Grace's genius is stressed; she is not offered as an example to more mortal beings.
99. Horace Greeley even went so far as to apply this remedy to the "dissatisfactions" of Margaret Fuller. In his autobiography, *Recollections of a Busy Life* (New York, 1868) he says that "noble and great as she was, a good husband and two or three bouncing babies would have emancipated her from a deal of cant and nonsense" (p. 178).
100. *Sphere and Duties of Woman*, p. 64.
101. *A Sermon: Preached March 13, 1808, for the Benefit of the Society Instituted in the City of New-York, for the Relief of Poor Widows with Small Children* (New York, 1808), pp. 13, 14.

102. *Lady's Magazine and Museum: A Family Journal* (London) IV (Jan. 1831), 6. This magazine is included partly because its editorials proclaimed it "of interest to the English speaking lady at home and abroad" and partly because it shows that the preoccupation with True Womanhood was by no means confined to the United States.
103. *Sphere and Duties of Woman*, p. 102.
104. "Matrimony," *Lady's Amaranth*, II (Dec. 1839), 271.
105. Elizabeth Doten, "Marrying for Money," *The Lily of the Valley*, n.v. (1857), p. 112.
106. *Letters to Mothers*, p. 9.
107. "Maternal Relation," *Ladies' Casket* (New York, 1850?), p. 85. The importance of the mother's role was emphasized abroad as well as in America. *Godey's* recommended the book by the French author Aimée-Martin on the education of mothers to "be read five times," in the original if possible (XIII, Dec. 1842, 201). In this book the highest ideals of True Womanhood are upheld. For example: "Jeunes filles, jeune épouses, tendres mères, c'est dans votre âme bien plus que dans les lois du législateur que reposent aujourd'hui l'avenir de l'Europe et les destinées du genre humain," L. Aimée-Martin, *De l'Education des Meres de famille ou De la civilisation du genre humain par les femmes* (Bruxelles, 1857), II, 527.
108. *Maternal Association of the Amity Baptist Church:* Annual Report (New York, 1847), p. 2: "Suffer the little children to come unto to me and forbid them not, is and must ever be a sacred commandment to the Christian woman."
109. For example, Daniel Webster, "The Influence of Woman," in *The Young Ladies' Reader* (Philadelphia, 1851), p. 310.
110. Mrs. Emma C. Embury, "Female Education," *Ladies' Companion*, VIII (Jan. 1838), 18. Mrs. Embury stressed the fact that the American woman was not the "mere plaything of passion" but was in strict training to be "the mother of statesmen."
111. "How May An American Woman Best Show Her Patriotism?" *Ladies' Wreath*, III (1851), 313. Elizabeth Wetherell was the pen name of Susan Warner, author of *The Wide Wide World* and *Queechy*.
112. Henry F. Harrington, "Female Education," *Ladies' Companion*, IX (1838), 293, and "Influence of Woman—Past and Present," *Ladies' Companion*, XIII (1840), 245.
113. Mrs. E. Little, "What Are the Rights of Women?" *Ladies' Wreath*, II (1848–49), 133.
114. *Female Influence*, p. 18.
115. Ibid., p. 23.
116. Even the women reformers were prone to use domestic images, i.e. "sweep Uncle Sam's kitchen clean," and "tidy up our country's house."
117. The "Animus and Anima" of Jung amounts almost to a catalogue of the nineteenth-century masculine and female traits, and the female hysterics whom Freud saw had much of the same training as the nineteenth-century American woman. Betty Friedan, *The Feminine Mystique* (New York, 1963), challenges the whole concept of True Womanhood as it hampers the "fulfillment" of the twentieth-century woman.

Catharine Beecher and the Education of American Women

Joan N. Burstyn

Catharine Beecher is only grudgingly accorded a place among the heroines of American history. The eldest child of Lyman Beecher, a renowned Congregationalist minister, Catharine Beecher is admired for her contributions to the education of women: the school she founded in 1823, Hartford Female Seminary, is acknowledged to have been one of the finest of its time; and her later work arranging for women from the East to teach in frontier communities, and founding the first normal schools in the West for women teachers is applauded. But the deeper significance of her work is ignored. She is known to have been a forthright, even a dogmatic woman, who cut a rather ridiculous figure in old age when, with corkscrew curls a-bobbing, she spoke out against women's suffrage, insisting that the development of woman's profession was more important than the vote.

Beecher's aspirations for women meet with little sympathy today, for most people do not believe in the possibility of equal but separate spheres of influence for men and women, and this disbelief leads people to overlook the radical nature of many of Beecher's ideas. She argued that each woman, like each man, should be educated for a career, and she set out to define a professional structure for each type of work women should engage in. She was sensitive to the trend to professionalization, believing passionately that women would achieve equal status only when they had professionalized their work. Over the years her ideas on women's sphere became less conventional as her work led her into unforeseen paths. Thus, after she discovered that Governor William Slade was not prepared to subordinate himself to her plans once he took charge of the committees to transport women teachers to the West, she abandoned her belief that a man should act as head of such an organization. But all her life she upheld *"distinctive divisions of responsibility"* [1] for men and women, and, like many of her contemporaries, she was convinced that one could judge the civilization of a society by the extent to which men's and women's jobs had been differentiated.[2]

Beecher does not stand alone among women educational reformers in believing that women had a different role in life from men. Because she was active until the 1870s, when few women reformers espoused this idea, one forgets that she was born in 1800 and formulated many of her educational ideas while she was running her first school which opened in 1823. Emma Willard, thirteen years older than Beecher, began Troy Female Seminary only two years earlier. Like Beecher, Willard believed women should undertake serious intellectual study but their education should be different from men's. Both women stepped outside women's conventional role, and through their work changed society's idea of what that role should be, but neither of them rebelled against the notion that women should lead different lives from men. Each felt herself to be a preceptor, not a rebel. Their similar attitudes were perhaps due to their similar family experiences: each had a father who respected both her intellect and her femininity; each had male relatives who actively supported her work throughout her life.

Looking back at the eighteenth and nineteenth centuries, one senses that the dichotomy between ascription and achievement has been crucial in dividing people on the issue of women's role. A growing tension has developed during the last two hundred years between those believing that womankind has a certain role to play in life, and those believing that each woman has to fulfill herself in whatever way she chooses. The former *ascribe* one role to all women, while the latter allow each woman to *achieve* whatever role she desires, choosing from a variety of possible roles unlabelled as to sex. A study of Catharine Beecher shows that while she believed women had an ascribed role different from men's, within that role she envisaged professional structures based on achievement.

An occupation becomes professionalized when people systematize the knowledge needed to perform it. They draw generalizations from the specific knowledge of individual practitioners, and publish these generalizations so that those wishing to become practitioners may learn them and become qualified for the occupation. Those who draw up the generalizations become experts in the field, explaining and expanding its content. They may themselves be practitioners, though the tendency of professionalization is to divide and subdivide work within an occupation so that the practitioner becomes a different person from the researcher. Whatever number of job categories develop within a profession, each category develops a hierarchy within it—some people get further up the career ladder than others—and each category becomes exclusive—some do not qualify for the job.[3]

Beecher's prescience on the need for women to professionalize their work was astounding. Her career in education spans fifty-five years of activity from 1823, when she opened her school in Hartford, Connecticut, to 1878 when she died in Elmira, New York, while planning to get public schools to adopt courses, in Home Economics. When she began her work, few occupations in the country had been professionalized, although the general outline of professionalization, as it applied to the content of a field, was established, and institutions were beginning to emerge for the training of professionals. Catharine Beecher knew about these; she was brought up in Litchfield, Connecticut, where Judge Tapping Reeve conducted the first Law School in the country, and her father, Lyman Beecher, was responsible for founding in 1824 the Connecticut *Observer,* in which Thomas Gallaudet published one of the first plans in the United States for a seminary for the training of teachers.[4] Moreover, in one of her first works, in 1829, Beecher lamented that, in the past, education had been neither an honored nor an honorable profession. The practitioners of other professions, law, divinity, and medicine, were united by their professional interest, and by periodicals in which they recorded their experiments.

The duties of all other professions are deemed of so much consequence that *years* must be spent, even after a liberal education, in preparation for these *peculiar* duties, and the public are so tenacious lest these professions should be filled by persons not properly prepared, that none may be admitted, but upon an examination before those qualified by study and experience to judge of the acquisitions of each candidate.[5]

Beecher recognized the exclusive nature of a profession. She saw the need to select school teachers, and to educate them for their work, but her belief in an ascribed role for women led her to ignore the logic of selecting practitioners for women's work of running a home and bringing up very young children. She strove to professionalize women's work, but she never discussed one consequence of her claim that a woman needed to be educated to run a home well—the creation of a group of housewives who, since they were uneducated, were inadequate for the job.

Beecher assumed that a million or more children in the western United States had ignorant, even depraved parents. Her twofold mission was to teach mothers how to care for their families, and to prepare teachers to educate children from unfortunate homes. Clearly the two parts of her mission were in conflict. If Beecher had succeeded in educating all mothers, there would have been no need for the kind of teachers she envisaged. Beecher, however, dealt with immediate problems, attacking them in as many ways as she could. She believed that each person could find salvation by leading a socially useful life but she knew that most people needed help. That some time in the future a society of upright individuals would have no need for helpers was not her concern; she was living in the present when help was needed. Her task, and the task she set for other educated women, was to provide it.[6]

Beecher defined woman's work as educating young children, caring for newborn babies, children, and the sick, and attending to the management of the household, which included designing and furnishing new houses, selecting and managing the fuel supplies of kitchen stoves and furnaces, selecting and preparing foods, planning and making clothes. Having defined woman's work, Beecher proceeded to generalize her individual experience, systematize the work women had to do, and publish the results. When she found the available textbooks for children unsatisfactory, she wrote her own: an arithmetic, and a geography text written jointly with her sister, in 1833; a moral instructor in 1838; a book on physiology and calisthenics in 1856. Her ideas were innovative: she stressed the teaching of concepts in place of memorization of details; she urged teachers to show how one subject linked to another, and she insisted on the use of apparatus to demonstrate ideas.

In 1841 she brought out the first of her books systematizing women's work in the home, *A Treatise on Domestic Economy*, the first textbook in its field to be acknowledged by a state board of education.[7] The book reveals why Beecher felt it was important to systematize the work of running a house. Today many fail to comprehend the complexities of everyday life for the majority of women in the 1840s. Used to tumble-dry fabrics, we have forgotten the labor of ironing; accustomed to ready-made clothes, we do not think of the skills needed to make patterns or sew by hand every stitch of clothing, every sheet, every curtain. Consumers of frozen processed foods, we tend to laugh at Beecher's preoccupation with domestic affairs, but the sales of this and her other books on housekeeping indicate how useful her contemporaries found her work.[8] Moreover she adapted her ideas to changing times: *The American Woman's Home* (1869), which she wrote with her sister, Harriet Beecher Stowe, contrasts in many ways with her earlier *Domestic Economy*.[9] The Beecher sisters' design for "a Christian house" has been described as one of the most daring innovations of its time. The plumbing and heating were located in a central unit, and a movable storage wall converted two living rooms into a large airy bedroom.[10] In domestic architecture, as in teaching, Beecher was an innovator. Her intention was that women should keep the designing of houses, and the designing of schools, within their sphere of influence.

Like many other women of her generation Beecher was dogged by ill health. With great skill, she generalized her own experience and turned her missionary work into the area of preventive medicine. After an informal survey of existing conditions, she concluded that healthy, vigorous women were hard to find. Beecher then outlined ways to improve the health of women in *Letters to the People on Health and Happiness* (1855), and *Physiology and Calisthenics* (1856). She not only introduced calisthenics into each school and college that she founded (she had been one of the pioneers in the United States to use calisthenics in the 1820s), but in her later years she traveled widely in the East, urging public school administrators to introduce the subject. No assessment has yet been made of the considerable impact of her work on the health of American women. It would be interesting to assess Beecher's role in the history of preventive medicine, and to see how many other women followed her lead in that profession.

Beecher also wrote several books on religion. As in her other endeavors, she was among those of her denomination who led their generation in reinterpreting Calvinism. The story of her harrowing religious experience after the death of her fiance, Alexander Fisher, is well known although it is difficult to appreciate how fearful was her quest for evidence that Fisher's soul had been saved. The God the Beechers had been brought up to believe in was capricious:

> Having deprived man of the means of salvation this uncontrollable egotist held him responsible for his failure to achieve it, and as if this were not enough, he then inflicted on the helpless soul and body unmentionable torture forever and ever.[11]

Small wonder that in the end Catharine Beecher chose to reject the attributes of her father's God, but she never rejected her father. The bond between them was strong, and he stood always as her model: like him, she informed the public of her solutions to personal problems; like him she saw herself as a missionary. But where Lyman saw religious conversion as his mission, believing that no amount of "natural goodness" could save a soul, but only the saving grace of God, granted to men in a moment of religious revelation, Catharine believed that conversion was unnecessary. By living an upright, unselfish life one made the conditions for one's salvation. She denied the essential depravity of human nature, and her work in education confirmed her belief that "the infant mind is the creation of God and we impeach his wisdom or goodness when we deny that it is rightly constructed." [12] Like some other educational reformers of her time, she revolted against the gloomy Calvinism of her youth with an intense effort to demonstrate the essential goodness of the child. Her mission was to educate young children and their parents to lead Christian lives, and to this end she wrote several books on religious education.

Had Catharine Beecher dealt only with the systematization of women's work, hers would have been an important contribution to the history of women. But she was not content to leave to chance the application of her ideas on domestic economy, health, and education. Through her contact with the teachers she sent to the West, she ensured that her books were used in their teaching, and her ideas spread to the housewives of the frontier. Beecher had great political acumen. From our vantage point we can see that she acted on a stage far larger than that of her contemporaries, Zilpah Grant or Emma Willard.[13] She broke away from the day-to-day burden of running an institution to publicize her ideas through her own organizations and her writing. With a missionary zeal born of her family's dedication to God's work, she envisioned an audience of hundreds of thousands. Like her brothers and her sister, Harriet, Catharine manifested a subtle blend of personal ambition and missionary zeal.[14] To promote education in the West, she wrote thirty-three books by the end of her life. Each added to her renown, although her ostensible object was to add profits from their sales to the coffers of her enterprises. As she wrote to Mary Lyon about her arithmetic text:

> If it is simply as good as any other, the object to which its profits are devoted is a sufficient reason for the friends of education to exert themselves in promoting its introduction.[15]

Beecher's ideas on how to proceed in her missionary work took form slowly. During her first years in Cincinnati, her father's house, his church, and Lane Theological Seminary were filled with discussions about how to educate the settlers in the West, and by 1835, in *An Essay on the Education of Female Teachers,* written at the request of the American Lyceum, Beecher had formulated her plans. The country was about to be submerged in ignorance and vice. Millions of children were growing up in the West "without any means of instruction," while "thousands of degraded foreigners and their ignorant families, are pouring into this nation at every avenue." [16] In this tirade against immigrants, Beecher echoed her father's antagonism to the Irish Catholic immigrants of Boston.

Her fear of the spread of Roman Catholicism was a mainspring in her missionary zeal, and her views on the subject did not change. When she was seventy years old, while addressing an audience in Boston, she argued that one reason why she opposed female suffrage was that it would give the vote to "that vast mass of ignorant women whose consciences and votes would be controlled by a foreign and domestic priesthood." [17] Yet Beecher's anti-Catholicism was muted by her respect for the way the Catholic church treated women; it provided, she said, "posts of competence, usefulness, and honor, in her service, for women of every rank and of every description of talents." [18] When her school in Cincinnati failed for lack of funds in 1837, and became a Catholic girls' school, Beecher realized that Catholics could muster greater support for women's education than could Protestants, and she urged Protestant clergymen more actively to support women in their attempts to join the fight against ignorance.[19]

The remedy for ignorance, Beecher concluded in her 1835 paper, was for the wealthy and intelligent to finance a vast educational program for moral and religious education. She wished women to become teachers, for traditionally the early education of the family had been a mother's task. If some mothers were failing to carry out that task well, then other women should take it over. Her arguments were politically astute although, to our ears, they have so great a ring of expediency as to demean women. Men, she claimed, had so many exciting, profitable occupations open to them that they would scarcely wish to take over the "sedentary, confining, and toilsome duties of teaching ... young children," particularly when they would earn "a scanty pittance":

> And therefore it is, that females must be trained and educated for this employment. And, most happily, it is true, that the education necessary to fit a woman to be a teacher, is exactly the one that best fits her for that domestic relation she is primarily designed to fill.[20]

Under the guise of "woman's role," the wily Catharine Beecher was staking out a new territory for women. They were to be trained for their work, as men were trained for theirs; women were to become teachers; they were to leave their families, and friends to travel alone to frontier lands, and by their own efforts, to support themselves.

During the next few years Beecher fleshed out her plans and presented them at meetings around the country in talks later published as books. Like the rest of her family and with their help, she decided to rely on private individuals to fund her schemes. She envisaged two sets of local committees: one in the East to select women teachers and to arrange a brief training session for them before they traveled West; the other in the West to arrange jobs for the teachers, to welcome them when they arrived, and to make sure they were comfortably settled. Beecher was convinced that, in the long run, each western state would have to establish its own college for the training of teachers, and her second plan was to establish such colleges according to her own designs.

Beecher was particularly fortunate to live in an environment with access to innovative ideas in many fields. The Beecher family was close-knit, and her brother Edward, particularly, gave Catharine constant support.[21] When she moved to Hartford, he was headmaster of Hartford Academy. Aspiring to more prestigious tasks than keeping school, in 1830 he was offered the presidency of Illinois College. His father had already been offered the presidency of Lane Theological Seminary. And Catharine? What was more prestigious for a woman to do than carry out the many chores of running a girls' school? It is no coincidence that she longed to found women's colleges with the same endowment and the same division of labor prevailing in men's colleges.

She pleaded for endowments for her Hartford School, and later for her colleges in Milwaukee, Wisconsin, Quincy, Illinois, and Dubuque,

Iowa. When her pleas were often unsuccessful, her bitterness was due in part to her knowledge that large endowments were forthcoming for men's but not for women's education.[22] Her father and her brother had been successful in raising money to support their colleges. Her organization, the American Women's Educational Association, sought $20,000 for each college but failed to raise it; the Society for the Promotion of Collegiate and Theological Education at the West, founded in 1843 with the help of Lyman and Edward Beecher, netted $367,745.58 in twenty-one years, with an additional $100,000 which "went directly from the Society's field to the several institutions for endowments." [23] Lane Seminary was free of debt by 1850, the year Lyman Beecher retired; Illinois College, which Edward Beecher had left in 1844, by 1858.[24]

Beecher's ideas on the need for endowments and her ideas on the governance of colleges were formed early while she was running the Hartford Female Seminary. Even at this date she referred to the need for a proper division of labor for women teachers. Over twenty years later when the Milwaukee Normal Institute and High School was founded, Beecher herself chose the first teachers "subject to the advice and consent of the Trustees who act on the part of the citizens of the place." [25] But later vacancies were to be "supplied by the nomination of the teachers themselves, confirmed by the Trustees. The four teachers are to be in all respects, *equal* in authority and rank, and the various responsibilities and duties are to be so divided that each teacher will be responsible for certain departments." [26] This plan of governance followed closely Beecher's conception of how a college should be governed. She wrote in 1851:

> In colleges, each professor is the head of his own department; and neither the president nor any of his colleagues have a right to interfere—not so much even as to give advice—much less to control. The corporation is the only body that can exercise the power of advice and control over the faculty. The president has no more power than any of his colleagues. He is only *primus inter pares* (the first among equals), and acts as the presiding officer of the faculty. In some of our universities . . . the office of president is omitted entirely, as needless.[27]

Beecher's first attempt to run a school according to what she called "the college plan" was the Western Female Institute in Cincinnati, which she founded in 1833. Yet faculty responsibility for college governance was then an innovation in American colleges. One would like to know who influenced Beecher's thinking on this subject: possibly her fiancé, Alexander Fisher, Professor of Mathematics at Yale until his death in 1822; possibly her brother Edward, an undergraduate at Yale from 1818 to 1822, and a tutor there in 1825. Under President Jeremiah Day (1817–1846), Yale was in the forefront of the movement for faculty governance. Day discussed all matters of policy with the assembled faculty, and together they decided how to act.

> The principle that a new professor or other officer connected with instruction should not be appointed without the consent of his future colleagues seems to have been observed with particular scrupulousness.[28]

By 1830 other colleges in the East had followed Yale's example, but in many colleges the President and Trustees retained their former power, and, in some cases, did not relinquish it until the twentieth century. In drawing up her plans for female colleges Beecher chose the innovative model of faculty responsibility.[29]

In 1835 when she first outlined her plans for educating children in the West, Beecher exhorted her compatriots, with a breathtaking urgency, to endow seminaries for women teachers:

> We must educate the nation, or be dashed in pieces, amid all the terrors of the wild fanaticism, infidel recklessness, and political strife, of an ungoverned, ignorant, and unprincipled populace.[30]

But it took time to organize support. When at last it was forthcoming and the Ladies Society for the Promotion of Education at the West was founded in Boston (later to be merged with the Board of National Popular Education founded by Governor Slade), Beecher spent several years arranging the transportation of teachers from the East to the West, and had no time to plan the founding of seminaries. Only after she had broken away from the Board of National Popular Education, was she able to concentrate on establishing seminaries in the West. To aid her, she persuaded a group of women in New York, in 1852, to found the American Women's Educational Association, dedicated to providing endowments for the colleges she set up.[31]

By then the movement to establish state normal schools was under way, and many reformers had turned to public funding as the only way to meet the enormous demand for qualified teachers.[32] Many welcomed public institutions as a means of overcoming the bitter denominational strife which had marked the first half of the century.

Beecher herself deplored denominationalism, insisting that the local committees to found colleges in connection with the AWEA be non-denominational.

With the opening of normal programs in city high schools and the founding of state normal schools, the training of teachers took a different route from that envisaged by Catharine Beecher. The model for such schools was European, linking them to primary and secondary schools rather than to universities. At the same time a growing number of people felt that women's colleges should offer a truly liberal education, not one that was narrowly vocational. Thus it was that Beecher's plans for her colleges began to seem outdated even as she came to found them.

There was a particular irony in this, since Beecher realized that with their new aspirations for a liberal education, women were jeopardizing their control over their traditional sphere of influence. They were opting out of the process of professionalization, which still continued apace. In 1862 the Morrill Act had set up land-grant colleges where the study of agriculture was to be systematized. With some bitterness Beecher commented in 1870:

> The care of a house, the conduct of a home, the management of children, the instruction and government of servants, are as deserving of scientific treatment and scientific professors and lectureships as are the care of farms, the management of manure and crops, and the raising and care of stock.[33]

There was support for her position, especially in the West. Iowa State College began to offer Domestic Economy as a subject in the Ladies' Course in 1871, and other agricultural colleges soon followed.[34] Those who ran other institutions, however, were out of sympathy with Beecher's desire that women should master "the principles of hydraulics, as applied in constructing cisterns, boilers, water pipes, faucets and other modern conveniences," [35] urging that women's colleges should pattern themselves on the best men's colleges and offer sound education in the liberal arts.

Beecher achieved a great deal in her attempt to professionalize women's work. She systematized its content, drawing generalizations and introducing innovations. Her zealous tone, however, was that of a missionary teaching the unenlightened masses; she does not seem to have had much feeling for the intellectual discourse among colleagues within a discipline which is a hallmark of professional life. In some areas, such as Home Economics, women continued Beecher's work after her death in 1878. In others, such as domestic engineering, men took over. As Beecher had foreseen, education was a crucial factor in deciding who was to become a professional; women were often handicapped by their lack of education when they competed with men to professionalize an occupation. In the first decade of the present century midwives were assailed by highly educated obstetricians (predominantly men) in a fierce controversy over licensing. Male obstetricians argued that midwives should not be licensed; rather they should be eliminated in favor of trained doctors. One writer charged that midwives had contributed nothing to obstetrics, although they were responsible for delivering half the babies in the country.[36] In retrospect one can see that the problem was not that midwives were incapable—some writers acknowledged that their practical apprenticeship made them more capable than doctors with their theoretical training—but that they were uneducated. Not even attempts to change the training given midwives so that it became more professional could save the occupation from virtual extinction during the next thirty years.[37]

Although Beecher did not ensure that women kept control of all work traditionally theirs, she did help ensure that teaching was accepted as a career for women. Through the organizations she started, hundreds of women teachers moved to the West during the turbulent years of early settlement. Beecher encouraged the founding through private subscription of normal schools for women in Wisconsin, Illinois, and Iowa before those states established their own normal schools. The normal schools and seminaries Beecher founded were designed to provide for women the same kind of teaching experience that college teaching provided men.

Beecher believed that men and women each had an ascribed sphere of influence. She saw that men were professionalizing their work to advantage, and wished women to do the same. She sensed that if women refused, men would do it for them. She objected to the kind of factory work women textile workers were asked to do because men had organized the work traditionally carried out by women. Her fears for women were well founded; the history of occupations since 1800 has been one of men's encroachment into work traditionally organized by women. The process by which an occupation becomes professionalized includes a division of jobs, so that the practitioner becomes a different person from the organizer and the researcher. Men's entry into women's sphere has been at the organizational and research levels; women have been left to carry out the practice. Obviously, at the same time, women have encroached on work traditionally performed by men, since both sexes have abandoned the notion of ascribed spheres of influence. But few women have received jobs in men's traditional sphere at the levels of organization and research. These levels, on the whole, have been denied them, and women have been left, in this sphere as in the one traditionally their own, to carry out the practice. Men and women today cannot subscribe to Catharine Beecher's belief in equal but separate spheres for the sexes, but they can appreciate the importance of her attempts to ensure to women their share of top jobs in an occupational hierarchy.[38]

NOTES

1. *Woman Suffrage and Woman's Profession* (Hartford, 1871), p. 7.
2. For a discussion of how this opinion was used by others to oppose higher education for women see: Joan N. Burstyn, "Brain and Intellect: Science Applied to a Social Issue, 1860–1875," *Actes du XIIe Congrès International d'Histoire des Sciences*, ix, 13–16 (Paris, 1971); and Joan N. Burstyn, "Higher Education for Women: the Opposition in England During the Nineteenth Century" (Ph.D. dissertation, University of London, 1968), chapter 5.
3. For a discussion of professionalization in our own time see Ernest Greenwood, "Attributes of a Profession," in *Man, Work, and Society*, eds. S. Nosow and W.H. Form (New York, 1962), pp. 206–18.
4. Gallaudet's article appeared in the *Connecticut Observer*, Jan. 4, 1825 and was later published as a pamphlet entitled "Plan of a Seminary for the Education of Instructors of Youth." (Boston, 1825).
5. Catharine E. Beecher, *Suggestions Respecting Improvements in Education* (Hartford, 1829), p. 5.
6. Beecher shared some of Horace Mann's commitment to perfectionism, although, like her brother Henry Ward Beecher, she was most concerned to temper the excesses of democracy. For a comparison of their ideas and hers see John L. Thomas, "Romantic Reform in America, 1815–1865," *Ante-Bellum Reform*, ed. David Brion Davis (New York, 1967), pp. 153–76; and William C. McLaughlin, *The Meaning of Henry Ward Beecher: An Essay on the Shifting Values of Mid-Victorian America 1840–1870* (New York, 1970), passim.
7. The *Treatise on Domestic Economy* was placed in the Massachusetts State Library by the Massachusetts Board of Education in 1843. For Beecher's role in founding Home Economies as a professional subject see Charlotte E. Biester, "Prelude–Catharine Beecher," *Journal of Home Economics* 51 (Sept., 1959): 549–51; James M. Fitch, "When Housekeeping Became a science," *American Heritage*, XII (August, 1961), 34–37.
8. The popularity of Beecher's books on domestic economy can be gauged from the fact that the *Treatise on Domestic Economy* was reprinted fifteen times between 1841 and 1856, when the third edition was published. *The American Woman's Home* (1869), which is listed as a revision of the

Treatise on Domestic Economy, was reprinted twice in 1870; *The New Housekeeper's Manual,* published in 1873 and reprinted in 1874, incorporated a revision of *The American Woman's Home.*

9. For a discussion of the changes see: Fitch, "When Housekeeping Became a science," pp. 35–36.

10. The importance of this design in the history of American domestic architecture is described by John A. Kouwenhoven, *The Arts in Modern American Civilization* (New York, 1967), pp. 60–61.

11. Martha Bacon, "Miss Beecher in Hell," *American Heritage,* XIV (Dec., 1962), 29.

12. Catharine E. Beecher as quoted in Lyman Beecher Stowe, *Saints Sinners and Beechers* (Indianapolis, 1934), p. 99.

13. *Zilpah Grant,* 1794–1874, became preceptress of Adams Female Academy, Londonderry, N.H., in 1824, and in 1829 organized Ipswich Female Seminary, Mass., which she ran for ten years. She became a member of the American Women's Educational Association and for several years assisted Beecher in preparing teachers for the West.

   Emma Willard, 1787–1870, opened Middlebury Female Seminary, 1814. She later moved to Waterford and in 1821 to Troy where she founded Troy Female Seminary. She sought vainly for the New York Legislature to support state-aided schools for girls. She retired from managing Troy Female Seminary in 1838 and devoted her time to advising and speaking. Like Catharine Beecher she wrote a number of books on the education of women.

14. Mae E. Harveson, *Catharine Esther Beecher, Pioneer Educator* (Philadelphia, 1932), p. 89, discusses the Beechers' reputation of being opportunists. They certainly managed to fulfill their ambitions for personal recognition while carrying out their missionary endeavors, and it may be here that the key to their so-called opportunism lies. They sought two kinds of immortality which the world views as inimical: immortality as individuals, through work that remained individual to them, such as books, and immortality as God's missionaries, remembered only through their influence on others.

15. Catharine E. Beecher as quoted in Harveson, *Catharine Esther Beecher,* p. 85.

16. Catharine E. Beecher, *An Essay on the Education of Female Teachers* (New York, 1835), p. 16.

17. Catharine E. Beecher, *Woman Suffrage and Woman's Profession,* p. 11.

18. Catharine E. Beecher, *The True Remedy for the Wrongs of Woman, with a History of an Enterprise Having That for Its Object* (Boston, 1851), p. 51.

19. In Catharine E. Beecher, *An Address to the Protestant Clergy of the United States* (New York, 1846).

20. Catharine E. Beecher, *An Essay on the Education of Female Teachers,* p. 18.

21. Robert Merideth, *The Politics of the Universe* (Nashville, 1968), p. 32. The whole chapter, "The Inward Man," illuminates the close emotional and intellectual ties between Catharine and Edward.

22. Lyman Beecher Stowe suggests that Catharine Beecher's lack of success in raising money arose in part from her refusal to allow her schools to

belong to one religious sect *(Saints Sinners and Beechers,* p. 115).

23. "Western College Society," *American Journal of Education* 15 (1865): 263.
24. "Western College Society," p. 264.
25. "Milwaukee Normal Institute and High School," Beecher-Stowe Collection, Schlesinger Library, Radcliffe College, Folder 321 (Newspaper cutting pasted into the Records of the American Women's Education Association).
26. "Milwaukee Normal Institute. . . ."
27. Catharine E. Beecher, *The True Remedy for the Wrongs of Woman,* p. 54.
28. Richard Hofstadter, *Academic Freedom in the Age of the College* (New York, 1961), p. 235.
29. Not until after World War I was the governance of Vassar College reorganized with "the guaranty of academic freedom and the principle of conference on all vital questions." (Henry Noble MacCracken, *The Hickory Limb* (New York, 1950), p. 205); while Mt. Holyoke College waited until 1929 before the President agreed to the setting up of an Advisory Committee of the Faculty on Appointments, Reappointments and Promotions with whom the President would consult "before making appointments to any grades of professional rank." (*Bulletin of the American Association of University Professors* 15 (April, 1929): 320–21.
30. Catharine E. Beecher, *An Essay on the Education of Female Teachers,* p. 18.
31. The difference between secondary and college education was ill-defined with regard both to the age of the student body, and the purpose of instruction; but with the development of public high schools definite sequences of instruction began to emerge. Beecher used a variety of names to describe the institutions she set up. The ones she set up in the West were definitely postsecondary; she sometimes referred to them as colleges, sometimes as seminaries. She regarded the high schools attached to them as model schools for student teachers to work in, as well as sources of future teachers. Her concept of a seminary or college included literary studies but went beyond that to encompass, also, training for all the pursuits that made up "woman's profession."
32. James P. Wickersham, *A History of Education in Pennsylvania* (Lancaster, 1886), p. 521, describes the role of the County Superintendents in Pennsylvania in encouraging the development of public support for teacher training. Several volumes of the *Amercan Journal of Education* contain articles on the growth of state support; especially useful is Volume XIII (1863) with several articles on the subject including " 'Normal Schools and Teachers' Seminaries,' Historical Development," 753–57.
33. Catharine E. Beecher, *Woman Suffrage and Woman's Profession,* p. 26.
34. Mabel Newcomer, *A Century of Higher Education for American Women* (New York, 1959), p. 90.
35. Catharine E. Beecher, *Woman Suffrage and Woman's Profession,* p. 27.
36. Charles E. Ziegler, "The Elimination of the Midwife," *Journal of the American Medical Association* LX (1913): 33–36.
37. There are a number of contemporary articles, as well as the one cited above, on the controversy between midwives and obstetricians including: A.B. Emmons and J.L. Huntington, "The Midwife: her future in the

United States," *American Journal of Obstetrics and Gynecology,* LXV (1912): 393-404; J. Whitridge Williams, "Medical Education and the Midwife Problem in the United States," *Journal of the American Medical Association* LVIII (1912): 1-7; Abraham Jacobi, "The Best Means of Combating Infant Mortality," *Journal of the American Medical Association* LVIII (1912): 1735-44. (Jacobi wrote in favor of educating midwives, not eliminating them.)

38. Since this article was written, there has been published Kathryn K. Sklar, *Catharine Beecher: A Study in American Domesticity* (New Haven, 1973). Particularly relevant to this article are pp. 170-75, 180-82, 265-70.

Family Limitation, Sexual Control, and Domestic Feminism in Victorian America

Daniel Scott Smith

The history of women is inextricably connected with the social evolution of the family. The revitalization of the American feminist movement and the surge of interest in social history among professional historians during the past decade have combined to make the study of women in the family a crucial concern. The central insight of new feminism—the critical relationship of family structure and roles to the possibilities for full participation by women in the larger society—provides an immediate impetus to the historical study of that relationship. To isolate a central historical question conceptually, however, is far easier than to examine it empirically. Women in the family do not generate written documents describing their ordinary life experiences. It is easier, for example, to describe historical attitudes toward women's proper role than to determine what the roles actually were at any given time. Only painstaking research into local history, a systematic study of personal documents describing ordinary behavior, and tracing life histories of women through manuscript lists can bridge this major gap in the historiography of American women.[1] At this point, then, a different approach seems necessary and useful.

An examination of three rather well-established quantitative indicators showing the relationship of the entire population of American women to the family suggests the hypothesis that over the course of the nineteenth century the average woman experienced a great increase in power and autonomy *within* the family. The important contribution women made to the radical decline in nineteenth-century marital fertility provides the central evidence for this hypothesis. Empirical data on the details of family limitation and the control of sexuality in the nineteenth century unfortunately are limited. However, an analysis of nineteenth-century sexual ideology supports the theory that women acquired an increasing power over sex and reproduction within marriage. The hypothesis that women's power increased within the nineteenth-century family also accords well with such important themes as the narrow social base of the women's movement in America before the late nineteenth century, the flourishing of women's groups opposed to female suffrage, and the centrality of the attack on aspects of male culture in such movements as temperance. A long-term perspective is essential for understanding the history of women in the family. I shall suggest how the situation of women varied in three periods: the preindustrial (seventeenth and eighteenth century); industrial (nineteenth century); and the postindustrial (recent) phases of American society.

From the colonial period to the present, *an overwhelming majority—from eighty-nine to ninety-six percent—of American women surviving past the age of forty-five have married* (Table 1). The proportion who never married was highest for those born in the last four decades of the nineteenth century. Small percentage changes represent, of course, thousands of women. While marriage was overwhelmingly the typical experience for American women, before the present century roughly a third of all females did not survive long enough to be eligible for marriage.[2] In addition, the numerically tiny minority who remained single had a far larger historical importance than their percentage would suggest. For example, 30.1 percent of forty-five to forty-nine-year-old native-white female college graduates in 1940 were unmarried.[3] Before the marked increase in life-expectancy in the late nineteenth and early twentieth century, the average American woman married in her early-to-mid-twenties, survived with her husband for some three decades, and, if widowed, spent an additional decade or so in widowhood.[4]

The implications of these figures for historians of women are obvious but must still be emphasized. Labor historians now realize that most workers historically did not belong to unions, black historians have been conscious that most Negroes were not in civil-rights organizations, and urban historians have discovered that groups other than politicians and elites dwell in cities. The search for the history of "anonymous Americans" has generally focused on population elements that in one sense or another have been defined as "social problems." For these groups there exists at least some information imbedded in contemporary myths and prejudices. It will be more difficult to write

TABLE I

Percentage of American Women Who Never Married

Census or survey, and birth cohort		Age at enumeration	Percentage never-married
1910	1835–38	70–74	7.3
	1840–44	65–69	7.1
	1845–49	60–64	8.0
	1850–54	55–59	7.7
	1855–59	50–54	8.9
	1860–64	45–49	10.0
1940	1865–69	70–74	11.1
	1870–74	65–69	10.9
	1875–79	60–64	10.4
	1880–84	55–59	8.7
	1885–89	50–54	8.8
	1890–94	45–49	8.6
1950	1895–99	50–54	7.7
	1900–04	45–49	8.0
1960	1905–09	50–54	7.6
	1910–14	45–49	6.5
1965	1915–19	45–49	4.8
1969	1921–25	45–49	4.5
	1926–30	40–44	5.0

SOURCE: Calculated from Irene B. Taeuber, "Growth of the population of the United States in the Twentieth Century," Table 11, p. 40 in *Demographic and Social Aspects of Population Growth,* eds., Charles F. Westoff and Robert Parke, Jr., vol. 1, U.S. Commission on Population Growth and the American Future (Washington: Government Printing Office, 1972).

the history of the average or model American woman, a person substantively akin to William Graham Sumner's Forgotten Man. She was, in 1880, for example, a thirty-eight-year-old white wife of a farmer living eight miles west-by-south of Cincinnati and the mother eventually of five or six children.[5] Intensive study of local records may reveal a surprising degree of social participation in church and voluntary associations and perhaps performance in other roles as well. Yet the primary statuses of the modal woman were those of wife and mother.

While nearly all American women have married, *married American women did not work outside the home until the twentieth century,* with the major increase coming in the last three decades (Table 2). Only one white married woman in forty was classified in the labor force in 1890 and only one in seven in 1940; today two-fifths of all married women are working according to official definition.[6] The increase in labor-force participation for single women in the twentieth century has been less dramatic. More generally, many indicators (an increase in single-person households for the young and widowed, the disappearance of boarders and lodgers from family units, the decline in the age at marriage, an increase in premarital intercourse, and the legalization of abortion and no-fault divorce) point to an emerging post-industrial family pattern in the post-World-War-II period. This major shift in the family has important implications for the periodization of women's history.

The statistical trend presents an interesting historical problem. During the nineteenth century, some ninety percent of women got married, over ninety-five percent of the married were not employed outside the home, yet *women progressively bore fewer and fewer children.* The average number born to a white woman surviving to menopause fell from 7.04 in 1800 to 6.14 in 1840, to 4.24 in 1880, and finally to 3.56 in 1900 (Table 3). The same decline is also apparent in U.S. census data on completed fertility.[7] Between 1800 and 1900 the total fertility rate decreased by half. By the late nineteenth century, France was the only European country whose fertility rate was lower than America's.[8] Despite the demographic effects of a later marriage age and of more women remaining permanently single, from one-half to three-fourths of the nineteenth-century decline in fertility may be attributed to the reduction of fertility within marriage.[9]

TABLE 2

Female Participation in the Labor Force (in percentage)

		White only		Native-white, age 35-44	
Year	Total	Single	Married	Single	Married
1830 [a]	(7)	—	—	—	—
1890 [a]	12.1	35.2	2.5	39.3	2.3
1940 [a]	26.9	47.9	14.6	73.6	17.9
1960 [a]	34.1	45.5	29.6	76.5	29.9

	All Women			Age 35-44		
	Single	Married, husband present	Widowed, divorced, separated	Single	Married, husband present	Widowed, divorced, separated
1950 [b]	50.5	23.8	37.8	83.6	28.5	65.4
1960 [b]	44.1	30.5	40.0	79.7	36.2	67.4
1972 [b]	54.9	41.5	40.1	71.5	48.6	71.7

[a] Stanley Lebergott, *Manpower in Economic Growth* (New York: McGraw-Hill, 1964), Table A-10, p. 519.

[b] Bureau of Labor Statistics, summarized in *The New York Times*, January 31, 1973, p. 20.

TABLE 3

Total Fertility Rates (TFR) for Whites, 1800-1968

Year	TFR	Year	TFR	Year	TFR
1800	7.04	1860	5.21	1920	3.17
1810	6.92	1870	4.55	1930	2.45
1820	6.73	1880	4.24	1940	2.19
1830	6.55	1890	3.87	1950	3.00
1840	6.14	1900	3.56	1960	3.52
1850	5.42	1910	3.42	1968	2.36

SOURCES: For 1800-1960 Ansley J. Coale and Melvin Zelnik, *New Estimates of Fertility and Population in the United States* (Princeton: Princeton University Press, 1963), Table 2, p. 36; 1968 calculated from Irene B. Taueber, "Growth of the Population of the United States in the Twentieth Century," in *Demographic and Social Aspects of Population Growth*, eds. Charles F. Westoff and Robert Parke, Jr., U.S. Commission on Population Growth and the American Future, vol. 1 (Washington, D.C.: Government Printing Office, 1972), Table 7, p. 33.

The decline in marital fertility is of critical importance in structuring the possibilities open to the average woman. A fifteen-to-twenty-year cycle of conception-birth-nursing-weaning-conception (broken not infrequently by spontaneous abortions) at the height of active adulthood obviously limits chances for social and economic participation as well as for individual development. Child-rearing must be added to this onerous cycle. The great transition in fertility is a central event in the history of woman. A dominant theme in the history is that women have not shaped their own lives. Things are done to women, not by them. Thus it is important to examine the extent to which nineteenth-century women did gain control over their reproductive lives.

Many forces, to be mentioned later, were clearly at work in curbing fertility, but the power of the wife to persuade or coerce her husband into practicing birth control deserves examination. While women did employ contraceptive methods in the nineteenth century (principally douching and the sponge), the major practices involved the control of male sexuality—*coitus interruptus* (withdrawal) and abstinence.[10] Following Kraditor's excellent definition of the essence of feminism as the demand for autonomy, sexual control of the husband by the wife can easily be subsumed under the label of "domestic feminism." [11]

Before marshalling empirical data showing the strengthening of the position of women within the nineteenth-century American family, it is first necessary to consider certain misconceptions about women's place in the industrial and preindustrial periods. Many of the recent interpretations of the history of American women have been devoted to an autopsy of the "failure" of women's suffrage. According to Kraditor, late nineteenth-and early-twentieth-century American women became conservative and were co-opted into the general progressive movement.[12] In Degler's view, women lacked an ideology that could properly guide them to full status as human beings.[13] For O'Neill, the "failure" lay in the refusal of the movement to assault the ideology and reality of the conjugal family structure that sustained women's inferior position.[14] This "what-went-wrong" approach implicitly assumes the constancy of woman's role within the family, and, more damagingly, interprets the behavior and responses of women as deviations from a preconceived standard rather than as responses to their actual situations. The turn toward conservatism and the leadership of active American women, for example, is seen as a tactical mistake rather than as the result of interaction between the leaders and their female constituency.

The extremely low percentage of married women in the nineteenth-century labor force suggests that the domestic-sphere versus social-participation dichotomy is not appropriate for the interpretation of women's history during the industrial period. If the average woman in the last century failed to perceive her situation through the modern feminist insight, this did not mean she was not increasing her autonomy, exercising more power, or even achieving happiness within the domestic sphere. Rather than examining Victorian culture and especially the Victorian family at its heart through a twentieth-century perspective, it is more useful and revealing to contrast nineteenth-century values and institutions with their preindustrial antecedents.

Misconceptions about women in the preindustrial family fit integrally into the pessimistic view of the Victorian era derived from the modern feminist perspective. Having portrayed the nineteenth century as something of a nadir for women, by implication, all other eras must be favorable by comparison. In order to show that women are not inevitably entrapped by the family, it has seemed important to emphasize that somewhere or sometime the status and role of women were quite different. While cross-culture evidence supports this argument adequately, more compelling are conclusions drawn from as little as two centuries ago in American or Western culture. Historians, however, have been properly cautious about more than hinting at a Golden Age for the preindustrial American woman. There is, to be sure, a sharp difference between the preindustrial and industrial family and the corresponding position of women in each. A conjugal family system, in the sense of the centrality of the married pair, in contrast to the dominance of the family line, did emerge in the United States during the early nineteenth century.[15]

The effects of this shift for women are complex. The conventional belief in the more favorable position of the average woman in preindustrial society rests on three arguments: the intimacy and complementary nature of sex roles in an undifferentiated economy; Aries' thesis that the boundary between the preindustrial family and society was very permeable; and finally, in the American case, the favorable implications for women of the relative female and labor scarcity on the frontier. The first argument may be compared to George Fitzhugh's defense of slavery, but extreme subordination and superordination do not require a highly differentiated economy and society. The very absence of complexity in the preindustrial family doubtless contributed to the subordination of women. While the identity of the place of work and residence in an agricultural economy inevitably meant some sharing of productive tasks by husband and wife, the husband's presence, given the prevailing ideological and cultural values, deterred the wife from gaining a sense of autonomy. Just as the gender stereotypes of masculine and feminine were not as rigidly defined as in the Victorian period, the prestige attached to the status of wife and mother was less than in the nineteenth century. Social prestige depended on the position of the woman's family in the hierarchical structure of preindustrial society. Daughters and wives shared in the deference paid to important families. When this system collapsed in the nineteenth century, women of high-status families experienced considerable deprivation compared to their high-ranking colonial counterparts. Women born to more modest circumstances, however, derived enhanced status from the shift away from deference and ascription.

Although Aries has little to say about women, his thesis that the line between the Western preindustrial family and community was not sharply delineated is of considerable importance here.[16] There does exist scattered evidence of women's nonfamilial activity, e.g., voting, operating businesses, etc., in the preindustrial period. The incidence of women's nonfamilial activity over time, its relationship to family and conventional sex roles, and finally, its importance in the social structure as a whole have not been explored. The existing social history of colonial women has successfully demonstrated that wider participation was not unknown.[17] The details of such nonfamilial participation have been much more fully researched for the colonial period than for the nineteenth century. Spinsters almost certainly were more marginal and deviant in preindustrial American society than during the nineteenth century. Only widows who controlled property may have been in a more favorable position. While changes in colonial America law permitted a married woman to exercise certain rights, these innovations related mainly to acting as a stand-in for a husband.[18] By negating the impact of male absence because of travel and death, these modifications in colonial law made the family a more efficient economic unit; historians should not confuse a response to high mortality and slow transportation with normative support for women's being outside the family. In fact, nonfamilial participation by preindustrial women must generally be viewed as a substitution for the activities of absent husbands. In effect, a woman's activity outside the preindustrial family was a *familial* responsibility.

Systematic evidence comparing the position of women in the preindustrial and industrial phases of American society is scarce; what exists points to the comparatively unfavorable place of women in the earlier stage. In most populations, for example, women live considerably longer than men. Yet this was not the case in four (Andover, Hingham, Plymouth and Salem) of the five seventeenth-century New

England communities studied to date. Only in seventeenth-century Ipswich did the typical pattern of longer survival for adult females exist.[19] In Hingham, furthermore, an inverse relationship between family
wealth and mortality is apparent only for eighteenth-century married
women, not for their husbands or children.[20] Literacy is a good index
of the potential to perform complex tasks. The scattered published
data on the frequency of signatures on documents suggest that there
may have been some narrowing of the historic differential between
male and female literacy during the eighteenth century. The gap,
however, was not fully closed until the nineteenth century.[21] The sex
differential in literacy is, of course, also a class differential. Compared
to those of preindustrial men, the burdens of life were harsh for
women, particularly those of low status. Finally, the resemblance in
that era of the sexual act itself to the Hobbesian state of nature is
revealing. Marital sex, succinctly summarized by Shorter as "simple
up-and-down, man on top, woman on bottom, little foreplay, rapid
ejaculation, masculine unconcern with feminine orgasm," [22] perhaps
mirrored the broader social relationship between men and women.

It may be argued that America was not Europe and that the relative
strength of the woman's movement in nineteenth-century America can
be attributed to a decline from a more favorable situation during the
colonial period. The existence of protest, however, is not an index of
oppression, but rather a measure of the ambiguities and weaknesses of
the system of control. It is ironic that the Turnerian frontier theory,
implicity biased by its emphasis on male experience, survives most
strongly in the field of women's history.[23] As Domar has shown,
however, labor scarcity and free land are intimately related to the
institutions of slavery and serfdom.[24] The economic factor associated
with the exceptional freedom of white American males was a precondition of the equally exceptional degree of suppression of blacks. For
a group to gain from favorable economic conditions, it must be able to
benefit from the operation of the market. While this was true for
single women in the nineteenth century (but not in the preindustrial
period), it decidedly was not true for married women. Wives were not
free to strike a better bargain with a new mate. What appears to be
crucial in determining the turn toward freedom or suppression of the
vulnerable group are the ideology and values of the dominant group.[25]
Neither the position of the labor force nor of women can be mecha-
nistically reduced to simple economic factors.[26]

The empirical basis for the importance of the frontier in the history
of women is not impressive. On the nineteenth-century frontier at
least, the high male-to-female sex ratio was a transitory phenome-

non.[27] For the entire American population, the high rate of natural increase during the colonial period quickly narrowed the differential in the sex ratio created by immigration.[28] The truth left in the frontier argument is also ironic. Women's suffrage undeniably came earlier in the West. That development, as Grimes has argued, reflected the potential usefulness of women as voters along the conservative wife-mother line rather than a recognition of Western women as citizens per se.[29] Farber's interesting analyses of the East-Midwest variation in marriage prohibition statutes points to a relative emphasis on the conjugal family in the newer areas of the country. Midwestern states tend to prohibit marriages of cousins while certain affinal marriages are illegal in the East and South.[30] In summary, then, the frontier and the general newness of social institutions in America benefitted women chiefly as part of the elevation of conjugality in family structure.

The majority of women in nineteenth-century families had good reason to perceive themselves as better off than their preindustrial forebearers. This shift involved not merely the level of material comfort but, more importantly, the quality of social and familial relationships. Since being a wife and mother was now evaluated more positively, women recognized an improvement within their "sphere" and thus channelled their efforts within and not beyond the family unit. It is not surprising that contemporary and later critics of the Victorian family referred to it as patriarchal, since that was the older form being superseded. If a descriptive label with a Latin root is wanted, however, "matriarchal" would be more suitable for the nineteenth-century family. Men had inordinate power within the Victorian family, but it was as husbands—not as fathers. The conservative conception of woman's role focused, after all, on the submissive wife rather than the submissive daughter.[31] Nineteenth-century women, once married, did not retain crucial ties to their family of birth; marriage joined individuals and not their families.[32]

While the interpretation being advanced here stresses the significance of the new autonomy of women within the family as an explanation of the decline of fertility during the nineteenth century, this is not to deny the importance of economic, instrumental, or "male" considerations. The shift from agriculture, the separation of production from the family, the urbanization of the population, and the loss of child labor through compulsory education doubtless also contributed. Indeed, the wife's demand for a smaller family may have been so successful precisely because it was not contrary to the rational calculations of her husband. Since the fertility decline was nationwide and affected urban and rural areas simultaneously, attitudes and values as well as structural factors are obviously of relevance.[33] The romantic cult of childhood, for example, may have induced a change from quantitative to qualitative fertility goals on the part of parents.

The social correlates of lower fertility found in modern populations are relevant to this discussion of the history of American fertility. A common finding of cross-national studies, for example, is a strong negative relationship between fertility and female participation in the labor force.[34] The American historical record, however, does not provide much support for this theory. During the 1830–1890 period, there was probably only a slight increase in the labor-force participation of married women and yet marital fertility continuously declined.[35] During both the post-World-War-II baby boom and the fertility decline since 1957, labor-force activity of married women increased.[36] For lower fertility, what is important is the meaning women assign to themselves and their work, either in or out of the home.[37] Since work is compatible with a traditional orientation for women,[38] the converse may also be true. Finally, the strong relationship between lower fertility and the educational attainment of a woman may involve more than a response to the higher financial return of nonfamilial activity for the better educated.[39] Education may be a proxy variable for the degree to which a woman defines her life in terms of self rather than others.

Some quantitative support for the hypothesis that the wife significantly controlled family planning in the nineteenth century derives from a comparison of sex ratios of last children in small and large families, and an analysis of the sex composition of very small families in Hingham, Massachusetts. Most studies indicate that men and women equally prefer boys to girls.[40] Given a residue of patriarchal bias in nineteenth-century values, it is not an unlikely assumption that women would be more satisfied than men with girl children. A suggestive psychological study supports this notion. In a sample of Swedish women expecting their first child, those preferring a boy were found to have less of a sense of personal autonomy. Of the eleven of the eighty-one women in the sample who considered themselves dominant in their marriages, only two wanted sons. The "no-preference" women were better adjusted psychologically and scored higher on intelligence tests.[41] In short, the less autonomous and adjusted the woman, the more likely she is to want her first child to be a boy.

In Hingham marriages formed between 1821 and 1860, the last child was more likely to be a girl in small families and a boy in the larger families (see Table 4). The difference between the sex ratios of the final child in families with one to four children as compared to those with five and more is statistically significant only at the 0.1 level.

Given the complexity of the argument here, this is not impressive. Small families, however, tended to contain only girls. Sixty percent of only children were girls (twenty-one of thirty-five): twenty-seven percent and seventeen percent of two-child families were both girls (fourteen) and boys (nine) respectively; and fourteen percent and six percent of three-child families were all girls (nine) and all boys (four) respectively. The independent probability of these differences is less than one in ten, one in four, and one in twenty respectively. With a slight biological tendency toward males in births to young women, these figures suggest that differing sex-preferences of husbands and wives may explain the pattern. On the other hand, twentieth-century sex-ratio samples show either no difference or a bias toward males in the sex ratio of the last-born child.[42] In the absence of very marked differences in the preference of husbands and wives and with less than perfect contraceptive methods available to nineteenth-century couples, no extreme relationship should appear. This quantitative pattern does suggest that the Victorian family had a domestic-feminist rather than a patriarchal orientation.

TABLE 4

Sex ratio of last versus other children of stated parity and the probability of having another child according to sex of the last child: Hingham women in complete families marrying before age twenty-five between 1821 and 1860.

| | Sex ratio | | Parity progression ratios | | |
Parity	Last	Not last	Male last	Female last	Difference
1	57(22)	124(242)	.944	.885	+.059
2	113(32)	82(211)	.848	.855	−.037
3	69(49)	83(165)	.789	.756	+.033
4	83(42)	114(124)	.776	.716	+.060
5	107(31)	114(94)	.758	.746	+.012
6	237(22)	74(66)	.596	.826	−.230
7	150(20)	77(46)	.625	.764	−.139
8& +	124(47)	105(86)	.628	.667	−.039

NOTE: Sample sizes in parentheses. Chi-Square (1–4) vs. (5 and more) 2.882, significant at 0.1 level.
SOURCE: Daniel Scott Smith, "Population, Family and Society in Hingham, Massachusetts, 1635–1880," (unpublished Ph.D. dissertation, University of California, Berkeley, 1973), p. 360.

Recognition of the desirability and even the existence of female control of marital sexual intercourse may be found in nineteenth-century marital advice literature. In these manuals, "marital excess," i.e., too-frequent coitus, was a pervasive theme. Although conservative writers, such as William Alcott, proclaimed that "the submissive wife should do everything for your husband which your strength and a due regard to your health would admit," [43] women rejected submission. In fact, Dio Lewis claimed that marital excess was the topic best received by his female audience during his lecture tours of the 1850s. The Moral Education Society, according to Lewis, asserted the right "of a wife to be her own person, and her sacred right to deny her husband if need be; and to decide how often and when she should become a mother." [44] The theme of the wife's right to control her body and her fertility was not uncommon. "It is a woman's right, not her privilege, to control the surrender of her person; she should have pleasure or not allow access unless she wanted a child." [45]

It should be emphasized that both the husband and the wife had good (albeit different) reasons for limiting the size of their family. In most marriages, perhaps, these decisions were made jointly by the couple. Nor is it necessarily true that the wife imposed abstinence on her husband. While *coitus interruptus* is the male contraceptive par excellence, the wife could assist "with voluntary [though unspecified] effort." [46] Withdrawal was, according to one physician, "so universal it may be called a national vice, so common that it is unblushingly acknowledged by its perpetrators, *for the commission of which the husband is even eulogized by his wife and applauded by her friends* [italics added]." [47] In the marriage manuals, withdrawal was the most denounced means of marital contraception and, it may be inferred, the most common method in actual practice.

There are serious questions about the applicability of this literary evidence to actual behavior. Even among the urban middle classes (presumably the consumers of these manuals and tracts) reality and ideology probably diverged considerably. Historical variation in sexual ideology doubtless is much greater than change in actual sexual behavior.[48] The antisexual themes of the nineteenth century should not, however, be ignored. One may view this ideology as the product of underlying social circumstances—the conscious tip, so to speak, of the submerged iceberg of sexual conflict. While the influence of this literature is difficult to assess, its functions can be examined. It can be argued that antisexual themes had little to do with family limitation. Nor was contraception universally condemned by respectable opinion. The *Nation* in June 1869 called family limitation "not the noblest motive of action, of course; but there is something finely human about it." [49] Male sexual self-control was necessary, it has been suggested, to produce ordered, disciplined personalities who could focus relentlessly on success in the marketplace.[50] The conventional interpretation of these antisexual themes, of course, is that Victorian morality was but another means for suppressing women. The trouble with these arguments is that men more than women should be expected to favor, support, and extend the operation of this morality.

To understand the function of this ideology we must examine the market system involving the exchanges of services between women and men. In historical, preindustrial, hierarchical society, male control and suppression of female sexuality focused especially on the paternal control of daughters. This system of control existed for the establishment of marriage alliances and for the protection of one's females from the intrusions of social inferiors. Sexual restrictiveness need not, however, imply direct male domination. In a system of equality between males in which females are denied access to other resources, a sexually restrictive ideology is predictable. Nineteenth-century mate-choice was more or less an autonomous process uncontrolled by elders. American women, as Tocqueville and others noted, had considerable freedom before marriage. Lacking economic resources, however, they could bargain with their only available good—sex. The price of sex, as of other commodities, varies inversely with the supply. Since husbands were limited by the autonomy of single women in finding sexual gratification elsewhere, sexual restrictiveness also served the interests of married women. Futhermore, in a democratic society, men could not easily violate the prerogatives of their male equals by seducing their wives. Thus Victorian morality functioned in the interest of both single and married women.[51] By having an effective monopoly on the supply of sexual gratification, married women could increase the "price" since their husbands still generally expressed a traditional uncontrolled demand for sex. Instead of being "possessed," women could now bargain. Respectable sexual ideology argued, it is true, that men should substitute work for sex. This would reduce the price that wives could exact. At the same time, according to the prevailing sexual ideology, marital sex was the least dangerous kind. In contrast to masturbation or prostitution, marital intercourse was evaluated positively. But, contrary to these ideological trends, prostitution appears to have increased during the nineteenth century. Whether or not prostitution was a substitute for marital sex or merely a reflection of the relative incease in the proportion of unattached males created by late marriage and high geographical mobility is uncertain. This brief economic analysis of the supply and demand of sex at least suggests the possibility that Victorian morality had distincly feminist overtones.

In principle, Victorian sexual ideology did advance the interest of individual women. Whether or not this represented a genuine feminist ideology depends to some extent on the behavior of women as a group. The evidence seems to be fairly clear on this point. If women as individuals had wished to maximize their advantage, they could have furthered the devaluation of non-marital sex for men by drawing more firmly the line between "good" and "bad" women, between the lady and the whore. While mothers may have done this on an individual basis, for example, by threatening their daughters with the dishonor of being a fallen woman, collectively they tended to sympathize with the prostitute or fallen woman and condemn the male exploiter or seducer.[52] The activity of the New York Female Moral Reform Society is an instructive case in point.[53]

Historians have had some difficulty in interpreting the antisexual theme in nineteenth-century women's history. Although Rosenberg recognizes the implicit radicalness of the assault on the double standard and the demand for a reformation in male sexual behavior, she tends to apologize for the failure of sexual reformers to link up with the "real" feminism represented by Sarah Grimke's feminist manifesto.[54] More serious is the distortion of the central question of the periodization of women's history. Cott's labeling of the first half of the nineteenth century as a question of "the cult of domesticity vs. social change," Kraditor's similar choice of "the family vs. autonomy," and Lerner's dichotomy of "the lady and the mill girl" all perpetuate the half-truth that the family served only as a source of social stability and change for women occurred only outside of the family.[55] I am arguing here, however, that the domestic roles of women and the perceptions that developed out of these roles were not an alternative to social change but presented a significant and positive development for nineteenth-century women.

Linking the decline of marital fertility to women's increasing autonomy within the family—the concept of "domestic feminism"—conflicts with several other theories held by scholars. To stress the failure of the woman's movement to support family limitation, as the Bankses do in their analyses for England, ignores the possibility of a parallel domestic feminist movement. It may be more to the point that anti-feminists blamed the revolt against maternity and marital sexual intercourse on the public feminists.[56] The Bankses suggest that individual feminists may have fought a battle to gain control over their own reproduction.[57] The nineteenth-century neo-Malthusians and the woman's movement had different purposes; the former attempted to control the fertility of "others," i.e., the working classes, while the latter sought reforms in its own interest. Since mechanical means of contraception were associated with nonmarital sex of a kind exploitative of women, the opposition of women to these devices was an expression of the deeper hostility to the double standard.

A more serious objection to identifying the increasing power and automony of women within the family as feminism is, of course, the existence of the parallel tradition of "real" or "public" feminism. This tradition—linking Wollstonecraft, Seneca Falls, Stanton, Anthony, and Gilman—at least partially recognized the centrality of the role and position of women in the family to the general subjugation of women in society. In contrast, the goals of domestic feminism, at least in its intitial stage, were situated entirely within marriage. Clearly some explanation is needed of why both strands of feminism existed. A possible answer relates to the evolution of the family in the process of modernization. With the democratization of American society, prestige ascribed by birth declined. Women born into families of high social status could not obtain deference if they remained single; even if a woman married a man of equally high status, his position would not assure her prestige; his status depended on his achievement. The satisfactory and valued performance of the roles of wife and mother could not compenstate for the loss of status associated with the family line in preindustrial society. Thus public feminism would be most attractive to women of high social origin.[58] This conception of the woman as an atomistic person and citizen naturally drew on the Enlightenment attack on traditional social ties. The modeling of the Seneca Falls manifesto on the Declaration of Independence is suggestive in this regard.[59]

The liberal origins of public feminism were both its strength and its weakness. Because it emphasized a clear standard of justice and stressed the importance of human individuality, it was consistent with the most fundamental values in American political history. But it was also limiting as a political ideology in that it cast its rhetoric against nearly obsolete social forms that had little relevance in the experience of the average American woman, i.e., patriarchalism and arbitrary male authority. Paradoxically, public feminism was simultaneously behind and ahead of the times. Resting on eighteenth-century notions, it clashed with the romantic and sentimental mood of the nineteenth century. The social basis of the appeal of public feminism—the opportunity for married women to assume both family and social roles—would not be created for the average woman until the postindustrial period.

Domestic feminism, on the other hand, was a nineteenth-century creation, born out of the emerging conjugal family and the social stresses accompanying modern economic growth. Instead of postulating woman as an atom in competitive society, domestic feminism viewed woman as a person in the context of relationships with others. By defining the family as a community, this ideology allowed women to engage in something of a critique of male, materialistic, market society and simultaneously proceed to seize power within the family. Women asserted themselves within the family much as their husbands were attempting to assert themselves outside the home. Critics such as de Tocqueville concluded that the Victorian conjugal family was really a manifestation of selfishness and a retreat from the older conception of community as place. As one utopian-communitarian put it, the basic social question of the day was "whether the existence of the marital family is compatible with that of the universal family which the term 'Community' signifies." [60]

Community—"that mythical state of social wholeness in which each member has his place and in which life is regulated by cooperation rather than by competition and conflict," [61]—is not fixed historically in one social institution. Rather, as Kirk Jeffrey has argued, the nineteenth-century home was conceived of as a utopian community—at once a retreat, refuge and critique of the city.[62] Jeffrey, however, does not fully realize the implications of his insight. He admits that the literature of the utopian home demanded that husbands consult their wives, avoid sexual assault on them, and even consciously structure their own behavior on the model of their spouses. Yet he still concludes that "there seems little doubt that they (women) suffered a notable decline in autonomy and morale during the three-quarters of a century following the founding of the American republic." [63] He suggests that women who engaged in writing, social activities, political reform, drug use, and sickliness were "dropping out" of domesticity. On the contrary, these responses reflect both the time and autonomy newly available to women. The romantic ideal of woman as wife and mother in contrast to the Enlightenment model of woman as person and citizen did not have entirely negative consequences—particularly for the vast majority of American women who did not benefit from the position of their family in society.

The perspective suggested above helps to explain why the history of the suffrage movement involved a shift from the woman-as-atomistic-person notion toward the ideology of woman-as-wife-and-mother. Drawing on the perceptions gained from their rise within the family, women finally entered politics in large numbers at the turn of the twentieth century. Given the importance of family limitation and sexual control in domestic feminism, it is not surprising that women were involved in and strongly supported the temperance and social purity movements—reform attempts implicitly attacking male culture. Since these anti-male responses and attitudes were based on the familial and social experience of women, it seems beside the point to infer psychological abnormality from this emphasis.[64]

In an important sense, the traditions of domestic and public feminism merged in the fight for suffrage in the early twentieth century. In a study of "elite" women surveyed in 1913, Jensen found that mothers of completed fertility actually exhibited more support for suffrage than childless married women.[65] Women in careers involving more social interaction, for example, medicine, law, administration, tended to favor suffrage more strongly than women in more privatistic occupations, for example, teaching, writing, art.[66] In short, the dichotomy between women trapped or suppressed within marriage and women seeking to gain freedom through social participation does not accurately represent the history of American women in the nineteenth century.

It has been argued that historians must take seriously the changing roles and behavior of women within the Victorian conjugal family. That women eventually attained a larger arena of activity was not so much an alternative to the woman-as-wife-and-mother as an extension of the progress made within the family itself. Future research doubtless will qualify, if not completely obviate, the arguments presented in this essay. Although power relationships within contemporary marriages are poorly understood by social scientists, this critical area very much needs a historical dimension.[67] The history of women must take into account major changes in the structure of society and the family. During the preindustrial period, women (mainly widows) exercised power as replacements for men. In the industrializing phase of the last century, married women gained power and a sense of autonomy within the family. In the postindustrial era, the potentiality for full social participation of women clearly exists. The construction of these historical stages inevitably involves oversimplification. Drawing these sharp contrasts, however, permits the historian to escape from the present-day definition of the situation. Once it is clear just what the long-run course of change actually was, more subtlety and attention to the mechanism of change will be possible in the analysis of women's history.

NOTES

1. The attempt to examine systematically the lives of ordinary women is well underway; for example, see Theodore Hershberg, "A Method for the Computerized Study of Family and Household Structure Using the Manuscript Schedules of the U.S. Census of Population," *Family in Historical Perspective Newsletter* 3 (1973): 6–20.
2. For the suggestive illustration of the impact of changing mortality on the average female, see Peter R. Uhlenberg, "A Study of Cohort Life Cycles: Cohorts of Native-Born Massachusetts Women, 1830–1920," *Population Studies* 23 (1969): 407–20.
3. Wilson H. Grabill, Clyde V. Kiser, and Pascal K. Whelpton, *The Fertility of American Woman* (New York: John Wiley & Sons, Inc., 1958), Table 67, p. 145.
4. Robert V. Wells, "Demographic Change and the Life Cycle of American Families," *Journal of Interdisciplinary History* 2 (1971): Table 2, p. 282.
5. This modal woman was constructed from the median age of household heads (less four years) from U.S. Bureau of the Census, *Historical Statistics of the United States, Colonial Times to 1957* (Washington, D.C.: Government Printing Office, 1960), Series A-263, p. 16; from the center of population gravity, from *U.S. Statistical Abstract* (87th ed., 1966), Table 11; from the mean number (5.6) of children born to rural-farm women in the north-central region born between 1835 and 1844 and married only once, U.S. Bureau of the Census, Sixteenth Census, *Population: Differential Fertility 1940 and 1910, Women by Number of Children ever Born* (Washington, D.C.: Government Printing Office, 1945), Table 81, p. 237; and from the fact that 51.3 percent of the workforce in 1880 was employed in agriculture, Stanley Lebergott, *Manpower in Economic Growth* (New York: McGraw Hill, 1964), Table A-1, p. 510.
6. Some working women may have been counted as housewives by the census takers. Lebergott, *Manpower*, pp. 70–73, however, makes a cogent case for accepting the census figures.
7. Grabill *et al.*, *Fertility*, Table 9, p. 22.
8. Ansley J. Coale and Melvin Zelnik, *New Estimates of Fertility and Population in the United States* (Princeton: Princeton University Press, 1963), p. 41.
9. Yasukichi Yasuba, *Birth Rates of the White Population in the United States, 1800-1860* (Baltimore: Johns Hopkins Press, 1961), Table IV–9, p. 119, attributes 64.3 percent of the Connecticut fertility decline between 1774 and 1890 and 74.3 percent of the New Hampshire decline between 1774 and 1890 to change in marital fertility. Longer birth intervals and an earlier age at the termination of childbearing contributed nearly equally to the decrease in marital fertility. See Daniel Scott Smith, "Change in American Family Structure before the Demographic Transition: The Case of Hingham, Massachusetts," (unpublished paper presented to the American Society for Ethnohistory, October 1972), p. 3.
10. For a summary of the importance of withdrawal in the history of European contraception, see D. V. Glass, *Population: Policies and Movements in Europe* (New York: Augustus M. Kelley, Booksellers, 1967), p. 46–50.

11. For this definition, see Aileen S. Kraditor, *Up from the Pedestal* (Chicago: Quadrangle Books, 1968), p. 5.

12. Aileen S. Kraditor, *The Ideas of the Woman Suffrage Movement* (New York: Anchor Books, 1971).

13. Carl N. Degler, "Revolution without Ideology: The Changing Place of Women in America," *Daedalus* 93 (1964): 653–70.

14. William L. O'Neill, *Everyone Was Brave* (Chicago: Quadrangle Books, 1969).

15. My use of the term conjugal is intended to be much broader than the strict application to household composition. On the relatively unchanging conjugal (or nuclear) structure of the household see Peter Laslett, ed., *Household and Family in Past Time* (Cambridge: Cambridge University Press, 1972). For an empirical demonstration of the types of changes involved see my article, "Parental Power and Marriage Patterns: An Analysis of Historical Trends in Hingham, Massachusetts," in the special historical issue of *Journal of Marriage and the Family* 35 (1973).

16. Phillipe Aries, *Centuries of Childhood: A Social History of Family Life,* trans. Robert Baldick (New York: Vintage Books, 1962).

17. Julia Cherry Spruill, *Women's Life and Work in the Southern Colonies* (Chapel Hill: University of North Carolina Press, 1938) and Elisabeth Anthony Dexter, *Colonial Women of Affairs* (Boston: Houghton Mifflin Company, 1924).

18. Richard B. Morris, *Studies in the History of American Law,* 2nd ed. (Philadelphia: Joseph M. Mitchell Co., 1959), pp. 126–200.

19. Maris Vinovskis, "Mortality Rates and Trends in Massachusetts before 1860," *Journal of Economic History* 32 (1972): 198–99. In the eighteenth century women began to live longer than men with the exception again of Ipswich.

20. Daniel Scott Smith, "Population, Family and Society in Hingham, Massachusetts, 1635–1880," (unpublished Ph.D. dissertation, University of California, Berkeley, 1973), pp. 225–27.

21. Scattered American data are available in Lawrence A. Cremin, *American Education: The Colonial Experience, 1607–1783* (New York: Harper Torchbooks, 1970), pp. 526, 533, 540. Also see Carlo M. Cipolla, *Literacy and Development in the West* (Baltimore: Penguin Books, 1969), Table 1, p. 14. Professor Kenneth Lockridge of the University of Michigan, who is undertaking a major study of literacy in early America has written me, however, that women using a mark may have been able to read.

22. Edward Shorter, "Capitalism, Culture and Sexuality: Some Competing Models," *Social Science Quarterly* 53 (1972): 339.

23. David M. Potter, "American Women and the American Character," in *History and American Society: Essays of David M. Potter,* ed. Don E. Fehrenbacher (New York: Oxford University Press, 1973), pp. 227–303.

24. Evsey D. Domar, "The Causes of Slavery or Serfdom: A Hypothesis," *Journal of Economic History* 30 (1970): 18–32.

25. See Edmund S. Morgan, "Slavery and Freedom: An American Paradox," *Journal of American History* 59 (1972): 3–29.

26. Stanley Engerman, "Some Considerations Relating to Property Rights in Man," *Journal of Economic History* 33 (1973): 56–65.

27. Jack E. Eblen, "An Analysis of Nineteenth Century Frontier Populations," *Demography* 2 (1965): 399–413.
28. See Herbert Moller, "Sex Composition and Correlated Culture Patterns of Colonial America," *William and Mary Quarterly* 2 (1945): 113–53 for data on sex ratios.
29. Alan P. Grimes, *The Puritan Ethic and Woman Suffrage* (New York: Oxford University Press, 1967).
30. Bernard Farber, *Comparative Kinship Systems* (New York: John Wiley & Sons, Inc., 1968), pp. 23–46.
31. Walter E. Houghton, *The Victorian Frame of Mind* (New Haven: Yale University Press, 1957), pp. 348–53.
32. See Smith, "Parental Power and Marriage Patterns..." *Journal of Marriage and the Family* 35 (1973).
33. Grabill *et al., Fertility*, pp. 16–19. For insights based on differentials in census child-woman ratios see Yasuba, *Birth Rates*, as well as Colin Forster and G.S.L. Tucker, *Economic Opportunity and White American Fertility Ratios, 1800–1860* (New Haven: Yale University Press, 1972). For a brief statement of the structural argument see Richard Easterlin, "Does Fertility Adjust to the Environment?" *American Economic Review* 61 (1971): 394–407.
34. John D. Kasarda, "Economic Structure and Fertility: A Comparative Analysis," *Demography* 8 (1971): 307–17.
35. Lebergott, *Manpower*, p. 63.
36. Kingsley Davis, "The American Family in Relation to Demographic Change," in *Demographic and Social Aspects of Population Growth*, eds. Charles F. Westoff and Robert Parke, Jr. (Washington, D.C.: Government Printing Office, 1972), p. 245.
37. One study involving seven Latin American cities has suggestively concluded that the "wife's motivation for employment, her education, and her preferred role seem to exert greater influence on her fertility than her actual role of employee or homemaker." Paula H. Hass, "Maternal Role Incompatibility and Fertility in Urban Latin America," *Journal of Social Issues* 28 (1972): 111–27.
38. Virginia Yans McLaughlin, "Patterns of Work and Family Organization: Buffalo's Italians," *Journal of Interdisciplinary History* 2 (1971): 299–314.
39. For the relationship between fertility and individual characteristics see the special issue of the *Journal of Political Economy* 81, pt. 2 (1973) on "new economic approaches to fertility."
40. See the summary by Gerald E. Markle and Charles B. Nam, "Sex Determination: Its Impact on Fertility," *Social Biology* 18 (1971): 73–82.
41. N. Uddenberg, P.E. Almgren and A. Nilsson, "Preference for Sex of Child among Pregnant Women," *Journal of Biosocial Science* 3 (1971): 267–80.
42. In a study of early twentieth century *Who's Who*, cited by Markle and Nam, the sex ratio of the last child was 117.4 in 5,466 families. No differences appear in Harriet L. Fancher, "The Relationship between the Occupational Status of Individuals and the Sex Ratio of their Offspring," *Human Biology* 28 (1966): 316–22.
43. William A. Alcott, *The Young Man's Wife, or Duties of Women in the Marriage Role* (Boston: George W. Light, 1837), p. 176.

44. Dio Lewis, *Chastity, or Our Secret Sins* (New York: Canfield Publishing Company, 1888), p. 18.
45. Henry C. Wright, *Marriage and Parentage* (Boston: Bela Marsh, 1853), pp. 242–55.
46. Anon, *Satan in Society* (Cincinnati: C.V. Vent, 1875), p. 153.
47. Ibid., p. 152.
48. For a discussion of the gradualness of change in sexual behavior see Daniel Scott Smith, "The Dating of the American Sexual Revolution: Evidence and Interpretation," in *The American Family in Social-Historical Perspective*, ed. Michael Gordon (New York: St. Martin's Press, 1973), pp. 321–55.
49. Quoted by George Humphrey Napheys, *The Physical Life of Women* (Philadelphia: H.C. Watts Co., 1882), p. 119.
50. Peter C. Cominos, "Late Victorian Sexual Respectability and the Social System," *International Review of Social History* 8 (1963): 18–48, 216–50.
51. Although the basic argument here was formulated independently, Randall Collins, "A Conflict Theory of Sexual Stratification," *Social Problems* 19 (1971): 3–21; and David G. Berger and Morton C. Wenger, "The Ideology of Virginity," (paper read at the 1972 meeting of the National Council on Family Relations) were very helpful in developing this theme.
52. On attitudes toward prostitution, see Margaret Wyman, "The Rise of the Fallen Woman," *American Quarterly* 3 (1951): 167–77; and Robert E. Riegel, "Changing American Attitudes Toward Prostitution," *Journal of the History of Ideas* 29 (1968): 437–52.
53. Carroll Smith-Rosenberg, "Beauty, the Beast and the Militant Woman: a Case Study in Sex Roles in Jacksonian America," *American Quarterly* 23 (1971): 562–84.
54. Ibid.
55. Nancy F. Cott, *Root of Bitterness* (New York: E.P. Dutton & Co., Inc., 1972), pp. 11–14; Kraditor, *Up From the Pedestal*, p. 21; Gerda Lerner, "The Lady and the Mill Girl: Changes in the Status of Women in the Age of Jackson," *Midcontinent American Studies Journal* 10 (1969): 5–14.
56. J.A. and Olive Banks, *Feminism and Family Planning in Victorian England* (Liverpool: Liverpool University Press, 1964); esp. pp. 53–57.
57. Ibid., p. 125.
58. In his book, *Daughters of the Promised Land* (Boston: Little, Brown, 1970), Page Smith argues that many prominent feminists had strong fathers. It might be that the true relationship, if any in fact exists, is between public feminism and high status fathers.
59. Robert A. Nisbet, *The Sociological Tradition* (New York: Basic Books, 1966), ch. 3, esp. 47–51.
60. Quoted by John L. Thomas, "Romantic Reform in America, 1815–1865," *American Quarterly* 17 (1965): 677.
61. Charles Abrams, *The Language of Cities* (New York: Viking Press, 1971), p. 60.
62. Kirk Jeffrey effectively develops this theme in "The Family as Utopian Retreat from the City: The Nineteenth Century Contribution" in *The Family, Communes and Utopian Societies*, ed. Sallie Teselle (New York: Harper Torchbooks, 1972), pp. 21–41.

63. Ibid., p. 30.
64. For a psychological emphasis see James R. McGovern, "Anna Howard Shaw: New Approaches to Feminism," *Journal of Social History* 3 (1969–70): 135–53.
65. Richard Jensen, "Family, Career, and Reform: Women Leaders of the Progressive Era," in *The American Family in Social-Historical Perspective,* Table 7, p. 277.
66. Ibid., Table 2, p. 273.
67. An analysis of recent literature of this important topic is presented by Constantina Safilios-Rothschild, "The Study of Family Power Structure: A Review 1960–1969," *Journal of Marriage and the Family* 32 (1970): 539–52.

The Female World of Love and Ritual: Relations Between Women in Nineteenth-Century America

Carroll Smith-Rosenberg

The female friendship of the nineteenth century, the long-lived, intimate, loving friendship between two women, is an excellent example of the type of historical phenomena which most historians know something about, which few have thought much about, and which virtually no one has written about.[1] It is one aspect of the female experience which consciously or unconsciously we have chosen to ignore. Yet an abundance of manuscript evidence suggests that eighteenth- and nineteenth-century women routinely formed emotional ties with other women. Such deeply felt, same-sex friendships were casually accepted in American society. Indeed, from at least the late eighteenth through the mid-nineteenth century, a female world of varied and yet highly structured relationships appears to have been an essential aspect of American society. These relationships ranged from the supportive love of sisters, through the enthusiasms of adolescent girls, to sensual avowals of love by mature women. It was a world in which men made but a shadowy appearance.[2]

Defining and analyzing same-sex relationships involves the historian in deeply problematical questions of method and interpretation. This is especially true since historians, influenced by Freud's libidinal theory, have discussed these relationships almost exclusively within the context of individual psychosexual developments or, to be more explicit, psychopathology.[3] Seeing same-sex relationships in terms of a dichotomy between normal and abnormal, they have sought the origins of such apparent deviance in childhood or adolescent trauma and detected the symptoms of "latent" homosexuality in the lives of both those who later became "overtly" homosexual and those who did not. Yet theories concerning the nature and origins of same-sex relationships are frequently contradictory or based on questionable or arbitrary data. In recent years such hypotheses have been subjected to criticism both from within and without the psychological professions. Historians who seek to work within a psychological framework, therefore, are faced with two hard questions: Do sound psychodynamic theories concerning the nature and origins of same-sex relationships exist? If so, does the historical datum exist which would permit the use of such dynamic models?

I would like to suggest an alternative approach to female friendships—one which would view them within a cultural and social setting rather than from an exclusively individual psychosexual perspective. Only by thus altering our approach will we be in the position to evaluate the appropriateness of particular dynamic interpretations. Intimate friendships between men and men and women and women existed in a larger world of social relations and social values. To interpret such friendships more fully they must be related to the structure of the American family and to the nature of sex-role divisions and of male-female relations both within the family and in society generally. The female friendship must not be seen in isolation; it must be analyzed as one aspect of women's overall relations with one another. The ties between mothers and daughters, sisters, female cousins and friends, at all stages of the female life cycle constitute the most suggestive framework for the historian to begin an analysis of intimacy and affection between women. Such an analysis would not only emphasize general cultural patterns rather than the internal dynamics of a particular family or childhood; it would shift the focus of the study from a concern with deviance to that of defining configurations of legitimate behavioral norms and options.[4]

This analysis will be based upon the correspondence and diaries of women and men in thirty-five families between the 1760s and the 1880s. These families, though limited in number, represented a broad range of the American middle class, from hard-pressed pioneer families and orphaned girls to daughters of the intellectual and social elite.

It includes families from most geographic regions, rural and urban, and a spectrum of Protestant denominations ranging from Mormon to orthodox Quaker. Although scarcely a comprehensive sample of America's increasingly heterogeneous population, it does, I believe, reflect accurately the literate middle class to which the historian working with letters and diaries is necessarily bound. It has involved an analysis of many thousands of letters written to women friends, kin, husbands, brothers, and children at every period of life from adolescence to old age. Some collections encompass virtually entire life spans; one contains over 100,000 letters as well as diaries and account books. It is my contention that an analysis of women's private letters and diaries which were never intended to be published permits the historian to explore a very private world of emotional realities central both to women's lives and to the middle-class family in nineteenth-century America.[5]

The question of female friendships is peculiarly elusive; we know so little or perhaps have forgotten so much. An intriguing and almost alien form of human relationship, they flourished in a different social structure and amidst different sexual norms. Before attempting to reconstruct their social setting, therefore, it might be best first to describe two not atypical friendships. These two friendships, intense, loving, and openly avowed, began during the women's adolescence and, despite subsequent marriages, and geographic separation, continued throughout their lives. For nearly half a century these women played a central emotional role in each other's lives, writing time and again of their love and of the pain of separation. Paradoxically to twentieth-century minds, their love appears to have been both sensual and platonic.

Sarah Butler Wister first met Jeannie Field Musgrove while vacationing with her family at Stockbridge, Massachusetts, in the summer of 1849.[6] Jeannie was then sixteen, Sarah fourteen. During the two subsequent years spent together in boarding school, they formed a deep and intimate friendship. Sarah began to keep a bouquet of flowers before Jeannie's portrait and wrote complaining of the intensity and anguish of her affection.[7] Both young women assumed nom de plumes, Jeannie a female name, Sarah a male one: they would use these secret names into old age.[8] They frequently commented on the nature of their affection: "If the day should come," Sarah wrote Jeannie in the spring of 1861, "when you failed me either through your fault or my own, I would forswear all human friendship, thenceforth." A few months later Jeannie commented: "Gratitude is a word I should never use toward you. It is perhaps a misfortune of such intimacy and love that it makes one regard all kindness as a matter of course, as one has always found it, as natural as the embrace in meeting." [9]

Sarah's marriage altered neither the frequency of their correspondence nor their desire to be together. In 1864, when twenty-nine, married, and a mother, Sarah wrote to Jeannie: "I shall be entirely alone [this coming week]. I can give you no idea how desperately I shall want you...." After one such visit Jeannie, then a spinster in New York, echoed Sarah's longing: "Dear darling Sarah! How I love you & how happy I have been! You are the joy of my life.... I cannot tell you how much happiness you gave me, nor how constantly it is all in my thoughts.... My darling how I long for the time when I shall see you...." After another visit Jeannie wrote: "I want you to tell me in your next letter, to assure me, that I am your dearest.... I do not doubt you, & I am not jealous but I long to hear you say it once more & it seems already a long time since your voice fell on my ear. So just fill a quarter page with caresses & expressions of endearment. Your silly Angelina." Jennie ended one letter: "Goodby my dearest, dearest lover—ever your own Angelina." And another, "I will go to bed ... [though] I could write all night—A thousand kisses—I love you with my whole soul—your Angelina."

When Jeannie finally married in 1870 at the age of thirty-seven, Sarah underwent a period of extreme anxiety. Two days before Jeannie's marriage Sarah, then in London, wrote desperately: "Dearest darling—How incessantly have I thought of you these eight days—all today—the entire uncertainty, the distance, the long silence—are all new features in my separation from you, grevious to be borne.... Oh Jeannie. I have thought & thought & yearned over you these two days. Are you married I wonder? My dearest love to you whenever and *who*ever you are." [10] Like many other women in this collection of thirty-five families, marriage brought Sarah and Jeannie physical separation; it did not cause emotional distance. Although at first they may have wondered how marriage would affect their relationship, their affection remained unabated throughout their lives, underscored by their loneliness and their desire to be together. [11]

During the same years that Jeannie and Sarah wrote of their love and need for each other, two slightly younger women began a similar odyssey of love, dependence and—ultimately—physical, though not emotional, separation. Molly and Helena met in 1868 while both attended the Cooper Institute School of Design for Women in New York City. For several years these young women studied and explored the city together, visited each other's families, and formed part of a social network of other artistic young women. Gradually, over the years, their initial friendship deepened into a close intimate bond which continued throughout their lives. The tone of the letters which Molly wrote to Helena changed over the years from "My dear Helena," and signed "your attached friend," to "My dearest Helena," "My Dearest," "My Beloved," and signed "Thine always," or "thine Molly." [12]

The letters they wrote to each other during these first five years permit us to reconstruct something of their relationship together. As Molly wrote in one early letter:

> I have not said to you in so many or so few words that I was happy with you during those few so incredibly short weeks but surely you do not need words to tell you what you must know. Those two or three days so dark without, so bright with firelight and contentment within I shall always remember as proof that, for a time, at least—I fancy for quite a long time—we might be sufficient for each other. We know that we can amuse each other for many idle hours together and now we know that we can also work together. And that means much, don't you think so?

She ended: "I shall return in a few days. Imagine yourself kissed many times by one who loved you so dearly."

The intensity and even physical nature of Molly's love was echoed in many of the letters she wrote during the next few years, as, for instance in this short thank-you note for a small present: "Imagine yourself kissed a dozen times my darling. Perhaps it is well for you that we are far apart. You might find my thanks so expressed rather overpowering. I have that delightful feeling that it doesn't matter much what I say or how I say it, since we shall meet so soon and forget in that moment that we were ever separated.... I shall see you soon and be content." [13]

At the end of the fifth year, however, several crises occurred. The relationship, at least in its intense form, ended, though Molly and Helena continued an intimate and complex relationship for the next half-century. The exact nature of these crises is not completely clear, but it seems to have involved Molly's decision not to live with Helena, as they had originally planned, but to remain at home because of parental insistence. Molly was now in her late twenties. Helena responded with anger and Molly became frantic at the thought that Helena would break off their relationship. Though she wrote distraught letters and made despairing attempts to see Helena, the relationship never regained its former ardor—possibly because Molly had a male suitor. [14] Within six months Helena had decided to marry a man who was, coincidentally, Molly's friend and publisher. Two years later Molly herself finally married. The letters toward the end of this period discuss the transition both women made to having male lovers—Molly spending much time reassuring Helena, who seemed depressed about the end of their relationship and with her forthcoming marriage.[15]

It is clearly difficult from a distance of 100 years and from a post-Freudian cultural perspective to decipher the complexities of Molly and Helena's relationship. Certainly Molly and Helena were lovers—emotionally if not physically. The emotional intensity and pathos of their love becomes apparent in several letters Molly wrote Helena during their crisis: "I wanted so to put my arms round my girl of all the girls in the world and tell her ... I love her as wives do love their husbands, as *friends* who have taken each other for life—and believe in her as I believe in my God. ... If I didn't love you do you suppose I'd care about anything or have ridiculous notions and panics and behave like an old fool who ought to know better. I'm going to hang on to your skirts. ... You can't get away from [my] love." Or as she wrote after Helena's decision to marry: "You know dear Helena, I really was in love with you. It was a passion such as I had never known until I saw you. I don't think it was the noblest way to love you." The theme of intense female love was one Molly again expressed in a letter she wrote to the man Helena was to marry: "Do you know sir, that until you came along I believe that she loved me almost as girls love their lovers. *I know I loved her so.* Don't you wonder that I can stand the sight of you." This was in a letter congratulating them on their forthcoming marriage.[16]

The essential question is not whether these women had genital contact and can therefore be defined as heterosexual or homosexual. The twentieth-century tendency to view human love and sexuality within a dichotomized universe of deviance and normality, genitality and platonic love, is alien to the emotions and attitudes of the nineteenth century and fundamentally distorts the nature of these women's emotional interaction. These letters are significant because they force us to place such female love in a particular historical context. There is every indication that these four women, their husbands and families—all eminently respectable and socially conservative—considered such love both socially acceptable and fully compatible with heterosexual marriage. Emotionally and cognitively, their heterosocial and their homosocial worlds were complementary.

One could argue, on the other hand, that these letters were but an example of the romantic rhetoric with which the nineteenth century surrounded the concept of friendship. Yet they possess an emotional intensity and a sensual and physical explicitness that is difficult to dismiss. Jeannie longed to hold Sarah in her arms; Molly mourned her physical isolation from Helena. Molly's love and devotion to Helena, the emotions that bound Jeannie and Sarah together, while perhaps a phenomenon of nineteenth-century society were not the less real for their Victorian origins. A survey of the correspondence and diaries of eighteenth- and nineteenth-century women indicates that Molly, Jeannie, and Sarah represented one very real behavioral and emotional option socially available to nineteenth-century women.

This is not to argue that individual needs, personalities, and family dynamics did not have a significant role in determining the nature of particular relationships. But the scholar must ask if it is historically possible and, if possible, important, to study the intensely individual aspects of psychosexual dynamics. Is it not the historian's first task to explore the social structure and the world view which made intense and sometimes sensual female love both a possible and an acceptable emotional option? From such a social perspective a new and quite different series of questions suggests itself. What emotional function did such female love serve? What was its place within the hetero- and homosocial worlds which women jointly inhabited? Did a spectrum of love-object choices exist in the nineteenth century across which some individuals, at least, were capable of moving? Without attempting to answer these questions it will be difficult to understand either nineteenth-century sexuality or the nineteenth-century family.

Several factors in American society between the mid-eighteenth and the mid-nineteenth centuries may well have permitted women to form a variety of close emotional relationships with other women. American society was characterized in large part by rigid gender-role differentiation within the family and within society as a whole, leading to the emotional segregation of women and men. The roles of daughter and mother shaded imperceptibly and ineluctably into each other, while the biological realities of frequent pregnancies, childbirth, nursing, and menopause bound women together in physical and emotional intimacy. It was within just such a social framework, I would argue, that a specifically female world did indeed develop, a world built around a generic and unself-conscious pattern of single-sex or homosocial networks. These supportive networks were institutionalized in social conventions or rituals which accompanied virtually every important event in a woman's life, from birth to death. Such female relationships were frequently supported and paralleled by severe social restrictions on intimacy between young men and women. Within such a world of emotional richness and complexity devotion to and love of other women became a plausible and socially accepted form of human interaction.

An abundance of printed and manuscript sources exists to support such a hypothesis. Etiquette books, advice books on child rearing, religious sermons, guides to young men and young women, medical texts, and school curricula all suggest that late eighteenth- and most nineteenth-century Americans assumed the existence of a world composed of distinctly male and female spheres, spheres determined by the immutable laws of God and nature.[17] The unpublished letters and diaries of Americans during this same period concur, detailing the existence of sexually segregated worlds inhabited by human beings with different values, expectations, and personalities. Contacts between men and women frequently partook of a formality and stiffness quite alien to twentieth-century America and which today we tend to define as "Victorian." Women, however, did not form an isolated and oppressed sub-category in male society. Their letters and diaries indicate that women's sphere had an essential integrity and dignity that grew out of women's shared experiences and mutual affection and that, despite the profound changes which affected American social structure and institutions between the 1760s and the 1870s, retained a constancy and predictability. The ways in which women thought of and interacted with each other remained unchanged. Continuity, not discontinuity, characterized this female world. Molly Hallock's and Jeannie Fields's words, emotions, and experiences have direct parallels in the 1760s and the 1790s.[18] There are indications in contemporary sociological and psychological literature that female closeness and support networks have continued into the twentieth century—not only among ethnic and working-class groups but even among the middle class.[19]

Most eighteenth- and nineteenth-century women lived within a world bounded by home, church, and the institution of visiting—that endless trooping of women to each others' homes for social purposes. It was a world inhabited by children and by other women.[20] Women helped each other with domestic chores and in times of sickness, sorrow, or trouble. Entire days, even weeks, might be spent almost exclusively with other women.[21] Urban and town women could devote virtually every day to visits, teas, or shopping trips with other women. Rural women developed a pattern of more extended visits that lasted weeks and sometimes months, at times even dislodging husbands from their beds and bedrooms so that dear friends might spend every hour of every day together.[22] When husbands traveled, wives routinely

moved in with other women, invited women friends to teas and sup-
pers, sat together sharing and comparing the letters they had received
from other close women friends. Secrets were exchanged and cherished, and the husband's return at times viewed with some ambivalence.[23]

Summer vacations were frequently organized to permit old friends
to meet at water spas or share a country home. In 1848, for example, a
young matron wrote cheerfully to her husband about the delightful
time she was having with five close women friends whom she had
invited to spend the summer with her; he remained at home alone to
face the heat of Philadelphia and a cholera epidemic.[24] Some ninety
years earlier, two young Quaker girls commented upon the vacation
their aunt had taken alone with another woman; their remarks were
openly envious and tell us something of the emotional quality of these
friendships: "I hear Aunt is gone with the Friend and won't be back
for two weeks, fine times indeed I think the old friends had, taking
their pleasure about the country . . . and have the advantage of that
fine woman's conversation and instruction, while we poor young girls
must spend all spring at home. . . . What a disappointment that we are
not together. . . ."[25]

Friends did not form isolated dyads but were normally part of
highly integrated networks. Knowing each other, perhaps related to
each other, they played a central role in holding communities and kin
systems together. Especially when families became geographically mobile women's long visits to each other and their frequent letters filled
with discussions of marriages and births, illness and deaths, descriptions of growing children, and reminiscences of times and people past
provided an important sense of continuity in a rapidly changing society.[26] Central to this female world was an inner core of kin. The ties
between sisters, first cousins, aunts, and nieces provided the underlying
structure upon which groups of friends and their network of female
relatives clustered. Although most of the women within this sample
would appear to be living within isolated nuclear families, the emotional ties between nonresidential kin were deep and binding and
provided one of the fundamental existential realities of women's
lives.[27] Twenty years after Parke Lewis Butler moved with her husband to Louisiana, she sent her two daughters back to Virginia to
attend school, live with their grandmother and aunt, and be integrated
back into Virginia society.[28] The constant letters between Maria Inskeep and Fanny Hampton, sisters separated in their early twenties
when Maria moved with her husband from New Jersey to Louisiana,
held their families together, making it possible for their daughters to

feel a part of their cousins' network of friends and interests.[29] The Ripley daughters, growing up in western Massachusetts in the early 1800s, spent months each year with their mother's sister and her family in distant Boston; these female cousins and their network of friends exchanged gossip-filled letters and gradually formed deeply loving and dependent ties.[30]

Women frequently spent their days within the social confines of such extended families. Sisters-in-law visited each other and, in some families, seemed to spend more time with each other than with their husbands. First cousins cared for each other's babies—for weeks or even months in times of sickness or childbirth. Sisters helped each other with housework, shopped and sewed for each other. Geographic separation was borne with difficulty. A sister's absence for even a week or two could cause loneliness and depression and would be bridged by frequent letters. Sibling rivalry was hardly unknown, but with separation or illness the theme of deep affection and dependency re-emerged.[31]

Sisterly bonds continued across a lifetime. In her old age a rural Quaker matron, Martha Jefferis, wrote to her daughter Anne concerning her own half-sister, Phoebe: "In sister Phoebe I have a real friend—she studies my comfort and waits on me like a child. . . . She is exceedingly kind and this to all other homes (set aside yours) I would prefer—it is next to being with a daughter." Phoebe's own letters confirmed Martha's evaluation of her feelings. "Thou knowest my dear sister," Phoebe wrote, "there is no one . . . that exactly feels [for] thee as I do, for I think without boasting I can truly say that my desire is for thee." [32]

Such women, whether friends or relatives, assumed an emotional centrality in each others' lives. In their diaries and letters they wrote of the joy and contentment they felt in each others' company, their sense of isolation and despair when apart. The regularity of their correspondence underlines the sincerity of their words. Women named their daughters after one another and sought to integrate dear friends into their lives after marriage.[33] As one young bride wrote to an old friend shortly after her marriage: "I want to see you and talk with you and feel that we are united by the same bonds of sympathy and congeniality as ever." [34] After years of friendship one aging woman wrote of another: "Time cannot destroy the fascination of her manner . . . her voice is music to the ear. . . ." [35] Women made elaborate presents for each other, ranging from the Quakers' frugal pies and breads to painted velvet bags and phantom bouquets.[36] When a friend died, their grief was deeply felt. Martha Jefferis was unable to write to her daughter for three weeks because of the sorrow she felt at the death of a dear friend. Such distress was not unusual. A generation earlier a young Massachusetts farm woman filled pages of her diary with her grief at the death of her "dearest friend" and transcribed the letters of condolence other women sent her. She marked the anniversary of Rachel's death each year in her diary, contrasting her faithfulness with that of Rachel's husband who had soon remarried.[37]

These female friendships served a number of emotional functions. Within this secure and empathetic world women could share sorrows, anxieties, and joys, confident that other women had experienced similar emotions. One mid-nineteenth-century rural matron in a letter to her daughter discussed this particular aspect of women's friendships: "To have such a friend as thyself to look to and sympathize with her—and enter into all her little needs and in whose bosom she could with freedom pour forth her joys and sorrows—such a friend would very much relieve the tedium of many a wearisome hour. . . ." A generation later Molly more informally underscored the importance of this same function in a letter to Helena: "Suppose I come down . . . [and] spend Sunday with you quietly," she wrote Helena ". . . that means talking all the time until you are relieved of all your latest troubles, and I of mine. . . ."[38] These were frequently troubles that apparently no man could understand. When Anne Jefferis Sheppard was first married, she and her older sister Edith (who then lived with Anne) wrote in detail to their mother of the severe depression and anxiety which they experienced. Moses Sheppard, Anne's husband, added cheerful postscripts to the sisters' letters—which he had clearly not read—remarking on Anne's and Edith's contentment. Theirs was an emotional world to which he had little access.[39]

This was, as well, a female world in which hostility and criticism of other women were discouraged, and thus a milieu in which women could develop a sense of inner security and self-esteem. As one young woman wrote to her mother's longtime friend: "I cannot sufficiently thank you for the kind unvaried affection & indulgence you have ever shown and expressed both by words and actions for me. . . . Happy would it be did all the world view me as you do, through the medium of kindness and forbearance."[40] They valued each other. Women, who had little status or power in the larger world of male concerns, possessed status and power in the lives and worlds of other women.[41]

An intimate mother-daughter relationship lay at the heart of this female world. The diaries and letters of both mothers and daughters attest to their closeness and mutual emotional dependency. Daughters routinely discussed their mother's health and activities with their own friends, expressed anxiety in cases of their mother's ill health and concern for her cares.[42] Expressions of hostility which we would today consider routine on the part of both mothers and daughters seem to have been uncommon indeed. On the contrary, this sample of families indicates that the normal relationship between mother and daughter was one of sympathy and understanding.[43] Only sickness or great geographic distance was allowed to cause extended separation. When marriage did result in such separation, both viewed the distance between them with distress.[44] Something of this sympathy and love between mothers and daughters is evident in a letter Sarah Alden Ripley, at age sixty-nine, wrote her youngest and recently married daughter: "You do not know how much I miss you, not only when I struggle in and out of my mortal envelop and pump my nightly potation and no longer pour into your sympathizing ear my senile gossip, but all the day I muse away, since the sound of your voice no longer rouses me to sympathy with your joys or sorrows.... You cannot know how much I miss your affectionate demonstrations."[45] A dozen aging mothers in this sample of other thirty families echoed her sentiments.

Central to these mother-daughter relations is what might be described as an apprenticeship system. In those families where the daughter followed the mother into a life of traditional domesticity, mothers and other older women carefully trained daughters in the arts of housewifery and motherhood. Such training undoubtedly occurred throughout a girl's childhood but became more systematized, almost ritualistic, in the years following the end of her formal education and before her marriage. At this time a girl either returned home from boarding school or no longer divided her time between home and school. Rather, she devoted her energies on two tasks: mastering new domestic skills and participating in the visiting and social activities necessary to finding a husband. Under the careful supervision of their mothers and of older female relatives, such late-adolescent girls temporarily took over the household management from their mothers, tended their young nieces and nephews, and helped in childbirth, nursing, and weaning. Such experiences tied the generations together in shared skills and emotional interaction.[46]

Daughters were born into a female world. Their mother's life expectations and sympathetic network of friends and relations were among the first realities in the life of the developing child. As long as the mother's domestic role remained relatively stable and few viable alternatives competed with it, daughters tended to accept their mother's world and to turn automatically to other women for support and intimacy. It was within this closed and intimate female world that the young girl grew toward womanhood.

One could speculate at length concerning the absence of that mother-daughter hostility today considered almost inevitable to an adolescent's struggle for autonomy and self-identity. It is possible that taboos against female aggression and hostility were sufficiently strong to repress even that between mothers and their adolescent daughters. Yet these letters seem so alive and the interest of daughters in their mothers' affairs so vital and genuine that it is difficult to interpret their closeness exclusively in terms of repression and denial. The functional bonds that held mothers and daughters together in a world that permitted few alternatives to domesticity might well have created a source of mutuality and trust absent in societies where greater options were available for daughters than for mothers. Furthermore, the extended female network—a daughter's close ties with her own older sisters, cousins, and aunts—may well have permitted a diffusion and a relaxation of mother-daughter identification and so have aided a daughter in her struggle for identity and autonomy. None of these explanations are mutually exclusive; all may well have interacted to produce the degree of empathy evident in those letters and diaries.

At some point in adolescence, the young girl began to move outside the matrix of her mother's support group to develop a network of her own. Among the middle class, at least, this transition toward what was at the same time both a limited autonomy and a repetition of her mother's life seemed to have most frequently coincided with a girl's going to school. Indeed education appears to have played a crucial role in the lives of most of the families in this study. Attending school for a few months, for a year, or longer, was common even among daughters of relatively poor families, while middle-class girls routinely spent at least a year in boarding school.[47] These school years ordinarily marked a girl's first separation from home. They served to wean the daughter from her home, to train her in the essential social graces, and, ultimately, to help introduce her into the marriage market. It was not infrequently a trying emotional experience for both mother and daughter.[48]

In this process of leaving one home and adjusting to another, the mother's friends and relatives played a key transitional role. Such older women routinely accepted the role of foster mother; they supervised the young girl's deportment, monitored her health and introduced her to their own network of female friends and kin.[49] Not infrequently women, friends from their own school years, arranged to send their daughters to the same school so that the girls might form bonds paralleling those their mothers had made. For years Molly and Helena wrote of their daughters' meeting and worried over each others' children. When Molly finally brought her daughter east to school, their first act on reaching New York was to meet Helena and her daughters. Elizabeth Bordley Gibson virtually adopted the daughters of her school chum, Eleanor Custis Lewis. The Lewis daughters soon began to write Elizabeth Gibson letters with the salutation "Dearest Mama." Eleuthera DuPont, attending boarding school in Philadelphia at roughly the same time as the Lewis girls, developed a parallel relationship with her mother's friend, Elizabeth McKie Smith. Eleuthera went to the same school and became a close friend of the Smith girls and eventually married their first cousin. During this period she routinely called Mrs. Smith "Mother." Indeed Eleuthera so internalized the sense of having two mothers that she casually wrote her sisters of her "Mamma's" visits at her "mother's" house—that is at Mrs. Smith's.[50]

Even more important to this process of maturation than their mother's friends were the female friends young women made at school. Young girls helped each other overcome homesickness and endure the crises of adolescence. They gossiped about beaux, incorporated each other into their own kinship systems, and attended and gave teas and balls together. Older girls in boarding school "adopted" younger ones, who called them "Mother."[51] Dear friends might indeed continue this pattern of adoption and mothering throughout their lives; one woman might routinely assume the nurturing role of pseudomother, the other the dependency role of daughter. The pseudomother performed for the other woman all the services which we normally associate with mothers: she went to absurd lengths to purchase items her "daughter" could have obtained from other sources, gave advice and functioned as an idealized figure in her "daughter's" imagination. Helena played such a role for Molly, as did Sarah for Jeannie. Elizabeth Bordley Gibson bought almost all Eleanor Parke Custis Lewis's necessities—from shoes and corset covers to bedding and harp strings—and sent them from Philadelphia to Virginia, a procedure that sometimes took months. Eleanor frequently asked Elizabeth to take back her purchases, have them redone, and argue with shopkeepers about prices. These were favors automatically asked and complied with. Anne Jefferis Sheppard made the analogy very explicitly in a letter to her own mother written shortly after Anne's marriage, when she was feeling depressed about their separation: "Mary Paulen is truly kind, almost acts the part of a mother and trys to aid and *comfort me,* and also to *lighten my new cares.*"[52]

A comparison of the references to men and women in these young women's letters is striking. Boys were obviously indispensable to the elaborate courtship ritual girls engaged in. In these teenage letters and diaries, however, boys appear distant and warded off—an effect produced both by the girl's sense of bonding and by a highly developed and deprecatory whimsy. Girls joked among themselves about the conceit, poor looks or affectations of suitors. Rarely, especially in the eighteenth and early nineteenth centuries, were favorable remarks exchanged. Indeed, while hostility and criticism of other women were so rare as to seem almost tabooed, young women permitted themselves to express a great deal of hostility toward peer-group men.[53] When unacceptable suitors appeared, girls might even band together to harass them. When one such unfortunate came to court Sophie DuPont she hid in her room, first sending her sister Eleuthera to entertain him and then dispatching a number of urgent notes to her neighboring sister-in-law, cousins, and a visiting friend who all came to Sophie's support. A wild female romp ensued, ending only when Sophie banged into a door, lacerated her nose, and retired, with her female cohorts, to bed. Her brother and the presumably disconcerted suitor were left alone. These were not the antics of teenagers but of women in their early and mid-twenties.[54]

Even if young men were acceptable suitors, girls referred to them formally and obliquely: "The last week I received the unexpected intelligence of the arrival of a friend in Boston," Sarah Ripley wrote in her diary of the young man to whom she had been engaged for years and whom she would shortly marry. Harriet Manigault assiduously kept a lively and gossipy diary during the three years preceding her marriage, yet did not once comment upon her own engagement nor indeed make any personal references to her fiance—who was never identified as such but always referred to as Mr. Wilcox.[55] The point is not that these young women were hostile to young men. Far from it; they sought marriage and domesticity. Yet in these letters and diaries men appear as an other or out group, segregated into different schools, supported by their own male network of friends and kin, socialized to different behavior, and coached to a proper formality in courtship behavior. As a consequence, relations between young women and men frequently lacked the spontaneity and emotional intimacy that characterized the young girls' ties to each other.

Indeed, in sharp contrast to their distant relations with boys, young women's relations with each other were close, often frolicsome, and surprisingly long lasting and devoted. They wrote secret missives to each other, spent long solitary days with each other, curled up together in bed at night to whisper fantasies and secrets.[56] In 1862 one young woman in her early twenties described one such scene to an absent friend: "I have sat up to midnight listening to the confidences of Constance Kinney, whose heart was opened by that most charming of all situations, a seat on a bedside late at night, when all the household are asleep & only oneself & one's confidante survive in wakefulness. So she has told me all her loves and tried to get some confidences in return but being five or six years older than she, I know better. . . ." [57] Elizabeth Bordley and Nelly Parke Custis, teenagers in Philadelphia in the 1790s, routinely secreted themselves until late each night in Nelly's attic, where they each wrote a novel about the other.[58] Quite a few young women kept diaries, and it was a sign of special friendship to show their diaries to each other. The emotional quality of such exchanges emerges from the comments of one young girl who grew up along the Ohio frontier:

> Sisters CW and RT keep diaries & allow me the inestimable pleasure of reading them and in turn they see mine—but O shame covers my face when I think of it; theirs is so much better than mine, that every time. Then I think well now I *will* burn mine but upon second thought it would deprive me the pleasure of reading theirs, for I esteem it a very great privilege indeed, as well as very improving, as we lay our hearts open to each other, it heightens our love & helps to cherish & keep alive that sweet soothing friendship and endears us to each other by that soft attraction.[59]

Girls routinely slept together, kissed and hugged each other. Indeed, while waltzing with young men scandalized the otherwise flighty and highly fashionable Harriet Manigault, she considered waltzing with other young women not only acceptable but pleasant.[60]

Marriage followed adolescence. With increasing frequency in the nineteenth century, marriage involved a girl's traumatic removal from her mother and her mother's network. It involved, as well, adjustment to a husband, who, because he was male came to marriage with both a different world view and vastly different experiences. Not surprisingly, marriage was an event surrounded with supportive, almost ritualistic, practices. (Weddings are one of the last female rituals remaining in twentieth-century America.) Young women routinely spent the months preceding their marriage almost exclusively with other women—at neighborhood sewing bees and quilting parties or in a round of visits to geographically distant friends and relatives. Ostensibly they went to receive assistance in the practical preparations for their new home—sewing and quilting a trousseau and linen—but of equal importance, they appear to have gained emotional support and reassurance. Sarah Ripley spent over a month with friends and relatives in Boston and Hingham before her wedding; Parke Custis Lewis exchanged visits with her aunts and first cousins throughout Virginia.[61] Anne Jefferis, who married with some hesitation, spent virtually half a year in endless visiting with cousins, aunts, and friends. Despite their reassurance and support, however, she would not marry Moses Sheppard until her sister Edith and her cousin Rebecca moved into the groom's house, met his friends, and explored his personality.[62] The wedding did not take place until Edith wrote to Anne: "I can say in truth I am entirely willing thou shouldst follow him even away in the Jersey sands believing if thou are not happy in thy future home it will not be any fault on his part. . . ."[63]

Sisters, cousins, and friends frequently accompanied newlyweds on their wedding night and wedding trip, which often involved additional family visiting. Such extensive visits presumably served to wean the daughter from her family of origin. As such they often contained a note of ambivalence. Nelly Custis, for example, reported homesickness and loneliness on her wedding trip. "I left my Beloved and revered Grandmamma with sincere regret," she wrote Elizabeth Bordley. "It was sometime before I could feel reconciled to traveling without her." Perhaps they also functioned to reassure the young woman herself, and her friends and kin, that though marriage might alter it would not destroy old bonds of intimacy and familiarity.[64]

Married life, too, was structured about a host of female rituals. Childbirth, especially the birth of the first child, became virtually a *rite de passage*, with a lengthy seclusion of the woman before and after delivery, severe restrictions on her activities, and finally a dramatic reemergence.[65] This seclusion was supervised by mothers, sisters, and loving friends. Nursing and weaning involved the advice and assistance of female friends and relatives. So did miscarriage.[66] Death, like birth, was structured around elaborate unisexed rituals. When Nelly Parke Custis Lewis rushed to nurse her daughter who was critically ill while away at school, Nelly received support, not from her husband, who remained on their plantation, but from her old school friend, Elizabeth Bordley. Elizabeth aided Nelly in caring for her dying daughter, cared for Nelly's other children, played a major role in the elaborate funeral arrangements (which the father did not attend), and frequently visited the girl's grave at the mother's request. For years Elizabeth continued to be the confidante of Nelly's anguished recollections of her lost daughter. These memories, Nelly's letters make clear, were for Elizabeth alone. "Mr. L. knows nothing of this," was a frequent comment.[67] Virtually every collection of letters and diaries in my sample contained evidence of women turning to each other for comfort when facing the frequent and unavoidable deaths of the eighteenth and nineteenth centuries.[68] While mourning for her father's death, Sophie DuPont received elaborate letters and visits of condolence—all from women. No man wrote or visited Sophie to offer sympathy at her father's death.[69] Among rural Pennsylvania Quakers, death and mourning rituals assumed an even more extreme same-sex form, with men or women largely barred from the deathbeds of the other sex. Women relatives and friends slept with the dying woman, nursed her, and prepared her body for burial.[70]

Eighteenth- and nineteenth-century women thus lived in emotional proximity to each other. Friendships and intimacies followed the biological ebb and flow of women's lives. Marriage and pregnancy, childbirth and weaning, sickness and death involved physical and psychic trauma which comfort and sympathy made easier to bear. Intense bonds of love and intimacy bound together those women who, offering each other aid and sympathy, shared such stressful moments.

These bonds were often physical as well as emotional. An undeniably romantic and even sensual note frequently marked female relationships. This theme, significant throughout the stages of a woman's life, surfaced first during adolescence. As one teenager from a struggling pioneer family in the Ohio Valley wrote in her diary in 1808: "I laid with my dear R[ebecca] and a glorious good talk we had until about 4 [A.M.]—O how hard I do *love* her. . . ." [71] Only a few years later Bostonian Eunice Callender carved her initials and Sarah Ripley's into a favorite tree, along with a pledge of eternal love, and then waited breathlessly for Sarah to discover and respond to her declaration of affection. The response appears to have been affirmative.[72] A half-century later urbane and sophisticated Katherine Wharton commented upon meeting an old school chum: "She was a great pet of mine at school & I thought as I watched her light figure how often I had held her in my arms—how dear she had once been to me." Katie maintained a long intimate friendship with another girl. When a young man began to court this friend seriously, Katie commented in her diary that she had never realized "how deeply I loved Eng and how fully." She wrote over and over again in that entry: "Indeed I love her!" and only with great reluctance left the city that summer since it meant also leaving Eng with Eng's new suitor.[73]

Peggy Emlen, a Quaker adolescent in Philadelphia in the 1760s, expressed similar feelings about her first cousin, Sally Logan. The girls sent love poems to each other (not unlike the ones Elizabeth Bordley wrote to Nelly Custis a generation later), took long solitary walks together, and even haunted the empty house of the other when one was out of town. Indeed Sally's absences from Philadelphia caused Peggy acute unhappiness. So strong were Peggy's feelings that her brothers began to tease her about her affection for Sally and threatened to steal Sally's letters, much to both girls' alarm. In one letter that Peggy wrote the absent Sally she elaborately described the depth and nature of her feelings: "I have not words to express my impatience to see My Dear Cousin, what would I not give just now for an hours sweet conversation with her, it seems as if I had a thousand things to say to thee, yet when I see thee, everything will be forgot thro' joy. . . . I have a very great friendship for several Girls yet it dont give me so much uneasiness at being absent from them as from thee. . . . [Let us] go and spend a day down at our place together and there unmolested enjoy each others company." [74]

Sarah Alden Ripley, a young, highly educated woman, formed a similar intense relationship, in this instance with a woman somewhat older than herself. The immediate bond of friendship rested on their atypically intense scholarly interests, but it soon involved strong emotions, at least on Sarah's part. "Friendship," she wrote Mary Emerson, "is fast twining about her willing captive the silken hands of dependence, a dependence so sweet who would renounce it for the apathy of self-sufficiency?" Subsequent letters became far more emotional, almost conspiratorial. Mary visited Sarah secretly in her room, or the two women crept away from family and friends to meet in a nearby woods. Sarah became jealous of Mary's other young woman friends. Mary's trips away from Boston also thrust Sarah into periods of anguished depression. Interestingly, the letters detailing their love were not destroyed but were preserved and even reprinted in a eulogistic biography of Sarah Alden Ripley. [75]

Tender letters between adolescent women, confessions of loneliness and emotional dependency, were not peculiar to Sarah Alden, Peggy Emlen, or Katie Wharton. They are found throughout the letters of the thirty-five families studied. They have, of course, their parallel today in the musings of many female adolescents. Yet these eighteenth- and nineteenth-century friendships lasted with undiminished, indeed often increased, intensity throughout the women's lives. Sarah Alden Ripley's first child was named after Mary Emerson. Nelly Custis Lewis's love for and dependence on Elizabeth Bordley Gibson only increased after her marriage. Eunice Callender remained enamored of her cousin Sarah Ripley for years and rejected as impossible the suggestion by another woman that their love might some day fade away.[76] Sophie DuPont and her childhood friend, Clementina Smith, exchanged letters filled with love and dependency for forty years while another dear friend, Mary Black Couper, wrote of dreaming that she, Sophie, and her husband were all united in one marriage. Mary's letters to Sophie are filled with avowals of love and indications of ambivalence toward her own husband. Eliza Schlatter, another of Sophie's intimate friends, wrote to her at a time of crisis: "I wish I could be with you present in the body as well as the mind & heart—I would turn your *good husband out of bed*—and snuggle into you and we would have a long talk like old times in Pine St.—I want to tell you so many things that are not *writable. . . ."* [77]

Such mutual dependency and deep affection is a central existential reality coloring the world of supportive networks and rituals. In the case of Katie, Sophie, or Eunice—as with Molly, Jeannie, and Sarah—their need for closeness and support merged with more intense demands for a love which was at the same time both emotional and sensual. Perhaps the most explicit statement concerning women's lifelong friendships appeared in the letter abolitionist and reformer Mary Grew wrote about the same time, referring to her own love for her dear friend and lifelong companion, Margaret Burleigh. Grew wrote, in response to a letter of condolence from another woman on Burleigh's death: "Your words respecting my beloved friend touch me deeply. Evidently . . . you comprehend and appreciate, as few persons do . . . the nature of the relation which existed, which exists, between her and myself. Her only surviving niece . . . also does. To me it seems to have been a closer union than that of most marriages. We know there have been other such between two men and also between two women. And why should there not be. Love is spiritual, only passion is sexual." [78]

How then can we ultimately interpret these long-lived intimate female relationships and integrate them into our understanding of Victorian sexuality? Their ambivalent and romantic rhetoric presents us with an ultimate puzzle: the relationship along the spectrum of human emotions between love, sensuality, and sexuality.

One is tempted, as I have remarked, to compare Molly, Peggy, or Sophie's relationships with the friendships adolescent girls in the twentieth century routinely form—close friendships of great emotional intensity. Helena Deutsch and Clara Thompson have both described these friendships as emotionally necessary to a girl's psychosexual development. But, they warn, such friendships might shade into adolescent and postadolescent homosexuality.[79]

It is possible to speculate that in the twentieth century a number of cultural taboos evolved to cut short the homosocial ties of girlhood and to impel the emerging women of thirteen or fourteen toward heterosexual relationships. In contrast, nineteenth-century American society did not taboo close female relationships but rather recognized them as a socially viable form of human contact—and, as such, acceptable throughout a woman's life. Indeed it was not these homosocial ties that were inhibited but rather heterosexual leanings. While closeness, freedom of emotional expression, and uninhibited physical contact characterized women's relationships with each other, the opposite was frequently true of male-female relationships. One could thus argue that within such a world of female support, intimacy, and ritual it was only to be expected that adult women would turn trustingly and lovingly to each other. It was a behavior they had observed and learned since childhood. A different type of emotional landscape existed in the nineteenth century, one in which Molly and Helena's love became a natural development.

Of perhaps equal significance are the implications we can garner from this framework for the understanding of heterosexual marriages in the nineteenth century. If men and women grew up as they did in relatively homogeneous and segregated sexual groups, then marriage represented a major problem in adjustment. From this perspective we could interpret much of the emotional stiffness and distance that we associate with Victorian marriage as a structural consequence of contemporary sex-role differentiation and gender-role socialization. With marriage both women and men had to adjust to life with a person who was, in essence, a member of an alien group.

I have thus far substituted a cultural or psychosocial for a psychosexual interpretation of women's emotional bonding. But there are psychosexual implications in this model which I think it only fair to make more explicit. Despite Sigmund Freud's insistence on the bisexuality of us all or the recent American Psychiatric Association decision on homosexuality, many psychiatrists today tend explicitly or implicitly to view homosexuality as a totally alien or pathological behavior—as totally unlike heterosexuality. I suspect that in essence they may have adopted an explanatory model similar to the one used in discussing schizophrenia. As a psychiatrist can speak of schizophrenia and of a borderline schizophrenic personality as both ultimately and fundamentally different from a normal or neurotic personality, so they also think of both homosexuality and latent homosexuality as states totally different from heterosexuality. With this rapidly dichotomous model of assumption, "latent homosexuality" becomes the indication of a disease in progress—seeds of a pathology which belie the reality of an individual's heterosexuality.

Yet at the same time we are well aware that cultural values can effect choices in the gender of a person's sexual partner. We, for instance, do not necessarily consider homosexual-object choice among men in prison, on shipboard or in boarding schools a necessary indication of pathology. I would urge that we expand this relativistic model and hypothesize that a number of cultures might well tolerate or even encourage diversity in sexual and nonsexual relations. Based on my research into this nineteenth-century world of female intimacy, I would further suggest that rather than seeing a gulf between the normal and the abnormal we view sexual and emotional impulses as part of a continuum or spectrum of affect gradations strongly effected by cultural norms and arrangements, a continuum influenced in part by observed and thus learned behavior. At one end of the continuum lies committed heterosexuality, at the other uncompromising homosexuality; between, a wide latitude of emotions and sexual feelings. Certain cultures and environments permit individuals a great deal of freedom in moving across this spectrum. I would like to suggest that the nineteenth century was such a cultural environment. That is, the supposedly repressive and destructive Victorian sexual ethos, may have been more flexible and responsive to the needs of particular individuals than those of mid-twentieth century.

NOTES

1. The most notable exception to this rule is now eleven years old: William R. Taylor and Christopher Lasch, "Two Kindred 'Spirits': Sorority and Family in New England, 1839–1846," *New England Quarterly* 36 (1963): 25–41. Taylor has made a valuable contribution to the history of women and the history of the family with his concept of "sororial" relations. I do not, however, accept the Taylor-Lasch thesis that female friendships developed in the mid-nineteenth century because of geographic mobility and the breakup of the colonial family. I have found these friendships as frequently in the eighteenth century as in the nineteenth and would hypothesize that the geographic mobility of the mid-nineteenth century eroded them as it did so many other traditional social institutions. Helen Vendler *(Review of Notable American Women, 1607–1950,* ed. Edward James and Janet James, *New York Times* [November 5, 1972]: sec. 7) points out the significance of these friendships.
2. I do not wish to deny the importance of women's relations with particular men. Obviously, women were close to brothers, husbands, fathers, and sons. However, there is evidence that despite such closeness relationships

between men and women differed in both emotional texture and frequency from those between women. Women's relations with each other, although they played a central role in the American family and American society, have been so seldom examined either by general social historians or by historians of the family that I wish in this article simply to examine their nature and analyze their implications for our understanding of social relations and social structure. I have discussed some aspects of male-female relationships in two articles: "Puberty to Menopause: The Cycle of Feminity in Nineteenth-Century America," *Feminist Studies* 1 (1973): 58–72, and, with Charles Rosenberg, "The Female Animal: Medical and Biological Views of Women in 19th Century America," *Journal of American History* 59 (1973): 331–56.

3. See Freud's classic paper on homosexuality, "Three Essays on the Theory of Sexuality," in *The Standard Edition of the Complete Psychological Works of Sigmund Freud*, trans. James Strachey (London: Hogarth Press, 1953), 7:135–72. The essays originally appeared in 1905. Prof. Roy Shafer, Department of Psychiatry, Yale University, has pointed out that Freud's view of sexual behavior was strongly influenced by nineteenth-century evolutionary thought. Within Freud's schema, genital heterosexuality marked the height of human development (Shafer, "Problems in Freud's Psychology of Women," *Journal of the American Psychoanalytic Association* 22 [1974]: 459–85).

4. For a novel and most important exposition of one theory of behavioral norms and options and its application to the study of human sexuality, see Charles Rosenberg, "Sexuality, Class and Role," *American Quarterly* 25 (1973): 131–53.

5. See, e.g., the letters of Peggy Emlen to Sally Logan, 1768–72, Wells Morris Collection, Box 1, Historical Society of Pennsylvania; and the Eleanor Parke Custis Lewis Letters, Historical Society of Pennsylvania, Philadelphia.

6. Sarah Butler Wister was the daughter of Fanny Kemble and Pierce Butler. In 1859 she married a Philadelphia physician, Owen Wister. The novelist Owen Wister is her son. Jeannie Field Musgrove was the half-orphaned daughter of constitutional lawyer and New York Republican politician David Dudley Field. Their correspondence (1855–98) is in the Sarah Butler Wister Papers, Wister Family Papers, Historical Society of Pennsylvania.

7. Sarah Butler, Butler Place, S.C., to Jeannie Field, New York, September 14, 1855.

8. See, e.g., Sarah Butler Wister, Germantown, Pa., to Jeannie Field, New York, September 25, 1862, October 21, 1863; or Jeannie Field, New York, to Sarah Butler Wister, Germantown, July 3, 1861, January 23 and July 12, 1863.

9. Sarah Butler Wister, Germantown, to Jeannie Field, New York, June 5, 1861, February 29, 1864; Jeannie Field to Sarah Butler Wister, November 22, 1861, January 4 and June 14, 1863.

10. Sarah Butler Wister, London, to Jeannie Field Musgrove, New York, June 18 and August 3, 1870.

11. See, e.g., two of Sarah's letters to Jeannie: December 21, 1873, July 16, 1878.

12. This is the 1868-1920 correspondence between Mary Hallock Foote and Helena, a New York friend (the Mary Hallock Foote Papers are in the Manuscript Division, Stanford University). Wallace E. Stegner has written a fictionalized biography of Mary Hallock Foote *(Angle of Repose* [Garden City, N.Y.: Doubleday & Co., 1971]). See, as well, her autobiography: Mary Hallock Foote, *A Victorian Gentlewoman in the Far West: The Reminiscences of Mary Hallock Foote*, ed. Rodman W. Paul (San Marino, Calif.: Huntington Library, 1972). In many ways these letters are typical of those women wrote to other women. Women frequently began letters to each other with salutations such as "Dearest," "My Most Beloved," "You Darling Girl," and signed them "tenderly" or "to my dear dear sweet friend, good-bye." Without the least self-consciousness, one woman in her frequent letters to a female friend referred to her husband as "my other love." She was by no means unique. See, e.g., Annie to Charlene Van Vleck Anderson, Appleton, Wis., June 10, 1871, Anderson Family Papers, Manuscript Division, Stanford University; Maggie to Emily Howland, Philadelphia, July 12, 1851, Howland Family Papers, Phoebe King Collection, Friends Historical Library, Swarthmore College; Mary Jane Burleigh to Emily Howland, Sherwood, N.Y., March 27, 1872, Howland Family Papers, Sophia Smith Collection, Smith College; Mary Black Couper to Sophia Madeleine DuPont, Wilmington, Del.: n.d. [1834] (two letters), Samuel Francis DuPont Papers, Eleutherian Mills Foundation, Wilmington, Del.; Phoebe Middleton, Concordeville, Pa., to Martha Jefferis, Chester County, Pa., February 22, 1848; and see in general the correspondence (1838-49) between Rebecca Biddle of Philadelphia and Martha Jefferis, Chester County, Pa., Jefferis Family Correspondence, Chester County Historical Society, West Chester, Pa.; Phoebe Bradford Diary, June 7 and July 13, 1832, Historical Society of Pennsylvania; Sarah Alden Ripley, to Abba Allyn, Boston, n.d. [1818-20], and Sarah Alden Ripley to Sophia Bradford, November 30, 1854, in the Sarah Alden Ripley Correspondence, Schlesinger Library, Radcliffe College; Fanny Canby Ferris to Anne Biddle, Philadelphia, October 11 and November 19, 1811, December 26, 1813, Fanny Canby to Mary Canby, May 27, 1801, Mary R. Garrigues to Mary Canby, five letters n.d., [1802-8], Anne Biddle to Mary Canby, two letters, n.d., May 16, July 13 and November 24, 1806, June 14, 1807, June 5, 1808, Anne Sterling Biddle Family Papers, Friends Historical Society, Swarthmore College; Harriet Manigault Wilcox Diary, August 7, 1814, Historical Society of Pennsylvania. See as well the correspondence between Harriet Manigault Wilcox's mother, Mrs. Gabriel Manigault, Philadelphia, and Mrs. Henry Middletown, Charleston, S.C., between 1810 and 1830, Cadwalader Collection, J. Francis Fisher Section, Historical Society of Pennsylvania. The basis and nature of such friendships can be seen in the comments of Sarah Alden Ripley to her sister-in-law and long-time friend, Sophia Bradford: "Hearing that you are not well reminds me of what it would be to lose your loving society. We have kept step together through a long piece of road in the weary journey of life. We have loved the same beings and wept together over their graves" (Mrs. O.J. Wister and Miss Agnes Irwin, eds., *Worthy Women of Our First Century* [Philadelphia: J.B. Lippincott & Co., 1877] p. 195).

13. Mary Hallock [Foote] to Helena, n.d. [1869–70], n.d. [1871–72], Folder 1, Mary Hallock Foote Letters, Manuscript Division, Stanford University.

14. Mary Hallock [Foote] to Helena, September 15 and 23, 1873, n.d. [October 1873], October 12, 1873.

15. Mary Hallock [Foote] to Helena, n.d. [January 1874], n.d. [Spring 1874].

16. Mary Hallock [Foote] to Helena, September 23, 1873; Mary Hallock [Foote] to Richard, December 13, 1873. Molly's and Helena's relationship continued for the rest of their lives. Molly's letters are filled with tender and intimate references, as when she wrote, twenty years later and from 2,000 miles away: "It isn't because you are good that I love you—but for the essence of you which is like perfume" (n.d. [1890s?]).

17. I am in the midst of a larger study of adult gender-roles and gender-role socialization in America, 1785–1895. For a discussion of social attitudes toward appropriate male and female roles, see Barbara Welter, "The Cult of True Womanhood: 1820–1860," *American Quarterly* 18 (Summer 1966): 151–74; Ann Firor Scott, *The Southern Lady: From Pedestal to Politics, 1830–1930* (Chicago: University of Chicago Press, 1970), chaps. 1–2; Smith-Rosenberg and Rosenberg.

18. See, e.g., the letters of Peggy Emlen to Sally Logan, 1768–72, Wells Morris Collection, Box 1, Historical Society of Pennsylvania; and the Eleanor Parke Custis Lewis Letters, Historical Society of Pennsylvania.

19. See esp. Elizabeth Botts, *Family and Social Network* (London: Tavistock Publications, 1957); Michael Young and Peter Willmott, *Family and Kinship in East London,* rev. ed. (Baltimore: Penguin Books, 1964).

20. This pattern seemed to cross class barriers. A letter that an Irish domestic wrote in the 1830s contains seventeen separate references to women and but only seven to men, most of whom were relatives and two of whom were infant brothers living with her mother and mentioned in relation to her mother (Ann McGrann, Philadelphia, to Sophie M. DuPont, Philadelphia, July 3, 1834, Sophie Madeleine DuPont Letters, Eleutherian Mills Foundation).

21. Harriett Manigault Diary, June 28, 1814, and passim; Jeannie Field, New York, to Sarah Butler Wister, Germantown, April 19, 1863; Phoebe Bradford Diary, January 30, February 19, March 4, August 11, and October 14, 1832, Historical Society of Pennsylvania; Sophie M. DuPont, Brandywine, to Henry DuPont, Germantown, July 9, 1827, Eleutherian Mills Foundation.

22. Martha Jefferis to Anne Jefferis Sheppard, July 9, 1843; Anne Jefferis Sheppard to Martha Jefferis, June 28, 1846; Anne Sterling Biddle Papers, passim, Biddle Family Papers, Friends Historical Society, Swarthmore College; Eleanor Parke Custis Lewis, Virginia, to Elizabeth Bordley Gibson, Philadelphia, November 24 and December 4, 1820, November 6, 1821.

23. Phoebe Bradford Diary, January 13, November 16–19, 1832, April 26 and May 7, 1833; Abigail Brackett Lyman to Mrs. Catling, Litchfield, Conn., May 3, 1801, collection in private hands; Martha Jefferis to Anne Jefferis Sheppard, August 28, 1845.

24. Lisa Mitchell Diary, 1860s, passim, Manuscript Division, Tulane University; Eleanor Parke Custis Lewis to Elizabeth Bordley [Gibson] February 5, 1822; Jeannie McCall, Cedar Park, to Peter McCall, Philadelphia, June

30, 1849, McCall Section, Cadwalader Collection, Historical Society of Pennsylvania.

25. Peggy Emlen to Sally Logan, May 3, 1769.

26. For a prime example of this type of letter, see Eleanor Parke Custis Lewis to Elizabeth Bordley Gibson, passim, or Fanny Canby to Mary Canby, Philadelphia, May 27, 1801; or Sophie M. DuPont, Brandywine, to Henry DuPont, Germantown, February 4, 1832.

27. Place of residence is not the only variable significant in characterizing family structure. Strong emotional ties and frequent visiting and correspondence can unite families that do not live under one roof. Demographic studies based on household structure alone fail to reflect such emotional and even economic ties between families.

28. Eleanor Parke Custis Lewis to Elizabeth Bordley Gibson, April 20 and September 25, 1848.

29. Maria Inskeep to Fanny Hampton Correspondence, 1823–60, Inskeep Collection, Tulane University Library.

30. Eunice Callender, Boston, to Sarah Ripley [Stearns], September 24 and October 29, 1803, February 16, 1805, April 29 and October 9, 1806, May 26, 1810.

31. Sophie DuPont filled her letters to her younger brother Henry (with whom she had been assigned to correspond while he was at boarding school) with accounts of family visiting (see, e.g., December 13, 1827, January 10 and March 9, 1828, February 4 and March 10, 1832; also Sophie DuPont to Victorine DuPont Bauday, September 26 and December 4, 1827, February 22, 1828; Sophie M. DuPont, Brandywine, to Clementina B. Smith, Philadelphia, January 15, 1830; Eleuthera DuPont, Brandywine, to Victorine DuPont Bauday, Philadelphia, April 17, 1821, October 20, 1826; Evelina DuPont [Biderman] to Victorine DuPont Bauday, October 18, 1816). Other examples, from the Historical Society of Pennsylvania, are Harriett Manigault [Wilcox] diary, August 17, September 8, October 19 and 22, December 22, 1814; Jane Zook, Westtown School, Chester County, Pa., to Mary Zook,, November 13, December 7 and 11, 1870, February 26, 1871; Eleanor Parke Custis [Lewis] to Elizabeth Bordley [Gibson], March 30, 1796, February 7 and March 20, 1798; Jeannie McCall to Peter McCall, Philadelphia, November 12, 1847; Mary B. Ashew Diary, July 11 and 13, August 17, Summer and October 1858, and, from a private collection, Edith Jefferis to Anne Jefferis Sheppard, November 1841, April 5, 1842; Abigail Brackett Lyman, Northampton, Mass., to Mrs. Catling, Litchfield, Conn., May 13, 1801; Abigail Brackett Lyman, Northampton, to Mary Lord, August 11, 1800. Mary Hallock Foote vacationed with her sister, her sister's children, her aunt, and a female cousin in the summer of 1874; cousins frequently visited the Hallock farm in Milton, N.Y. In later years Molly and her sister Bessie set up a joint household in Boise, Idaho (Mary Hallock Foote to Helena, July [1874?] and passim). Jeannie Field, after initially disliking her sister-in-law, Laura, became very close to her, calling her "my little sister" and at times spending virtually every day with her (Jeannie Field [Musgrove] New York, to Sarah Butler Wister, Germantown, March 1, 8, and 15, and May 9, 1863).

32. Martha Jefferis to Anne Jefferis Sheppard, January 12, 1845; Phoebe

Middleton to Martha Jefferis, February 22, 1848. A number of other women remained close to sisters and sisters-in-law across a long lifetime (Phoebe Bradford Diary, June 7, 1832, and Sarah Alden Ripley to Sophia Bradford, cited in Wister and Irwin, p. 195).

33. Rebecca Biddle to Martha Jefferis, 1838–49, passim; Martha Jefferis to Anne Jefferis Sheppard, July 6, 1846; Anne Jefferis Sheppard to Rachael Jefferis, January 16, 1865; Sarah Foulke Farquhar [Emlen] Diary, September 22, 1813, Friends Historical Library, Swarthmore College; Mary Garrigues to Mary Canby [Biddle], 1802–08, passim; Anne Biddle to Mary Canby [Biddle], May 16, July 13, and November 24, 1806, June 14, 1807, June 5, 1808.

34. Sarah Alden Ripley to Abba Allyn, n.d., Schlesinger Library.

35. Phoebe Bradford Diary, July 13, 1832.

36. Mary Hallock [Foote] to Helena, December 23 [1868 or 1869]; Phoebe Bradford Diary, December 8, 1832; Martha Jefferis and Anne Jefferis Sheppard letters, passim.

37. Martha Jefferis to Anne Jefferis Sheppard, August 3, 1849; Sarah Ripley [Stearns] Diary, November 12, 1808, January 8, 1811. An interesting note of hostility or rivalry is present in Sarah Ripley's diary entry. Sarah evidently deeply resented the husband's rapid remarriage.

38. Martha Jefferis to Edith Jefferis, March 15, 1841; Mary Hallock Foote to Helena, n.d. [1874–75?]; see also Jeannie Field, New York, to Sarah Butler Wister, Germantown, May 5, 1863, Emily Howland Diary, December 1879, Howland Family Papers.

39. Anne Jefferis Sheppard to Martha Jefferis, September 29, 1841.

40. Frances Parke Lewis to Elizabeth Bordley Gibson, April 29, 1821.

41. Mary Jane Burleigh, Mount Pleasant, S.C., to Emily Howland, Sherwood, N.Y., March 27, 1872, Howland Family Papers; Emily Howland Diary, September 16, 1879, January 21 and 23, 1880; Mary Black Couper, New Castle, Del., to Sophie M. DuPont, Brandywine, April 7, 1834.

42. Harriet Manigault Diary, August 15, 21, and 23, 1814, Historical Society of Pennsylvania; Polly [Simmons] to Sophie Madeleine DuPont, February 1822; Sophie Madeleine DuPont to Victorine Bauday, December 4, 1827; Sophie Madeleine DuPont to Clementina Beach Smith, July 24, 1828, August 19, 1829; Clementina Beach Smith to Sophie Madeleine DuPont, April 29, 1831; Mary Black Couper to Sophie Madeleine DuPont, December 24, 1828, July 21, 1834. This pattern appears to have crossed class lines. When a former Sunday school student of Sophie DuPont's (and the daughter of a worker in her father's factory) wrote to Sophie she discussed her mother's health and activities quite naturally (Ann McGrann to Sophie Madeleine DuPont, August 25, 1832; see also Elizabeth Bordley to Martha, n.d. [1797], Eleanor Parke Custis [Lewis] to Elizabeth Bordley [Gibson], May 13, 1796, July 1, 1798; Peggy Emlen to Sally Logan, January 8, 1786. All but the Emlen/Logan letters are in the Eleanor Parke Custis Lewis Correspondence, Historical Society of Pennsylvania).

43. Mrs. S.S. Dalton, "Autobiography" (Circle Valley, Utah, 1876), pp. 21–22, Bancroft Library, University of California, Berkeley; Sarah Foulke Emlen Diary, April 1809; Louisa G. Van Vleck, Appleton, Wis., to Charlena Van Vleck Anderson, Göttingen, n.d. [1875], Harriet Manigault Di-

ary, August 16, 1814, July 14, 1815; Sarah Alden Ripley to Sophy Fisher [early 1860s], quoted in Wister and Irwin (n. 12 above), p. 212. The Jefferis family papers are filled with empathetic letters between Martha and her daughters, Anne and Edith. See, e.g., Martha Jefferis to Edith Jefferis, December 26, 1836, March 11, 1837, March 15, 1841; Anne Jefferis Sheppard to Martha Jefferis, March 17, 1841, January 17, 1847, Martha Jefferis to Anne Jefferis Sheppard, April 17, 1848, April 30, 1849. A representative letter is this of March 9, 1837 from Edith to Martha: "My heart can fully respond to the language of my own precious Mother, that absence has not diminished our affection for each other, but has, if possible, strengthened the bonds that have united us together & I have had to remark how we had been permitted to mingle in sweet fellowship and have been strengthened to bear one another's burdens. . . ."

44. Abigail Brackett Lyman, Boston, to Mrs. Abigail Brackett (daughter to mother), n.d. [1797], June 3, 1800; Sarah Alden Ripley wrote weekly to her daughter, Sophy Ripley Fisher, after the latter's marriage (Sarah Alden Ripley Correspondence, passim); Phoebe Bradford Diary, February 25, 1833, passim, 1832–33; Louisa G. Van Vleck to Charlena Van Vleck Anderson, December 15, 1873, July 4, August 15 and 29, September 19, and November 9, 1875. Eleanor Parke Custis Lewis's long correspondence with Elizabeth Bordley Gibson contains evidence of her anxiety at leaving her foster mother's home at various times during her adolescence and at her marriage, and her own longing for her daughters, both of whom had married and moved to Louisiana (Eleanor Parke Custis [Lewis] to Elizabeth Bordley [Gibson], October 13, 1795, November 4, 1799, passim, 1820s and 1830s). Anne Jefferis Sheppard experienced a great deal of anxiety on moving two days' journey from her mother at the time of her marriage. This loneliness and sense of isolation persisted through her marriage until, finally a widow, she returned to live with her mother (Anne Jefferis Sheppard to Martha Jefferis, April 1841, October 16, 1842, April 2, May 22, and October 12, 1844, September 3, 1845, January 17, 1847, May 16, June 3, and October 31, 1849; Anne Jefferis Sheppard to Susanna Lightfoot, March 23, 1845, and to Joshua Jefferis, May 14, 1854). Daughters evidently frequently slept with their mothers—into adulthood (Harriett Manigault [Wilcox] Diary, February 19, 1815; Eleanor Parke Custis Lewis to Elizabeth Bordley Gibson, October 10, 1832). Daughters also frequently asked mothers to live with them and professed delight when they did so. See, e.g., Sarah Alden Ripley's comments to George Simmons, October 6, 1844, in Wister and Irwin, p. 185: "It is no longer 'Mother and Charles came out one day and returned the next,' for mother is one of us: she has entered the penetratice, been initiated into the mystery of the household gods, . . . Her divertissement is to mend the stockings . . . whiten sheets and napkins, . . . and take a stroll at evening with me to talk of our children, to compare our experiences, what we have learned and what we have suffered, and, last of all, to complete with pears and melons the cheerful circle about the solar lamp. . . ." We did find a few exceptions to this mother-daughter felicity (M.B. Ashew Diary, November 19, 1857, April 10 and May 17, 1858). Sarah Foulke Emlen was at first very hostile to her stepmother

(Sarah Foulke Emlen Diary, August 9, 1807), but they later developed a warm supportive relationship.

45. Sarah Alden Ripley to Sophy Thayer, n.d. [1861].

46. Mary Hallock Foote to Helena [Winter 1873] (no. 52); Jossie, Stevens Point, Wis., to Charlena Van Vleck [Anderson], Appleton, Wis., October 24, 1870; Pollie Chandler, Green Bay, Wis., to Charlena Van Vleck [Anderson], Appleton, n.d. [1870]; Eleuthera DuPont to Sophie DuPont, September 5, 1829; Sophie DuPont to Eleuthera DuPont, December 1827; Sophie DuPont to Victorine Bauday, December 4, 1827; Mary Gilpin to Sophie DuPont, September 26, 1827; Sarah Ripley Stearns Diary, April 2, 1809; Jeannie McCall to Peter McCall, October 27 [late 1840s]. Eleanor Parke Custis Lewis's correspondence with Elizabeth Bordley Gibson describes such an apprenticeship system over two generations—that of her childhood and that of her daughters. Indeed Eleanor Lewis's own apprenticeship was quite formal. She was deliberately separated from her foster mother in order to spend a winter of domesticity with her married sisters and her remarried mother. It was clearly felt that her foster mother's (Martha Washington) home at the nation's capital was not an appropriate place to develop domestic talents (October 13, 1795, March 30, May 13, and [Summer] 1796, March 18 and April 27, 1797, October 1827).

47. Education was not limited to the daughters of the well-to-do. Sarah Foulke Emlen, the daughter of an Ohio Valley frontier farmer, for instance, attended day school for several years during the early 1800s. Sarah Ripley Stearns, the daughter of a shopkeeper in Greenfield, Mass., attended a boarding school for but three months, yet the experience seemed very important to her. Mrs. S.S. Dalton, a Mormon woman from Utah, attended a series of poor country schools, and greatly valued her opportunity, though she also expressed a great deal of guilt for the sacrifices her mother made to make her education possible (Sarah Foulke Emlen Journal, Sarah Ripley Stearns Diary, Mrs. S.S. Dalton, "Autobiography").

48. Maria Revere to her mother [Mrs. Paul Revere], June 13, 1801, Paul Revere Papers, Massachusetts Historical Society. In a letter to Elizabeth Bordley Gibson, March 28, 1847, Eleanor Parke Custis Lewis from Virginia discussed the anxiety her daughter felt when her granddaughters left home to go to boarding school. Eleuthera DuPont was very homesick when away at school in Philadelphia in the early 1820s (Eleuthera DuPont, Philadelphia, to Victorine Bauday, Wilmington, Del., April 7, 1821; Eleuthera DuPont to Sophie Madeleine DuPont, Wilmington, Del., February and April 3, 1821).

49. Elizabeth Bordley Gibson, a Philadelphia matron, played such a role for the daughters and nieces of her lifelong friend, Eleanor Parke Custis Lewis, a Virginia planter's wife (Eleanor Parke Custis Lewis to Elizabeth Bordley Gibson, January 29, 1833, March 19, 1826, and passim through the collection). The wife of Thomas Gurney Smith played a similar role for Sophie and Eleuthera DuPont (see, e.g., Eleuthera DuPont to Sophie Madeleine DuPont, May 22, 1825; Rest Cope to Philema P. Swayne [niece] West Town School, Chester County, Pa., April 8, 1829, Friends

Historical Library, Swarthmore College). For a view of such a social pattern over three generations, see the letters and diaries of three generations of Manigault women in Philadelphia: Mrs. Gabrielle Manigault, her daughter, Harriett Manigault Wilcox, and granddaughter, Charlotte Wilcox McCall. Unfortunately the papers of the three women are not in one family collection (Mrs. Henry Middleton, Charleston, S.C., to Mrs. Gabrielle Manigault, n.d. [mid 1800s]; Harriett Manigault Diary, vol. 1; December 1, 1813, June 28, 1814; Charlotte Wilcox McCall Diary, vol. 1, 1842, passim. All in Historical Society of Philadelphia).

50. Frances Parke Lewis, Woodlawn, Va., to Elizabeth Bordley Gibson, Philadelphia, April 11, 1821, Lewis Correspondence; Eleuthera DuPont, Philadelphia, to Victorine DuPont Bauday, Brandywine, December 8, 1821, January 31, 1822; Eleuthera DuPont, Brandywine, to Margaretta Lammont [DuPont], Philadelphia, May 1823.

51. Sarah Ripley Stearns Diary, March 9 and 25, 1810; Peggy Emlen to Sally Logan, March and July 4, 1769; Harriett Manigault [Wilcox] Diary, vol. 1, December 1, 1813, June 28 and September 18, 1814, August 10, 1815; Charlotte Wilcox McCall Diary, 1842, passim; Fanny Canby to Mary Canby, May 27, 1801, March 17, 1804; Deborah Cope, West Town School, to Rest Cope, Philadelphia, July 9, 1828, Chester County Historical Society, West Chester, Pa.; Anne Zook, West Town School, to Mary Zook, Philadelphia, January 30, 1866, Chester County Historical Society, West Chester, Pa.; Mary Gilpin to Sophie Madeleine DuPont, February 25, 1829; Eleanor Parke Custis [Lewis] to Elizabeth Bordley [Gibson], April 27, July 2, and September 8, 1797, June 30, 1799, December 29, 1820; Frances Parke Lewis to Elizabeth Bordley Gibson, December 20, 1820.

52. Anne Jefferis Sheppard to Martha Jefferis, March 17, 1841.

53. Peggy Emlen to Sally Logan, March 1769, Mount Vernon, Va.; Eleanor Parke Custis [Lewis] to Elizabeth Bordley [Gibson], Philadelphia, April 27, 1797, June 30, 1799; Jeannie Field, New York, to Sarah Butler Wister, Germantown, July 3, 1861, January 16, 1863; Harriett Manigault Diary, August 3 and 11–13, 1814; Eunice Callender, Boston, to Sarah Ripley [Stearns], Greenfield, May 4, 1809. I found one exception to this inhibition of female hostility. This was the diary of Charlotte Wilcox McCall, Philadelphia (see, e.g., her March 23, 1842 entry).

54. Sophie M. DuPont and Eleuthera DuPont, Brandywine, to Victorine DuPont Bauday, Philadelphia, January 25, 1832.

55. Sarah Ripley [Stearns] Diary and Harriett Manigault Diary, passim.

56. Sophie Madeleine DuPont to Eleuthera DuPont, December 1827; Clementina Beach Smith to Sophie Madeleine DuPont, December 26, 1828; Sarah Foulke Emlen Diary, July 21, 1808, March 30, 1809; Annie Hethroe, Ellington, Wis., to Charlena Van Vleck [Anderson], Appleton, Wis., April 23, 1865; Frances Parke Lewis, Woodlawn, Va., to Elizabeth Bordley [Gibson], Philadelphia, December 20, 1820; Fanny Ferris to Debby Ferris, West Town School, Chester County, Pa., May 29, 1826. An excellent example of the warmth of women's comments about each other and the reserved nature of their references to men are seen in two entries in Sarah Ripley Stearn's diary. On January 8, 1811 she commented about a young woman friend: "The amiable Mrs. White of Princeton . . . one of

the loveliest most interesting creatures I ever knew, young fair and blooming ... beloved by everyone ... formed to please & to charm. ..." She referred to the man she ultimately married always as "my friend" or "a friend" (February 2 or April 23, 1810).

57. Jeannie Field, New York, to Sarah Butler Wister, Germantown, April 6, 1862.

58. Elizabeth Bordley Gibson, introductory statement to the Eleanor Parke Custis Lewis Letters [1850s], Historical Society of Pennsylvania.

59. Sarah Foulke [Emlen] Diary, March 30, 1809.

60. Harriett Manigault Diary, May 26, 1815.

61. Sarah Ripley [Stearns] Diary, May 17 and October 2, 1812; Eleanor Parke Custis Lewis to Elizabeth Bordley Gibson, April 23, 1826; Rebecca Ralston, Philadelphia, to Victorine DuPont [Bauday], Brandywine, September 27, 1813.

62. Anne Jefferis to Martha Jefferis, November 22 and 27, 1840, January 13 and March 17, 1841; Edith Jefferis, Greenwich, N.J., to Anne Jefferis, Philadelphia, January 31, February 6 and February 1841.

63. Edith Jefferis to Anne Jefferis, January 31, 1841.

64. Eleanor Parke Custis Lewis to Elizabeth Bordley, November 4, 1799. Eleanor and her daughter Parke experienced similar sorrow and anxiety when Parke married and moved to Cincinnati (Eleanor Parke Custis Lewis to Elizabeth Bordley Gibson, April 23, 1826). Helena DeKay visited Mary Hallock the month before her marriage; Mary Hallock was an attendant at the wedding; Helena again visited Molly about three weeks after her marriage; and then Molly went with Helena and spent a week with Helena and Richard in their new apartment (Mary Hallock [Foote] to Helena DeKay Gilder [Spring 1874] (no. 61), May 10, 1874 [May 1874], June 14, 1874 [Summer 1874]. See also Anne Biddle, Philadelphia, to Clement Biddle (brother), Wilmington, March 12 and May 27, 1827; Eunice Callender, Boston, to Sarah Ripley [Stearns], Greenfield, Mass., August 3, 1807, January 26, 1808; Victorine DuPont Bauday, Philadelphia, to Evelina DuPont [Biderman], Brandywine, November 25 and 26, December 1, 1813; Peggy Emlen to Sally Logan, n.d. [1769-70?]; Jeannie Field, New York, to Sarah Butler Wister, Germantown, July 3, 1861).

65. Mary Hallock to Helena DeKay Gilder [1876] (no. 81); n.d. (no. 83), March 3, 1884; Mary Ashew Diary, vol. 2, September-January, 1860; Louisa Van Vleck to Charlena Van Vleck Anderson, n.d. [1875]; Sophie DuPont to Henry DuPont, July 24, 1827; Benjamin Ferris to William Canby, February 13, 1805; Benjamin Ferris to Mary Canby Biddle, December 20, 1825; Anne Jefferis Sheppard to Martha Jefferis, September 15, 1884; Martha Jefferis to Anne Jefferis Sheppard, July 4, 1843, May 5, 1844, May 3, 1847, July 17, 1849; Jeannie McCall to Peter McCall, November 26, 1847, n.d. [late 1840s]. A graphic description of the ritual surrounding a first birth is found in Abigail Lyman's letter to her husband Erastus Lyman, October 18, 1810.

66. Fanny Ferris to Anne Biddle, November 19, 1811; Eleanor Parke Custis Lewis to Elizabeth Bordley Gibson, November 4, 1799, April 27, 1827; Martha Jefferis to Anne Jefferis Sheppard, January 31, 1843, April 4, 1844; Martha Jefferis to Phoebe Sharpless Middleton, June 4, 1846; Anne

Jefferis Sheppard to Martha Jefferis, August 20, 1843, February 12, 1844; Maria Inskeep, New Orleans, to Mrs. Fanny G. Hampton, Bridgeton, N.J., September 22, 1848; Benjamin Ferris to Mary Canby, February 14, 1805; Fanny Ferris to Mary Canby [Biddle], December 2, 1816.

67. Eleanor Parke Custis Lewis to Elizabeth Bordley Gibson, October-November 1820, passim.

68. Emily Howland to Hannah, September 30, 1866; Emily Howland Diary, February 8, 11, and 27, 1880; Phoebe Brandford Diary, April 12 and 13, and August 4, 1833; Eunice Callender, Boston, to Sarah Ripley [Stearns], Greenwich, Mass., September 11, 1802, August 26, 1810; Mrs. H. Middleton, Charleston, to Mrs. Gabrielle Manigault, Philadelphia, n.d. [mid 1800s]; Mrs. H.C. Paul to Mrs. Jeannie McCall, Philadelphia, n.d. [1840s]; Sarah Butler Wister, Germantown, to Jeannie Field [Musgrove], New York, April 22, 1864; Jeannie Field [Musgrove] to Sarah Butler Wister, August 25, 1861, July 6, 1862; S.B. Raudolph to Elizabeth Bordley [Gibson], n.d. [1790s]. For an example of similar letters between men, see Henry Wright to Peter McCall, December 10, 1852; Charles McCall to Peter McCall, January 4, 1860, March 22, 1864; R. Mercer to Peter McCall, November 29, 1872.

69. Mary Black [Couper] to Sophie Madeleine DuPont, February 1827, [November 1, 1834], November 12, 1834, two letters [late November 1834]; Eliza Schlatter to Sophie Madeleine DuPont, November 2, 1834.

70. For a few of the references to death rituals in the Jefferis papers see: Martha Jefferis to Anne Jefferis Sheppard, September 28, 1843, August 21 and September 25, 1844, January 11, 1846, summer 1848, passim; Anne Jefferis Sheppard to Martha Jefferis, August 20, 1843; Anne Jefferis Sheppard to Rachel Jefferis, March 17, 1863, February 9, 1868. For other Quaker families, see Rachel Biddle to Anne Biddle, July 23, 1854; Sarah Foulke Farquhar [Emlen] Diary, April 30, 1811, February 14, 1812; Fanny Ferris to Mary Canby, August 31, 1810. This is not to argue that men and women did not mourn together. Yet in many families women aided and comforted women and men, men. The same-sex death ritual was one emotional option available to nineteenth-century Americans.

71. Sarah Foulke [Emlen] Diary, December 29, 1808.

72. Eunice Callender, Boston, to Sarah Ripley [Stearns], Greenfield, Mass., May 24, 1803.

73. Katherine Johnstone Brinley [Wharton] Journal, April 26, May 30, and May 29, 1856, Historical Society of Pennsylvania.

74. A series of roughly fourteen letters written by Peggy Emlen to Sally Logan (1768–71) has been preserved in the Wells Morris Collection, Box 1, Historical Society of Pennsylvania (see esp. May 3 and July 4, 1769, January 8, 1768).

75. The Sarah Alden Ripley Collection, the Arthur M. Schlesinger, Sr., Library, Radcliffe College, contains a number of Sarah Alden Ripley's letters to Mary Emerson. Most of these are undated, but they extend over a number of years and contain letters written both before and after Sarah's marriage. The eulogistic biographical sketch appeared in Wister and Irwin (n. 12 above). It should be noted that Sarah Butler Wister was one of the editors who sensitively selected Sarah's letters.

76. See Sarah Alden Ripley to Mary Emerson, November 19, 1823. Sarah

Alden Ripley routinely, and one must assume ritualistically, read Mary Emerson's letters to her infant daughter, Mary. Eleanor Parke Custis Lewis reported doing the same with Elizabeth Bordley Gibson's letters, passim. Eunice Callender, Boston, to Sarah Ripley [Stearns], October 19, 1808.

77. Mary Black Couper to Sophie M. DuPont, March 5, 1832. The Clementina Smith-Sophie DuPont correspondence of 1,678 letters is in the Sophie DuPont Correspondence. The quotation is from Eliza Schlatter, Mount Holly, N.J., to Sophie Dupont, Brandywine, August 24, 1834. I am indebted to Anthony Wallace for informing me about this collection.

78. Mary Grew, Providence, R.I., to Isabel Howland, Sherwood, N.Y., April 27, 1892, Howland Correspondence, Sophia Smith Collection, Smith College.

79. Helena Deutsch, *Psychology of Women* (New York: Grune & Stratton, 1944), vol. 1, chaps. 1-3; Clara Thompson, *On Women,* ed. Maurice Green (New York: New American Library, 1971).

Women and Their Families on the Overland Trail to California and Oregon, 1842–1867

Johnny Faragher and Christine Stansell

I am not a wheatfield
nor the virgin forest

I never chose this place
yet I am of it now

—Adrienne Rich
"From an Old House in America"

From 1841 until 1867, the year in which the transcontinental railroad was completed, nearly 350,000 North Americans emigrated to the Pacific coast along the western wagon road known variously as the Oregon, the California, or simply the Overland Trail. This migration was essentially a family phenomenon. Although single men constituted the majority of the party which pioneered large-scale emigration on the Overland Trail in 1841, significant numbers of women and children were already present in the wagon trains of the next season. Families made up the preponderant proportion of the migrations throughout the 1840s. In 1849, during the overwhelmingly male Gold Rush, the number dropped precipitously, but after 1851 families once again assumed dominance in the overland migration.[1] The contention that "the family was the one substantial social institution" on the frontier is too sweeping, yet it is undeniable that the white family largely mediated the incorporation of the western territories into the American nation.[2]

The emigrating families were a heterogeneous lot. Some came from farms in the midwest and upper South, many from small midwestern towns, and others from northeastern and midwestern cities. Clerks and shopkeepers as well as farmers outfitted their wagons in Independence, St. Louis, or Westport Landing on the Missouri. Since costs for supplies, travel, and settlement were not negligible,[3] few of the very poor were present, nor were the exceptionally prosperous. The dreams of fortune which lured the wagon trains into new lands were those of modest men whose hopes were pinned to small farms or larger dry-goods stores, more fertile soil or more customers, better market prospects and a steadily expanding economy.

For every member of the family, the trip West was exhausting, toilsome, and often grueling. Each year in late spring, westbound emigrants gathered for the journey at spots along the Missouri River and moved out in parties of ten to several hundred wagons. Aggregates of nuclear families, loosely attached by kinship or friendship, traveled together or joined an even larger caravan.[4] Coast-bound families traveled by ox-drawn wagons at the frustratingly slow pace of fifteen to twenty miles per day. They worked their way up the Platte River valley through what is now Kansas and Nebraska, crossing the Rockies at South Pass in southwestern Wyoming by mid-summer. The Platte route was relatively easy going, but from present-day Idaho, where the roads to California and Oregon diverged, to their final destinations, the pioneers faced disastrous conditions: scorching deserts, boggy salt flats, and rugged mountains. By this time, families had been on the road some three months and were only at the midpoint of the journey: the environment, along with the wear of the road, made the last months difficult almost beyond endurance. Finally, in late fall or early winter the pioneers straggled into their promised lands, after six months and over two thousand miles of hardship.[5]

As this journey progressed, bare necessity became the determinant of most of each day's activities. The primary task of surviving and getting to the coast gradually suspended accustomed patterns of dividing work between women and men. All able-bodied adults worked all day in one way or another to keep the family moving. Women's work was no less indispensable than men's; indeed, as the summer wore on, the boundaries dividing the work of the sexes were threatened, blurred and transgressed.

The vicissitudes of the trail opened new possibilities for expanded work roles for women, and in the cooperative work of the family there existed a basis for a vigorous struggle for female-male equality. But most women did not see the experience in this way. They viewed it as a male enterprise from its very inception. Women experienced the breakdown of the sexual division of labor as a dissolution of their own autonomous "sphere." Bereft of the footing which this independent base gave them, they lacked a cultural rationale for the work they did, and remained estranged from the possibilities of the enlarged scope and power of family life on the trail. Instead, women fought *against* the forces of necessity to hold together the few fragments of female subculture left to them. We have been bequeathed a remarkable record of this struggle in the diaries, journals, and memoirs of emigrating women. In this study, we will examine a particular habit of living, or culture, in conflict with the new material circumstances of the Trail, and the efforts of women to maintain a place, a sphere of their own.

The overland family was not a homogeneous unit, its members imbued with identical aspirations and desires. On the contrary, the period of westward movement was also one of multiplying schisms within those families whose location and social status placed them in the mainstream of rational culture.[6] Child-rearing tracts, housekeeping manuals, and etiquette books by the hundreds proscribed and rationalized to these Americans a radical separation of the work responsibilities and social duties of mothers and fathers; popular thought assigned unique personality traits, spiritual capacities, and forms of experience to the respective categories of man, woman, and child.[7] In many families, the tensions inherent in this separatist ideology, often repressed in the everyday routines of the East, erupted under the strain of the overland crossing. The difficulties of the emigrants, while inextricably linked to the duress of the journey itself, also revealed family dynamics which had been submerged in the less eventful life "back home."

A full blown ideology of "woman's place" was absent in preindustrial America. On farms, in artisan shops, and in town marketplaces, women and children made essential contributions to family income and subsistence; it was the family which functioned as the basic unit of production in the colony and the young nation. As commercial exchanges displaced the local markets where women had sold surplus dairy products and textiles, and the workplace drifted away from the household, women and children lost their breadwinning prerogatives.[8]

In Jacksonian America, a doctrine of "sexual spheres" arose to facilitate and justify the segregation of women into the home and men into productive work.[9] While the latter attended to politics, economics, and wage-earning, popular thought assigned women the refurbished and newly professionalized tasks of child-rearing and housekeeping.[10] A host of corollaries followed on the heels of these shifts. Men were physically strong, women naturally delicate; men were skilled in practical matters, women in moral and emotional concerns; men were prone to corruption, women to virtue; men belonged in the world, women in the home. For women, the system of sexual spheres represented a decline in social status and isolation from political and economic power. Yet it also provided them with a psychological power base of undeniable importance. The "cult of true womanhood" was more than simply a retreat. Catharine Beecher, one of the chief theorists of "woman's influence," proudly quoted Tocqueville's observation that "in no country has such constant care been taken, as in America, to trace two clearly distinct lines of action for the two sexes, and to make them keep pace with the other, but in two pathways which are always different." [11] Neither Beecher nor her sisters were simply dupes of a masculine imperialism. The supervision of child-rearing, household economy, and the moral and religious life of the family granted women a certain degree of real autonomy and control over their lives as well as those of their husbands and children.

Indeed, recent scholarship has indicated that a distinctly female subculture emerged from "woman's sphere." By "subculture" we simply mean a "habit of living"—as we have used "culture" above—of a minority group which is self-consciously distinct from the dominant activities, expectations, and values of a society. Historians have seen female church groups, reform associations, and philanthropic activity as expressions of this subculture in actual behavior, while a large and rich body of writing by and for women articulated the subcultural impulses on the ideational level. Both behavior and thought point to child-rearing, religious activity, education, home life, associationism, and female communality as components of women's subculture. Female friendships, strikingly intimate and deep in this period, formed the actual bonds.[12] Within their tight and atomized family households, women carved out a life of their own.

At its very inception, the western emigration sent tremors through the foundations of this carefully compartmentalized family structure.

The rationale behind pulling up stakes was nearly always economic advancement,[13] since breadwinning was a masculine concern, the husband and father introduced the idea of going West and made the final decision. Family participation in the intervening time ran the gamut from enthusiastic support to stolid resistance. Many women cooperated with their ambitious spouses: "The motive that induced us to part with pleasant associations and the dear friends of our childhood days, was to obtain from the government of the United States a grant of land that 'Uncle Sam' had promised to give to the head of each family who settled in this new country." [14] Others, however, only acquiesced. "Poor Ma said only this morning, 'Oh, I wish we never had started,' " Lucy Cooke wrote her first day on the trail, "and she looks so sorrowful and dejected. I think if Pa had not passengers to take through she would urge him to return; not that he should be so inclined." [15] Huddled with her children in a cold, damp wagon, trying to calm them despite the ominous chanting of visiting Indians, another woman wondered "what had possessed my husband, anyway, that he should have thought of bringing us away out through this God forsaken country." Similar alienation from the "pioneer spirit" haunted Lavinia Porter's leave-taking:

> I never recall that sad parting from my dear sister on the plains of Kansas without the tears flowing fast and free.... We were the eldest of a large family, and the bond of affection and love that existed between us was strong indeed ... as she with the other friends turned to leave me for the ferry which was to take them back to home and civilization, I stood alone on that wild prairie. Looking westward I saw my husband driving slowly over the plain; turning my face once more to the east, my dear sister's footsteps were fast widening the distance between us. For the time I knew not which way to go, nor whom to follow. But in a few moments I rallied my forces ... and soon overtook the slowly moving oxen who were bearing my husband and child over the green prairie ... the unbidden tears would flow in spite of my brave resolve to be the courageous and valiant frontierswoman.[17]

Her dazed vacillation soon gave way to a private conviction that the family had made a dire mistake: "I would make a brave effort to be cheerful and patient until the camp work was done. Then starting out ahead of the team and my men folks, when I thought I had gone beyond hearing distance, I would throw myself down on the unfriendly desert and give way like a child to sobs and tears, wishing myself back home with my friends and chiding myself for consenting to take this wild goose chase." [18] Men viewed drudgery, calamity, and privation as trials along the road to prosperity, unfortunate but inevitable corollaries of the rational decision they had made. But to those women who were unable to appropriate the vision of the upwardly mobile pilgrimage, hardship and loss only testified to the inherent folly of the emigration, "this wild goose chase."

If women were reluctant to accompany their men, however, they were often equally unwilling to let them go alone. In the late 1840s, the conflict between wives and their gold-crazed husbands reveals the determination with which women enforced the cohesion of the nuclear family. In the name of family unity, some obdurate wives simply chose to blockbust the sexually segregated Gold Rush: "My husband grew enthusiastic and wanted to start immediately," one woman recalled, "but I would not be left behind. I thought where he could go I could and where I went I could take my two little toddling babies." [19] Her family departed intact. Other women used their moral authority to smash the enterprise in its planning stages. "We were married to live together," a wife acidly reminded her spouse when he informed her of his intention to join the Rush: "I am willing to go with you to any part of *God's Foot Stool* where you think you can do best, and under these circumstances you have no right to go where I cannot, and if you do you need never return for I shall look upon you as dead." [20] Roundly chastised, the man postponed his journey until the next season, when his family could leave with him. When included in the plans, women seldom wrote of their husbands' decisions to emigrate in their diaries or memoirs. A breadwinner who tried to leave alone, however, threatened the family unity upon which his authority was based; only then did a wife challenge his dominance in worldly affairs.[21]

There was an economic reason for the preponderance of families on the Trail. Women and children, but especially women, formed an essential supplementary work force in the settlements. The ideal wife in the West resembled a hired hand more than a nurturant Christian housekeeper.[22] Narcissa Whitman wrote frankly to aspiring settlers of the functional necessity of women on the new farms: "Let every young man bring a wife, for he will want one after he gets here, if he never did before." [23] In a letter from California, another seasoned woman warned a friend in Missouri that in the West women became "hewers of wood and drawers of water everywhere." [24] Mrs. Whitman's fellow missionary Elkanah Walker was unabashedly practical in beseeching his wife to join him: "I am tired of keeping an old bachelor's hall. I want someone to get me a good supper and let me take my ease and when I am very tired in the morning I want someone to get up and get breakfast and let me lay in bed and take my rest."[25] It would be both simplistic and harsh to argue that men brought their families West or married because of the labor power of women and children; there is no doubt, however, that the new Westerners appreciated the advantages of familial labor. Women were not superfluous; they were workers. The migration of women helped to solve the problem of labor scarcity, not only in the early years of the American settlement on the coast, but throughout the history of the continental frontier.[26]

In the first days of the overland trip, new work requirements were not yet pressing and the division of labor among family members still replicated familiar patterns. Esther Hanna reported in one of her first diary entries that "our men have gone to build a bridge across the stream, which is impassable," while she baked her first bread on the prairie.[27] Elizabeth Smith similarly described her party's day: "rainy ... Men making rafts. Women cooking and washing. Children crying."[28] When travel was suspended, "the men were generally busy mending wagons, harnesses, yokes, shoeing the animals etc., and the women washed clothes, boiled a big mess of beans, to warm over for several meals, or perhaps mended clothes."[29] At first, even in emergencies, women and men hardly considered integrating their work. "None but those who have cooked for a family of eight, crossing the plains, have any idea of what it takes," a disgruntled woman recalled: "My sister-in-law was sick, my niece was much younger than I, and consequently I had the management of all the cooking and planning on my young shoulders."[30] To ask a man to help was a possibility she was unable even to consider.[31]

The relegation of women to purely domestic duties, however, soon broke down under the vicissitudes of the Trail. Within the first few weeks, the unladylike task of gathering buffalo dung for fuel (little firewood was available *en route)* became women's work.[32] As one traveler astutely noted, "force of surroundings was a great leveler";[33] miles of grass, dust, glare, and mud erased some of the most rudimentary distinctions between female and male responsibilities. By summer, women often helped drive the wagons and the livestock.[34] At one Platte crossing, "the men drawed the wagons over by hand and the women all crossed in safety"; but at the next, calamity struck when the bridge collapsed, "and then commenced the hurry and bustle of repairing; all were at work, even the women and children."[35] Such crises, which compounded daily as the wagons moved past the Platte up the long stretches of desert and coastal mountains, generated equity in work; at times of Indian threats, for example, both women and men made bullets and stood guard.[36] When mountain fever struck the Pengra family as they crossed the Rockies, Charlotte relieved her incapacitated husband of the driving while he took care of the youngest child.[37] Only such severe afflictions forced men to take on traditionally female chores. While women did men's work, there is little evidence that men reciprocated.

Following a few days in the life of an overland woman discloses the magnitude of her work. During the hours her party traveled, Charlotte Pengra walked beside the wagons, driving the cattle and gathering buffalo chips. At night she cooked, baked bread for the next noon meal, and washed clothes. Three successive summer days illustrate how trying these small chores could be. Her train pulled out early on a Monday morning, only to be halted by rain and a flash flood; Mrs. Pengra washed and dried her family's wet clothes in the afternoon while doing her daily baking. On Tuesday the wagons pushed hard to make up for lost time, forcing her to trot all day to keep up. In camp that night there was no time to rest. Before going to bed, she wrote, "Kept busy in preparing tea and doing other things preparatory for the morrow. I baked a cracker pudding, warm biscuits and made tea, and after supper stewed two pans of dried apples, and made two loaves of bread, got my work done up, beds made, and child asleep, and have written in my journal. Pretty tired of course." The same routine devoured the next day and evening: "I have done a washing. Stewed apples, made pies and baked a rice pudding, and mended our wagon cover. Rather tired." And the next: "baked biscuits, stewed berries, fried meat, boiled and mashed potatoes, and made tea for supper, afterward baked bread. Thus you see I have not much rest." [38] Children also burdened women's work and leisure. During one quiet time, Helen Stewart retreated in mild defiance from her small charges to a tent in order to salvage some private time: "It exceeding hot ... some of the men is out hunting and some of them sleeping. The children is grumbling and crying and laughing and howling and playing all around." [39] Although children are notably absent in women's journals, they do appear, frightened and imploring, during an Indian scare or a storm, or intrude into a rare and precious moment of relaxation, "grumbling and crying." [40]

Because the rhythm of their chores was out of phase with that of the men, the division of labor could be especially taxing to women. Men's days were toilsome but broken up at regular intervals with periods of rest. Men hitched the teams, drove or walked until noon, relaxed at dinner, traveled until the evening camp, unhitched the oxen, ate supper, and in the evening sat at the campfire, mended equipment, or stood guard. They also provided most of the labor in emergencies, pulling the wagons through mires, across treacherous river crossings, up long grades, and down precipitous slopes. In the pandemonium of a steep descent,

> you would see the women and children in advance seeking the best way, some of them slipping down, or holding on to the rocks, now taking an "otter slide," and then a run til some natural obstacle presented itself to stop their accelerated progress and those who get down safely without a hurt or a bruise, are fortunate indeed. Looking back to the train, you would see some of the men holding on to the wagons, others slipping under the oxen's feet, some throwing articles out of the way that had fallen out, and all have enough to do to keep them busily occupied.[41]

Women were responsible for staying out of the way and getting themselves and the children to safety, men for getting the wagons down. Women's work, far less demanding of brute strength and endurance, was nevertheless distributed without significant respite over all waking hours: mealtimes offered no leisure to the cooks. "The plain fact of the matter is," a young woman complained,

> we *have no time for sociability.* From the time we get up in the morning, until we are on the road, it is hurry scurry to get breakfast and put away the things that necessarily had to be pulled out last night—while under way there is no room in the wagon for a visitor, nooning is barely long enough to eat a cold bite—and at night all the cooking utensils and provisions are to be gotten about the camp fire, and cooking enough to last until the next night.[42]

After supper, the men gathered together, "lolling and smoking their pipes and guessing, or maybe betting, how many miles we had covered during the day," [43] while the women baked, washed, and put the children to bed before they finally sat down. Charlotte Pengra found "as I was told before I started that there is no rest in such a journey." [44]

Unaccustomed tasks beset the travelers, who were equipped with only the familiar expectation that work was divided along gender lines. The solutions which sexual "spheres" offered were usually irrelevant to the new problems facing families. Women, for example, could not afford to be delicate: their new duties demanded far greater stamina and hardiness than their traditional domestic tasks. With no tradition to deal with the new exigencies of fuel-gathering, cattle-driving, and cooking, families found that "the division of labor in a party . . . was a prolific cause of quarrel." [45] Within the Vincent party, "assignments to duty were not accomplished without grumbling and objection . . . there were occasional angry debates while the various burdens were being adjusted," while in "the camps of others who sometimes jogged along the trail in our company . . . we saw not a little fighting . . . and these bloody fisticuffs were invariably the outcome of disputes over division of labor." [46] At home, these assignments were familiar and accepted, not subject to questioning. New work opened the division of labor to debate and conflict.

By midjourney, most women worked at male tasks. The men still retained dominance within their "sphere," despite the fact that it was no longer exclusively masculine. Like most women, Lavinia Porter was responsible for gathering buffalo chips for fuel. One afternoon, spying a grove of cottonwoods half a mile away, she asked her husband to branch off the trail so that the party could fell trees for firewood, thus easing her work. "But men on the plains I had found were not so accomodating, nor so ready to wait upon women as they were in more civilized communities." Her husband refused and Porter fought back: "I was feeling somewhat under the weather and unusually tired, and crawling into the wagon told them if they wanted fuel for the evening meal they could get it themselves and cook the meal also, and laying my head down on a pillow, I cried myself to sleep." [47] Later that evening her husband awakened her with a belated dinner he had prepared himself, but despite his conciliatory spirit their relations were strained for weeks: "James and I had gradually grown silent and taciturn and had unwittingly partaken of the gloom and somberness of the dreary landscape." [48] No longer a housewife or a domestic ornament, but a laborer in a male arena, Porter was still subordinate to her husband in practical matters.

Lydia Waters recorded another clash between new work and old consciousness: "I had learned to drive an ox team on the Platte and my driving was admired by an officer and his wife who were going with the mail to Salt Lake City." Pleased with the compliment, she later overheard them "laughing at the thought of a woman driving oxen." [49] By no means did censure come only from men. The officer's wife as well as the officer derided Lydia Waters, while her own mother indirectly reprimanded teenaged Mary Ellen Todd. "All along our journey, I had tried to crack that big whip," Mary Ellen remembered years later:

> Now while out at the wagon we kept trying until I was fairly successful. How my heart bounded a few days later when I chanced to hear father say to mother, "Do you know that Mary Ellen is beginning to crack the whip." Then how it fell again when mother replied, "I am afraid it isn't a very lady-like thing for a girl to do." After this, while I felt a secret joy in being able to have a power that set things going, there was also a sense of shame over this new accomplishment.[50]

To understand Mrs. Todd's primness, so incongruous in the rugged setting of the Trail, we must see it in the context of a broader struggle on the part of women to preserve the home in transit. Against the leveling forces of the Plains, women tried to maintain the standards of cleanliness and order that had prevailed in their homes back East:

> Our caravan had a good many women and children and although we were probably longer on the journey owing to their presence—they exerted a good influence, as the men did not take such risks with Indians ... were more alert about the care of teams and seldom had accidents; more attention was paid to cleanliness and sanitation and, lastly, but not of less importance, meals were more regular and better cooked thus preventing much sickness and there was less waste of food.[51]

Sarah Royce remembered that family wagons "were easily distinguished by the greater number of conveniences, and household articles they carried." [52] In the evenings, or when the trains stopped for a day, women had a chance to create with these few props a flimsy facsimile of the home.

Even in camp women had little leisure time, but within the "hurry scurry" of work they managed to recreate the routine of the home. Indeed, a female subculture, central to the communities women had left behind, reemerged in these settings. At night, women often clustered together, chatting, working, or commiserating, instead of joining the men: "High teas were not popular, but tatting, knitting, crocheting, exchanging recipes for cooking beans or dried apples or swopping food for the sake of variety kept us in practice of feminine occupations and diversions." [53] Besides using the domestic concerns of the Trail to reconstruct a female sphere, women also consciously invoked fantasy:

"Mrs. Fox and her daughter are with us and everything is so still and quiet we can almost imagine ourselves at home again. We took out our Daguerrotypes and tried to live over again some of the happy days of 'Auld Lang Syne.' " [54] Sisterly contact kept "feminine occupations" from withering away from disuse: "In the evening the young ladies came over to our house and we had a concert with both guitars. Indeed it seemed almost like a pleasant evening at home. We could none of us realize that we were almost at the summit of the Rocky Mountains." [55] The hostess added with somewhat strained sanguinity that her young daughter seemed "just as happy sitting on the ground playing her guitar as she was at home, although she does not love it as much as her piano." [56] Although a guitar was no substitute for the more refined instrument, it at least kept the girl "in practice with feminine occupations and diversions": unlike Mary Ellen Todd, no big whip would tempt her to unwomanly pleasure in the power to "set things going."

But books, furniture, knick-knacks, china, the daguerrotypes that Mrs. Fox shared, or the guitars of young musicians—the "various articles of ornament and convenience"—were among the first things discarded on the epic trash heap which trailed over the mountains. On long uphill grades and over sandy deserts, the wagons had to be lightened; any materials not essential to survival were fair game for disposal. Such commodities of woman's sphere, although functionally useless, provided women with a psychological lifeline to their abandoned homes and communities, as well as to elements of their identities which the westward journey threatened to mutilate or entirely extinguish.[57] Losing homely treasures and memorabilia was yet another defeat within an accelerating process of dispossession.

The male-directed venture likewise encroached upon the Sabbath, another female preserve. Through the influence of women's magazines, by mid-century Sunday had become a veritable ladies' day; women zealously exercised their religious influence and moral skill on the day of their families' retirement from the world. Although parties on the Trail often suspended travel on Sundays, the time only provided the opportunity to unload and dry the precious cargo of the wagons—seeds, food, and clothing—which otherwise would rot from dampness. For women whose creed forbade any worldly activity on the Sabbath, the work was not only irksome and tedious but profane.

This is Sabath it is a beautiful day but indeed we do not use it as such for we have not traveled far when we stop in a most lovely place oh it is such a beautiful spot and take everything out of our wagon to air them and it is well we done it as the flower was damp and there was some of the other ones flower was rotten ... and we baked and boiled and washed oh dear me I did not think we would have abused the sabeth in such a manner. I do not see how we can expect to get along but we did not intend to do so before we started.[58]

Denied a voice in the male sphere that surrounded them, women were also unable to partake of the limited yet meaningful power of women with homes. On almost every Sunday, Helen Stewart lamented the disruption of a familiar and sustaining order of life, symbolized by the household goods strewn about the ground to dry: "We took everything out the wagons and the side of the hill is covered with flower biscut meat rice oat meal clothes and such a quantity of articles of all discertions to many to mention and childre[n] included in the number. And hobos that is neather men nor yet boys being in and out hang about." [59]

The disintegration of the physical base of domesticity was symptomatic of an even more serious disruption in the female subculture. Because the wagon trains so often broke into smaller units, many women were stranded in parties without other women. Since there were usually two or more men in the same family party, some male friendships and bonds remained intact for the duration of the journey. But by midway in the trip, female companionship, so valued by nineteenth-century women, was unavailable to the solitary wife in a party of hired men, husband, and children that had broken away from a larger train. Emergencies and quarrels, usually between men, broke up the parties. Dr. Powers, a particularly ill-tempered man, decided after many disagreements with others in his train to make the crossing alone with his family. His wife shared neither his misanthropy nor his grim independence. On the day they separated from the others, she wrote in her journal: "The women came over to bid me goodbye, for we were to go alone, all alone. They said there was no color in my face. I felt as if there was none." She perceived the separation as a banishment, almost a death sentence: "There is something peculiar in such a parting on the Plains, one there realizes what a goodbye is. Miss Turner and Mrs. Hendricks were the last to leave, and they bade me adieu the tears running down their sunburnt cheeks. I felt as though my last friends were leaving me, for what—as I thought then—was a Maniac." [60] Charlotte Pengra likewise left Missouri with her family in a large train. Several weeks out, mechanical problems detained some of the wagons, including those of the other three women. During the month they were separated, Pengra became increasingly dispirited and anxious: "The roads have been good today—I feel lonely and almost disheartened.... Can hear the wolves howl very distinctly. Rather ominis, perhaps you think.... Feel very tird and lonely—our folks not having come—I fear some of them ar sick." Having waited as long as possible for the others, the advance group made a major river crossing. "Then I felt that indeed I had left all my friends," Pengra wrote, "save my husband and his brother, to journey over the dreaded Plains, without one female acquaintance even for a companion—of course I wept and grieved about it but to no purpose." [61]

Others echoed her mourning. "The whipporwills are chirping," Helen Stewart wrote, "they bring me in mind of our old farm in pensillvania the home of my childhood where I have spent the happiest days I will ever see again. ... I feel rather lonesome today oh solitude solitude how I love it if I had about a dozen of my companions to enjoy it with me." [62] Uprootedness took its toll in debilitation and numbness. After a hard week, men "lolled around in the tents and on their blankets seeming to realize that the 'Sabbath was made for man,' " [63] resting on the palpable achievements of miles covered and rivers crossed. In contrast, the women "could not fully appreciate physical rest, and were rendered more uneasy by the continual passing of emigrant trains all day long. ... To me, much of the day was spent in meditating over the past and in forebodings for the future." [64]

The ultimate expression of this alienation was the pressure to turn back, to retrace steps to the old life. Occasionally anxiety or bewilderment erupted into open revolt against going on.

> This morning our company moved on, except one family. The woman got mad and wouldn't budge or let the children go. He had the cattle hitched on for three hours and coaxed her to go, but she wouldn't stir. I told my husband the circumstances and he and Adam Polk and Mr. Kimball went and each one took a young one and crammed them in the wagon, and the husband drove off and left her sitting. ... She cut across and overtook her husband. Meantime he sent his boy back to camp after a horse he had left, and when she came up her husband said, "Did you meet John?" "Yes," was the reply, "and I picked up a stone and knocked out his brains." Her husband went back to ascertain the truth and while he was gone she set fire to one of the wagons. ... He saw the flames and came running and put it out, and then mustered spunk enough to give her a good flogging.[65]

Short of violent resistance, it was always possible that circumstances would force a family to reconsider and turn back. During a cholera scare in 1852, "women cried, begging their men to take them back." [66] When the men reluctantly relented, the writer observed that "they did the hooking up of their oxen in a spiritless sort of way," while "some of the girls and women were laughing." [67] There was little lost and much regained for women in a decision to abandon the migration.

Both sexes worked, and both sexes suffered. Yet women lacked a sense of inclusion and a cultural rationale to give meaning to the suffering and the work; no augmented sense of self or role emerged from augmented privation. Both women and men also complained, but women expanded their caviling to a generalized critique of the whole enterprise. Margaret Chambers felt "as if we had left all civilization behind us" [68] after crossing the Missouri, and Harriet Ward's cry from South Pass—"Oh, shall we ever live like civilized beings again?" [69]—reverberated through the thoughts of many of her sisters. Civilization was far more to these women than law, books, and municipal government; it was pianos, church societies, daguerrotypes, mirrors—in short, their homes. At their most hopeful, the exiles perceived the Trail as a hellish but necessary transition to a land where they could renew their domestic mission: "Each advanced step of the slow, plodding cattle carried us farther and farther from civilzation into a desolate, barbarous country. . . . But our new home lay beyond all this and was a shining beacon that beckoned us on, inspiring our hearts with hope and courage." [70] At worse, temporary exigencies became in the minds of the dispossessed the omens of an irrevocable exile: "We have been travelling with 25-18-14-129-64-3 wagons—now all alone—how dreary it seems. Can it be that I have left my quiet little home and taken this dreary land of solitude in exchange?" [71]

Only a minority of the women who emigrated over the Overland Trail were from the northeastern middle classes where the cult of true womanhood reached its fullest bloom. Yet their responses to the labor demands of the Trail indicate that "womanliness" had penetrated the values, expectations, and personalities of midwestern farm women as well as New England "ladies." "Woman's sphere" provided them with companionship, a sense of self-worth, and most important, independence from men in a patriarchal world. The Trail, in breaking down sexual segregation, offered women the opportunities of socially essential work. Yet this work was performed in a male arena, and many women saw themselves as draftees rather than partners.

Historians have generally associated "positive work roles" [72] for women with the absence of narrowly defined notions of "woman's place." In the best summary of literature on colonial women, for example, the authors of *Women in American Society* write: "In general, neither men nor women seemed concerned with defining what women were or what their unique contribution to society should be. ... Abstract theories about the proper role of women did not stand in the way of meeting familial and social needs." [73] Conversely, the ascendancy of "true womanhood" and the doctrine of sexual spheres coincided with the declining importance of the labor of middle- and upper-class women in a rapidly expanding market economy. On the Overland Trail, cultural roles and self-definitions conflicted with the immediate necessities of the socioeconomic situation. Women themselves fought to preserve a circumscribed role when material circumstances rendered it dysfunctional. Like their colonial great-grandmothers on premarket subsistence farms, they labored at socially indispensable tasks. Yet they refused to appropriate their new work to their own ends and advantage. In their deepest sense of themselves they remained estranged from their function as "able bodies."

It could be argued that the time span of the trip was not long enough to alter cultural values. Yet there is evidence that the tensions of the Trail haunted the small and isolated market farms at the journey's end. [74] Women in the western settlements continued to try to reinstate a culture of domesticity, although their work as virtual hired hands rendered obsolete the material base of separate arenas for women and men.

The notion of subculture employed in this and other studies of nineteenth-century women is hazy and ill-defined. We need to develop more rigorous conceptions of society, culture, and subculture, and to clarify the paradoxes of women's position, both isolated and integrated, in the dominant social and cultural movements of their time. Nonetheless, the journals of overland women are irrefutable testimony to the importance of a separate female province. Such theorists as Catharine Beecher were acutely aware of the advantages in keeping life divvied up, in maintaining "two pathways which are always different" for women and men. [75] The women who traveled on the Overland Trail experienced first hand the tribulations of integration which Beecher and her colleagues could predict in theory.

NOTES

1. The 1841 Bidwell-Bartelson party of about fifty people included only five women—three of them wives—and ten children. Contemporary figures for

.the forties' migrations indicate that men made up roughly fifty percent of the parties, women and children the other fifty percent. These proportions prevailed until the Gold Rush. In contrast, the composition of the 1849 emigration was men—ninety-two percent, women—six percent, and children—two percent; in 1850, men—ninety-seven percent, women and children—three percent. In 1852 the proportions shifted toward the pre-1849 norm: men—seventy percent, women—thirteen percent, children—twenty percent. These percentages are rough estimates, and indicate no more than trends.

For overall figures see Merrill Mattes, *The Great Platte River Road* (Lincoln, Nebraska: Nebraska State Historical Society, 1969), p. 23. For the early forties' on the Oregon Trail, see David Lavender, *Westward Vision: The Story of the Oregon Trail* (New York: McGraw-Hill, 1963), pp. 349-50, 365. For the California branch: George R. Stewart, *The California Trail: An Epic With Many Heroes* (New York: McGraw-Hill, 1962), pp. 8, 54-55, 85, 147, 187, 195, 232, 303, 310. For the Gold Rush: Georgia Willis Read, "Women and Children on the Oregon-California Trail in the Gold-Rush Years," *Missouri Historical Review* 34 (1944–1945): 6.

2. Arthur W. Calhoun, *A Social History of the American Family from Colonial Times to the Present* 3 vols. (New York: Barnes & Noble, 1945) 2:11. Calhoun's statement has stood up well to demographic tests; after analysis of nineteenth-century census data, Jack Eblen concludes that "the deeply entrenched ideal and institution of the family provided the mechanism by which people were bound together during the process of cultural transplantation and adaptation" ("An Analysis of Nineteenth Century Frontier Populations," *Demography* 2, no. 4 [1965]: 341).

3. A simple enumeration of the special equipment necessary for the trip indicates the expense. Each family needed a light wagon, harnesses, and a team, usually oxen; the team alone could easily cost two hundred dollars. Arms and ammunition were purchased specially for the trip; such weapons as shotguns and rifles cost around twenty-five dollars. Since there was practically no chance for resupply along the route, a family had to stock for the entire six-month trip, a considerable investment that only the economically stable could afford. For a discussion and details see Mattes, *Great Platte River Road*, pp. 37-50; Stewart, *The California Trail*, pp. 106-26.

4. Neighbors and friends often moved as a "party," later joining a larger train. Brothers, cousins, and their families, or parents and one or two married children and their families, might set out together. Conjugal and parental ties usually survived under stress, while other relations disintegrated or exploded. Interestingly, the most enduring extrafamilial bonds may have been between nuclear families and the single men who traveled with them. The latter saved money by attaching themselves to family parties rather than outfitting a wagon alone. Some paid for their passage, while others worked as drivers or cattle drovers. For examples of various groupings, see Phoebe Goodell Judson, *A Pioneer's Search for an Ideal Home* (Bellingham, Washington: United Printing, Binding and Stationery Co., 1925), pp. 15-17; Mary E. Ackley, *Crossing the Plains and Early Days in California* (San Francisco: the author, 1928), p. 17; Sarah J. Cummins, *Autobiography and Reminiscences* (Walla Walla, Oregon: The

Walla Walla Bulletin, 1920), p. 22; Mrs. J.T. Gowdy, *Crossing the Plains: Personal Recollections of the Journey to Oregon in 1852* (Dayton, Oregon: n.p., 1906), p. 1; Nancy A. Hunt, "By Ox Team to California," *Overland Monthly* 67 (April 1916): 10; Mrs. M.A. Looney, *A Trip Across the Plains in the Year of 1852 with Ox Teams* (McMinnville, Oregon: n.p., 1915), p. 8; and Mrs. Lee Whipple-Halsam, *Early Days in California: Scenes and Events of the '60s as I Remember Them* (Jamestown, California: n.p., 1923), p. 8.

5. For a recent revision of work on the Overland Trail see Mattes, *The Great Platte River Road.*

6. Most of the research on the Victorian family has been based on middle- and upper-class northeastern and mid-western families. We do not yet know to what extent the ideology of domesticity affected poor, proletarianized, or southern families.

   Although our suggestions about the geographic and class composition of the migrations are generally accepted ones, they remain hypothetical in the absence of demographic research. An overwhelming majority of the women who kept the journals upon which much of our research is based *did* come from the northeastern and midwestern middle class. Nevertheless, until we know much more about the inarticulate families from backwoods Missouri, we cannot pretend to describe the "normative" experience of the overland family. Our interpretation is limited to families whose structure and consciousness were rooted in American bourgeois culture.

7. The ten volumes of Sarah Hale's *Ladies' Magazine* (1828–1837) are rich primary sources for antebellum ideals of sex roles and the family. For secondary works see the introductory pieces in Nancy Cott, ed., *Root of Bitterness* (Boston: E.P. Dutton, 1972), and Kathryn Kish Sklar, *Catharine Beecher* (New Haven: Yale University Press, 1973). A relatively inaccessible essay remains one of the most illuminating treatments of the period: Nancy Osterud, "Sarah Josepha Hale: A Study of the History of Women in Nineteenth Century America" (unpublished honors thesis, Harvard College, 1971).

8. See Cott, *Root of Bitterness,* pp. 11–14; Alice Clark, *Working Life of Women in the Seventeenth Century* (London: G. Routledge & Sons, 1919); Elisabeth Dexter, *Colonial Women of Affairs: Women in Business and Professions in America Before 1776* (Boston: Houghton Mifflin Co., 1924); Alice M. Earle, *Home Life in Colonial Days* (New York: Macmillan Co., 1898); Nancy Osterud, "The New England Family, 1790–1840" (unpublished manuscript, Old Sturbridge Village Education Department; Sturbridge, Mass., n.d.).

9. We do not use "productive" as a value judgement but as a historically specific concept: labor which produces surplus value within the capitalist mode of production. Within the work process itself, both men's *and* women's labor was "useful," but only men's, in the accepted sex-division, resulted in the creation of commodities. For a provocative discussion of this problem see Ian Gough, "Marx's Theory of Productive and Unproductive Labor," *New Left Review* 76 (November-December 1972): 47–72, and Lise Vogel, "The Earthly Family," *Radical America* 7 (July-October 1973): 9–50.

10. See Sklar, *Catharine Beecher*, and Ann D. Gordon, Mari Jo Buhle, and Nancy E. Schrom, "Women in American Society," *Radical America* (1972): 25–33.

11. Quoted in Catharine Beecher, *A Treatise on Domestic Economy* (New York: Harper Brothers, 1858), p. 28.

12. The most comprehensive account to date of domesticity, culture, and sexual spheres is Sklar, *Catharine Beecher;* see especially pp. 151–67 and 204–16. For the cultural importance of reform to women, see Carroll Smith-Rosenberg, "Beauty, the Beast, and the Militant Woman: A Case Study in Sex Roles in Jacksonian America," *American Quarterly* 23 (Fall 1971): 562–84 and Gail Parker, *The Oven Birds: American Women on Womanhood 1820–1920* (New York: Doubleday and Co., 1972), pp. 1–56. Nancy Cott's argument in *Root of Bitterness*, pp. 3–4, is a concise summary of the subculture argument. See Ann Douglas Wood, "The 'Scribbling Women' and Fanny Fern: Why Women Wrote," *American Quarterly* 23 (Spring 1971): 1–24, and "Mrs. Sigourney and the Sensibility of the Inner Space," *New England Quarterly* 45 (June 1972): 163–81 for women's cultural impulses in literature.

13. The Great Pacific migration began in the wake of the depression of 1837–40. The Pacific Northwest and California seemed to offer unfailing markets at Hudson's Bay forts, Russian settlements, even the massive Orient. The Pacific itself was to be the great transportation network that backwoods farmers needed so desperately. The 1841 migration was the result of the work of the Western Emigration Society, specifically organized to overcome the economic problems of the depressed Midwest. In short, the coast was rich in fertile, free land and unlimited chances for economic success. See Lavender, *Westward Vision*, pp. 327–28. The major exception to this generalization is the Mormon emigration.

14. Judson, *A Pioneer's Search*, p. 9.

15. Lucy Rutledge Cooke, *Crossing the Plains in 1852 . . . as told in Letters Written During the Journey* (Modesto, California: the author, 1923), p. 5. See also James Robertson, *A Few Months in America* (London: n.p., 1855), p. 150; Nancy A. Hunt, "By Ox-Team," p. 9; and Elias Johnson Draper, *An Autobiography* (Fresno, California: the author, 1904), p. 9.

16. Margaret M. Hecox, *California Caravan: the 1846 Overland Trail Memoir of Margaret M. Hecox* (San Jose, California: Harlan-Young Press, 1966), p. 31.

17. Lavinia Honeyman Porter, *By Ox Team to California: A Narrative of Crossing the Plains in 1860* (Oakland, California: the author, 1910), p. 7; see also Margaret White Chambers, *Reminiscences* (n.p.: n.p., 1903), pp. 5–7.

18. Porter, *By Ox Team*, p. 41.

19. Luzena Stanley Wilson, *Luzena Stanley Wilson, '49er* (Oakland, California: The Eucalyptus Press, 1937), p. 1.

20. Mary Jane Hayden, *Pioneer Days* (San Jose, California: Murgotten's Press, 1915), pp. 7–8.

21. Our sample of women's diaries and memoirs is by definition biased toward those women who successfully challenged their husbands. A more comprehensive view requires reading another set of journals—those of men who left their families behind. This work, as a part of a general

history of the family, women, and men on the Overland Trail, is now in progress: John Faragher, "Women, Men and Their Families on the Overland Trail" (Ph.D. thesis, Yale University, in progress).

22. For a particularly striking record of marriage proposals, see *Mollie: The Journal of Mollie Dorsey Sanford in Nebraska and Colorado Territories, 1857-66* (Lincoln, Nebraska: University of Nebraska Press, 1959), pp. 20, 58, 59, 74, 91.

23. Quoted in Nancy Ross, *Westward the Women* (New York: Alfred A. Knopf, 1944), p. 110.

24. Mrs. John Wilson, quoted in Read, "Women and Children on the Oregon-California Trail in the Gold-Rush Years," p. 7.

25. Ross, *Westward the Women*, p. 111.

26. See Mari Sandoz's biography of her father, *Old Jules* (Lincoln, Nebraska: University of Nebraska Press, 1955) for a dramatic illustration of a male homesteader's functional view of wives and children.
    The conventional view that the American west was predominantly male dies hard. Jack Eblen, in "Nineteenth Century Frontier Populations," conclusively demonstrates that the sex ratio in the West was little different from that in the East: women were nearly always present in numbers equal to men. See Christine Stansell, "Women on the Plains." *Women's Studies* (forthcoming).

27. Esther Allen, *Canvas Caravans: Based on the Journal of Esther Belle McMillan Hanna* (Portland, Oregon: Binfords & Mort, 1946), p. 18.

28. Mrs. Elizabeth Dixon Smith Geer, "Diary," in Oregon Pioneer Association, *Transactions of the Thirty-fifth Annual Reunion* (1907), p. 169.

29. Catherine Margaret Haun, quoted in Read, "Women and Children on the Oregon-California Trail in the Gold-Rush Years," p. 9.

30. Chambers, *Reminiscences*, p. 8.

31. See Adrietta Applegate Hixon, *On to Oregon! A True Story of a Young Girl's Journey Into the West* (Wesler, Idaho: Signal-American Printers, 1947), p. 17, for one of the few instances in the diaries when men took on women's work.

32. See Charles Howard Crawford, *Scenes of Earlier Days: In Crossing the Plains to Oregon, and Experiences of Western Life* (Chicago: Quadrangle, 1962), p. 9, for an account of women's resistance to assuming this particular responsibility.

33. Cummins, *Autobiography and Reminiscences*, p. 28.

34. See Gowdy, *Crossing the Plains*, p. 2; John Barnett, *Long Trip in a Prairie Schooner* (Whittier, California: Western Stationary Co., 1928), p. 105; and Lydia Milner Waters, "A Trip Across the Plains in 1855," *Quarterly of the Society of California Pioneers* 6 (June 1929): 66.

35. Charlotte Emily Pengra, "Diary of Mrs. Byron J. Pengra" (unpublished typescript in Lane County Historical Society, Eugene, Oregon, n.d.), p. 8.

36. Mary Burrell, "Mary Burrell's Book" (manuscript diary, Beinecke Library, Yale University), no pagination; Cummins, *Autobiography*, p. 27; E. Allene Dunham, *Across the Plains in a Covered Wagon* (Milton, Iowa: n.p., n.d.), p. 10.

37. Pengra, "Diary" p. 5.

38. Ibid., pp. 6, 8-9, 12.

39. Helen Marnie Stewart, "Diary" (unpublished typescript at Lane County Historical Society, Eugene, Oregon, 1961), p. 13.

40. The place of children in the structure of the overland family is an intriguing question that we are reserving for more research and reflection. On the basis of their infrequent appearance in the journals, it seems that in this area, too, nineteenth-century patterns were more modified. Many historians have pointed to the antebellum period as the time when "the child" emerged from obscurity to a special social status. In the overland sources, however, children over the age of five are rarely discussed except as younger and more vulnerable members of the working group, requiring little extra or special attention.

41. Elizabeth Wood, "Journal of a Trip to Oregon, 1851," *Oregon Historical Society Quarterly* 17 (1926): 4.

42. Helen M. Carpenter, "A Trip Across the Plains in an Ox Wagon, 1857" (manuscript diary, Huntington Library, San Marino, California), pp. 27–28.

43. Hixon, *On to Oregon!* p. 17.

44. Pengra, "Diary," p. 5.

45. Emery T. Bray, ed., *Bray Family Geneology and History* (n.p.: n.p., 1927), p. 10.

46. Ibid.

47. Porter, *By Ox Team to California,* p. 43.

48. Ibid., p. 118.

49. Waters, "A Trip Across the Plains in 1855," p. 77.

50. Hixon, *On to Oregon!* p. 45.

51. Catherine Haun in Read, "Women and Children During the Gold-Rush Years," p. 9. See also Hixon, *On to Oregon!* p. 15 and *passim;* and William Smedley, "Across the Plains in Sixty-two," *The Trail* 19 (March 1927): 11.

52. Sarah Royce, *A Frontier Lady: Recollections of the Gold Rush and Early California* (New Haven: Yale University Press, 1932), pp. 8–9.

53. Haun in Read, "Women and Children During the Gold-Rush Years," p. 9.

54. Harriet Sherril Ward, *Prairie Schooner Lady: The Journal of Harriet Sherril Ward* (Los Angeles: Westernlore Press, 1959), p. 60.

55. Ibid., p. 95. See also Celinda E. Hines, "Diary of Celinda E. Hines," in Oregon Pioneer Association, *Transactions of the Forty-sixth Annual Reunion* (1918), pp. 82–83 and *passim.*

56. Ward, *Prairie Schooner Lady,* p. 69.

57. See Narcissa Whitman, "Diary," (manuscript, Beinecke Library, Yale University), p. 18, or in any one of its many unpublished versions—see e.g., *Oregon Historical Quarterly* 35 (1936). Also Esther and Joseph Lyman, "Letters About the Lost Wagon Train of 1853" (unpublished typescript in Lane County Historical Society, Eugene, Oregon), p. 6; and Georgia Read and Ruth Gaines, eds., *Gold Rush: the Journals, Drawings, and Other Papers of J. Goldsborough Bruff . . . April 2, 1849-July 20, 1851* (New York: n.p., 1949), p. 45 and *passim.*

58. Stewart, "Diary," entry for June 6, 1853. See also Whitman, "Diary," p. 21; Pengra, "Diary," p. 3; and Royce, *Frontier Lady,* p. 11.

59. Stewart, "Diary," entry for June 12, 1853.

60. Mrs. Mary Rockwood Power, "The Overland Route: Leaves from the Journal of a California Emigrant," *Amateur Book Collector* 1 (November 1950): 6.

61. Pengra, "Diary," entries for May 2, 3, 8, and 10, and entries for June 5, 24, and July 7, 1853. See also, Royce, *Frontier Lady,* p. 9; and Mrs. Mary A. Frink, *Journal of the Adventures of a Party of California Gold-Seekers* (Oakland, California: n.p., 1897), p. 67.
62. Stewart, "Diary," entry for May 1, 1853.
63. Judson, *A Pioneer's Search,* p. 23.
64. Ibid.
65. Geer, "Diary," pp. 165–66.
66. Hixon, *On to Oregon!* p. 18.
67. Ibid.
68. Chambers, *Reminiscences,* p. 7.
69. Ward, *Prairie Schooner Lady,* p. 128. See also Allen, *Canvas Caravans,* p. 28.
70. Judson, *A Pioneer's Search,* p. 18.
71. Maria Parsons Belshaw, "Diary of a Bride Written on the Trail in 1853," *Oregon Historical Society Quarterly* 33 (March-December 1932): 334.
72. Cott, *Root of Bitterness,* p. 5.
73. Gordon, Buhle, and Schrom, *Women in American Society,* p. 22.
74. Stansell, "Women on the Plains."
75. Catharine Beecher, *Domestic Economy,* p. 28.

The Hysterical Woman:
Sex Roles and Role Conflict
in Nineteenth-Century America

Carroll Smith-Rosenberg

Hysteria was one of the classic diseases of the nineteenth century. It was a protean ailment characterized by such varied symptoms as paraplegia, aphonia, hemi-anaesthesia, and violent epileptoid seizures. Under the broad rubric of hysteria, nineteenth-century physicians gathered cases which might today be diagnosed as neurasthenia, hypochondriasis, depression, conversion reaction, and ambulatory schizophrenia. It fascinated and frustrated some of the century's most eminent clinicians; through its redefinition Freud rose to international fame, while the towering reputation of Charcot suffered a comparative eclipse. Psychoanalysis can historically be called the child of the hysterical woman.

Not only was hysteria a widespread and—in the intellectual history of medicine—significant disease, it remains to this day a frustrating and ever-changing illness. What was diagnosed as hysteria in the nineteenth century is not necessarily related to the hysterical character as defined in the twentieth century, or again to what the Greeks meant by hysteria when they christened the disease millennia ago. The one constant in this varied history has been the existence in virtually every era of Western culture of some clinical entity called hysteria; an entity which has always been seen as peculiarly relevant to the female experience, and one which has almost always carried with it a pejorative implication.

For the past half century and longer, American culture has defined hysteria in terms of individual psychodynamics. Physicians and psychologists have seen hysteria as a "neurosis" or character disorder, the product of an unresolved Oedipal complex. Hysterical women, fearful of their own sexual impulses—so the argument went—channeled that energy into psychosomatic illness. Characteristically, they proved unable to form satisfying and stable relationships.[1] More recently psychoanalysts such as Elizabeth Zetzel have refined this Freudian hypothesis, tracing the roots of hysteria to a woman's excessively ambivalent preoedipal relation with her mother and to the resulting complications of oedipal development and resolution.[2] Psychologist David Shapiro has emphasized the hysterical woman's impressionistic thought pattern.[3] All such interpretations focus exclusively on individual psychodynamics and relations within particular families.

Yet hysteria is also a socially recognized behavior pattern and as such exists within the larger world of cultural values and role relationships. For centuries hysteria has been seen as characteristically female—the hysterical woman the embodiment of a perverse or hyper femininity.[4] Why has this been so? Why did large numbers of women "choose" the character traits of hysteria as their particular mode of expressing malaise, discontent, anger or pain?[5] To begin to answer this question, we must explore the female role and role socialization. Clearly not all women were hysterics; yet the parallel between the hysteric's behavior and stereotypic femininity is too close to be explained as mere coincidence. To examine hysteria from this social perspective means necessarily to explore the complex relationships that exist between cultural norms and individual behavior, between behavior defined as disease and behavior considered normal.

Using nineteenth-century America as a case study,[6] I propose to explore hysteria on at least two levels of social interaction. The first involves an examination of hysteria as a social role within the nineteenth-century family. This was a period when, it has been argued, social and structural change had created stress within the family and when, in addition, individual domestic role alternatives were few and rigidly defined. From this perspective hysteria can be seen as an alternate role option for particular women incapable of accepting their life situation. Hysteria thus serves as a valuable indicator both of domestic stress and of the tactics through which some individuals sought to resolve that stress. By analyzing the function of hysteria within the family and the interaction of the hysteric, her family, and the interceding—yet interacting—physician, I also hope to throw light upon the role of women and female-male relationships within the larger world of nineteenth-century American society. Secondly, I will attempt to raise some questions concerning female role socialization, female personality options, and the nature of hysterical behavior.[7]

I

It might be best to begin with a brief discussion of three relatively well known areas: first, the role of women in nineteenth-century American society; second, the symptoms which hysterical women presented and which established the definition of the disease, and lastly, the response of male physicians to their hysterical patients.

The ideal female in nineteenth-century America was expected to be gentle and refined, sensitive and loving. She was the guardian of religion and spokeswoman for morality. Hers was the task of guiding the more worldly and more frequently tempted male past the maelstroms of atheism and uncontrolled sexuality. Her sphere was the hearth and the nursery; within it she was to bestow care and love, peace and joy. The American girl was taught at home, at school, and in the literature of the period, that aggression, independence, self-assertion and curiosity were male traits, inappropriate for the weaker sex and her limited sphere. Dependent throughout her life, she was to reward her male protectors with affection and submission. At no time was she expected to achieve in any area considered important by men and thus highly valued by society. She was, in essence, to remain a child-woman, never developing the strengths and skills of adult autonomy. The stereotype of the middle class woman as emotional, pious, passive and nurturant was to become increasingly rigid throughout the nineteenth century.[8]

There were significant discontinuities and inconsistencies between such ideals of female socialization and the real world in which the American woman had to live. The first relates to a dichotomy between the ideal woman and the ideal mother. The ideal woman was emotional, dependent and gentle—a born follower. The ideal mother, then and now, was expected to be strong, self-reliant, protective, an efficient caretaker in relation to children and home. She was to manage the family's day-to-day finances, prepare foods, make clothes, compound drugs, serve as family nurse—and, in rural areas, as physician as well.[9] Especially in the nineteenth century, with its still primitive obstetrical practices and its high child mortality rates, she was expected to face severe bodily pain, disease and death—and still serve as the emotional support and strength of her family.[10] As S. Weir Mitchell, the eminent Philadelphia neurologist wrote in the 1880s, "We may be sure that our daughters will be more likely to have to face at some time the grim question of pain than the lads who grow up beside them. . . . To most women . . . there comes a time when pain is a grim presence in their lives." Yet, as Mitchell pointed out, it was boys whom society taught from early childhood on to bear pain stoically, while girls were encouraged to respond to pain and stress with tears and the expectation of elaborate sympathy.[11]

Contemporaries noted routinely in the 1870s, 1880s and 1890s that middle-class American girls seemed ill-prepared to assume the responsibilities and trials of marriage, motherhood and maturation. Frequently women, especially married women with children, complained of isolation, loneliness, and depression. Physicians reported a high incidence of nervous disease and hysteria among women who felt overwhelmed by the burdens of frequent pregnancies, the demands of children, the daily exertions of housekeeping and family management.[12] The realities of adult life no longer permitted them to elaborate and exploit the role of fragile, sensitive and dependent child.

Not only was the Victorian woman increasingly ill-prepared for the trials of childbirth and childrearing, but changes were also at work within the larger society which were to make her particular socialization increasingly inappropriate. Reduced birth and mortality rates, growing population concentration in towns, cities and even in rural areas, a new, highly mobile economy, as well as new patterns of middle class aspiration—all reached into the family altering that institution, affecting domestic relations and increasing the normal quantity of infrafamilial stress.[13] Women lived longer; they married later and less often. They spent less and less time in the primary processing of food, cloth and clothing. Increasingly, both middle and lower class women took jobs outside the home until their marriages—or permanently if unable to secure a husband.[14] By the post-Civil War years, family limitation—with its necessary implication of altered domestic roles and relationships—had become a real option within the decision-making processes of every family.[15]

Despite such basic social, economic and demographic changes, however, the family and gender role socialization remained relatively inflexible. It is quite possible that many women experienced a significant level of anxiety when forced to confront or adapt in one way or another to these changes. Thus hysteria may have served as one option or tactic offering particular women otherwise unable to respond to these changes a chance to redefine or restructure their place within the family.

So far this discussion of role socialization and stress has emphasized primarily the malaise and dissatisfaction of the middle class woman. It is only a covert romanticism, however, which permits us to assume that the lower class or farm woman, because her economic functions within her family were more vital than those of her decorative and economically secure urban sisters, escaped their sense of frustration, conflict or confusion. Normative prescriptions of proper womanly behavior were certainly internalized by many poorer women. The desire to marry and the belief that a woman's social status came not from the exercise of her own talents and efforts but from her ability to attract a competent male protector were as universal among lower class and farm women as among middle and upper class urban women. For some of these women—as for their urban middle class sisters—the traditional female role proved functional, bringing material and psychic rewards. But for some it did not. The discontinuity between the child and adult female roles, along with the failure to develop substantial ego strengths, crossed class and geographic barriers—as did hysteria itself. Physicians connected with almshouses, and later in the century with urban hospitals and dispensaries, often reported hysteria among immigrant and tenement house women.[16] Sex differentiation and class distinctions both play a role in American social history, yet hysteria seems to have followed a psychic fault line corresponding more to distinctions of gender than to those of class.

Against this background of possible role conflict and discontinuity, what were the presenting symptoms of the female hysteric in nineteenth-century America? While physicians agreed that hysteria could afflict persons of both sexes and of all ages and economic classes (the male hysteric was an accepted clinical entity by the late nineteenth century), they reported that hysteria was most frequent among women between the ages of fifteen and forty and of the urban middle and upper middle classes. Symptoms were highly varied. As early as the seventeenth century, indeed, Sydenham had remarked that "the frequency of hysteria is no less remarkable than the multiformity of the shapes it puts on. Few maladies are not imitated by it; whatever part of the body it attacks, it will create the proper symptom of that part."[17] The nineteenth-century physician could only concur. There were complaints of nervousness, depression, the tendency to tears and chronic fatigue, or of disabling pain. Not a few women thus afflicted showed a remarkable willingness to submit to long-term, painful therapy—to electric shock treatment, to blistering, to multiple operations, even to amputations.[18]

The most characteristic and dramatic symptom, however, was the hysterical "fit." Mimicking an epileptic seizure, these fits often occurred with shocking suddenness. At other times they "came on" gradually, announcing their approach with a general feeling of depression, nervousness, crying or lassitude. Such seizures, physicians generally agreed, were precipitated by a sudden or deeply felt emotion—fear, shock, a sudden death, marital disappointment—or by physical trauma. It began with pain and tension, most frequently in the "uterine area." The sufferer alternately sobbed and laughed violently, complained of palpitations of the heart, clawed her throat as if strangling and, at times, abruptly lost the power of hearing and speech. A death-like trance might follow, lasting hours, even days. At other times violent convulsions—sometimes accompanied by hallucinations—seized her body.[19] "Let the reader imagine," New York physician E. H. Dixon wrote in the 1840s:

> the patient writhing like a serpent upon the floor, rending her garments to tatters, plucking out handsful of hair, and striking her person with violence—with contorted and swollen countenance and fixed eyes resisting every effort of bystanders to control her . . .[20]

Finally the fit subsided; the patient, exhausted and sore, fell into a restful sleep.

During the first half of the nineteenth century physicians described hysteria principally though not exclusively in terms of such episodes. Symptoms such as paralysis and contracture were believed to be caused by seizures and categorized as infraseizure symptoms. Beginning in mid-century, however, physicians became increasingly flexible in their diagnosis of hysteria and gradually the fit declined in significance as a pathognomonic symptom.[21] Dr. Robert Carter, a widely-read British authority on hysteria, insisted in 1852 that at least one hysterical seizure must have occurred to justify a diagnosis of hysteria. But, he admitted, this seizure might be so minor as to have escaped the notice even of the patient herself; no subsequent seizures were necessary.[22] This was clearly a transitional position. By the last third of the nineteenth century the seizure was no longer the central phenomenon defining hysteria; physicians had categorized hysterical symptoms which included virtually every known human ill. They ranged from loss of sensation in part, half or all of the body, loss of taste, smell, hearing, or vision, numbness of the skin, inability to swallow, nausea, headaches, pain in the breast, knees, hip, spine or neck, as well as contracture or paralysis of virtually any extremity.[23]

Hysterical symptoms were not limited to the physical. An hysterical female character gradually began to emerge in the nineteenth-century medical literature, one based on interpretations of mood and personality rather than on discrete physical symptoms—one which grew closely to resemble twentieth-century definitions of the "hysterical personality." Doctors commonly described hysterical women as highly impressionistic, suggestible, and narcissistic. Highly labile, their moods changed suddenly, dramatically, and for seemingly inconsequential reasons. Doctors complained that the hysterical woman was egocentric in the extreme, her involvement with others consistently superficial and tangential. While the hysterical woman might appear to physicians and relatives as quite sexually aroused or attractive, she was, doctors cautioned, essentially asexual and not uncommonly frigid.[24]

Depression also appears as a common theme. Hysterical symptoms not infrequently followed a death in the family, a miscarriage, some financial setback which forced the patient to become self-supporting; or they were seen by the patient as related to some long-term, unsatisfying life situation—a tired school teacher, a mother unable to cope with the demands of a large family.[25] Most of these women took to their beds because of pain, paralysis or general weakness. Some remained there for years.

The medical profession's response to the hysterical woman was at best ambivalent. Many doctors—and indeed a significant proportion of society at large—tended to be caustic, if not punitive towards the hysterical woman. This resentment seems rooted in two factors: first, the baffling and elusive nature of hysteria itself, and second, the relation which existed in the physicians' minds between their categorizing of hysteria as a disease and the role women were expected to play in society. These patients did not function as women were expected to function, and, as we shall see, the physician who treated them felt threatened both as a professional and as a rejected male. He was the therapist thwarted, the child untended, the husband denied nurturance and sex.

During the second half of the nineteenth century, the newly established germ theory and discoveries by neurologists and anatomists for the first time made an insistence on disease specificity a *sine qua non* for scientific respectability. Neurology was just becoming accepted as a speciality, and in its search for acceptance it was particularly dependent on the establishment of firm, somatically-based disease entities.[26]

If hysteria *was* a disease, and not the imposition of self-pitying women striving to avoid their traditional roles and responsibilities—as was frequently charged, it must be a disease with a specific etiology and a predictable course. In the period 1870 to 1900, especially, it was felt to be a disease rooted in some specific organic malfunction.

Hysteria, of course, lacked all such disease characteristics. Contracture or paralysis could occur without muscular atrophy or change in skin temperature. The hysteric might mimic tuberculosis, heart attacks, blindness or hip disease, while lungs, heart, eyes and hips remained in perfect health.[27] The physician had only his patient's statement that she could not move or was wracked with pain. If concerned and sympathetic, he faced a puzzling dilemma. As George Preston wrote in his 1897 monograph on hysteria:

> In studying the ... disturbances of hysteria, a very formidable difficulty presents itself in the fact that the symptoms are purely subjective. ... There is only the bald statement of the patient. ... No confirming symptoms present themselves ... and the appearance of the affected parts stands as contradictory evidence against the patient's word.[28]

Equally frustrating and medically inexplicable were the sudden changes in the hysteric's symptoms. Paralysis or anaesthesia could shift from one side of the body to the other, from one limb to another. Headaches would replace contracture of a limb, loss of voice, the inability to taste. How could a physician prescribe for such ephemeral symptoms? "Few practitioners desire the management of hysterics," one eminent gynecologist, Samuel Ashwell, wrote in 1833. "Its symptoms are so varied and obscure, so contradictory and changeable, and if by chance several of them, or even a single one be relieved, numerous others almost immediately spring into existence." [29] Half a century later, neurologist Charles K. Mills echoed Ashwell's discouraging evaluation. "Hysteria is pre-eminently a chronic disease," he warned. "Deceptive remissions in hysterical symptoms often mislead the unwary practitioner. Cures are sometimes claimed where simply a change in the character of the phenomena has taken place. It is a disease in which it is unsafe to claim a conquest." [30]

Yet physicians, especially newly established neurologists with urban practices, were besieged by patients who appeared to be sincere, respectable women sorely afflicted with pain, paralysis or uncontrollable "nervous fits." "Looking at the pain evoked by ideas and beliefs," S. Weir Mitchell, America's leading expert on hysteria wrote in 1885, "we are hardly wise to stamp these pains as non-existent." [31] Despite the tendency of many physicians to contemptuously dismiss the hysterical patient when no organic lesions could be found, neurologists such as Mitchell, George M. Beard, or Charles L. Dana sympathized with these patients and sought to alleviate their symptoms.

Such pioneer specialists were therefore in the position of having defined hysteria as a legitimate disease entity, and the hysterical woman as sick, when they were painfully aware that no organic etiology had yet been found. Cautiously, they sought to formally define hysteria in terms appropriately mechanistic. Some late nineteenth-century physicians, for example, still placing a traditional emphasis on hysteria's uterine origins, argued that hysteria resulted from "the reflex effects of utero-ovarian irritation." [32] Others, reflecting George M. Beard's work on neurasthenia, defined hysteria as a functional disease caused either by "metabolic or nutritional changes in the cellular elements of the central nervous system." Still others wrote in terms of a malfunction of the cerebral cortex.[33] All such explanations were but hypothetical gropings for an organic explanation—still a necessity if they were to legitimate hysteria as a disease.[34]

The fear that hysteria might after all be only a functional or "ideational" disease—to use a nineteenth-century term—and therefore not really a disease at all, underlies much of the writing on hysteria as well as the physicians' own attitudes toward their patients. These hysterical women might after all be only clever frauds and sensation-seekers—morally delinquent and, for the physician, professionally embarrassing.

Not surprisingly, a compensatory sense of superiority and hostility permeated many physicians' discussions of the nature and etiology of hysteria. Except when called upon to provide a hypothetical organic etiology, physicians saw hysteria as caused either by the indolent, vapid and unconstructive life of the fashionable middle and upper class woman, or by the ignorant, exhausting and sensual life of the lower or working class woman. Neither were flattering etiologies. Both denied the hysteric the sympathy granted to sufferers from unquestionably organic ailments.

Any general description of the personal characteristics of the well-to-do hysteric emphasized her idleness, self-indulgence, her deceitfulness and "craving for sympathy." Petted and spoiled by her parents, waited upon hand and foot by servants, she had never been taught to exercise self-control or to curb her emotions and desires.[35] Certainly she had not been trained to undertake the arduous and necessary duties of wife and mother. "Young persons who have been raised in luxury and too often in idleness," one late-nineteenth-century physician lectured, "who have never been called upon to face the hardships of life, who have never accustomed themselves to self-denial, who have abundant time and opportunity to cultivate the emotional and sensuous, to indulge the sentimental side of life, whose life purpose is too often an indefinite and self-indulgent idea of pleasure, these are the most frequent victims of hysteria."[36] Sound education, outside interests such as charity and good works, moral training, systematic outdoor exercise and removal from an overly sympathetic family were among the most frequent forms of treatment recommended. Mothers, consistently enough, were urged to bring up daughters with a strong sense of self-discipline, devotion to family needs, and a dread of uncontrolled emotionality.[37]

Emotional indulgence, moral weakness and lack of will power characterized the hysteric in both lay and medical thought. Hysteria, S. Weir Mitchell warned, occurred in women who had never developed habitual restraint and "rational endurance"—who had early lost their power of "self-rule." [38] "The mind and body are deteriorated by the force of evil habit," Charles Lockwood wrote in 1895, "morbid thought and morbid impulse run through the poor, weak, unresisting brain, until all mental control is lost, and the poor sufferer is ... at the mercy of ... evil and unrestrained passions, appetites and morbid thoughts and impulses." [39]

In an age when will, control, and hard work were fundamental social values, this hypothetical etiology necessarily implied a negative evaluation of those who succumbed to hysteria. Such women were described as weak, capricious and, perhaps most important, morbidly suggestible.[40] Their intellectual abilities were meager, their powers of concentration eroded by years of self-indulgence and narcissistic introspection.[41] Hysterical women were, in effect, children, and ill-behaved, difficult children at that. "They have in fact," Robert Carter wrote, "all the instability of childhood, joined to the vices and passions of adult age...." [42]

Many nineteenth-century critics felt that this emotional regression and instability was rooted in woman's very nature. The female nervous system, doctors argued, was physiologically more sensitive and thus more difficult to subject to the will. Some physicians assumed as well that woman's blood was "thinner" than man's, causing nutritional inadequacies in the central nervous system and an inability to store nervous energy—a weakness, Mary Putnam Jacobi stressed, women shared with children. Most commonly, a woman's emotional states generally, and hysteria in particular, were believed to have the closest ties to her reproductive cycle.[43] Hysteria commenced with puberty and ended with menopause, while ailments as varied as menstrual pain and irregularity, prolapsed or tipped uterus, uterine tumor, vaginal infections and discharges, sterility, could all—doctors were certain—cause hysteria. Indeed, the first question routinely asked hysterical women was "are your courses regular? "[44] Thus a woman's very physiology and anatomy predisposed her to hysteria; it was, as Thomas Laycock put in, "the natural state" in a female, a "morbid state" in the male.[45] In an era when a sexual perspective implied conflict and ambivalence, hysteria was perceived by physician and patient as a disease both peculiarly female and peculiarly sexual.

Hysteria could also result from a secret and less forgivable form of sexuality. Throughout the nineteenth century, physicians believed that masturbation was widespread among America's females and a frequent cause of hysteria and insanity. As early as 1846, E. H. Dixon reported that masturbation caused hysteria "among females even in society where physical and intellectual culture would seem to present the strongest barriers against its incursions. . . ." Other physicians concurred, reporting that harsh public and medical reactions to hysterical women were often based on the belief that masturbation was the cause of their behavior.[46]

Masturbation was only one form of sexual indulgence. A number of doctors saw hysteria among lower class women as originating in the sensuality believed to characterize their class. Such tenement-dwelling females, doctors reported, "gave free reign to . . . 'passions of the baser sort,' not feeling the necessity of self-control because they have to a pitiably small degree any sense of propriety or decency." Hysteria, another physician reported, was found commonly among prostitutes, while virtually all physicians agreed that even within marriage sexual excess could easily lead to hysteria.[47]

Expectedly, conscious anger and hostility marked the response of a good many doctors to their hysterical patients. One New York neurologist called the female hysteric a willful, self-indulgent and narcissistic person who cynically manipulated her symptoms. "To her distorted vision," he complained, "there is but one commanding personage in the universe—herself—in comparison with whom the rest of mankind are nothing." Doctors admitted that they were frequently tempted to use such terms as "willful" and "evil," "angry" and "impatient" when describing the hysteric and her symptoms.[48] Even the concerned and genteel S. Weir Mitchell, confident of his remarkable record in curing hysteria, described hysterical women as "the pests of many households, who constitute the despair of physicians, and who furnish those annoying examples of despotic selfishness, which wreck the constitutions of nurses and devoted relatives, and in unconscious or half-conscious self-indulgence destroy the comfort of everyone about them." He concluded by quoting Oliver Wendell Holmes' acid judgment that "a hysterical girl is a vampire who sucks the blood of the healthy people about her." [49]

Hysteria as a chronic, dramatic and socially accepted sick role could thus provide some alleviation of conflict and tension, but the hysteric purchased her escape from the emotional—and frequently—from the sexual demands of her life only at the cost of pain, disability, and an intensification of woman's traditional passivity and dependence. Indeed a complex interplay existed between the character traits assigned women in Victorian society and the characteristic symptoms of the nineteenth-century hysteric: dependency, fragility, emotionality, narcissism. (Hysteria has, after all, been called in that century and this a stark caricature of femininity.) Not surprisingly the hysteric's peculiar passive aggression and her exploitive dependency often functioned to cue a corresponding hostility in the men who cared for her or lived with her. Whether father, husband, or physician, they reacted with ambivalence and in many cases with hostility to her aggressive and never-ending demands.

II

What inferences concerning woman's role and female-male relationships can be drawn from this description of nineteenth-century hysteria and of medical attitudes toward the female patient? What insights does it allow into patterns of stress and resolution within the traditional nuclear family?

Because traditional medical wisdom had defined hysteria as a disease, its victims could expect to be treated as sick and thus to elicit a particular set of responses—the right to be seen and treated by a physician, to stay in bed and thus be relieved of their normal day-to-day responsibilities, to enjoy the special prerogatives, indulgences, and sympathy the sick role entailed. Hysteria thus became one way in which conventional women could express—in most cases unconsciously—dissatisfaction with one or several aspects of their lives.

The effect of hysteria upon the family and traditional sex role differentiation was disruptive in the extreme. The hysterical woman virtually ceased to function within the family. No longer did she devote herself to the needs of others, acting as self-sacrificing wife, mother, or daughter. Through her hysteria she could and in fact did force others to assume those functions. Household activities were reoriented to answer the hysterical woman's importunate needs. Children were hushed, rooms darkened, entertaining suspended, a devoted nurse recruited. Fortunes might be spent on medical bills or for drugs and operations. Worry and concern bowed the husband's shoulders; his home had suddenly become a hospital and he a nurse. Through her illness, the bedridden woman came to dominate her family to an extent that would have been considered inappropriate—indeed shrewish—in a healthy woman. Taking to one's bed, especially when suffering from dramatic and ever-visible symptoms, might also have functioned as a mode of passive aggression, especially in a milieu in which weakness was rewarded and in which women had since childhood been taught not to express overt aggression. Consciously or unconsciously, she had thus opted out of her traditional role.

Women did not accomplish this redefinition of domestic roles without the aid of the men in their family. Doctors commented that the hysteric's husband and family often, and unfortunately, rewarded her symptoms with elaborate sympathy. "The hysteric's credit is usually first established," as one astute mid-century clinician pointed out, "by those who have, at least, the wish to believe them." [50] Husbands and fathers were not alone in their cooperation; the physician often played a complex and in a sense emotionally compromising role in legitimizing the female hysteric's behavior. As an impartial and professionally skilled observer, he was empowered to judge whether or not a particular woman had the right to withdraw from her socially allotted duties. At the same time, these physicians accepted as correct, indeed as biologically inevitable, the structure of the Victorian family and the division of sex roles within it. He excused the woman only in the belief that she was ill and that she would make every effort to get well and resume her accustomed role. It was the transitory and unavoidable nature of the sick role that made it acceptable to family and physician as an alternate mode of female behavior.[51]

The doctor's ambivalence toward the hysterical woman, already rooted as we have seen in professional and sexual uncertainties, may well have been reinforced by his complicitory role within the family. It was for this reason that the disease's erratic pattern, its chronic nature, its lack of a determinable organic etiology, and the patient's seeming failure of will, so angered him. Even if she were not a conscious malingerer, she might well be guilty of self-indulgence and moral delinquency. By diagnosing her as ill, he had in effect created or permitted the hysterical woman to create a bond between himself and her. Within the family configuration he had sided with her against her husband or other male family members—men with whom he would normally have identified.[52]

The quintessential sexual nature of hysteria further complicated the doctor's professional stance. As we have already seen, the hysterical patient in her role as woman may well have mobilized whatever ambivalence towards sex a particular physician felt. In a number of cases, moreover, the physician also played the role of oedipal father figure to the patient's child-woman role, and in such instances his complicity was not only moral and intellectual but sexual as well. These doctors had become part of a domestic triangle—a husband's rival, the fatherly attendant of a daughter. This intra-family role may therefore go far to explain the particularly strident and suspicious tone which characterized much of the clinical discussion of hysteria. The physician had, by his alertness to deception and self-indulgence and by his therapeutic skills, to prevent the hysterical woman from using her disease to avoid her feminine duties—and from making him an unwitting accomplice in her deviant role. While tied to her as physician and thus legitimizer of her sick role, he had also to preserve his independence.

Although much of this interpretation must remain speculative, both the tone and substance of contemporary medical reaction to the female hysteric tends to confirm these inferences. Physicians were concerned with—and condemned—the power which chronic illness such as hysteria gave a woman over her family. Many women, doctors noted with annoyance, enjoyed this power and showed no inclination to get well: it is hardly coincidental that most late-nineteenth-century authorities agreed that removal from her family was a necessary first step in attempting to cure the hysterical patient.[53]

Not only did the physician condemn the hysteric's power within her family, he was clearly sensitive to her as a threat to his own prestige and authority. It is evident from their writings that many doctors felt themselves to be locked in a power struggle with their hysterical patients. Such women, doctors claimed, used their symptoms as weapons in asserting autonomy in relation to their physician; in continued illness was their victory. Physicians perceived hysterical women as unusually intractable and self-assertive. Although patients and women, they reserved the right to judge and approve their male physician's every action. Indeed, much of the medical literature on hysteria is devoted to providing doctors with the means of winning this war of wills. Physicians felt that they must dominate they hysteric's will; only in this way, they wrote, could they bring about her permanent cure. "Do not flatter yourselves . . . that you will gain an easy victory," Dr. L. C. Grey told a medical school class in 1888:

On the contrary, you must expect to have your temper, your ingenuity, your nerves tested to a degree that cannot be surpassed even by the greatest surgical operations. I maintain that the man who has the nerve and the tact to conquer some of these grave cases of hysteria has the nerve and the tact that will make him equal to the great emergencies of life. Your patient must be taught day by day ... by steady resolute, iron-willed determination and tact—that combination which the French ... call "the iron hand beneath the velvet glove." [54]

"Assume a tone of authority which will of itself almost compel submission," Robert Carter directed. "If a patient ... interrupts the speaker, she must be told to keep silence and to listen; and must be told, moreover, not only in a voice that betrays no impatience and no anger, but in such a manner as to convey the speaker's full conviction that the command will be immediately obeyed." [55]

Much of the treatment prescribed by physicians for hysteria reflects, in its draconic severity, their need to exert control—and, when thwarted, their impulse to punish. Doctors frequently recommended suffocating hysterical women until their fits stopped, beating them across the face and body with wet towels, ridiculing and exposing them in front of family and friends, showering them with icy water. "The mode adopted to arrest this curious malady," a physician connected with a large mental hospital wrote,

consists in making some strong and sudden impression on the mind through ... the most potent of all impressions, fear. ... Ridicule to a woman of sensitive mind, is a powerful weapon ... but there is no emotion equal to fear and the threat of personal chastisement ... They will listen to the voice of authority.[56]

When, on the other hand, the hysterical patient proved tractable, gave up her fits or paralyses and accepted the physician as saviour and moral guide, he no longer had to appear in the posture of chastising father. He could respond to his hysterical patient with fondness, sympathy, and praise. No longer was she thwarting him with "temper, tears, tricks, and tantrums"—as one doctor chose to title a study of hysteria.[57] Her cure demonstrated that he had mastered her will and body. The successful father-like practitioner had restored another wayward woman to her familial duties. Thomas Addis Emmett, pioneer gynecological specialist, recalled with ingenuous candor his mode of treating hysterics:

the patient ... was a child in my hands. In some respects the power gained was not unlike that obtained over a wild beast except that in one case the domination would be due to fear, while with my patient as a rule, it would be the desire to please me and to merit my approval from the effort she would make to gain her self-control. I have at times been depressed with the responsibility attending the blind influence I have often been able to gain over the nervous women under my influence.[58]

Not surprisingly, S. Weir Mitchell ended one of his treatises on hysteria with the comment that doctors, who knew and understood all women's petty weaknesses, who could govern and forgive them, made the best husbands.[59] Clearly the male physician who treated the hysterical woman was unable to escape the sex role relations that existed within nineteenth-century society generally.

III

The hysterical female thus emerges from the essentially male medical literature of the nineteenth century as a "child-woman," highly impressionable, labile, superficially sexual, exhibitionistic, given to dramatic body language and grand gestures, with strong dependency needs and decided ego weaknesses. She resembled in many ways the personality type referred to by Guze in 1967 as a "hysterical personality," or by Kernberg in 1968 as an "infantile personality." [60] But in a very literal sense these characteristics of the hysteric were merely hypertrophied versions of traits and behavior commonly reinforced in female children and adolescents. At a time when American society accepted egalitarian democracy and free will as transcendent social values, women, as we have seen, were nevertheless routinely socialized to fill a weak, dependent and severely limited social role. They were sharply discouraged from expressing competition or mastery in such "masculine" areas as physical skill, strength and courage, or in academic or commercial pursuits, while at the same time they were encouraged to be coquettish, entertaining, nonthreatening and nurturant. Overt anger and violence were forbidden as unfeminine and vulgar. The effect of this socialization was to teach women to have a low evaluation of themselves, to significantly restrict their ego functions to low prestige areas, to depend on others and to altruistically wish not for their own worldly success, but for that of their male supporters.

In essence, then, many nineteenth-century women reached maturity with major ego weaknesses and with narrowly limited compensatory ego strengths, all of which implies, I think, a generic relationship between this pattern of socialization and the adoption of hysterical behavior by particular individuals. It seems plausible to suggest that a certain percentage of nineteenth-century women faced with stress developing out of their own peculiar personality needs or because of situational anxieties might well have defended themselves against such stress by regressing towards the childish hyper-femininity of the hysteric. The discontinuity between the roles of courted woman and pain-bearing, self-sacrificing wife and mother, the realities of an unhappy marriage, the loneliness and chagrin of spinsterhood may all have made the petulant infantilism and narcissistic self-assertion of the hysteric a necessary alternative to women who felt unfairly deprived of their promised social role and who had few strengths with which to adapt to a more trying one. Society had indeed structured this regression by consistently reinforcing those very emotional traits characterized in the stereotype of the female—and caricatured in the symptomatology of the hysteric. At the same time, the nineteenth-century female hysteric also exhibited a significant level of hostility and aggression—rage—which may have led in turn to her depression and to her self-punishing psychosomatic illnesses. In all these ways, then, the hysterical woman can be seen as both product and indictment of her culture.

I must conclude with a caution. The reasons why individuals displayed that pattern of behavior called by nineteenth-century physicians "hysteria" must in individual cases remain moot. What this paper has sought to do is to suggest why certain symptoms were available and why women, in particular, tended to resort to them. It has sought as well to use the reactions of contemporaries to illuminate female-male and intrafamilial role realities. As such it has dealt with hysteria as a social role produced by and functional within a specific set of social circumstances.

NOTES

1. For a review of the recent psychiatric literature on hysteria see Aaron Lazare, "The Hysterical Character in Psychoanalytic Theory: Evolution and Confusion," *Archives of General Psychiatry*, XXV (August, 1971), pp. 131–37; Barbara Ruth Easser and S.R. Lesser, "Hysterical Personality: A Reevaluation," *Psychoanalytic Quarterly*, XXXIV (1965), pp. 390–405, and Marc H. Hollander, "Hysterical Personality," *Comments on Contemporary Psychiatry*, I (1971), pp. 17–24.
2. Elizabeth Zetzel, *The Capacity for Emotional Growth, Theoretical and Clinical Contributions to Psychoanalysis, 1943-1969* (London: Hogarth Press, 1970), Chap. 1-f, "The So-Called Good Hysteric."

3. David Shapiro, *Neurotic Styles,* (New York: Basic Books, 1965).
4. The argument can be made that hysteria exists among men and therefore is not exclusively related to the female experience; the question is a complex one, and I am presently at work on a parallel study of male hysteria. There are, however, four brief points concerning male hysteria that I would like to make. First, to this day hysteria is still believed to be principally a female "disease" or behavior pattern. Second, the male hysteric is usually seen by physicians as somehow different. Today it is a truism that hysteria in males is found most frequently among homosexuals; in the nineteenth century men diagnosed as hysterics came almost exclusively from a lower socioeconomic status than their physicians—immigrants, especially "new immigrants," miners, railroad workers, blacks. Third, since it was defined by society as a female disease, one may hypothesize that there was some degree of female identification among the men who assumed a hysterical role. Lastly, we must recall that a most common form of male hysteria was battle fatigue and shell shock. I should like to thank Erving Goffman for the suggestion that the soldier is in an analogous position to women regarding autonomy and power.
5. The word choose, even in quotes, is value-laden. I do not mean to imply that hysterical women consciously chose their behavior. I feel that three complex factors interacted to make hysteria a real behavioral option for American women: first, the various experiences that caused a woman to arrive at adulthood with significant ego weaknesses; second, certain socialization patterns and cultural values which made hysteria a readily available alternate behavior pattern for women, and third, the secondary gains conferred by the hysterical role in terms of enhanced power within the family. Individual cases presumably each represented their own peculiar balance of these factors, all of which will be discussed in this paper.
6. Nineteenth-century hysteria has attracted a good number of students: two of the most important are Henri F. Ellenberger, *The Discovery of the Unconscious* (New York: Basic Books, 1970), and Ilza Veith, *Hysteria: The History of a Disease* (Chicago: University of Chicago Press, 1965). Ellenberger and Veith approach hysteria largely from the framework of intellectual history. For a review of Veith see Charles E. Rosenberg, "Historical Sociology of Medical Thought," *Science,* CL (October 15, 1965), p. 330. For two studies which view nineteenth-century hysteria from a more sociological perspective see Esther Fischer-Homberger, "Hysterie und Misogynie: Ein Aspekt der Hysteriegeschichte," *Gesnerus,* XXVI (1969), pp. 117–27, and Marc H. Hollander, "Conversion Hysteria: A Post-Freudian Reinterpretation of Nineteenth-Century Psychosocial Data," *Archives of General Psychiatry,* XXVI (1972), pp. 311–14.
7. I would like to thank Reneé Fox, Cornelia Friedman, Erving Goffman, Charles E. Rosenberg and Paul Rosenkrantz for having read and criticized this paper. I would also like to thank my clinical colleagues Philip Mechanick, Henry Bachrach, Ellen Berman, and Carol Wolman of the Psychiatry Department of the University of Pennsylvania for similar assistance. Versions of this paper were presented to the Institute of the Pennsylvania Hospital, the Berkshire Historical Society, and initially, in October 1971, at the Psychiatry Department of Hannehmann Medical College, Philadelphia.

8. This summary of woman's role and role socialization is drawn from a larger study of male and female gender roles and gender role socialization in the United States from 1785 to 1895 on which I am presently engaged. This research has been supported by both the Grant Foundation, New York City and the National Institute of Child Health and Human Development, N.I.H. It ts difficult to refer succinctly to the wide range of sources on which this paragraph is based. Such a role model appears in virtually every nineteenth-century woman's magazine, in countless guides to young women and young wives and in etiquette books. For a basic secondary source see Barbara Welter, "The Cult of True Womanhood," *American Quarterly*, XVIII (1966), pp. 151–74. For an excellent overall history of women in America see Eleanor Flexner, *Century of Struggle* (Cambridge, Massachusetts: Harvard University Press, 1959).

9. For the daily activities of a nineteenth-century American housewife see, for example, *The Maternal Physician: By an American Matron* (New York: Isaac Riley, 1811. Reprinted New York: Arno Press, 1972); Hugh Smith, *Letters to Married Ladies* (New York: Bliss, White and G. & C. Carvill, 1827); John S. C. Abbott, *The Mother at Home* (Boston: Crocker and Brewster, 1833); Lydia H. Sigourney, *Letters to Mothers* (New York: Harper & Brothers, 1841); Mrs. C.A. Hopkinson, *Hints for the Nursery or the Young Mother's Guide* (Boston: Little, Brown & Company, 1836); Catharine Beecher and Harriet Beecher Stowe, *The American Woman's Home* (New York: J.B. Ford & Company, 1869). For an excellent secondary account of the southern woman's domestic life see Anne Firor Scott, *The Southern Lady* (Chicago: University of Chicago Press, 1970).

10. Nineteenth-century domestic medicine books, gynecological textbooks, and monographs on the diseases of women provide a detailed picture of women's diseases and health expectations.

11. S. Weir Mitchell, *Doctor and Patient* (Philadelphia: J.B. Lippincott Company, 1887), pp. 84, 92.

12. See among others Edward H. Dixon, *Woman and Her Diseases* (New York: Charles H. Ring, 1846), pp. 135–36; Alice Stockham, *Tokology: A Book for Every Woman* (Chicago: Sanitary Publishers, 1887), p. 83; Sarah A. Stevenson, *Physiology of Women*, 2nd edn. (Chicago: Cushing, Thomas & Co., 1881), p. 91; Henry Pye Chavasse, *Advice to a Wife and Counsel to a Mother* (Philadelphia: J.B. Lippincott, 1891), p. 97. A Missouri physician reported the case of a twenty-eight year old middle class woman with two children. Shortly after the birth of her second child, she missed her period, believed herself to be pregnant for a third time and succumbed to hysterical symptoms: depression, headaches, vomiting and seizures. Her doctor concluded that she had uterine disease, exacerbated by pregnancy. He aborted her and reported a full recovery the following day. George J. Engelmann, "A Hystero-Psychosis Epilepsy Dependent upon Erosions of the Cervix Uteri," *St. Louis Clinic Record* (1878), pp. 321–24. For similar cases, see A.B. Arnold, "Hystero-Hypochondriasis," *Pacific Medical Journal*, XXXIII (1890), pp. 321–24, and George J. Engelmann, "Hystero-neurosis," *Transactions of the American Gynecological Association*, II (1877), pp. 513–18.

13. For a study of declining nineteenth-century birth rates see Yasukichi

Yasuba, *Birth Rates of the White Population in the United States, 1800–1860* (Baltimore: Johns Hopkins University Press, 1962) and J. Potter, "American Population in the Early National Period," in *Proceedings of Section V of the Fourth Congress of the International Economic History Association,* Paul Deprez, ed. (Winnipeg, 1970), pp. 55–69.

14. For a useful general discussion of women's changing roles see Eleanor Flexner, op. cit.

15. For a discussion of birth control and its effect on domestic relations see Carroll Smith-Rosenberg and Charles E. Rosenberg, "The New Woman and the Troubled Man: Medical and Biological Views of Women in Nineteenth-century America," *Journal of American History* (in press).

16. William A. Hammond, *On Certain Conditions of Nervous Derangement* (New York: G.P. Putnam's Sons, 1881), p. 42; S. Weir Mitchell, *Lectures on the Diseases of the Nervous System, Especially in Women,* 2nd edn. (Philadelphia: Lea Brothers & Co., 1885), pp. 114, 110; Charles K. Mills, "Hysteria," in *A System of Practical Medicine by American Authors,* William Pepper, ed., assisted by Louis Starr, vol. V, "Diseases of the Nervous System," (Philadelphia: Lea Brothers & Co., 1883), p. 213; Charles E. Lockwood, "A Study of Hysteria and Hypochondriasis," *Transactions of the New York State Medical Association,* XII (1895), pp. 340–51. E.H. Van Deusen, Superintendent of the Michigan Asylum for the Insane, reported that nervousness, hysteria and neurasthenia were common among farm women and resulted, he felt, from the social and intellectual deprivation of their isolated lives. Van Deusen, "Observations on a Form of Nervous Prostration," *American Journal of Insanity,* XXV (1869), p. 447. Significantly most English and American authorities on hysteria were members of a medical elite who saw the wealthy in their private practices and the very poor in their hospital and dispensary work. Thus the observation that hysteria occurred in different social classes was often made by the very same clinicians.

17. Thomas Sydenham, "Epistolary Dissertation," in *The Works of Thomas Sydenham, M.D. . . . with a Life of the Author,* R.G. Latham, ed., 2 vols. (London: New Sydenham Society, 1850), II, p. 85.

18. Some women diagnosed as hysterics displayed quite bizarre behavior—including self-mutilation and hallucinations. Clearly a certain percentage of these women would be diagnosed today as schizophrenic. The majority of the women diagnosed as hysterical, however, did not display such symptoms, but rather appear from clinical descriptions to have had a personality similar to that considered hysterical by mid-twentieth-century psychiatrists.

19. For three typical descriptions of such seizures, see Buel Eastman, *Practical Treatise on Diseases Peculiar to Women and Girls* (Cincinnati: C. Cropper & Son, 1848), p. 40; Samuel Ashwell, *A Practical Treatise on the Diseases Peculiar to Women* (London: Samuel Highley, 1844), pp. 210–12; William Campbell, *Introduction to the Study and Practice of Midwifery and the Diseases of Children* (London: Longman, Rees, Orme, Brown, Green & Longman, 1833), pp. 440–42.

20. E.H. Dixon, op. cit., p. 133.

21. For examples of mid-nineteenth-century hysterical symptoms see Colombat de L'Isère, *A Treatise on the Diseases and Special Hygiene of Females,*

trans. with additions by Charles D. Meigs, (Philadelphia: Lea and Blanchard, 1845), pp. 522, 527–30; Gunning S. Bedford, *Clinical Lectures on the Diseases of Women and Children* (New York: Samuel S. & W. Wood, 1855), p. 373.

22. Robert B. Carter, *On the Pathology and Treatment of Hysteria* (London: John Churchill, 1853), p. 3.

23. See, for example, F.C. Skey, *Hysteria* (New York: A. Simpson, 1867), pp. 66, 71, 86; Mary Putnam Jacobi, "Hysterical Fever," *Journal of Nervous and Mental Disease*, XV (1890), pp. 373–88; Landon Carter Grey, "Neurasthenia: Its Differentiation and Treatment," *New York Medical Journal*, XLVIII (1888), p. 421.

24. See, for example, George Preston, *Hysteria and Certain Allied Conditions* (Philadelphia: P. Blakiston, Son & Co., 1897), pp. 31, 53; Charles E. Lockwood, op. cit., p. 346; Buel Eastman, op. cit., p. 39; Thomas More Madden, *Clinical Gynecology* (Philadelphia: J.B. Lippincott, 1895), p. 472.

25. See W. Symington Brown, *A Clinical Handbook on the Diseases of Women* (New York: William Wood & Company, 1882); Charles L. Dana, "A Study of the Anaesthesias of Hysteria," *American Journal of the Medical Sciences* (October, 1890), p. 1; William S. Playfair, *The Systematic Treatment of Nerve Prostration and Hysteria* (Philadelphia: Henry C. Lea's Son & Co., 1883), p. 29.

26. For a discussion of the importance of creating such organic etiologies in the legitimization of an increasingly large number of such "functional" ills, see Charles E. Rosenberg, "The Place of George M. Beard in Nineteenth-Century Psychiatry," *Bulletin of the History of Medicine*, XXXVI (1962), pp. 245-259. See also Owsei Temkin's discussion in his classic history of epilepsy, *The Falling Sickness,* 2nd ed., rev. (Baltimore: Johns Hopkins University Press, 1971), of the importance placed by neurologists in the late nineteenth century upon the differentiation of epilepsy and hysteria.

27. William Campbell, op. cit., pp. 440–41; Walter Channing, *Bed Case: Its History and Treatment* (Boston: Ticknor and Fields, 1860), pp. 41–42, 49. Charles L. Mix, "Hysteria: Its Nature and Etiology," *New York Medical Journal*, LXXII (August, 1900), pp. 183–89.

28. George Preston, op. cit., pp. 96–97.

29. Samuel Ashwell, op. cit., p. 226.

30. Charles K. Mills, op. cit., p. 258.

31. S. Weir Mitchell, *Lectures on the Diseases of the Nervous System*, op. cit., p. 66.

32. Thomas More Madden, op. cit., p. 474. The uterine origin of hysteria was by far the most commonly held opinion throughout the eighteenth and nineteenth centuries. Some believed it to be the exclusive cause, others to be among the most important causes. For three typical examples see: Alexander Hamilton, *A Treatise on the Management of Female Complaints and of Children in Early Infancy* (Edinburgh: Peter Hill, 1792), pp. 51-53. George J. Engelmann, "Hystero-Neurosis," op. cit., note 12; Augustus P. Clarke, "Relations of Hysteria to Structural Changes in the Uterus and its Adnexa," *American Journal of Obstetrics*, XXXIII (1894), pp. 477–83. The uterine theory came under increasing attack during the

late nineteenth century. See Hugh J. Patrick, "Hysteria: Neurasthenia," *International Clinics*, III (1898), pp. 183–84; F.C. Skey, op. cit., p. 68.

33. Robert Barnes, *Medical and Surgical Diseases of Women* (Philadelphia: H.C. Lea, 1874), p. 101; S.D. Hopkins, "A Case of Hysteria Simulating Organic Disease of the Brain," *Medical Fortnightly*, XI (July 1897), p. 327; C.D. Mills, op. cit., p. 218; J. Leonard Corning, *A Treatise on Hysteria and Epilepsy* (Detroit: George S. Davis, 1888), p. 2; August A. Eshner, "Hysteria in Early Life," read before the Philadelphia County Medical Society, June 23, 1897.

34. For examples of such concern and complexity, see A.A. King, "Hysteria," *The American Journal of Obstetrics*, XXIV (May, 1891), pp. 513–15; Marshall Hall, *Commentaries Principally on the Diseases of Females* (London: Sherwood, Gilbert and Piper, 1830), p. 118; C. L'Isère, op. cit., p. 530.

35. Robert B. Carter, op. cit., p. 140; J.L. Corning, op. cit., p. 70; Mills, op. cit., p. 218.

36. Preston, op. cit., p. 36.

37. See, for example: Mitchell, *Lectures on the Diseases of the Nervous System*, p. 170; Rebecca B. Gleason, M.D., of Elmira, New York, quoted by M.L. Holbrook, *Hygiene of the Brain and Nerves and the Cure of Nervousness* (New York: M.L. Holbrook & Company, 1878), pp. 270–71.

38. S. Weir Mitchell, *Fat and Blood* (Philadelphia: J.B. Lippincott, 1881), pp. 30–31.

39. Lockwood, op. cit., pp. 342–43; virtually every authority on hysteria echoed these sentiments.

40. Alexander Hamilton, op. cit., p. 52; Dixon, op. cit., pp. 142–43; Ashwell, op. cit., p. 217; Mills, op. cit., p. 230.

41. Walter Channing, op. cit., p. 28.

42. Robert B. Carter, op. cit., p. 113.

43. Mary P. Jacobi, op. cit., pp. 384–88; M.E. Dirix, *Woman's Complete Guide to Health* (New York: W.A. Townsend & Adams, 1869), p. 24; E.B. Foote, *Medical Common Sense* (New York: Published by the author, 1864), p. 167.

44. Reuben Ludlum, *Lectures, Clinical and Didactic, on the Diseases of Women* (Chicago: C.S. Halsey, 1872), p. 87; Robert Barnes, op. cit., p. 247. In 1847, the well-known Philadelphia gynecologist, Charles D. Meigs, had asked his medical school class the rhetorical question: "What is her erotic state? What the protean manifestations of the life force developed by a reproductive irritation which you call hysteria." Meigs, *Lectures on the Distinctive Characteristics of the Female*, delivered before the Class of Jefferson Medical College, January 5, 1847 (Philadelphia: T.K. & P.G. Collins, 1847), p. 20.

45. Thomas Laycock, *Essay on Hysteria*, pp. 76, 103, 105. See also Graham J. Barker-Benfield, "The Horrors of the Half-Known Life" (unpublished Ph.D. thesis, University of California at Los Angeles, 1969) and Ann Douglas Wood, "The Fashionable Diseases: Women's Complaints and Their Treatment in Nineteenth Century America," *Journal of Interdisciplinary History* (in press) for a speculative psychoanalytic approach to gynecological practice in nineteenth-century America.

46. Dixon, op. cit., p. 134; J. Leonard Corning, op. cit., p. 70; William Murray, *A Treatise on Emotional Disorders of the Sympathetic System of*

the Nerves (London: John Churchill, 1866). An extensive nineteenth-century masturbation literature exists. See, for example, Samuel Gregory, *Facts and Important Information for Young Women on the Self-Indulgence of the Sexual Appetite* (Boston: George Gregory, 1857), and Calvin Cutter, *The Female Guide: Containing Facts and Information upon the Effects of Masturbation* (West Brookfield, Mass.: Charles A. Mirick, 1844). Most general treatises on masturbation refer to its occurrence in females.

47. Preston, op. cit., p. 37; Carter, op. cit., pp. 46, 90. Nineteenth-century physicians maintained a delicate balance in their view of the sexual etiology of hysteria. Any deviation from moderation could cause hysteria or insanity: habitual masturbation, extended virginity, over-indulgence, prostitution, or sterility.

48. Skey, op. cit., p. 63.

49. Mitchell, *Lectures on the Diseases of the Nervous System*, p. 266; S. Weir Mitchell, *Fat and Blood*, op. cit., p. 37.

50. Carter, op. cit., p. 58.

51. For an exposition of this argument see Erving Goffman, "Insanity of Place," *Psychiatry*, XXXII (1969), pp. 357–88.

52. Such complaints are commonplace in the medical literature. See Mitchell, *Lectures*, p. 67; Mitchell, *Doctor and Patient*, op. cit., p. 117; Robert Thornton, *The Hysterical Women: Trials, Tears, Tricks and Tantrums* (Chicago: Donohue & Henneberry, 1893), pp. 97–98; Channing, op. cit., pp. 35–37; L'Isère, op. cit., p. 534.

53. The fact that the physician was at the same time employed and paid by the woman or her family—in a period when the profession was far more competitive and economically insecure than it is in midtwentieth century—implied another level of stress and ambiguity.

54. Channing, op. cit., p. 22; Thomas A. Emmett, *Principles and Practices of Gynecology* (Philadelphia: H.C. Lea, 1879), p. 107; L.C. Grey, "Clinical Lecture," p. 132.

55. Carter, op. cit., p. 119; Ashwell, op. cit., p. 227.

56. Skey, op. cit., p. 60.

57. Robert Thornton, op. cit.

58. Thomas A. Emmett, *Incidents of My Life* (New York: G.P. Putnam's Sons, 1911), p. 210. These are Emmett's recollections at the end of a long life. It is interesting that decades earlier Emmett, in discussing treating hysterical women, had confessed in hostile frustration that "in fact the physician is helpless...." Emmett, *Principles and Practices*, op. cit., p. 107.

59. Mitchell, *Doctor and Patient*, pp. 99–100.

60. Samuel Guze, "The Diagnosis of Hysteria: What are We Trying to Do," *American Journal of Psychiatry*, CXXIV (1967), pp. 494–98; Otto Kernberg, "Borderline Personality Organization," *Journal of the American Psychoanalytical Association*, XV (1967), pp. 641–85. For a critical discussion of the entire problem of diagnosis, see Henry Bachrach, "In Defense of Diagnosis," *Psychiatry* (in press).

WOMEN
IN TWENTIETH-CENTURY
SOCIETY

Women found new opportunities for participation in American society in the twentieth century. The woman's rights movement had successfully fought against most of the legal restrictions imposed on women. In 1920 they won their greatest victory—the passage of the nineteenth amendment granting women the right to vote. But more substantial changes in the lives of women were effected by the economic growth, urbanization and the "revolution in manners and morals" of the twentieth century.

Changing economic patterns and social mores were reflected in a revised feminine ideal—the assertive, independent, sexually knowledgeable "new woman." James McGovern traces the origins of this new model to expanding urbanization in the pre-World War I period, which weakened the supervisory functions of family, church and small town community. The growing acceptance of women working outside the home further undermined the viability of the nineteenth-century ideal of true womanhood. The requirements of the workplace modified Victorian strictures of appropriate female behavior; qualities such as piety and purity became less important as women entered a competitive economic and sexual marketplace. Changes in medical and psychological opinion which stressed women's sexuality, along with the growing availability of birth control measures, also fostered the growing popularity of the "new woman."

By the 1920s, the sexually adventurous, fun-loving flapper with her bobbed hair, makeup, short skirt and informal manner had become a popular culture figure. There was, however, a utilitarian side to the image of this "new woman." Kenneth Yellis explores the relationship between the practical requirements of the working woman and changes in her dress and behavior. He points out that in order to allow ease of movement, for example, clothes for working women had to be lighter and more flexible than the corseted, voluminous apparel of the Victorian age. The more androgynous look of the flapper costume in which breasts and hips were all but hidden, helped to diffuse the tensions inherent in a heterosexual work environment.

These changes in sexual and social mores, however, did not conflict with the belief that women's primary vocation was marriage and motherhood. The new psychology supported traditional female roles by asserting that women needed to find fulfillment as wives and mothers in order to prevent the development of neuroses or emotional disorders. The emphasis on heterosexual courtship reflected this intensified belief in the necessity of marriage for women. Domesticity was made even more compelling as notions of creative and scientific household management and childrearing were popularized.

The persistence of traditional sex role divisions was reflected in the employment patterns of women in the twentieth century. Though more women were working than ever before, they continued to face discrimination in hiring practices, wages and promotions. During the Depression, for example, legislation passed by both the federal and state governments served to restrict and even prohibit married women from working. Furthermore, as women came to predominate in certain occupations, such as clerical work, these positions became overwhelmingly underpaid and low in status. Despite the expansion of educational opportunities in the twentieth century, women were unable to compete in higher level management and professional occupations. Their persistence in pursuing careers in the face of almost insurmountable legal, social and economic obstacles is the subject of Frank Stricker's article on career women in the twentieth century.

Despite the rapid political, social and economic changes that have characterized the United States in the twentieth century, adherence to a social structure based on sex role divisions continues to be the dominant factor in women's lives. The notion that the social roles of women are both different from and subordinate to those of men is the foundation for the continuing resistance to women's full and equal participation in American society.

SELECTED READINGS

Chafe, William. *The American Woman: Her Changing Social, Economic, and Political Roles, 1920–1970.* New York: Oxford University Press, 1972.

Chafe, William. *Women and Equality: Changing Patterns in American Culture.* New York: Oxford University Press, 1977.

Dye, Nancy Schrom. "Creating a Feminist Alliance: Sisterhood and Class Conflict in the New York Women's Trade Union League." *Feminist Studies* 2 (1975): 24–38.

Epstein, Cynthia Fuchs. *Woman's Place: Options and Limits in Professional Careers.* Berkeley, Los Angeles and London: University of California Press, 1971.

Freedman, Estelle B. "The New Woman: Changing Views of Women in the 1920's." *Journal of American History* 61 (Sept. 1974): 372–93.

Gordon, Linda. *Woman's Body, Woman's Right: A Social History of Birth Control in America.* New York: Grossman, 1976.

Huber, Joan, ed. *Changing Women in a Changing Society.* Chicago: University of Chicago Press, 1973.

Jensen, Richard. "Family, Career and Reform: Women Leaders in the Progressive Era." In *The American Family in Social-Historical Perspective,* ed. Michael Gordon. New York: St. Martin's Press, 1973, pp. 267–80.

Lemons, J. Stanley. *The Woman Citizen: Social Feminism in the 1920's.* Urbana: University of Illinois Press, 1973.

O'Neill, William L. "Divorce in the Progressive Era." *American Quarterly* 17 (1965): 203–17.

O'Neill, William L. *Everyone Was Brave: The Rise and Fall of Feminism in America.* Chicago: Quadrangle Books, 1969.

Rothman, Sheila M. *Woman's Proper Place: A History of Changing Ideals and Practices, 1870 to the Present.* New York: Basic Books, 1978.

Scott, Anne Firor. "After Suffrage: Southern Women in the Twenties." *Journal of Southern History* 30 (Aug. 1964): 298–318.

Smith, Daniel Scott. "The Dating of the American Sexual Revolution: Evidence and Interpretation." In *The American Family in Social-Historial Perspective,* ed. Michael Gordon. New York: St. Martin's Press, 1973.

Smuts, Robert W. *Women and Work in America.* New York: Columbia University Press, 1959.

The American Woman's
Pre-World War I
Freedom in Manners and Morals

James R. McGovern

The Twenties have been alternately praised or blamed for almost everything and its opposite;[1] but most historians hold, whether to praise or to condemn, that this decade launched the revolution in manners and morals through which we are still moving today. This judgment seems to be part of an even more inclusive one in American historiography to exceptionalize the Twenties. No other decade has invited such titles of historical caricature as *The Jazz Age, This Was Normalcy, Fantastic Interim,* or *The Perils of Prosperity.* Richard Hofstadter's classic, *The Age of Reform,* subtly reinforces this view by seeing the Twenties as "Entr'acte," an interim between two periods of reform, the Progressive era and the New Deal, which themselves display discontinuity.[2]

Revisionism, in the form of a developmental interpretation of the relationship between the Progressive era and the Twenties, has been gaining strong support in recent years. De-emphasizing the disruptive impact of World War I, Henry F. May asked whether the 1920s could be understood fully "without giving more attention to the old regime."[3] He declared that "Immediately prewar America must be newly explored," especially "its inarticulate assumptions—assumptions in such areas as morality, politics, class and race relations, popular art and literature, and family life." [4] May pursued his inquiry in *The End of American Innocence* and showed that for the purposes of intellectual history, at least, the Twenties were not as significant as the preceding decade.[5] Political historians have been reassessing the relationship of the Progressive era to the Twenties as well. Arthur Link has demonstrated that progressivism survived World War I,[6] and J. Joseph Huthmacher has established continuity between progressivism and the New Deal in the immigrant's steadfast devotion to the ameliorative powers of the government.[7] Together with May's analysis, their writings suggest that the 1920s are much more the result of earlier intrinsic social changes than either the sudden, supposedly traumatic experiences of the war or unique developments in the Twenties. Since this assertion is certain to encounter the formidable claims that the 1920s, at least in manners and morals, amounted to a revolution, its viability can be tested by questioning if the American woman's "emancipation" in manners and morals occurred even earlier than World War I.

Even a casual exploration of the popular literature of the Progressive era reveals that Americans then described and understood themselves to be undergoing significant changes in morals. "Sex o'clock in America" struck in 1913,[8] about the same time as "The Repeal of Reticence." [9] One contemporary writer saw Americans as liberated from the strictures of "Victorianism," now an epithet deserving criticism, and exulted, "Heaven defend us from a return to the prudery of the Victorian regime!" [10] Conditions were such that another commentator asked self-consciously, "Are We Immoral?" [11] And still another feared that the present "vice not often matched since [the time of] the Protestant Reformation" might invite a return to Puritanism.[12] Yet, historians have not carefully investigated the possibility that the true beginnings of America's "New Freedom" in morals occurred prior to 1920.[13] The most extensive, analytical writing on the subject of changing manners and morals is found in Frederick L. Allen's *Only Yesterday* (1931), William Leuchtenburg's *The Perils of Prosperity* (1958), May's *The End of American Innocence* (1959), and George Mowry's *The Urban Nation* (1965).

Allen and Leuchtenburg apply almost identical sharp-break interpretations, respectively entitling chapters "The Revolution in Manners and Morals" and "The Revolution in Morals." [14] Both catalogue the same types of criteria for judgment. The flapper, as the "new woman" was called, was a creature of the 1920s. She smoked, drank, worked, and played side by side with men. She became preoccupied with sex—

shocking and simultaneously unshockable. She danced close, became freer with her favors, kept her own latchkey, wore scantier attire which emphasized her boyish, athletic form, just as she used makeup and bobbed and dyed her hair. She and her comradely beau tried to abolish time and succeeded, at least to the extent that the elders asked to join the revelry. Although there were occasional "advance signals" of "rebellion" before the war, it was not until the 1920s that the code of woman's innocence and ignorance crumbled.

May, who comes closest to an understanding of the moral permissiveness before the 1920s, describes in general terms such phenomena of the Progressive era as the "Dance Craze," birth control, the impact of the movies, and the "white-slave panic." [15] He focuses on the intellectuals, however, and therefore overlooks the depth of these and similar social movements. This causes him to view them as mere "Cracks in the Surface" of an essentially conservative society. He quotes approvingly of the distinction made by the *Nation* "between the fluttering tastes of the half-baked intellectuals, attracted by all these things, and the surviving soundness of the great majority." [16] His treatment also ignores one of the most significant areas of changing manners and morals as they affected the American woman: the decided shift in her sex role and identification in the direction of more masculine norms. Again, *The End of American Innocence* does not convincingly relate these changes to the growth of the cities. Perhaps these limitations explain Mowry's preference for a "sharp-break" interpretation, although he wrote seven years after May.

Mowry, who acknowledges especial indebtedness to Leuchtenburg,[17] is emphatic about the "startling" changes in manners and morals in the 1920s.[18] He highlights "the new woman of the twenties" [19] whose "modern feminine morality and attitudes toward the institution of marriage date from the twenties." [20] Mowry concedes to the libidos of progressives only the exceptional goings-on in Greenwich Village society.

These hypotheses, excluding May's, hold that the flapper appeared in the postwar period mainly because American women en masse then first enjoyed considerable social and economic freedom. They also emphasize the effect of World War I on morals.[21] By inference, of course, the Progressive era did not provide a suitable matrix. But an investigation of this period establishes that women had become sufficiently active and socially independent to prefigure the "emancipation" of the 1920s.

A significant deterioration of external controls over morality had occurred before 1920. One of the consequences of working and living conditions in the cities, especially as these affected women, was that Americans of the period 1900-1920 had experienced a vast dissolution of moral authority, which formerly had centered in the family and the small community. The traditional "straight and narrow" could not serve the choices and opportunities of city life.[22] As against primary controls and contacts based on face-to-face association where the norms of family, church, and small community, usually reinforcing each other, could be internalized, the city made for a type of "individualization" through its distant, casual, specialized, and transient clusters of secondary associations.[23] The individual came to determine his own behavioral norms.

The "home is in peril" became a fact of sociological literature as early as 1904.[24] One of the most serious signs of its peril was the increasing inability of parents to influence their children in the delicate areas of propriety and morals.[25] The car, already numerous enough to affect dating and pre-marital patterns,[26] the phone coming to be used for purposes of romantic accommodation,[27] and the variety of partners at the office or the factory,[28] all together assured unparalleled privacy and permissiveness between the sexes.

Individualization of members served to disrupt confidence between generations of the family, if not to threaten parents with the role of anachronistic irrelevance. Dorothy Dix observed in 1913 that there had been "so many changes in the conditions of life and point of view in the last twenty years that the parent of today is absolutely unfitted to decide the problems of life for the young man and woman of today. This is particularly the case with women because the whole economic and social position of women has been revolutionized since mother was a girl." [29] Magazine articles lamented "The Passing of the Home Daughter" who preferred the blessed anonymity of the city to "dying of asphyxiation at home!" [30] The same phenomenon helps to explain the popularity in this period of such standardized mothers as Dorothy Dix, Beatrice Fairfax, and Emily Post, each of whom was besieged with queries on the respective rights of mothers and daughters.

Woman's individualization resulted mainly because, whether single or married, gainfully employed or not, she spent more time outside her home. Evidence demonstrates that the so-called job and kitchen revolutions were already in advanced stages by 1910. The great leap forward in women's participation in economic life came between 1900 and 1910; the percentage of women who were employed changed only slightly from 1910 to 1930. A comparison of the percentages of gainfully employed women aged sixteen to forty-four between 1890 and 1930 shows that they comprised 21.7 percent of Americans employed in 1890, 23.5 percent in 1900, 28.1 percent in 1910, 28.3 percent in

1920, and 29.7 percent in 1930.[31] While occupational activity for women appears to stagnate from 1910 to 1920, in reality a considerable restructuring occurred with women leaving roles as domestics and assuming positions affording more personal independence as clerks and stenographers.[32]

Married women, especially those in the upper and middle classes, enjoyed commensurate opportunities. Experts in household management advised women to rid themselves of the maid and turn to appliances as the "maid of all service." [33] Statistics on money expended on those industries which reduced home labor for the wife suggest that women in middle-income families gained considerable leisure after 1914. [34] This idea is also corroborated from other sources,[35] especially from the tone and content of advertising in popular magazines when they are compared with advertising at the turn of the century. Generally speaking, women depicted in advertising in or about 1900 are well rounded, have gentle, motherly expressions, soft billowy hair, and delicate hands. They are either sitting down or standing motionless; their facial expressions are immobile as are their corseted figures.[36] After 1910, they are depicted as more active figures with more of their activity taking place outside their homes.[37] One woman tells another over the phone: "Yes[,] drive over right away—I'll be ready. My housework! Oh that's all done. How do I do it? I just let electricity do my work nowadays." [38] Vacuum cleaners permitted the housewife to "Push the Button—and Enjoy the Springtime!" [39] Van Camp's "Pork and Beans" promised to save her "100 hours yearly," [40] and Campbell's soups encouraged, "Get some fun out of life," since it was unnecessary to let the "three-meals-a-day problem tie you down to constant drudgery." [41] Wizard Polish, Minute Tapioca, and Minute Gelatine also offered the same promise. The advertising image of women became more natural, even nonchalant. A lady entertaining a friend remarks: "I don't have to hurry nowadays. I have a Florence Automatic Oil Stove in my kitchen." [42] It had become "so *very* easy" to wax the floors that well-dressed women could manage them.[43] And they enjoyed a round of social activities driving the family car.[44]

It was in this setting that the flapper appeared along with her older married sister who sought to imitate her. No one at the office or in the next block cared much about their morals as long as the one was efficient and the other paid her bills on time. And given the fact that both these women had more leisure and wished "to participate in what men call 'the game of life' " rather than accept "the mere humdrum of household duties," [45] it is little wonder that contemporaries rightly assessed the danger of the situation for traditional morals by 1910.

The ensuing decade was marked by the development of a revolution in manners and morals; its chief embodiment was the flapper who was urban based and came primarily from the middle and upper classes. Young—whether in fact or fancy—assertive, and independent, she experimented with intimate dancing, permissive favors, and casual courtships or affairs. She joined men as comrades, and the differences in behavior of the sexes were narrowed. She became in fact in some degree desexualized. She might ask herself, "Am I Not a Boy? Yes, I Am—Not." [46] Her speech, her interest in thrills and excitement, her dress and hair, her more aggressive sexuality, even perhaps her elaborate beautification, which was a statement of intentions, all point to this. Women, whether single or married, became at once more attractive and freer in their morals and paradoxically less feminine. Indeed, the term sexual revolution as applied to the Progressive era means reversal in the traditional role of women just as it describes a pronounced familiarity of the sexes.

The unmarried woman after 1910 was living in the "Day of the Girl." [47] Dorothy Dix described "the type of girl that the modern young man falls for" in 1915 as a "husky young woman who can play golf all day and dance all night, and drive a motor car, and give first aid to the injured if anybody gets hurt, and who is in no more danger of swooning than he is." [48] Little wonder she was celebrated in song as "A Dangerous Girl"; the lyrics of one of the popular songs for 1916 read, "You dare me, you scare me, and still I like you more each day. But you're the kind that will charm; and then do harm; you've got a dangerous way." [49] The "most popular art print ... ever issued" by *Puck* depicts a made-up young lady puckering her lips and saying "Take It From Me!" [50] The American girl of 1900 was not described in similar terms. The lovely and gracious Gibson Girl was too idealized to be real.[51] And when young lovers trysted in advertising, they met at Horlick's Malted Milk Bar; he with his guitar, and she with her parasol.[52] Beatrice Fairfax could still reply archaically about the need for "maidenly reserve" to such queries as those on the proprieties of men staring at women on the streets.[53] And the *Wellesley College News* in 1902 reported that students were not permitted to have a Junior Prom because it would be an occasion for meeting "promiscuous men," although the college sanctioned "girl dances." [54]

The girls, however, dispensed with "maidenly reserve." In 1910, Margaret Deland, the novelist, could announce a "Change in the Feminine Ideal."

> This young person ... with surprisingly bad manners—has gone to college, and when she graduates she is going to earn her

own living . . . she won't go to church; she has views upon marriage and the birth-rate, and she utters them calmly, while her
mother blushes with embarrassment; she occupies herself, passionately, with everything except the things that used to occupy
the minds of girls.[55]

Many young women carried their own latchkeys.[56] Meanwhile, as
Dorothy Dix noted, it had become "literally true that the average
father does not know, by name or sight, the young man who visits his
daughter and who takes her out to places of amusement." [57] She was
distressed over the widespread use by young people of the car which
she called the "devil's wagon." [58] Another writer asked: "Where Is
Your Daughter This Afternoon?" "Are you sure that she is not being
drawn into the whirling vortex of afternoon 'trots' . . . ?" [59] Polly, Cliff
Sterrett's remarkable comic-strip, modern girl from *Polly and Her Pals,*
washed dishes under the shower and dried them with an electric fan;
and while her mother tried hard to domesticate her, Polly wondered,
"Gee Whiz! I wish I knew what made my nose shine!" [60]
Since young women were working side by side with men and recreating more freely and intimately with them, it was inevitable that they
behave like men. Older people sometimes carped that growing familiarity meant that romance was dead [61] or that "nowadays brides
hardly blush, much less faint." [62] And Beatrice Fairfax asked, "Has
Sweet Sixteen Vanished?" [63] But some observers were encouraged to
note that as girls' ways approximated men's, the sexes were, at least,
more comradely.[64] The modern unmarried woman had become a "Diana, Hunting in the Open." [65] Dorothy Dix reported that "nice girls,
good girls, girls in good positions in society—frankly take the initiative
in furthering an acquaintance with any man who happens to strike
their fancy." The new ideal in feminine figure, dress, and hair styles
was all semi-masculine. The "1914 Girl" with her "slim hips and boy-
carriage" was a "slim, boylike creature." [66] The "new figure is Amazo-
nia, rather than Miloan. It is boyish rather than womanly. It is strong
rather than soft." [67] Her dress styles, meanwhile, de-emphasized both
hips and bust while they permitted the large waist. The boyish coiffure
began in 1912 when young women began to tuck-under their hair with
a ribbon;[68] and by 1913–1914, Newport ladies, actresses like Pauline
Frederick, then said to be the prettiest girl in America, and the
willowy, popular dancer Irene Castle were wearing short hair.[69] By
1915, the *Ladies Home Journal* featured women with short hair on its
covers, and even the pure type of woman who advertised Ivory Soap
appeared to be shorn.[70]

The unmarried flapper was a determined pleasure-seeker whom novelist Owen Johnson described collectively as "determined to liberate their lives and claim the same rights of judgment as their brothers." [71] The product of a "feminine revolution startling in the shock of its abruptness," she was living in the city independently of her family. Johnson noted: "She is sure of one life only and that one she passionately desires. She wants to live that life to its fullest. . . . She wants adventure. She wants excitement and mystery. She wants to see, to know, to experience. . . ." She expressed both a "passionate revolt against the commonplace" and a "scorn of conventions." Johnson's heroine in *The Salamander*, Doré Baxter, embodied his views. Her carefree motto is reminiscent of Fitzgerald's flappers of the Twenties: " 'How do I know what I'll do to-morrow?' " [72] Her nightly prayer, the modest " 'O Lord! give me everything I want!' " [73] Love was her "supreme law of conduct," [74] and she, like the literary flappers of the Twenties, feared "thirty as a sort of sepulcher, an end of all things!" [75] Johnson believed that all young women in all sections of the country had "a little touch of the Salamander," each alike being impelled by "an impetuous frenzy . . . to sample each new excitement," both the "safe and the dangerous." [76] Girls "seemed determined to have their fling like men," the novelist Gertrude Atherton noted in *Current Opinion*, "and some of the stories [about them] made even my sophisticated hair crackle at the roots. . . ." [77] Beatrice Fairfax deplored the trends, especially the fact that "Making love lightly, boldly and promiscuously seems to be part of our social structure." [78] Young men and women kissed though they did not intend to marry.[79] And kissing was shading into spooning (" 'To Spoon' or 'Not to Spoon' Seems to Be the Burning Question with Modern Young America") [80] and even "petting," which was modish among the collegiate set.[81] In fact, excerpts from the diary of a co-ed written before World War I suggest that experimentation was virtually complete within her peer group. She discussed her "adventures" with other college girls. "We were healthy animals and we were demanding our rights to spring's awakening." As for men, she wrote, "I played square with the men. I always told them I was not out to pin them down to marriage, but that this intimacy was pleasant and I wanted it as much as they did. We indulged in sex talk, birth control. . . . We thought too much about it." [82]

One of the most interesting developments in changing sexual behavior which characterized these years was the blurring of age lines between young and middle-aged women in silhouette, dress, and cosmetics.[83] A fashion commentator warned matrons, "This is the day of the figure. . . . The face alone, no matter how pretty, counts for nothing unless the body is as straight and yielding as every young girl's."[84] With only slight variations, the optimum style for women's dress between 1908 and 1918 was a modified sheath, straight up and down and clinging.[85] How different from the styles of the high-busted, broad-hipped mother of the race of 1904 for whom Ella Wheeler Wilcox, the journalist and poet, advised the use of veils because "the slightest approach to masculinity in woman's attire is always unlovely and disappointing."[86]

The sloughing off of numerous undergarments and loosening of others underscored women's quickening activity and increasingly self-reliant morals. Clinging dresses and their "accompanying lack of undergarments" eliminated, according to the president of the New York Cotton Exchange, "at least twelve yards of finished goods for each adult female inhabitant."[87] Corset makers were forced to make adjustments too and use more supple materials.[88] Nevertheless, their sales declined.[89]

The American woman of 1910, in contrast with her sister of 1900, avidly cultivated beauty of face and form. In fact, the first American woman whose photographs and advertising image we can clearly recognize as belonging to our times lived between 1910 and 1920. "Nowadays," the speaker for a woman's club declared in 1916, "only the very poor or the extremely careless are old or ugly. You can go to a beauty shop and choose the kind of beauty you will have."[90] Beautification included the use of powder, rouge, lipstick, eyelash and eyebrow stain. Advertising was now manipulating such images for face powder as "Mother tried it and decided to keep it for herself,"[91] or "You can have beautiful Eyebrows and Eyelashes.... Society women and actresses get them by using Lash-Brow-Ine."[92] Nearly every one of the numerous advertisements for cosmetics promised some variation of "How to Become Beautiful, Fascinating, Attractive."[93]

In her dress as well as her use of cosmetics, the American woman gave evidence that she had abandoned passivity. An unprecedented public display of the female figure characterized the period.[94] Limbs now became legs and more of them showed after 1910, although they were less revealing than the promising hosiery advertisements. Rolled down hose first appeared in 1917.[95] Dresses for opera and restaurant were deeply cut in front and back, and not even the rumor that Mrs. John Jacob Astor had suffered a chest cold as a result of wearing deep decolleté[96] deterred their wearers. As for gowns, "Fashion says—Evening gowns must be sleeveless ... afternoon gowns are made with semi-transparent yokes and sleeves."[97] Undoubtedly, this vogue for transparent blouses and dresses[98] caused the editor of the *Unpopular*

Review to declare: "At no time and place under Christianity, except the most corrupt periods in France ... certainly never before in America, has woman's form been so freely displayed in society and on the street." [99]

In addition to following the example of young women in dress and beautification, middle-aged women, especially those from the middle and upper classes, were espousing their permissive manners and morals.[100] Smoking and, to a lesser extent, drinking in public were becoming fashionable for married women of the upper class and were making headway at other class levels.[101] As early as 1910, a prominent clubwoman stated: "It has become a well-established habit for women to drink cocktails. It is thought the smart thing to do." [102] Even before Gertrude Atherton described in the novel *Black Oxen* the phenomenon of the middle-aged women who sought to be attractive to younger men, supposedly typifying the 1920s,[103] it was evident in the play "Years of Discretion." Written by Frederic Hatton and Fanny Locke Hatton, and staged by Belasco, the play was "welcomed cordially both in New York and Chicago" in 1912. It featured a widowed mother forty-eight years of age, who announces, "I intend to look under forty—lots under. I have never attracted men, but I know I can." [104] Again, "I mean to have a wonderful time. To have all sorts and kinds of experience. I intend to love and be loved, to lie and cheat." [105] Dorothy Dix was dismayed over "the interest that women ... have in what we are pleased to euphoniously term the 'erotic.' " She continued, "I'll bet there are not ten thousand women in the whole United States who couldn't get one hundred in an examination of the life and habits of Evelyn Nesbitt and Harry Thaw...." [106] Married women among the fashionable set held the great parties, at times scandalous ones which made the 1920s seem staid by comparison.[107] They hired the Negro orchestras at Newport and performed and sometimes invented the daring dances.[108] They conscientiously practiced birth control, as did women of other classes.[109] And they initiated divorce proceedings, secure in the knowledge that many of their best friends had done the same thing.

Perhaps the best insights on the mores and morals of this group are to be found in the writings of the contemporary, realistic novelist, Robert Herrick.[110] Herrick derived his heroines from "the higher income groups, the wealthy, upper middle, and professional classes among which he preferred to move." [111] His heroines resemble literary flappers of the 1920s in their repudiation of childbearing. "It takes a year out of a woman's life, of course, no matter how she is situated," they say, or, "Cows do that." [112] Since their lives were seldom more than a meaningless round of social experiences, relieved principally by romantic literature, many of them either contemplated or consented to infidelity. Thus Margaret Pole confesses to her friend, Conny Wood-yard, " 'I'd like to lie out on the beach and forget children and servants and husbands, and stop wondering what life is. Yes, I'd like a vacation—in the Windward Islands, with somebody who understood.' 'To wit, a man!' added Conny. 'Yes, a man! But only for the trip.' " [113] They came finally to live for love in a manner that is startlingly reminiscent of some of the famous literary women of the Twenties.[114]

Insights regarding the attitudes of married women from the urban lower middle class can be found in the diary of Ruth Vail Randall, who lived in Chicago from 1911 to the date of her suicide, March 6, 1920.[115] A document of urban sociology, the diary transcends mere personal experience and becomes a commentary on group behavior of the times. Mrs. Randall was reared in a family that owned a grocery store, was graduated from high school in Chicago, and was married at twenty to Norman B. Randall, then twenty-one. She worked after marriage in a department store and later for a brief period as a model. She looked to marriage, especially its romance, as the supreme fulfillment of her life and was bitterly disappointed with her husband. She began to turn to other men whom she met at work or places of recreation, and her husband left her. Fearing that her lover would leave her eventually as well, she killed him and herself.

The diary focuses on those conditions which made the revolution in morals a reality. The young couple lived anonymously in a highly mobile neighborhood where their morals were of their own making. Mrs. Randall did not want children; she aborted their only child.[116] She was also averse to the reserved "womanly" role, which her husband insisted that she assume.[117] She complained, "Why cannot a woman do all man does?" [118] She wished that men and women were more alike in their social roles.[119] She repudiated involvement in her home, resolved to exploit equally every privilege which her husband assumed, drank, flirted, and lived promiscuously. Telephones and cars made her extramarital liaisons possible. Even before her divorce, she found another companion; flouting convention, she wrote, "He and I have entered a marriage pact according to our own ideas." [120] Throughout her diary she entertained enormous, almost magical, expectations of love. She complained that her lovers no more than her husband provided what she craved—tenderness and companionship. Disillusionment with one of them caused her to cry out, "I am miserable. I have the utmost contempt for myself. But the lake is near and soon it will be warm. Oh, God to rest in your arms. To rest—and to have peace." [121]

That America was experiencing a major upheaval in morals during the Progressive era is nowhere better ascertained than in the comprehensive efforts by civic officials and censorial citizens to control them. Disapproval extended not only to such well-known staples as alcohol, divorce, and prostitution, but also to dancing, woman's dress, cabarets, theaters and movies, and birth control. "Mrs. Warren's Profession" was withdrawn from the New York stage in 1905 after a one night performance, the manager of the theater later being charged with offending public decency.[122] When a grand jury in New York condemned the "turkey trot and kindred dances" as "indecent," the judge who accepted the presentment noted that "Rome's downfall was due to the degenerate nature of its dancers, and I only hope that we will not suffer the same result." [123] Public dancing was henceforth to be licensed. Mayor John Fitzgerald personally assisted the morals campaign in Boston by ordering the removal from a store of an objectionable picture which portrayed a "show-girl" with her legs crossed.[124] Meanwhile, the "X-Ray Skirt" was outlawed in Portland, Oregon, and Los Angeles; [125] and the police chief of Louisville, Kentucky, ordered the arrest of a number of women appearing on the streets with slit skirts.[126] Witnessing to a general fear that the spreading knowledge of contraception might bring on sexual license, the federal and several state governments enacted sumptuary legislation.[127] And in two celebrated incidents, the offenders, Van K. Allison (1916) in Boston and Margaret Sanger (1917) in New York, were prosecuted and sent to jail.[128]

Public officials were apprehensive about the sweeping influence of the movies on the masses, "at once their book, their drama, their art. To some it has become society, school, and even church." [129] They proceeded to set up boards of censorship with powers to review and condemn movies in four states: Pennsylvania (1911), Ohio (1913), Maryland (1916), and Kansas (1917), and in numerous cities beginning with Chicago in 1907.[130] The Pennsylvania board, for example, prohibited pictures which displayed nudity, prolonged passion, women drinking and smoking, and infidelity. It protected Pennsylvanians from such films produced between 1915 and 1918 as "What Every Girl Should Know," "A Factory Magdalene," and "Damaged Goodness." [131]

Such determination proved unavailing, however, even as the regulatory strictures were being applied. According to one critic the "sex drama" using "plain, blunt language" had become "a commonplace" of the theater after 1910 and gave the "tender passion rather the worst for it in recent years." [132] Vice films packed them in every night, especially after the smashing success of "Traffic in Souls," which reportedly grossed $450,000.[133] In Boston the anti-vice campaign itself languished because there was no means of controlling "the kitchenette-apartment section." "In these apartment houses, there are hundreds of women who live as they please and who entertain as they will." [134] Mayor Fitzgerald's "show-girl," evicted from her saucy perch, gained more notoriety when she appeared in a Boston newspaper the following day.[135] Even Anthony Comstock, that indefatigable guardian of public morals, had probably come to look a bit like a comic character living beyond his times.[136]

When Mrs. Sanger was arrested for propagating birth control information in 1917, she confidently stated, "I have nothing to fear. ... Regardless of the outcome I shall continue my work, supported by thousands of men and women throughout the country." [137] Her assurance was well founded. Three years earlier her supporters had founded a National Birth Control League; and in 1919, this organization opened its first public clinic.[138] But most encouraging for Mrs. Sanger was the impressive testimony that many Americans were now practicing or interested in birth control.[139] When Paul B. Blanchard, pastor of the Maverick Congregational Church in East Boston, protested the arrest of Van K. Allison, he charged, "If the truth were made public and the laws which prevent the spreading of even oral information about birth control were strictly enforced how very few of the married society leaders, judges, doctors, ministers, and businessmen would be outside the prison dock!" [140]

The foregoing demonstrates that a major shift in American manners and morals occurred in the Progressive era, especially after 1910. Changes at this time, though developing out of still earlier conditions, represented such visible departures from the past and were so commonly practiced as to warrant calling them revolutionary. Too often scholars have emphasized the Twenties as the period of significant transition and World War I as a major cause of the phenomenon. Americans of the 1920s, fresh from the innovative wartime atmosphere, undoubtedly quickened and deepened the revolution. Women from smaller cities and towns contested what was familiar terrain to an already seasoned cadre of urban women and a formidable group of defectors. Both in their rhetoric and their practices, apparent even before the war, the earlier group had provided the shibboleths for the 1920s; they first asked, "What are Patterns for?" The revolution in manners and morals was, of course, but an integral part of numerous, contemporary, political and social movements to free the individual by reordering society. Obviously, the Progressive era, more than the 1920s, represents the substantial beginnings of contemporary American civilization.

The revolution in manners and morals, particularly as it affected women, took the twofold form of more permissive sexuality and diminished femininity. Women from the upper classes participated earlier, as is evidenced by their introductory exhibition of fashions, hair styles, dances, cosmetics, smoking, and drinking. Realistic novels concerned with marriage suggest that they entertained ideas of promiscuity and even infidelity before women of the lower classes. Yet the cardinal condition of change was not sophistication but urban living and the freedom it conferred. As technology and economic progress narrowed the gap between the classes, middle-class women and even those below were free to do many of the same things almost at the same time. Above all, the revolution in manners and morals after 1910 demonstrates that sexual freedom and the twentieth-century American city go together.

NOTES

1. Henry F. May, "Shifting Perspectives on the 1920's," *Mississippi Valley Historical Review* XLIII (1956): 405–27.
2. Richard Hofstadter, *The Age of Reform: From Bryan to F. D. R.* (New York, 1955), pp. 282–301.
3. May, "Shifting Perspectives on the 1920s," 426. See also Henry F. May, "The Rebellion of the Intellectuals, 1912–1917," *American Quarterly* VIII (1956): 115, wherein May describes 1912–1917 as a "pre-revolutionary or early revolutionary period."
4. May, "Shifting Perspectives on the 1920's," 427.
5. Henry F. May, *The End of American Innocence: A Study of the First Years of Our Own Time, 1912–1917* (New York, 1959).
6. Arthur S. Link, "What Happened to the Progressive Movement in the 1920's?" *American Historical Review* LXIV (1959): 833–51.
7. J. Joseph Huthmacher, "Urban Liberalism and the Age of Reform," *Mississippi Valley Historical Review* XLIX (1962): 231–41. Other political and economic historians concur on a developmental interpretation. Gerald D. Nash, *State Government and Economic Development: A History of Administrative Policies in California, 1849–1933* (Berkeley, 1964), pp. 250, 291, 326, views the period 1900–1933 as a unit because it was characterized by notable coordination and centralization of authority by agencies of state government in California. Donald C. Swain, *Federal Conservation Policy, 1921–1933* (Berkeley, 1963), p. 6, sees the national conservation program making continuous advances through the 1920s based upon beginnings in the Progressive period.
8. "Sex O'clock in America," *Current Opinion* LV (1913): 113–14. The

anonymous author borrowed the phrase from William M. Reedy, editor of the St. Louis *Mirror.*

9. Agnes Repplier, "The Repeal of Reticence," *Atlantic Monthly* CXIII (1914): 297–304, objected to the "obsession of sex which has set us all a-babbling about matters once excluded from the amenities of conversation" (p. 298). Articles on birth control, prostitution, divorce, and sexual morals between 1910 and 1914 were cumulatively more numerous per thousand among articles indexed in the *Reader's Guide to Periodical Literature* than for either 1919 to 1924 or 1925 to 1928. Hornell Hart, "Changing Social Attitudes and Interests," *Recent Social Trends in the United States: Report of the President's Research Committee on Social Trends* (2 vols., New York, 1933), I, p. 414.

10. H. W. Boynton, "Ideas, Sex and the Novel," *Dial* LX (1916): 361. In Robert W. Chambers, *The Restless Sex* (New York, 1918), p. 143, the heroine remarks, "What was all wrong in our Victorian mothers' days is all right now."

11. Arthur Pollock, "Are We Immoral?" *Forum* LI (1914): 52. Pollock remarks that "in our literature and in our life to-day sex is paramount."

12. "Will Puritanism Return?" *Independent* 77 (1914): 397.

13. Mark Sullivan, *Our Times: The War Begins* (New York, 1932), pp. 165–93, states in colorful and impressionistic terms that significant changes in moral attitudes had taken place in the Progressive era. He attributes much of this to the influence of Freud, Shaw, and Omar Khayyám. Preston William Slosson, *The Great Crusade and After: 1914–1928* (New York, 1930), describes the period 1914–1928 as a unit, but his material dealing with morals centers on the 1920s. For example, there are only five footnotes based on materials written between 1914 and 1919 in his chapter, "The American Woman Wins Equality," pp. 130–61. Samuel Eliot Morison makes brief mention of a "revolution in sexual morals" before 1920 in *The Oxford History of the American People* (New York, 1965), pp. 906–08.

14. Frederick Lewis Allen, *Only Yesterday: An Informal History of the Nineteen-Twenties* (New York, 1931), pp. 88–122; William E. Leuchtenburg, *The Perils of Prosperity: 1914–32* (Chicago, 1958), pp. 158–77.

15. May, *The End of American Innocence*, pp. 334–47, is lightly documented; there are only twelve footnotes to support his discussion of these and similar developments.

16. Ibid., p. 347. May's view of women's changing attitudes is contradicted by Margaret Deland: "Of course there were women a generation ago, as in all generations, who asserted themselves; but they were practically 'sports.' Now, the simple, honest woman ... the good wife, the good mother—is evolving ideals which are changing her life, and the lives of those people about her." Margaret Deland, "The Change in the Feminine Ideal," *Atlantic Monthly* CV (1910): 291.

17. George E. Mowry, *The Urban Nation: 1920–1960* (New York, 1965), p. 250.

18. Ibid., p. 23.

19. Ibid.

20. Ibid., p. 24.

21. "By 1930 more than ten million women held jobs. Nothing did more to

emancipate them." Leuchtenburg, *Perils of Prosperity*, p. 160. See also Allen, *Only Yesterday*, pp. 95–98. For estimates of the effects of World War I on morals, see Leuchtenburg, *Perils of Prosperity*, pp. 172–73; Allen, *Only Yesterday*, p. 94; Mowry, *Urban Nation*, p. 24.

22. Population in urban territory comprised only about twenty-eight percent of the total American population in 1880; but by 1920, approximately fifty-two percent were living there. Department of Commerce, Bureau of the Census, *Historical Statistics of the United States, Colonial Times to 1957* (Washington, 1960), p. 14.

23. Scott Nearing and Nellie M. S. Nearing, *Woman and Social Progress* (New York, 1912), pp. 137–41. The Nearings wrote: "The freedom which American women have gained through recent social changes and the significance of their consequent choice, constitutes one of the profoundest and at the same time one of the most inscrutable problems in American life." (p. 138). William I. Thomas, *The Unadjusted Girl: With Cases and Standpoint for Behavior Analysis* (Boston, 1923), p. 86. Ernest R. Mowrer, *Family Disorganization* (Chicago, 1927), pp. 6–8. Mowrer attributes "Family Disorganization" to the "conditions of city life" which resulted in a "rebellion against the old ideals of family life...."

24. George Elliott Howard, "Social Control and the Functions of the Family," Howard J. Rogers, ed., *Congress of Arts and Sciences: Universal Exposition, St. Louis, 1904* (8 vols., Boston, 1906), VII, p. 702.

25. Louise Collier Willcox, "Our Supervised Morals," *North American Review* CXCVIII (1913): 708, observes: "The time is past when parents supervised the morals of their children...."

26. There was a surprisingly large number of cars sold and used in America between 1910 and 1920. Approximately forty percent as many cars were produced each year between 1915 and 1917 as were manufactured between 1925 and 1927. *Facts and Figures of the Automobile Industry* (New York, 1929), pp. 6, 22. There were approximately 7,500,000 cars registered in 1919. "Existing Surfaced Mileage Total" on a scale of 1,000 miles was 204 in 1910, 332 in 1918, 521 in 1925, and 694 in 1930. *Historical Statistics of the United States*, p. 458. Newspapers reported the impact of the automobile on dating and elopements. For a moralistic reaction to the phenomenon, see Dorothy Dix, Boston *American*, Sept. 5, 1912. For an enthusiast of "mobile privacy" in this period, see F. Scott Fitzgerald, "Echoes of the Jazz Age," *Scribner's Magazine* XC (1931): 460. Fitzgerald wrote: "As far back as 1915 the unchaperoned young people of the smaller cities had discovered the mobile privacy of that automobile given to young Bill at sixteen to make him 'self-reliant.'"

27. Dorothy Dix, "A Modern Diana," Boston *American*, April 7, 1910.

28. Beatrice Fairfax, ibid., May 28, 1908; Dorothy Dix, ibid., Sept. 9, 1912.

29. Ibid., Aug. 21, 1913

30. Marion Harland, "The Passing of the Home Daughter," *Independent* LXXI (July 13, 1911): 90.

31. Sophonisba P. Breckinridge, *Women in the Twentieth Century: A Study of Their Political, Social and Economic Activities* (New York, 1933), p. 112. Overall percentages of women gainfully employed rose from nineteen percent of the total work force in 1890 to 20.6 percent in 1900, 24.3 percent in 1910, twenty-four percent in 1920, and 25.3 percent in 1930. Ibid., p. 108.

32. While the number of women who worked as domestics declined after 1910, large numbers of women were employed for the first time as clerks and stenographers. In fact, more women were employed in both these occupations between 1910 and 1920 than between 1920 and 1930. Ibid., pp. 129, 177.
33. Martha Bensley Bruere and Robert W. Bruere, *Increasing Home Efficiency* (New York, 1914), pp. 236–41.
34.

Item	Total Amount Expended in Millions of Dollars				
	1909	1914	1919	1923	1929
(a) canned fruits and vegetables	162	254	575	625	930
(b) cleaning and polishing preparations	6	9	27	35	46
(c) electricity in household operation	83	132	265	389	615.5
(d) mechanical appliances (refrigerators, sewing machines, washers, cooking)	152	175	419	535	804.1
Percentage of expenditures on household equipment to total expenditures	9.9%	9.2%	10.3%	11.6%	13.2%

(a-b) is found in William H. Lough, *High-Level Consumption: Its Behavior; Its Consequences* (New York, 1935), pp. 236, 241. These figures are tabulated in millions of dollars for 1935. Items (c-d) and the percentage of expenditure on household equipment to total expenditures were taken from James Dewhurst, *America's Needs and Resources: A New Survey* (New York, 1955), pp. 702, 704, 180.
35. Realistic novelists note the leisure of the middle-class women. David Graham Phillips, *The Hungry Heart* (New York, 1909) and *Old Wives for New* (New York, 1908); Robert Herrick, *Together* (New York, 1908), especially pp. 515–17.
36. For example, see *Cosmopolitan* XXXV (May-Oct, 1903); *Ladies Home Journal* XXI (Dec. 1903-May 1904). A notable exception, showing a woman riding a bicycle, may be found in ibid. (April 1904), p. 39.
37. *Ladies Home Journal* XXXIV (May 1917), for example shows a woman entertaining stylish women friends (34, 89, 92), driving the car or on an automobile trip (36–37, 74), economizing on time spent in housework (42), the object of "outdoor girl" ads (78), beautifying at a social affair or appearing very chic (102, 106). Perhaps the best illustration for woman's activity in advertisements was employed in *Ladies Home Journal* by Williams Talc Powder. It read, "After the game, the ride, the swim, the brisk walk, or a day at the sea-shore, turn for comfort to Williams Talc Powder." Ibid., XXXIV (July 1917): 74.
38. *Collier's* 56 (Nov. 27, 1915): 4.
39. *Cosmopolitan* LIX (June 1915), advertising section, 50.
40. *Collier's* 56 (Sept. 25, 1915): 22.
41. Ibid. (Nov. 27, 1915): 25.

42. *Ladies Home Journal* XXXV (April 1918): 58.

43. Ibid., 57.

44. Ibid., XXXIII (Jan. 1916): 46–47. Women drove their friends and families about in their cars. Ibid., XXXII (July 1915): 34–35; (Aug. 1915): 38–39; (Oct. 1915): 86; XXXIII (Nov. 1916): 71.

45. Susanne Wilcox, "The Unrest of Modern Women," *Independent* LXVII (July 8, 1909): 63.

46. Nell Brinkley, a nationally syndicated cartoonist and commentator on women's activities, asked this question of one of her young women. Boston *American,* July 14, 1913.

47. Nell Brinkley coined the phrase. Ibid., Nov. 14, 1916.

48. Ibid., May 4, 1915. See also *Ladies Home Journal* XXXII (July 1915), which depicts a young woman driving a speedboat while her boyfriend sits next to her.

49. Boston *American,* Oct. 1, 1916.

50. *Collier's* 56 (March 4, 1916): 38.

51. Emma B. Kaufman, "The Education of a Debutante," *Cosmopolitan* XXXV (Sept. 1903): 499–508.

52. *Cosmopolitan* XXXIX (Oct. 1905).

53. "Girls, Don't Allow Men to be Familiar," Boston *American,* June 17, 1904; ibid., July 15, 1905.

54. *Wellesley College News,* Feb. 20, 1902. Wellesley relented on "men dances" in 1913.

55. Deland, "The Change in the Feminine Ideal," 291.

56. Ibid., 289.

57. Boston *American,* May 6, 1910.

58. Ibid., Sept. 5, 1912.

59. Ethel Watts Mumford, "Where Is Your Daughter This Afternoon?" *Harper's Weekly* LVIII (Jan. 17, 1914): 28.

60. Boston *American,* Sept. 5, 1916; ibid., Jan. 4, 1914.

61. Alice Duer Miller, "The New Dances and the Younger Generation," *Harper's Bazaar* XLVI (May 1912): 250.

62. Deland, "Change in the Feminine Ideal," 293.

63. Boston *American,* March 24, 1916. In a letter to the editor of the New York *Times,* one critic of the "women of New York" complained that they seemed to be part of a "new race" or even a "super-sex." He waxed poetic: "Sweet seventeen is rouge-pot mad, And hobbles to her tasks blase, ... Where are the girls of yesterday?" New York *Times,* July 20, 1914.

64. Miller, "New Dances and the Younger Generation," 250. According to Helen Rowland, the woman was "no longer Man's plaything, but his playmate. ..." Helen Rowland, "The Emancipation of 'the Rib,' " *Delineator* LXXVII (March 1911): 233.

65. Boston *American,* April 7, 1910.

66. Ibid., March 20, 1914.

67. Ibid., June 11, 1916.

68. Ibid., Nov. 27, Dec. 8, 1912.

69. On Newport and Boston society women see ibid., July 6, 27, Aug. 10, 24, 1913. Pauline Frederick's picture may be found in ibid., Aug. 2, 1913. For Irene Castle, see Mr. and Mrs. Vernon Castle, *Modern Dancing* (New York, 1914), pp. 98, 105.

70. *Ladies Home Journal* XXXII (July and Sept. 1915); ibid. (Nov. 1915): 8.
71. Owen Johnson, *The Salamander* (Indianapolis, 1914), Foreword, n.p.
72. Ibid., 9.
73. Ibid., 129.
74. Ibid., 66.
75. Ibid., 61.
76. Ibid., Foreword, n.p. Chamber's young heroine Stephanie Cleland in *The Restless Sex*, p. 191, practiced trial marriage in order to learn by experience. See also Phillips, *Hungry Heart*, pp. 166–80; Terry Ramsaye, *A Million And One Nights: A History of the Motion Picture* (2 vols., New York, 1926), II, 702–04.
77. "Mrs. Atherton Tells of Her 'Perch of the Devil,' " *Current Opinion* LVII (Nov. 1914): 349.
78. Boston *American*, Feb. 8, 1917.
79. The "kiss of friendship" criticized by Fairfax had become a major issue of her mail by 1913. See, for example, ibid., July 5, 1913. Girls shocked her with inquiries as to whether it was permissable to "soul kiss" on a first date. Ibid., Feb. 13, 1914. An engaged girl asked whether it would be all right to kiss men other than her fiance. Ibid., May 2, 1916.
80. Ibid., Feb. 8, 1917.
81. Fitzgerald, "Echoes of the Jazz Age," 460.
82. Thomas, *Unadjusted Girl*, p. 95.
83. "Today in the world of fashion, all women are young, and they grow more so all the time," Doeuilet, "When All The World Looks Young," *Delineator* LXXXIII (Aug. 1913): 20. Advertisements used flattery or played up the value of youth for women and warned that they might age unless certain products were used. *Cosmopolitan* LIX (Nov. 1915): 112; ibid. (July 1915): 81; *Ladies Home Journal* XXXII (Nov. 1915): 65; *Cosmopolitan* LIX (Oct. 1915): 57.
84. Eleanor Chalmers, "Facts and Figures," *Delineator* LXXXIV (April 1914): 38.
85. Boston *American*, March 20, 1910; *Delineator* LXXXIX (Oct. 1916): 66.
86. Boston *American*, March 28, 1904.
87. New York *Tribune*, April 4, 1912; Eleanor Chalmers, "You and Your Sewing," *Delineator*, LXXXIII (Aug. 1913): 33.
88. Eleanor Chalmers, *Delineator* LXXXIV (April 1914): 38. The sense of relief these changes brought is amusingly described in Dorothy A. Plum, comp. *The Magnificent Enterprise: A Chronicle of Vassar College* (Poughkeepsie, 1961), pp. 43–44.
89. Percival White, "Figuring Us Out," *North American Review* CCXXVII (Jan. 1929): 69.
90. Boston *American*, Dec. 10, 1916.
91. *Delineator*, LXXXV (July 1914): 55.
92. Boston *American*, Sept. 3, 1916.
93. *Cosmopolitan* LIX (July 1915).
94. An editorial declared that women's dresses in 1913 had approached "the danger line of indecency about as closely as they could." New York *Times*, July 6, 1914.
95. *Ladies Home Journal* XXXIV (Oct. 1917): 98.
96. Boston *American*, June 8, 1907. "The conventions of evening dress have changed radically in the last four or five years. Not so very long ago a

high-necked gown was considered *au fait* for all evening functions except formal dinners and the opera. Nowadays, well-dressed women wear de-colleté dresses even for home dinners, and semi-decolleté gowns for restaurants and theaters." *Delineator* LXXV (Jan. 1910): 60.

97. *Cosmopolitan* LIX (July 1915).
98. *Ladies Home Journal* XXXII (Oct. 1915): 108; ibid XXXIII (Oct, 1916):82; ibid. XXXIII (Nov. 1916): 78–79; ibid. XXXIV (Jan. 1917): 53.
99. "The Cult of St. Vitus," *Unpopular Review* III (Jan.-March 1915): 94.
100. Boston *American,* July 6, 1912. Dix noted "flirtatious" middle-aged women were "aping the airs and graces of the debutante" and "trying to act kittenish" with men.
101. Ibid., Dec. 6, 10, 1912. Anita Stewart, a movie star who wrote "Talks to Girls," though personally opposed to smoking, admitted that "lots of my friends smoke" and "they are nice girls too." Ibid., Dec. 14, 1915. In 1916, the Boston *American* titled a column on a page devoted to women's interests "To Smoke or Not to Smoke." Ibid., April 12, 1916. The *Harvard Lampoon,* LXXI (June 20, 1916), 376, spoofed women smoking: it carried a heading "Roman Society Women Agree to Give Up Smoking" and a commentary below, "Oh, Nero, how times have changed! "
102. Boston *American,* March 7, 1910.
103. Leuchtenburg, *Perils of Prosperity,* pp. 174–75.
104. "'Years of Discretion'—A Play of Cupid at Fifty," *Current Opinion* LIV (Feb. 1913): 116.
105. Ibid., 117.
106. Boston *American,* April 10, 1908. Evelyn Nesbitt, the wife of Harry Thaw, was romantically involved with architect Stanford White, whom Shaw shot to death.
107. Ibid., Aug. 25, Sept. 1, 1912.
108. Most of the dances which became very popular after 1910, such as the Turkey Trot, the Bunny Hug, and the Grizzly Bear, afforded a maximum of motion in a minimum of space. The Chicken Flip was invented by a Boston society woman. Ibid., Nov. 11, 1912. See also "New Reflections on the Dancing Mania," *Current Opinion* LV (Oct. 1913): 262.
109. Louis I. Dublin, "Birth Control," *Social Hygiene* VI (Jan. 1920): 6.
110. Alfred Kazin, "Three Pioneer Realists," *Saturday Review of Literature* XX (July 8, 1939): 15. Herrick's biographer, Blake Nevius, declares, "It can be argued that Herrick is the most comprehensive and reliable social historian in American fiction to appear in the interregnum between Howells and the writers of the Twenties. . . ." Blake Nevius, *Robert Herrick: The Development of a Novelist* (Berkeley: 1962), Preface.
111. Nevius, *Robert Herrick,* p. 177.
112. Herrick, *Together,* pp. 91, 392.
113. Ibid., pp. 263, 250–51, 320–24.
114. Herrick describes the temperament of the modern woman as one of "mistress rather than the wife. . . . 'I shall be a person with a soul of my own. To have me man must win me not once, but daily.'" Ibid., p. 516. The last sentence above nearly duplicates Rosalind's statement to her beau in *This Side of Paradise,* "I have to be won all over again every time you see me." F. Scott Fitzgerald, *This Side of Paradise* (New York, 1920), p. 194.

115. Chicago *Herald and Examiner*, March 10–17, 1920.
116. Ibid., March 10, 1920.
117. Ibid., March 11, 1920.
118. Ibid.
119. Ibid., March 11, 12, 1920.
120. Ibid., March 13, 14, 1920.
121. Ibid., March 15, 1920.
122. New York *Tribune*, Nov. 1, 1905.
123. New York *Times*, May 28, 1913.
124. Ibid., Dec. 20, 1912.
125. Ibid., Aug. 20, 23, 1913.
126. Ibid., June 29, 1913.
127. Carol Flora Brooks, "The Early History of the Anti-Contraceptive Laws in Massachusetts and Connecticut," *American Quarterly* XVIII (1966): 3–23; George E. Worthington, "Statutory Restrictions on Birth Control," *Journal of Social Hygiene* IX (1923): 458–465.
128. Boston *American*, July 14, 21, 1916; New York *Times*, Feb. 6, 1917.
129. *Report of the Pennsylvania Board of Censors*, June 1, 1915 to Dec. 1, 1915 (Harrisburg, 1916), p. 6.
130. Ellis Paxson Oberholtzer, *The Morals of the Movie* (Philadelphia, 1922), pp. 115–23.
131. *Report of the Pennsylvania State Board of Censors*, 1915, pp. 14–15; ibid., 1916, pp. 24–25; ibid., 1917, pp. 8–9.
132. Boston *American*, Aug. 10, 1913.
133. Ramsaye, *A Million and One Nights*, II, 617.
134. Boston *American*, July 7, 1917.
135. Ibid., Dec. 20, 1912.
136. Heywood Broun, *Anthony Comstock: Roundsman of the Lord* (New York, 1927); Mary Alden Hopkins, "Birth Control and Public Morals: An Interview with Anthony Comstock," *Harper's Weekly* LX (May 22, 1915): 489–90.
137. Boston *American*, Jan. 4, 1917.
138. Norman E. Hines, "Birth Control in Historical and Clinical Perspective," *Annals of the American Academy of Political and Social Sciences* 160 (1932): 53.
139. Dublin, "Birth Control," 6.
140. Boston *American*, July 16, 1916. According to International News Service, "Mrs. Rose Pastor Stokes was literally mobbed by an eager crowd in Carnegie Hall when she offered, in defiance of the police, to distribute printed slips bearing a formula for birth control." Ibid., May 6, 1916.

Prosperity's Child:
Some Thoughts on the Flapper

Kenneth A. Yellis

John Held's drawings of the flapper are what one usually visualizes when one thinks of the 1920s, very much as Charles Dana Gibson's drawings of his wife conjure up the 1890s for us. This parallel is hardly accidental; to the extent that single images can characterize eras then surely both men captured what now strikes us as significant about their ages. Moreover, that both images were of women is not a superficial coincidence. In any epoch, what woman is perceived to be by men, by other women and by herself, and the way in which she wants to be perceived, all tell us a great deal about perception in that period.

An even more striking fact about this parallel domination of decades by images is that the flapper was the utter antithesis of the Gibson girl's long hair, high brow, thirty-six-inch bust, narrow, anatomically precise waist, broad hips and well-concealed legs. As an ideal physical type the Gibson girl was contradicted in every particular by the flapper, who bobbed her hair, concealed her forehead, flattened her chest, hid her waist, dieted away her hips and kept her legs in plain sight. The flapper could hardly have been a more thorough repudiation of the Gibson girl if that had been her intent, as, in a sense, it was.

Both the flapper and the Gibson girl were ideal types and as such they were emulated to greater or lesser degrees by many women. More importantly, however, both epitomized the then prevailing conceptions of woman and her role, and these conceptions were opposed to each other. The Gibson girl was maternal and wifely, while the flapper was boyish and single. The Gibson girl was the embodiment of stability. The flapper's aesthetic ideal was motion, her characteristics were intensity, energy, volatility. While the Gibson girl seems incapable of an immodest thought or deed, the flapper strikes us as brazen and at least capable of sin if not actually guilty of it. She refused to recognize the traditional moral code of American civilization, while the Gibson girl had been its guardian.

The thoroughness of the difference between the two images is remarkable in view of the short time that separated their ascendancies. Both were distinctly and indigenously American, but there the similarity ends. The Gibson girl strikes us as old-fashioned, clearly part of the nineteenth century, the girl who married your grandfather, perhaps, or great-grandfather. The flapper, on the other hand, seems less remote, distinctly modern, the first of the twentieth century types.

Moreover, those who were disturbed by social tendencies in the 1920s, the critics of the so-called "revolution in morals and manners," were aware that what appalled them about the flapper, her behavior and her dress, was precisely her modernity. They saw her for what she was, the utter repudiation of the Gibson girl, that is, of traditional morality and femininity. They saw, too, that she was not an isolated phenomenon but an extreme manifestation of changes in the life styles of American women. These changes were, of course, made visible in dress, and the critics responded to this surface revolution, and groped for its underlying causes. As defenders of the moral status quo, they harked back to the Gibson girl, while deploring her daughter.[1]

The Literary Digest throughout the 1920s concerned itself with "the present relaxation of morals and manners among young men and women," and reported the statements and counter-insurgency activities of the Pope, the Y.W.C.A., the Women's Auxiliary of the Episcopal Church, the editors of religious journals, educational leaders and college editors. A number of articles made perfectly clear how much importance was attached to the impending "demoralization" of the country.[2]

It emerges from these articles that modesty, chastity, morality and traditional concepts of masculinity and femininity all were perceived as indivisible and, in some sense, interchangeable. The anxiety that all were being undermined appears to have been fairly widespread. Thus, modern dress and modern behavior were attacked simultaneously. Appeals to the authority of tradition were made. A movement toward sumptuary legislation, for example, seems to have had some force, as well as one toward censorship of dancing. There was little geographical pattern to these movements, nor does the information contained in the articles in *The Literary Digest* suggest that the contributors' viewpoints might have been isolable in terms of age, or of rural or urban background. Their professions and the tone of the magazine do suggest, however, that the struggle between modernism and traditionalism was mostly waged within the large American middle class.

The morality under attack had been at least partly protected by the reserve of women of that class. Female education in the nineteenth century underscored "the importance of purity, health, hygiene, and the rigid control of sexual desire." Marriage was the precondition of physical love, but even then the enjoyment of sex was forbidden. Women were supposed to be the unwilling victims of animal desires, resigned to sexual intercourse solely for the benefit of the continuation of the race and because it was an inevitable concomitant of marriage.[3]

Therefore, when President Campbell of Sterling College, Kansas, remarked in the *Digest* that "This [younger] generation is sex mad," he was saying something very significant from his point of view. That there were, among the young, girls who were no longer willing to postpone intercourse until after the exchange of vows and who enjoyed it, constituted a threat of major proportions to American society. If women would no longer guard morality, who would? The college presidents, deans, student editors, religious leaders and others who wrote to the *Digest,* by and large, thought they were witnessing nothing less than the decline, decay and fall of civilization as they had known it. When the flapper raised her skirts above the knee and rolled her hose below it, the naked flesh of the lower limbs of respectable women was revealed for the first time since the fall of Rome; the connection of the two events was not seen as coincidental.

Furthermore, this "new woman" threatened not only traditional morality, but made an assault on the prerogatives of traditional masculinity as well, the final section of the modesty-chastity-morality-masculinity equation. Women were now competing with men in the business world to an unprecedented degree. Moreover, whereas the saloon had been a male preserve, women now drank with men in speakeasies. Women had now taken to swearing and smoking, using contraceptives and in general refusing to bear the burdens and accept the limitations as well as the prerogatives of femininity as it had long been understood. Women were now obtaining financial and, therefore, other kinds of independence in record numbers from their fathers and their husbands.[4]

The grounds on which the new woman was defended could only have served to heighten the fears of the "viewers with alarm." That women were now merely "yielding to normal human impulses" suggested that the nobility of women's impulses or their ability to resist them had weakened since the Gibson girl. It was said that the morality of the older generation no longer merited respect because that generation had fouled up the world; but arguing thus signified that authority itself was being challenged.

Again, modern clothing was defended as lighter, more flexible, better suited for busy, athletic women. But this, too, meant a dangerous change from the Gibson girl, who kept herself busy only with her need to appear decorous and reputable, and who had not engaged in active sport. Women now had business other than clothes, the details of which some even considered "petty." It became clear, too, that Eve was no longer willing to take the rap for the unclean thoughts aroused in men's minds when she discarded all but the meagerest, flimsiest clothing; she would wear what she liked and what suited her.

What was being challenged and defended was the Victorian-American conception of sexuality and of the roles of men and women with respect to each other and to society. Primarily a middle-class code, it was at least the acknowledged general standard. It held men to be the aggressor, woman the endurer in sex and in other activities; the children that resulted from this male aggression and female passivity were born and raised by the woman. It was a two-edged as well as a "double" standard, allotting to men all the liberties and prerogatives, but stigmatizing them as less moral creatures than women.

Freud wrote, and many of the correspondents of the *Digest* would have agreed, that for men to exercise sexual restraint is essential for the establishment, progress and maintenance of civilization. The first civilized man was the one who could deny himself the sexual satisfaction of putting out a fire by urinating on it, for it was he who mastered fire and used it, by taming the fire of his own passions. Since woman was physically incapable of extinguishing the fire this way, she was its proper guardian, so man took him a wife to stay by the hearth, to regulate sexuality.

But woman's new assertiveness, her unwillingness to keep the home fires burning, was a two-fold danger: it threatened to liberate destructive sexual fires and to let the fire of civilization die out for want of tending.[5] What's more, the death of the Gibson girl, the rejection of the traditional family relation by the new American woman was a

personal tragedy for the American male; he had found his love un-
true.[6]

Moreover, men had been culturally conditioned to being the initia-
tors and to finding women the passive recipients of sexual advances.
The new tendencies in dress and behavior portended an inversion in
this scheme, and men reacted vehemently. The flapper costume was
seen as a sexual assault, and it was obvious to the men that they were
its objects.[7]

A congeries of social and psychological factors, therefore, are bound
up in the question of dress and the deeper questions of behavior and
values which it symbolized. By looking at the tendencies which affected clothing one can find out a great deal about the women who
were wearing it. The flapper, however, is such a familiar image to us
that we need to examine her closely to realize what a complete break
she represented with almost every major style in the west since the
Middle Ages began.

The flapper wore her hair short in a "Ponjola" bob, a style initiated
in this country by the dancer Irene Castle in the mid-1910s, but still
considered radical at the end of the war. For hundreds of years women's hair—whether worn up or down, natural or wigged, powdered or
oiled—had been long. The flapper covered her head and forehead with
a cloche-style hat, tweezed her eyebrows, and used a whole range of
other cosmetic devices, including trying to make her mouth look small
and puckered, "bee-stung" like Clara Bow's. Her dresses were tight,
straight, short and rather plain, with a very low waist, usually about
the hips, low necks for evening wear, and short sleeves, or none at all.
She wore nude-colored silk or rayon stockings which she often rolled
below the knee, or omitted altogether in hot weather, and high-heeled
cut-out slippers or pumps. Underneath her outergarments she wore as
little as possible. The corset was replaced by a girdle or nothing at all,
and a brassière-like garment was worn to minimize the breasts.

The term "flapper" originated in England as a description of girls of
the awkward age, the mid-teens. The awkwardness was meant literally,
and a girl who flapped had not yet reached mature, dignified womanhood. The flapper "was supposed to need a certain type of clothing—
long, straight lines to cover her awkwardness—and the stores advertised these gowns as 'flapper-dresses.' "[8] It was in postwar America
that these gawky, boyish flappers became the aesthetic ideal.

The major component of this ideal was a displacement of exposure
and emphasis from the trunk to the limbs, "in order that the long lines
and graceful contours of the arm [and leg] may be fully appreciated."
The aesthetic ideal was, in a word, youth:

Long slender limbs and an undeveloped torso are typical of immaturity, and, if modesty has departed from the legs, it has now
moved upwards to the body, where any display of the (formerly
so much admired) characteristcs of the fuller figure is discounte-
nanced. The bosom must be small and virginal, and maturity . . .
is concealed as long as possible.[9]

This abandonment of the traditional female aesthetic paralleled the
rejection by many women of the passive sexual, social and economic
role from which it had derived its force and relevance.

All the previous kinds of clothing for women in the west were
appropriate for the kind of woman who existed at that time, but there
was no precedent for dressing the woman who seemed to be emerging
in the 1920s. But even without such a precedent, a proper dress for her
needs was found. It was much more light and comfortable than women's apparel had been for a long time, there were many fewer garments and the fabrics were less stiff and rigid, offering great flexibility
and freedom of movement. A greater variety of fabrics, colors, types
of clothing, and designs were available than ever before. Bones and
stays and long skirts seemed to have gone forever.

Economy, simplicity and durability were the watchwords. Inexpensive clothing that stayed out of one's way and could be cared for easily
was increasingly in demand and manufacturers made it available. Basic colors became important because of the economy and simple elegance they offered; black and beige were the most popular in the
1920s. Infinite permutations of a limited wardrobe were made possible
by a multitude of inexpensive and attractive accessories such as stockings, shoes, gloves, handbags and costume jewelry. As a number of
observers remarked, even the poorest women had it in their power to
dress comfortably and attractively for an active life with minimal cost
and care.[10]

The Lynds observed that in Middletown, at least, furnace-heated
houses and enclosed automobiles seemed to have obviated much of
the function of clothing as physical protection. Moreover, it seemed to
them that its moral function, at least for women, had been modified
considerably. They cited the Middletown high-school boy who confidently remarked that his generation's most important contribution to
civilization was the one-piece bathing suit for women. Middletown's
women and girls had shortened their skirts from the ground to the
knee and their "lower limbs have been emphasized by sheer silk stockings; more of the arms and neck are habitually exposed; while the
increasing abandonment of petticoats and corsets reveals more of the

natural contours of the body." A high-school girl in Middletown typically wore to school only a brassière, knickers (an undergarment), knee-length dress, low shoes and silk stockings. Though some in Middletown felt that these developments were "a violation of morals and good taste," a revue staged in the high-school auditorium featured locally prominent recent high-school alumnae dancing with backs bare to the waist and bare thighs.[11] Moreover, the contrast between the amount of clothing ordinarily worn by men and by women in the 1920s is suggestive:

> Men still cover the body modestly from chin to soles, but women are (or were) rolling up from below, down from above, and in from the sides. In summer, men wear four times as much clothes by weight as women.[12]

A certain amount of qualification is necessary here. Obviously not every American woman was a flapper, nor was the flapper herself uniform throughout the decade. Nevertheless, what was true of the flapper was true of fashionable women fairly generally, and somewhat less true of a whole range of women not strictly fashionable, but not totally out of it either. Perusal of the Sears, Roebuck catalogues for the decade is very suggestive in this respect. These catalogues were, presumably, important to women in areas and situations in which being strictly fashionable was not vital for their careers or social acceptance, such as women on farms or in towns out of the reach of the large urban department stores. But the styles in these catalogues, not only in dresses but in hats, coats, shoes, lingerie, cosmetics and accessories, were no more than three months behind what was readily available in New York department stores.

Moreover, the language of the descriptions of the items in the catalogue echoed *Vogue,* seeking to sell the garments by virtue of their fashionableness, their exactness in duplicating what was in New York shop windows and on Parisian manikins. Even the designs that Sears characterized as conservative were quite modish. And most importantly, the prices ranged from quite low to moderate, making it possible for most of the women who got the Sears catalogue to be very well dressed for a modest outlay.

Thus, the flapper was an ideal to be emulated, which it was possible for many women to do quite easily, and which they seem to have done. But what was the relation of this ideal to reality? Why did women seek to emphasize freedom and play down femininity in their dress? What made it possible and necessary for them to do so? One of the most frequent defenses women made of the current modes was their convenience. But convenience for what?

Increasingly in the postwar years, and as part of a long-term economic trend, women, whether married or single, were working to support themselves or to supplement their families' incomes. Moreover, they were penetrating all kinds of businesses and professions previously barely touched by ladylike hands. The economic independence, greater opportunity and ability to find personal satisfaction outside of the home life in which women had traditionally found fulfillment were both consequences and reinforcing causes of the social and sexual independence women were now beginning to exercise and which expressed itself in dress.

The ideal woman now, for those who did not work as well as for those who did, was self-sufficient, intelligent, capable and active. She possessed skills and had acquired needs unknown to her mother. The influx of well-educated single and married middle-class women into the professions, public service and business resulted in the creation of a new class of women who constituted a growing and lucrative market, especially for clothes. This market could easily be tapped if the right clothes were found, and they were. These working women were shrewd buyers, had more money to spend than their stay-at-home sisters, and greater need to spend it. Thus, the economic power of this group meant that working women increasingly became the standard-setters for other women in dress. Whether or not they bought a particular design in their lunch-hour shopping expeditions to the downtown stores could make or break a manufacturer, or a retailer.

Contemporaries were well aware that the entrance of women into the business world in large numbers was producing a radical change in clothing. For example, a home economics teacher wrote in 1926 that

> With the entrance of women into the business world the demand came for comfortable dress which did not hamper the wearer in any way, and would hold its own no matter in what situation its owner found herself. It must have lasting qualities as well, for the business woman like the business man, must not be bothered with constant repairs. It must be easy to put on. The designers set to work and the one-piece slip on gown was the result.[13]

All of which is true enough, and, indeed, the importance of the time-saving factor cannot be overemphasized. But the need for a change in clothing derived from more than the simple fact that now many women were working for a living and before they had not been.

Edward Sapir characterized woman as traditionally understood as "the one who pleases by being what she is and looking as she does rather than by doing what she does." As the "kept partner in marriage," she used fashion to emphasize perpetually her desirability. She was a status symbol, an "expensive luxury." [14] Veblen's analysis of fashion,[15] from which Sapir took off, applied very specifically to the Gibson girl.

According to Veblen, the importance of clothing is that one's expenditures on dress are always out where they can be plainly seen. Fashion is thus a popular and universal outlet for conspicuous display, especially since failure to come up to expected standards in this area can be mortifying. Thus, too, clothing's commercial value is largely determined by its fashionableness rather than by its utility. It is fashionable clothing that communicates to the onlooker what the wearer wants known about himself, that he is wealthy, nonproductive and leisured. For women especially, clothing demonstrates that the wearer does not and need not work and, indeed, cannot because of the impracticality of her attire, such as long hair, large hats, high-heeled shoes, elaborate skirts and draperies, corsets and so on. For Veblen then, the Gibson girl's femininity was bound up in her inability to do anything useful, symbolized and reinforced by her dress.

The Gibson girl was the manikin for the fashionable clothing which testified to her husband's ability to free her from work and on whom he hung the symbols of his prosperity. She was in this sense responsible for the "good name" of her household, living testimony to its economic as well as its moral respectability; this was her job. For the Gibson girl her grooming itself was her profession; to be her husband's "prized possession" was her career.

But in the postwar years many women were no longer content with this role of expensive chattel nor with the physical, economic, social and sexual limitations which it imposed on their lives. Many women could no longer "be satisfied with their [husbands'] esteem and with such agreeable objects as homes, gardens, and pretty clothes." [16] For one thing, the work environment itself induced many women to shift their emphasis toward practicality in dress. Energy was channeled into social modes of behavior. A premium was put on correct behavior and attire for the social situation, while less value was placed on attractiveness alone.

Thus it was possible to write in 1930 that "There seems to be . . . no essential factor in the nature, habits, or functions of the two sexes that would necessitate a striking difference of costume—other than the desire to accentuate sex differences themselves. . . ." [17] The tendency in the 1920s was toward the blurring of many such differences in dress. This drive toward greater simplicity and practicability in dress gained impetus from the change in life style that many women underwent. The advances and demands of technology enabled women to get the kind of clothing they needed. The growth of the sporting life had a similar effect. Tennis could not be played in croquet costume, any more than business could be conducted effectively in parlor dress. For women, athletics, like business, was no longer quite the frivolous matter it had been, and women brought a new seriousness to dress.

The economic independence that came with jobs meant that there were fewer "dependent women," either daughters or wives. The sacred institutions of the home and the family were being eroded: "For city dwellers the home was steadily becoming less of a shrine, more of a dormitory." [18] Women now dressed, not for doting fathers or loving husbands, but for the competitive arena and a social situation. While for the housewife such situations may be more or less infrequent, the career woman is exposed to them daily; she is continually surrounded and observed by her male and female peers and superiors. [19]

The new office situation made constant demands on women and necessitated a dress and grooming appropriate for it. Perfumes as well as natural body odors, for example, had to be minimal in "the enforced intimacy of heterosexual office work," so that the "physical being" may be de-emphasized and "the social role and the office" stressed. Sexuality had to be understated in order for the work of the office to continue smoothly. The career woman had to "conceal and control" her femininity, to "reduce herself to an *office*" by minimizing her "natural shape, smell, color, texture, and movement and to replace these by impersonal, neutral surfaces." [20] Hence, for example, the popularity of the colors black and beige in the 1920s.

While sexuality never disappears in the office situation it is usually muted and controlled, turned "from a raw physical relationship to a civilized game." [21] The exposure of some parts of the body does not contradict this principle. The parts exposed were those most remote from the explicitly sexual areas, while the waist was lowered and the breast bound to make their existence and exact location matters of some guesswork. The lowering of the forehead, shaping of eyebrows and emphasis on make-up tended, among other things, to make the eyes appear larger, more "battable," stressing the seductive, coquettish aspects of sexuality. Finally, it has been argued that exposure removes the aura of mystery which clothing lends to the female body, thereby making it possible for both sexes to concentrate on business, sexual curiosity and urge to display satisfied.

The office became a kind of hunting ground in which males were captured and tamed in their native habitat. But it was more important that a proper uniform for the office as social situation be devised. Clothes are a kind of communication, establishing a relationship between wearer and observer before a word has been exchanged. They evoke, if properly used, a predictable set of responses concerning identity, values, moods and attitudes. The importance of dress to the hurried world of business thus becomes clear: it can be a useful shortcut to acquiring information about others and telling them about oneself. One knows whom he is dealing with even in the most fleeting contact, what the hierarchies are and the status of persons on a day-to-day basis. Clothes, as a social uniform, identify the players and the name of the game as well.

The working woman, married or not, had a big economic edge over the nonworking woman, which she could use in sexual competition as well, aided by her greater proximity to men, her presence in the male arena. This put a great deal of pressure on women who did not have jobs to seek them. Moreover, there were often family economic needs compelling them to do so. Most growing families could use more money, and parents are able to spend less and less money on themselves as their children grow older, until the children become self-supporting. The long-term trend has been for families to have fewer children and for women to have them earlier in life so as to be able to return to work at the time of the family's greatest economic need.

Most observers in the 1920s remarked that the housewife herself seemed to be emerging toward emancipation. Smaller, centrally heated houses were easier to clean, and many other families lived in apartments. Canned and frozen foods began to dominate the American diet, along with store-bought baked goods. Out-of-home housekeeping services and the availability of inexpensive mechanical and electrical devices in the home also tended to ease the housewife's burden.[22] But the liberation of the housewife had just begun in the 1920s, hardly approaching the proportions it would later assume.

Nevertheless, the housewife's emancipation had gone sufficiently far to cause some concern in Middletown for the diffusion of activities once centered about the home. Technological advances were accepted, but always with a proviso: "fresh encroachments tend to be met by a reassertion of the traditional *noli tangere* attitude toward the 'sacred institution' of the home." At Middletown's Chautauqua, a speaker observed:

> We seem to be drifting away from the fundamentals in our home life. The home was once a sacred institution where the family spent most of its time. Now it is a physical service station except for the old and the infirm.[23]

If many people were wary and worried about where it would all end, women, by and large, seemed pleased that the boundaries of their universe now extended past the front gate.

Clothes were not only the symbol of this partial emancipation, but one of the tools which made it possible as well. As one woman wrote to *The Literary Digest:*

> Think of the ease of laundering the simple modern clothes, and of the time saved in fitting. Manufacturers turn out gowns in sizes by the gross, and almost any figure can wear them with little or no alteration.[24]

The ready-to-wear industry meant that Middletown's housewives no longer made their own or their families' clothes. The vast majority of them did only washing, ironing and occasional mending. The sales of yard goods and notions were down sharply compared to a generation before, and notions departments all over the country had begun carrying hardware, soap, sanitary goods and the like, in order to survive.[25] While Middletown's home economics courses still emphasized sewing, it was clear that for the foreseeable future Middletown's girls should have been taught the art of buying.

The impact of ready-made clothing on Middletown's home life was a reflection of the growth of the ready-to-wear clothing industry in America. The uneven movement of this sector of the economy toward rationalization pointed to a time not too far off when all Americans could be well- and fashionably-dressed within weeks of the debut of styles in Paris or New York. One expert remarked that the consumer no longer needed to be concerned overmuch with utility, durability or colorfastness when purchasing clothing; mass production, he argued rather sanguinely, enabled manufacturers to ensure the quality of their products.[26]

The combined effects of rationalization and prosperity had facilitated the diffusion of fashions and increased the market for them. Moreover, the high initial profits accruing from the introduction of a successful design put a premium on rapid and thorough distribution, quick turnover and the marketing of new styles as soon as they were born. Had it not been for large inventories, this process might have been even more rapid than it was.[27]

Clothes-making, once a function of the home and the job of the homemaker, had now become clothes-buying, dependent on the family's or individual's earning power. The Lynds reported that as late as 1910, newspaper advertisements for yard goods had been numerous in Middletown, while there had been almost none for ready-made dresses. By the 1920s the position was reversed.

The rise of the jobbing system, lending some rationality to the industry, was not favorable to the formerly common individualism and creativity. But it seemed perfectly well suited to the new, simpler styles. So, too, did mechanization. If the emphasis on cost-cutting reduced opportunities for individual workmanship, the popular modes left little room for such virtuosity in any case. Both the industry and the market moved toward simple, stylish, ready-made garments made quickly and distributed rapidly. The Sears, Roebuck catalogue for the fall-winter, 1929–30, featured a dress described in these terms:

Paris Sends You This Dress In the Smartest French Manner. . . .

From Paris to you . . . speeded across the ocean . . . rushed to our style studios in the heart of New York . . . Reproduced with deft rapidity . . . Adapted with exquisite skill to the needs and tastes of American women . . . *Parisian Style!!*

Mass production was manufacturing luxury for all: Paris originals, in two colors, available to all of the tens of thousands of women who wanted them, for only $10.95, postpaid.

Perhaps the greatest single fact that had made all of this possible was the implementation of the idea that women came in sizes, seven of which would fit half the women in the country. A bell-shaped distribution about two of the sizes was manufactured and bought by the department stores, a very efficient and profitable way of dressing the women of America.

The sizes developed were especially good for young figures, which is perhaps further explanation of the emphasis in this period on youthful styles: "It is estimated that approximately ninety percent of the young people between the ages of fifteen to nineteen may be fitted by the standard sizes for these ages, that about half the adults from twenty to forty-four may be cared for with standard sizes, but that only a third of the population from the age of forty-five up may be properly fitted with such standard sizes." [28] It seemed that technology was peculiarly suited to the needs of the young woman.

Although mass production in the apparel industry in the 1920s gave impetus to the drive toward simplicity and uniformity, it also worked in the direction of variety and multiplicity. It now became possible to offer consumers at reasonable prices a wide range of fabrics, textures, colors and styles, and also a greater number of types of garments, that is, clothing suited for specific occasions and needs, such as formal evening wear, town and afternoon dresses and suits, business wear, sports outfits, work clothing and many others. This diversification, and the diffusion of fashionable clothing, too, had the effect of breaking down the patent outward manifestations of class: "Only a connoisseur can distinguish Miss Astorbilt on Fifth Avenue from her father's stenographer or secretary." [29]

But the industry which had worked such a miracle on the face of America seemed utterly vulnerable to something called fashion, over which it had little control. Carried far forward and, alternately, overwhelmed by its uncharted ebbs and flows, the ready-to-wear industry was more victim than giant. It seemed unwilling to adapt for its own needs the marketing techniques (notably market research) which had gone so far toward regularizing the automobile industry, among others, in the 1920s.[30] If fashion could be controlled, American manufacturers were not the manipulators. The obvious place to look for the men pulling the threads is Paris.

The French clothing industry held roughly the same position in the French economy that the automobile industry now occupies in the United States. The establishments ranged from highly individualistic and creative to a very few mass production operations on the American model. Each of the twenty-five largest houses alone accounted for from 500 to 1000 new designs annually.

But the size of the industry did not disguise its lack of modernity. It relied almost entirely on accumulated prestige, the originality of its designers and the manual proficiency of the French seamstress. France was ill-equipped to compete with American mechanization in the large-volume production of simple styles; it hoped and agitated for the return of the more detailed, elaborate styles which would bestow the advantage once more to its skilled workers. The flapper, American in origin, was a bitter pill for the Parisian couturiers to swallow. Though partly sold to the world by Paris' prestige, this same prestige was put behind annual efforts to dethrone the flapper, efforts which did not succeed until 1930.

After World War I, Paris was faced with an unprecedented demand from a new clientele more interested in the correctness than the uniqueness of its dress. This, and the tubular silhouette, forced Paris to give up its emphasis on exclusiveness. Much of this financial pressure came from America and the incentive to sell to American manufacturers for duplication here was very great; the old fears of style piracy were overcome. Paris found itself reproducing its own models for sale to manufacturers all over the world. Several of the most successful Parisian houses got that way precisely because of their ability to sell in the American market. This was true of Lelong, Chanel, Premet and Patou, whose adoption of American modes and sales techniques led them to dominance of the French domestic and export markets.

In fact, Paris' more dismal moments came at precisely those times when it tried to buck American trends. The most notorious example was Paris' reaction to the short skirt, which it detested. During the depression of 1921–22, Paris predicted unequivocally that the short skirt was on its way out and that the straight silhouette would be altered as well. The reaction of the American industry to these pronouncements was characteristically sheeplike. Textile mills rejoiced at the anticipated use of greater yardage, while apparel manufacturers distributed garments with longer skirts to their customers, the wholesalers and retailers who, in turn, tried to pass them off on the consumer.

But American women weren't having any. Sales of garments with longer skirts slowed drastically while women hunted for the shorter ones. If they did buy the longer-skirted dresses they wore them once and then had them altered more to their liking at the retailers' expense. Throughout the fall of 1923 and the spring of 1924 the complaints of retailers whose alteration expenses were skyrocketing could be heard all the way to Paris. Thereafter, skirts continued their uninterrupted rise until they reached the top of the knee in 1927.[31]

This debacle had several less disastrous but equally intriguing counterparts. Throughout the 1920s, Paris predicted year in and year out that wider hats would be in, but they were always out. Every year between 1921 and 1928 the return of the tailored suit was heralded, but it never caught on. One observer commented with marked understatement that prewar claims to "fashion dictatorship" by several Parisian couturiers had been moderated by postwar developments.[32]

But if Paris was no dictator, the relative success of the great skirt counter-revolution of 1929–30 becomes an intriguing problem. The chronology is straightforward enough. In 1928, Paris started a series of inroads on the dominant styles: an occasional head replaced the cloche with a turban or a wider brim; the austere tubular chemise dress had been embellished with bows and panels, *godets* and shirring; the straight high hem was superseded by an uneven one of "dripping, flaring panels or slithering trains of ribbon width dangling below." During the summer of 1929 in the showings of fall fashions by the Paris houses skirts plummeted toward the floor. One observer at Patou's first show that season reported that "All the women are squirming about in their chairs. tugging at their skirts. Already they feel *démodée.*"[33]

It was not that easy to make American women at home feel uncomfortable with what they were wearing. The gradual incursions on the flapper mode had met with signs of awakening resistance. *The New York Times,* for example, noted "the general disinclination to follow the dictum of Paris that skirts be longer" among the marchers in the 1929 Easter parade.[34]

The evidence for considering 1929 as a kind of transitional year in the dominant female aesthetic is suggestive rather than strong, but is worth noting. Apparently women were willing to modify the prevailing mode but manufacturers, burnt several times before, were unsure of their ability to predict the relative acceptability of a change and tried to follow events.

The industry was warned that it would not prove easy to sell garments in the new style. The Merchandise and Research Bureau predicted resistance to the longer skirt and the new waistline and urged the trade to put special emphasis on the changes to make them more palatable. A merchandiser advised putting stress on the trend "toward a more formal way of living" and the desire to have clothes with "more of a made to order look." Such talk, however, apparently did little to instill confidence among the retailers of the salability of the new styles: "Retailers as yet are on the fence waiting for the consumer response to indicate their buying policies."[35]

It was not long before resistance materialized. Revealed in the comumns of the *New York Times* in letters to the editor, news stories and editorials, this resistance showed high sophistication, that is, an awareness of what clothing—especially the modes of the 1920s—represented to the wearer. Lucie R. Saylor's letter, which drew much support, merits lengthy citation:

> It has taken many centuries of hard, slow struggle to attain the present degree of freedom from cumbersome feminine clothes. If we women are willing to give up that freedom and the moral victory it represents just because Parisian modistes issue arbitrary

decrees and manufacturers want to sell more materials, we are scarcely worthy to have the vote and other hard-won modern liberties. Ankle-length skirts and confining waists—and the minds of those willing to wear them—belong to the Middle Ages or to the harem.

Several other female *Times* readers agreed. E.B.C. added that while the "society woman" or "grande dame" of whom little movement was required might be able to wear "Long, trailing gowns of fragile silks and velvets, trimmed with real lace ... what about the hordes of women and girls who travel in the subways and work in offices?" [36]

The revolt was sufficiently serious to warrant a *New York Times Magazine* article on it.[37] Noting that Paris had chosen "femininity" at the expense of "comfort or bank accounts" the author went on to say that feminine was meant "in its narrowest and most thoroughly traditional sense," a sense irrelevant to American women in 1929 but keyed to an idealization of French women before the fall, *i.e.*, their contamination by modern ideas. The French couturiers had indulged in "an orgy of nostalgia." But this same article struck an ambivalent note: "It would look as though women were persuaded that they were tired of simplicity and bored with freedom" and ready to accept a greater formality in some aspects or types of dress, especially evening wear. This hint of indecisiveness as to which role she wanted to play or perhaps her desire to play both if possible may be a vital clue toward an understanding of the American woman's ultimate acceptance of a more "feminine" costume.

The uncertainty continued over the winter. The *Times* observed that while the new modes were bought they were not worn except for formal evening wear. The Women's Federation sponsored a debate on the subject of skirt lengths whose outcome was predictably inconclusive. Manufacturers were likewise insecure. J. J. Goldman, founder of Associated Dress Industries, reported that the long skirt was curtailing sales, but predicted that it would be accepted by spring. A showing of New York designs for the spring, held more than a month before the Paris exhibitions to demonstrate independence, was conciliatory in intent, setting the length at six inches below the knee and moderating other extreme measures taken in the fall. A partial retreat was in evidence as well in the spring-summer shows in Paris, but this was evidently not rapid enough to please American manufacturers and merchandisers who by now had become angry with Paris' inability or unwillingness to develop clothes salable on the American market. The most recent experience in bucking consumer tastes at Paris' behest was

. too much: "Our endorsement of the very long skirt and the bizarre details last Fall," said Henry H. Finder, former President of the Industrial Council of Cloak, Suit and Skirt Manufacturers, Inc., "was a serious and costly mistake and we shall not permit it to occur again." [38]

Nevertheless, it was obvious that Paris had finally succeeded in doing what it had wanted to do all along: it had finally made the longer skirt stick. The Sears catalogues, starting with spring-summer 1930, reflected the winter compromises and were dominated by the new styles, with longer and fuller skirts, re-emphasized bust, waist and hips, tailored suits, prints and patterns, and larger hats. But the change had occurred *in* the American market. Some hypotheses on the nature of fashion may help illuminate these changes.

Although the machine threatened to obliterate class distinctions in dress, in a way it also helped to maintain them. The fact that of two identical garments one was mass-produced while the other was an "original" made by hand continued to give great prestige to the owner of the latter article: "The aesthetic value of a detected counterfeit in dress declines somewhat in the same proportion as the counterfeit is cheaper than its original." [39] The spread of fashion through a community is a function of the size of the middle class, which feels urgently the need to distinguish itself from the rest of the population. Thus the fashion cycle gains impetus from the drive of members of key affluent groups to emulate their superiors and dissociate themselves from their inferiors; the larger the middle class, the more rapid the turnover of modes.

Talking about groups makes it easy to forget that a large number of individual decisions are involved which are made on the basis of personal circumstances, relationships and needs. Fashion is a way of enabling individuals to belong where they want to belong, and to cut themselves off from undesired associations. It is an instrument of social mobility. Moreover, it is a legitimized outlet for personal self-expression, particularly valuable for persons who feel they live in a society in which the individual is devalued. Fashion is a kind of safety valve for aberrant individual or group tendencies, such as, in the 1920s, class consciousness in a democratic society, sexual curiosity in a puritanical one or individuality in a mass culture.

New fashions, of course, do not always find favor with the fashion following; certain conditions have to be met by the style itself and by the persons proposing it. A style which is too far out of the mainstream of public values, which satisfies neither articulated nor inarticulate needs, is liable to be abandoned quickly or not taken up at all.

This happened to the harem skirt, proposed in the 1910s, which apparently failed to pick up support because it symbolized an extreme form of the subjugation women were trying to escape. The farther out a style is, moreover, the greater the prestige needed by the initiator to make it catch on, but even the most modest innovation needs someone of stature behind it. What form of prestige is necessary varies according to social circumstances. By the 1920s the days of royal fashion plates were over and movie stars seemed to have replaced them as the great influences on American women.

This is no frivolous matter. The decision that a woman makes to follow one fashion leader and not another means that one has spoken to some important need and the other has not. When this process is repeated several million times, *i.e.*, sufficiently often to become a fashion trend, then we are dealing not with individual variations and impulses but with what amounts to a major social movement in which aesthetic and moral values are undergoing drastic and rapid change. On the surface this process seems to go on effortlessly. But previous to the change many women had to be groping about, feeling dissatisfied (perhaps unconsciously) with what they were wearing, wishing for some style of clothing that expressed *them* better, their needs and their aspirations. Having undergone what amounts to a change in identity by the 1920s many women needed a change of costume in order better to communicate what they thought about themselves and wanted thought about them, who they were.

The styles that predominated in the 1920s were urban in genesis, but there is reason to believe that they spread widely into small towns and rural areas. The automobile placed many previously isolated areas within easy reach of urban centers, becoming a tool for the penetration of urban modes and values into rural life. The Sears catalogue put city styles into country mailboxes. The Lynds reported that urban styles had taken over Middletown, and that family income did not seem to matter so much as that people felt obliged to wear them, to dress up all the time. Mass circulation newspapers and magazines, movies and radio tended to telescope distances and blur distinctions between small town and big city behavior patterns.

A number of major economic, social and technological trends, therefore, seem to have had similar influences and effects on the dress and behavior of many American women in the 1920s. Events, too, such as the war, the winning of suffrage and the prohibition experiment may have had the same kind of implications. The 1920s seem to have witnessed the emergence of a new woman whose behavior and appearnace constituted a major break with western, male-dominated civilization and was seen, in fact, as a dangerous threat to that civilization. The Lynds, among others, wondered if this woman's rise would continue uninterrupted and if the tendency toward greater emancipation and the dissolution of the home would go on.

For a short time, at least, their questions were answered by the Depression; the reversion or reaction toward more "feminine" attire was paralleled and facilitated by a retreat to the traditional family unit during the crisis period. The new woman seemed to go into eclipse during the period of anxiety, but the changed circumstances of World War II, including a manpower shortage, brought her out again.

Was the flapper a summer flower who withered in cold, hard times? Or was she a stage in a long-run development, temporarily retarded by crisis, while the men were able to haul the Gibson girl, or someone like her, down from the attic? Is the flapper, child of prosperity, the normal condition, or is the Gibson girl, daughter of scarcity, the real woman? [40]

The continuing and growing prosperity in the United States and Europe has afforded women, in this century, an opportunity to experiment with various life styles, value systems and social and personal roles. So far many different alternatives have proved satisfying to different women, ranging from traditional to avant-garde femininity. If prosperity continues it is likely that such diversity will be with us for the foreseeable future, but in the long run something more like the flapper than the Gibson girl will win out. The crisis would have to be very severe and the moral reaction very strong to induce modern woman to accept the values and limitations which she has already repudiated whenever she had the chance.

NOTES

1. In a letter to the *New York Times* (Feb. 25, 1930, p. 26) Andrew J. Haire expressed it this way: "Dear God, give us back our women! "
2. Cf. "Is the Younger Generation in Peril?" LXIX (May 14, 1921), 9–12, and *passim;* "Today's Morals and Manners—the Side of 'The Girls'," LXX (July 9, 1921), 34–42; "The Case Against the Younger Generation," LXXIII (June 17, 1922), 40 ff.
3. Andrew Sinclair, *Prohibition: The Era of Excess* (New York, 1962), p. 53.
4. See, for example, U.S. Bureau of Census, *Fifteenth Census of the United States: 1930,* "Population," Vol. V (Occupations), Washington, 1933, Tables 1–4, pp. 272–73, for impressive gains in the numbers and percentages of women working between 1890 and 1930, particularly married women. These figures also show impressive increases of women working in the "transportation and communication," "trade," "public service," "professional service," "domestic and personal service" and "clerical" sectors which overmatched massived declines in "agriculture" and "man-

ufacturing and mechanical" during this period. The report says: "In the percentages presented ... two very important facts stand out strikingly. The first is the marked increase during this period in the proportion of all women—and particularly in the proportion of all married women—gainfully occupied. The second is the striking increase in the proportion which married women form of all gainfully occupied women ..." (pp. 271–72).

5. Sigmund Freud, *Civilization and Its Discontents* (London, 1949, first published 1930), *passim*, esp. pp. 50 ff.
6. It is interesting and probably significant that it is in this period that the image of the woman as "victim" in American literature in a period darkened by the Gibson girl's shadow (Stephen Crane's Maggie, Theodore Dreiser's Jennie Gerhardt, David Graham Phillips' Susan Lenox) was replaced by woman as "the first great American grasping BITCH" (according to Dennis P. Kelly), that is, the flapper, in Fitzgerald (Daisy), Hemingway (Bret), Faulkner (Temple Drake) and others. If the American woman had turned on him, the American man would stigmatize her defection in deathless prose.
7. In further explanation of the vehemence of the reaction, the specter of homosexuality was also raised; that is, women were now dressing and behaving more like men, blurring the traditionally obvious superficial distinctions and increasing the chances of a mistake, i.e., making sexual advances toward or arousing desire in a person of the same sex. *Cf.* John C. Flügel, *The Psychology of Clothes* (London, 1930), p. 202. Freud also suggested that women bobbed their hair in order to compete with men for men's attention, due to the increase in overt homosexuality resulting from the trench experience in World War I. In any case, it is probably true that women were trying to attract men's attention, among other purposes, when they adopted male aggressiveness and changed their dress. In order to be nearer men, women needed to be more like men in certain ways so as to be admitted to the male arena.
8. Elizabeth Sage, *A Study of Costume* (New York, 1926), p. 216. See also, *O.E.D.*
9. Flügel, pp. 161–62.
10. Kurt and Gladys Lang, "Fashion: Identification and Differentiation in the Mass Society," in Mary Ellen Roach and Joanne Bubolz Eicher, *Dress Adornment and the Social Order* (New York, 1965), pp. 322 ff.
11. Robert S. and Helen M. Lynd, *Middletown* (New York, 1929), pp. 159–60.
12. Stuart Chase, *Prosperity—Fact or Myth?* (New York, 1929), p. 66.
13. Sage, p. 215.
14. Edward Sapir, "Fashion," in *Encyclopedia of the Social Sciences* (New York, 1931), VI, 142.
15. Thorstein Veblen, *The Theory of the Leisure Class* (New York, 1934).
16. Winifred Raushenbush, "The Idiot God Fashion," in *Woman's Coming of Age*, eds. Samuel D. Schmalhausen and V.F. Calverton (New York, 1931), p. 442.
17. Flügel, p. 201.
18. Frederick Lewis Allen, *Only Yesterday* (New York, 1964), p. 81.
19. Murray Wax, "Themes in Cosmetics and Grooming," in Roach and Eicher, p. 44.

20. Ibid., p. 39.
21. Ibid., pp. 42–45.
22. Siegfried Giedion characterizes the 1920s as the first decade in the "time of full mechanization." *Mechanization Takes Command* (New York, 1948), *passim.*
23. Lynds, pp. 177–78.
24. "To-Day's Morals . . . ," LXX, 36.
25. Paul H. Nystrom, *Economics of Fashion* (New York, 1928), p. 437.
26. Ibid., p. iii.
27. Sapir, pp. 141–43.
28. Nystrom, p. 463.
29. Chase, p. 65.
30. Nystrom, p. iv.
31. Ibid., p. 388.
32. Ibid., p. 396.
33. Edna Woolman Chase and Ilka Chase, *Always in Vogue* (New York, 1954), pp. 213 ff.
34. *New York Times,* Apr. 1, 1929, p. 3.
35. *New York Times,* Aug. 4, 1929, II, p. 8; Aug. 6, 1929, p. 42; Sept. 1, 1929, II, p. 14.
36. *New York Times,* Sept. 7, 1929, p. 16; Sept. 9, 1929, p. 24; Sept. 30, 1929, p. 30. See also the comments of Mrs. John C. Germann, Fannie Hurst and Viola Crawford in the same newspaper; Oct. 11, 1929, p. 30; Oct. 13, 1929, p. 28 and Oct. 21, 1929, p. 26, respectively.
37. Mildred Adams, "Revolt Rumbles in the Fashion World," Oct. 27, 1929, V, 4 *et passim.* Neither *Vogue* nor *Harper's Bazar* (sic) seems to have found occasion to underscore the drastic changes from the styles of the 1920s or to suggest that there was any resistance to this change. The tone of both suggest their belief that such a revolutionary shift in aesthetics was the most natural thing in the world and far be it from mere mortals to question the edicts of Paris, which were inscrutable in any case.
38. *New York Times:* Nov. 24, 1929, II, p. 8; Nov. 27, 1929, p. 29; Dec. 8, 1929, III, p. 2; Dec. 13, 1929, p. 36; Dec. 14, 1929, p. 40; Dec. 18, 1929, p. 13; Jan. 25, 1930, p. 1; Feb. 5, 1930, p. 25; May 8, 1930, p. 32 (see also "Paris Revives Skirt for Swimming Garb," Feb. 6, 1930, p. 11); Aug. 3, 1930, II, p. 18.
39. Veblen, p. 169.
40. The New Haven *Journal-Courier* for June 21, 1967, published a chart (prepared by Harris, Upham & Co., a brokerage firm) which showed that skirts and the Dow-Jones Industrial Average have tended to rise and fall together and that the long-term tendency for both was upward. While this holds great promise for the future, no claim is made here that the point is proved.

Cookbooks and Law Books:
The Hidden History of Career Women in Twentieth-Century America

Frank Stricker

I

A crucial problem in the history of American women in the twentieth century involves their participation in professional and business occupations. This is but one aspect of the role of women at work outside the home. Indeed, the majority of working women in this century were employed as domestics, garment workers, clerks, typists, and in a variety of other low-level jobs—not as professionals and business-women. For most of these the job was not a career or a means of personal fulfillment but a function of sheer economic necessity.[1] Yet even in work that seemed to leave little room for creativity, organizational expertise, and human control of the tasks, the job sometimes had attributes of a career. Women wished to work not merely to support their families, but for a measure of personal economic independence, or as a byproduct of escaping from dull country life, or simply for the sociability of working with other women.[2]

This paper, however, focuses on the special group of women in professional and business occupations, roughly corresponding to the census categories of "Professional, Technical, and Kindred Workers," and "Managers, Officials, and Proprietors." The category of "Professionals" has always included large numbers of school teachers and nurses, with smaller numbers of physicians, lawyers, college teachers, and the like. The category of "Managers, Officials, and Proprietors," included government officials, managers in industry, as well as owners of small businesses. Although women with career attitudes could be found outside these occupations, and although not all women in these occupations were career minded, the general categories roughly indicate the number of women in careers.

The career woman had serious goals in mind. She wanted economic independence and a job with intrinsic satisfactions. Along with the demand for political equality, the desire for a career was a central theme in early twentieth-century feminism. Although a career was not a real possibility for the majority of women, and although the career impulse was not identical with feminism, it did express the driving impulse of many advanced middle-class women.[3]

The feminist movement had reached its high point in 1920, when, after decades of struggle, women won a federal amendment granting the right to vote. In the years that followed, the movement fell on hard times. The largest number of activist women in the 1920s were "social feminists," women involved in service to society, often animated by an ideal of selfless sacrifice, and essentially conservative about women's role in the family. A small group of women in Alice Paul's Woman's Party, at odds with the social reformers, pushed for a federal equal rights amendment. Younger women were, on the whole, disaffected from both groups of feminists. They had turned away from reform and politics. In the age of the flapper, feminism seemed unfashionable.[4]

But if the feminist movement fell into disarray in the 1920s, what was actually happening to articulate educated women? What has been their history in career positions in the twentieth century? The problem that this paper deals with is the alleged decline of women's share of professional and business occupations, which is often located in the Twenties along with the difficulties of the feminist movement. The statistics do indicate a decline, although it sometimes occurs in previous or subsequent decades. For example, in 1920, one of seven doctorates was awarded to a woman; this ratio began declining in the Thirties until, in 1956, only one of ten doctorates were women. Women's proportion of total college enrollment peaked in the 1920s; their percentage of total college teaching faculty in the 1930s. In some areas not only women's share but their numbers declined. There were fewer female physicians in 1930 (8,388) than there had been in 1910 (9,015), the decline beginning in the 1910s. The number of female musicians and music teachers dropped from 84,478 in 1910 to 79,611 in 1930, losing twelve percent in the 1910s and gaining ten percent in the 1920s. Overall, women's proportion of the professional ranks reached a plateau in the 1920s and fell off in the following decade.[5]

It is, however, because of literary evidence rather than statistical facts that some historians have suggested that it was in the late 1920s that career women became disillusioned with their new role. Magazines like *Harper's, Scribner's,* and *The Forum* began publishing the confessions of professional and business-women who had apparently turned their backs on the workplace to find fulfillment at home.[6] "Feminist-New Style," as one author termed the younger generation, desired a measure of economic independence and satisfying work, but she would not sacrifice marriage and family for work. If forced to choose, she would give up her law book for the cookbook.[7]

As the 1920s came to a close, investigator Phyllis Blanchard discovered among young women "the first signs of disillusionment with the new freedom." The modern girl, "who has seen the loneliness of older unmarried friends, is beginning to discount the rewards from a material success that must be accomplished at the expense of love." [8] Even so staunch a feminist as Alice Beal Parsons had to admit that a new motto was finding its way into numerous magazines: "We are tired of our rights, give us our privileges again." [9] In short, within a decade of the high point of the woman suffrage movement, it seemed to contemporary observers that the tide had turned against woman's emancipation and that career women were going home.[10]

Having absorbed this information recent writers contend that women became disillusioned with the very ideals of economic independence and exciting work because the freer sexual morality of the period made love and marriage more attractive to women.[11]

Sociologist Jessie Bernard attaches to the 1920s the label, "Surging Flood of Disillusion," and argues that with success, the "éclat of the earlier years had spent itself." In the decade of the 1930s, academic women began "the headlong flight into maternity." Despite the lure of fellowships, "women turned their backs and ran to rock the cradle." [12] William O'Neill has argued that "the careerist myth had been deflated" and a "New Victorianism" encouraging sexual happiness for women in marriage, emerged in the 1920s.[13] The sexual revolution of the decade made romance and marriage more attractive than they had been in the Victorian period when women's sexual pleasure was discouraged. As a result, it is argued, the hardy and celibate spinster—the kind of woman who could devote herself wholeheartedly to a career— became an even rarer figure. Feminism itself was associated with flat heels and a lack of feminine charm.[14] According to this interpretation, the spread of a more sophisticated feminine mystique in the 1940s and 1950s was almost anticlimactic. Already in the 1920s, the career impulse was losing out to love and a marriage promising sexual fulfillment.[15]

In what follows I will argue against the theory of disillusionment on grounds first, that the evidence from the surveys of career intentions is inconclusive; second, that occupational statistics can be read in a non-regressive manner and that some of the explanations used for the decline are unnecessary or incorrect; third, that a woman's decision to marry was not necessarily the rejection of a career; fourth, that the public confessions of women who went home were less negative than has been supposed; and finally, that the assumptions of social scientists and psychologists must be distinguished from the complex attitudes of American women.

I will not deny that women were subject to job discrimination, the double burden of home and career, and, most of all, socialization from an early age to the domestic role. But obviously, many women received contrary pressures and went through experiences such as college education which raised opposite expectations. Women did receive strong pressures to marry, have a family, and follow a socially defined model of feminine beauty and submissiveness. But many of them also felt pressures to achieve, prepare for a career, and be intellectually alive (if only for their husbands' sakes). Our model of women's attitudes must be much more complex than the theory of disillusionment assumes, and it should view the formation of women's attitudes in the context of the varying and often contradictory social and economic forces pressing on them.[16]

II

Changes in the attitudes and aspirations of American women over the past fifty years cannot be measured with precision. In particular, the attitudes of younger women are hard to come by. They may be the most interesting, because women in their teens probably express career aspirations in a relatively pure form, before discrimination in the market place and the double burden of home and career become practical matters.

Perhaps for this reason, Lorine Pruette's 1924 survey of young women, most of them ages 15–17, shows a relatively high level of careerism. In fact, more than a third (thirty-five percent) said they would choose a career even if that meant giving up the possibility of marrying and having a family.[17]

Later surveys seemed to show a decline in career sentiment. A survey completed in 1930, of women ages eighteen to twenty-six, found only thirteen percent who were planning careers with no thought of marriage and who would forego marriage if it interfered with their careers. Phyllis Blanchard and Carolyn Manasses, the interviewers, concluded that young women were becoming disillusioned with the new freedom.[18] Several historians have followed their evaluation, citing similar surveys.[19]

But we must be cautious in using these surveys to demonstrate a decline of career sentiments. Each of them asks different questions of different groups. Each offers slightly different choices to the women. Even in Blanchard's group, thirty-eight percent of the total wanted to combine marriage and a career, a result that is not by itself evidence of a decline in career sentiment.[20] Elsewhere the evidence is also confusing, particularly if we are interested in dating the decline and fall of career attitudes. Of Vassar women surveyed in 1923, ninety percent wanted to marry; yet only seventy percent of the graduates of New Jersey's College for Women in 1930 agreed that marriage and family took precedence over a career.[21] In 1936 a majority of Pennsylvania State College Senior Women agreed that "a young woman cannot continue her business career after her wedding ... except in case of real financial need." [22] But half the Vassar College Seniors of 1937 would combine career and family if they could earn enough to pay for child-care and have some time for their children.[23]

The evidence of trends from the various career surveys is therefore somewhat ambiguous. One cannot feel secure in marking out long-range trends.[24] The apparently high interest of women in Pruette's 1924 survey in careers has much to do with the youth of those interviewed. Whether the lower number in Blanchard's survey who would forego marriage for a career represents a decline from previous periods among similar kinds of women is impossible to determine.

As time went on, women's career decisions grew more complex, with more and more potential career women planning some combination of vocation and domestic life. Even in the 1950s, when the feminine mystique reigned supreme, half the women in one survey of college students wanted a career, most with and some without marriage. Some twenty percent were determined career women. Others were willing to interrupt their work to have a family and then return to work, but some of these "would have preferred to carry on their careers without interruption" if part-time jobs and sufficient earnings for hiring domestic help were available.[25] With the spread of contraception and the lack of day-care facilities, it seems that many women made a pragmatic decision to withdraw temporarily from work, planning to return at a later date. Others, with plans for combining marriage and career, found out how difficult that was:

> I was definitely career-oriented when I was young. I had negative reactions to the thought of being tied down to housework. It seemed menial and extremely unrewarding to me. I planned to prepare for a career and, if I got married and had a family, to earn the money to hire a housekeeper. But that isn't the way it worked out. I had not gotten launched on a career by the time I was married, and we started having our family immediately ... there was no time to give thought to a career for many years.[26]

In short, the history of career women and potential career women is much more complex than a simple story of disillusionment or the supremacy of the feminine mystique. It must be full of the twists and turns, tensions and pragmatic decisions which constituted the story of thousands of women as they worked out their desire for a career and a personal life.

III

Along with surveys of career intentions, a widely used indicator of the progress of career women is the statistical evidence of women's share of professional and business occupations. Here the evidence for a decline in the 1920s—and in some cases the 1930s—is less than convincing. In the census category of "Managers, Officials, and Proprietors," the general pattern indicates slight but real increases after 1920. The numbers of businesswomen expanded at slightly higher rates than the numbers of businessmen in most decades. The job level which these women reached is another question; they did not win seats on the New York Stock Exchange or General Motors' Board of Directors. But those historians who find a deflation of the career ethic in the twenties and thirties have themselves utilized the broad census categories. Moreover, women's absence from the higher ranks must have resulted as much from discrimination as from lack of desire. Simply in terms of overall statistics, there was a gradual increase in women's share of business occupations.[27]

TABLE 1

Female Managers, Officials, Proprietors (except farm)

Year	Number	% of Total	Decennial Increase	Male Decennial Increase
1900	77,214	4.5%	—	—
1910	216,537	8.6%	180%	43%
1920	220,797	7.8%	2%	13%
1930	304,969	8.4%	38%	27%
1940	414,472	11.0%	36%	1%
1950	699,807	13.6%	69%	33%

Obviously women still gained a very small percentage of the total, but over the decades they increased their share of these and other business occupations. For example, the proportion of all real estate agents, managers, and superintendents who were women tripled from 1910 to 1920, from 2.3 percent to 6.1 percent of the total, doubled to 12.9 percent in 1930, and almost doubled again to 20.2 percent of the total in 1940.[28] Whether or not real estate work or any other business occupation expresses the highest ideals of feminism, the statistical evidence alone does not support a theory of progressive decline since the 1920s.[29]

In the other census category of significance for career women, "Professional, Technical, and Kindred Workers," the evidence indicates a decline after 1930. As suggested earlier, women increased their share steadily in the 1900s and 1910s, peaked in the 1920s, and lost ground in the 1930s and 1940s.[30]

TABLE 2

Women as a Percent of Total Professional Workers

1900	1910	1920	1930	1940	1950
35.2%	41.3%	44.1%	44.8%	41.5%	39.6%

The most drastic decline occurred in the decade of the Great Depression when the absolute number of female professionals increased by a mere 8.5 percent, the smallest decadal increase during the whole period.[31] Half the female professionals were schoolteachers and it cannot be accidental that the most substantial inroads against professional women occurred not during the sexual revolution of the 1920s but in the depression when school boards, state governments, and male teachers exerted terrific pressure against women teachers.[32] As a result, the number of female schoolteachers, which had risen from 635,207 in

1920 to 853,976 in 1930, actually dropped by the end of the thirties to 802,264.[33]

Other subcategories of professionals complicate the story. Not only the proportion but the number of female physicians declined, but the decline began in the 1910s, not in the 1920s.[34] The number of female editors and reporters doubled in the twenties and stabilized in the thirties—ironically the heyday of the woman reporter in American films.[35] Nurses, the second largest subcategory of female professionals after teachers, increased each decade until the 1940s. Nursing was an occupation that was highly segregated by sex, and, at least until recently, desperately underpaid. Still, as with teaching, it provided a channel for the aspirations of young women, many of them working-class and lower middle-class women whose real chances for more prestigious careers were limited for social and economic reasons.[36] In one particular area of professional endeavor, women's share quite clearly peaked in the twenties and began a long decline in the thirties.[37]

TABLE 3

Women's Share of Total

Year	College Teaching Faculty	Doctorates Awarded
1910	18.9%	10.0%
1920	30.1%	15.1%
1930	32.5%	15.4%
1940	26.5%	13.0%
1950	23.2%	9.2%
1959–60	19.4%	10.5%

The numbers of women college presidents, professors, and instructors increased from 2,928 in 1910 to 9,974 in 1920 and 19,930 in 1930, but stagnated in the depression, reaching only 20,124 by 1940.[38] The progress of female doctorates awarded yearly was more complex. The number rose and the proportion declined in the thirties.[39]

TABLE 4

Women Doctorates

Year	Number Awarded	Women as % of Total	% Decennial Increase
1920	90	15.1	—
1930	311	15.4	245.5
1940	419	13.0	34.7
1950	613	9.2	46.3
1960	1090	10.5	77.8

Here, quite clearly is a basic complexity in the professional world. If we look only at the percentages, women's proportion of the total doc-torates awarded peaked already in the 1920s; yet that would distort the fact that more than three times as many women were receiving doctorates at the end of the decade. That women failed to keep pace with men—much less catch up to them—is clear. But that is not evidence for claiming that women became "disillusioned" with careers, or, as Bernard has argued, that women turned their backs on academe to indulge in a "reproductive mania." [40] If it is assumed that women doctorates had serious career intentions, then more of them had them in 1940 than in 1920 (more of them, it might be noted, on a per capita as well as an absolute basis).

Women's proportion of the totals is a function of two factors—the rise or fall in the number of women receiving doctorates (factor one) as a percentage of the rise or fall in the total number of doctorates awarded, that is, including men (factor two). The tremendous increase of male doctorates, which makes a rising *number* of female Ph.D.'s a *declining percentage* of the total must be considered as an independent development, shaped largely by changes in the occupational and educational structure which encouraged doctoral training for men—and not by itself a factor whose growth indicates a decline in women's aspirations.

For the question really is, decline from what? The number of women with career aspirations in 1920 was small. The number of doctorates, for example, was a mere ninety in that year. A decade later, over 300 women received their doctorates, and with several pauses, more and more women took the doctorate in each succeeding decade down to the present. Taking another perspective, the results are similar if less dramatic. If we use the census categories of "Professional, Technical, and Kindred Workers," and "Managers, Officials, and Proprietors" as rough indicators of the number of women in careers, then the proportion of adult women in careers did not decline in the 1920s, but rose, stayed the same in the 1930s, and rose in the 1940s. There were three career women per 100 adult women in 1920, four in 1930, four in 1940, and five in 1950. In short, the mere use of only certain percentages, by making it appear that fewer women were interested in careers after the 1920s, is a distortion, indeed a rather dramatic distortion of the facts.[41]

IV

It is this use of unreliable proportions that sidetracks any search for explanations of the supposed decline among professional women. Thus when Jessie Bernard suggests that the decline in women's share of doctorates and college teaching positions was due to the "reproductive mania" that American women indulged in in the 1940s and 1950s, her own evidence suggests some reason for doubting a simple relationship between birth rates and careers. The birth rate and women's share in academic life declined simultaneously in the 1930s.[42] Furthermore, consider that between 1945 and 1957, when the fertility rates climbed from 85.9 to 122.9, the height of the baby boom, *the number* of women taking their doctorates tripled.[43]

Certainly women failed to keep pace with men, yet on a per capita basis, women's movement was not downward but upward. In part because of this, the question of women's social and economic roles was a very live issue, even in the 1950s when women's lives were supposedly dominated by babies.[44]

The relationship between marriage and fertility rates on the one side and careers on the other is, then, quite complex. It has been assumed by some writers that a rise in marriage rates proves a decline in the career impulse, and that the sexual revolution of the 1920s made marriage more attractive, sapping women's desire for an independent career.[45]

Several points can be made about this line of reasoning. First, marriage rates for women in the United States did not jump sharply in the 1920s. Second, even if they did rise for college women, that does not prove a decline in career aspirations.[46] Life is complicated. People hold several apparently conflicting desires at the same time. Or they postpone the fulfillment of one desire without actually giving it up. A rise in the marriage rates for college women is not incompatible with the possibility that women have found a comfortable way to keep their childbearing years restricted to a limited period, so as to permit them to return to work at a later period. As long-range historical trends indicate, a lower age of marriage seems to follow on the possibility of controlling fertility within marriage.[47] In and of itself, marriage and child-bearing may not be an absolute indicator of disillusionment with work outside the home.

In the 1910s and 1920s, women married at a rate that was only slightly higher than in preceding decades.[48] After all, marriage had always been the occupation for which most women were trained. What was new in the 1910s and 1920s was that although a few more women married than in the past, more and more combined marriage and a professional career. The proportion of all professional women who were married rose from 12.2 percent in 1910 to 19.3 percent in 1920 and 24.7 percent in 1930. The proportion of school teachers who were married rose from 9.7 percent in 1920 to 17.9 percent in 1930 and 24.6 percent in 1940.[49] Also, as time went on, some women dropped out temporarily to start a family, and then returned later to their careers. In one study, Astin found that ninety-one percent of the women who received their doctorates in 1957–58 were employed eight years later. The older the woman, the more likely she was to be at work; "the younger woman doctorate is more likely to have children at home." [50] There is thus no reason to take the unmarried state as the main criterion of career aspirations, for marriage and childbearing do not prove a decline in the career impulse, although they may complicate its realization for a period of life.

Beginning around the turn of the century, the marrying rate for college graduates has moved from a low proportion to a very high one approaching that for the whole population. The proportion of Vassarites who married within five and a half years of graduation began a steady rise in the 1890s. By 1936, fifty-one percent of the class of 1925 at Smith married; seventy-seven percent of the class of 1927 had already married.[51] A survey showed that the differences between all women and college graduates were narrowing in the 1940s, until, by 1947, eighty-seven percent of all adult women had ever been married and sixty-nine percent of all women college graduates.[62] By 1960, among all women, ages, thirty to thirty-four, almost as many college graduates as those with eight years of elementary schooling were married.[53]

There is no question that college women have married in greater numbers in each successive decade since the turn of the century. Hence, either the sexual revolution of the twenties—which O'Neill and Ryan emphasize—was not the main factor in diverting women from careers to marriage, or that revolution must be pushed back into the early 1900s or before.[54] In that case, the career disillusionment specific to the 1920s is left without an explanation. Whatever made marriage more attractive to college women or college women more attractive to men, and whatever attracted greater numbers of more "conventional women" to college was occurring by the turn of the century. No college president was a more determined feminist than M. Carey Thomas of Bryn Mawr, yet the percentage of Bryn Mawr graduates marrying rose and the percentage of childless graduates declined between the classes of 1896–1901 and 1902–1907.[55]

It seems obvious that the rising rates of marriage among women college graduates resulted in part from long-range changes in marriage patterns as well as compositional changes in and expansion of the college population. What is needed is a synthesis of the work of those who, like most historians, emphasize specific cultural and social factors in the history of career women, and the work of demographers who could fill in the long-term economic and social changes which have affected decisions to marry. On the whole historians and demographers have ignored one another's work. Demographers probably under-emphasize the significance of attitudinal changes and historians of feminism ignore the demographic factors that have shaped women's behavior regardless of the ebb and flow of career ideas.[56]

A final point: collective biographies of college women might give us hard data on the interaction of the new morality and career atti-tudes.[57] There is some reason to doubt that freer sexual attitudes led women to reject the independent professional life. Crystal Eastman, Vassar '03, lawyer and socialist activist, rejected Victorian sexual atti-tudes, yet wanted a child very badly. Although she married, she never gave up her independent career.[58] Phyllis Blanchard learned in college that sex was not "a degrading and disgusting phenomenon which men enjoyed but to which women submitted only because it was part of wifely duty," and she married. But she surrendered neither her per-sonal autonomy nor her career.[59] Another college graduate, writing anonymously in 1927, attacked the cold, asexual atmosphere of her women's college. She had married, but she expressed no desire to give up her career.[60] Even "Feminist-New Style," the younger woman who had been touched by the sexual revolution, wanted not only a family, but a job. She knew that "there is hardly a man who will never take advantage of his wife's economic dependence upon him or who will never assume that it gives him special prerogatives." [61] In fact, it ap-pears that the relationship between the new morality and the job could be the reverse of what we have been led to expect. Far from the freer sexual morality leading to the abandonment of the job, economic in-dependence could nurture sexual freedom, allowing some women to avoid marriage while having sexual relationships and others to seek fulfillment in marriage while maintaining careers.[62] In short, the rela-tionship between the sexual revolution and career aspirations was an extremely complex one. Until more case histories have been examined in detail, we will not be able to say with confidence what those rela-tionships were, but they may have been part of the same personality development of many college-educated women.

V

The foregoing is not meant to imply that balancing a marriage, family, and a job was not extremely difficult, or to deny that some women "went home." [63] We cannot ignore the fact that in the late 1920s and through the 1930s, magazines published many reports of women who went home.[64] In light of the statistics examined earlier, it seems clear that fewer went home than stayed on the job. Perhaps the novelty of career women had worn off by the late twenties; perhaps magazine publishers welcomed the confessions as confirmations of their own prejudices. Certainly the women who went home often felt the need to defend themselves because their friends continued as career women.

It seems certain that the fugitives were given disproportionate publicity. In 1939, the "Lady in the Shoe" explained why she had given up her job. In the very same magazine, buried amidst the advertisements on the fourth-to-last page, the editors summarized the results of their informal telephone survey of ten career women. Eight of the ten were sure they would not quit their jobs and six of these eight women had children. The two who thought they might quit gave as their reasons poor pay and dull work.[65] It seems unlikely that as many readers noticed this little survey as read the confession of the "Lady in the Shoe."

An obvious reason why some women did go home, or why younger women sometimes never ventured forth into the world of work in the 1920s and 1930s was that career women faced discrimination on the job—discrimination which was intensified in the Great Depression, particularly, as we have seen, in a few career lines where women were unusually articulate (e.g., teachers, journalists). Many young women may have anticipated discrimination and stopped short of their goals. Others went home because of low pay and lack of promotion.[66]

In fact, however, many who actually announced that they had quit their jobs did not write of on-the-job discrimination. The problems they articulated were more subtle. Their attitudes toward work and independence were more complicated than they appeared on first sight. A few women gave up their careers to service the career of a husband "who had offered me the greatest opportunity for happiness in life"—love itself. Lucy Tunis did seem content applying the skills learned in law school to the mysteries of a dinner recipe.[67] There is no question that women felt the pressure to fulfill stereotypes of sweet femininity, to tend to the children, to master the domestic arts, and to service a husband's career.[68] But these women did not always go home or stay home with an undivided commitment. Rarely did they reject on principle a woman's need for an independent income or the stimulation of some exciting work besides domestic chores.[69] Wrote one woman who was stranded in a small Midwestern town: "Housework as a life job bores and enrages me. Writing even such hack work as I do, lights up windows for my soul ... The thought of achieving even moderate success as a writer sends shivers up and down my spine." [70]

It was not so much that women repudiated the career as that many of them found it impossible to carry on. Husbands did not respect their wives' aspirations; "feminist" husbands offered no help with the housework or the children.[71] Husbands' careers necessitated moves to other cities which left the wives' careers up in the air.[72]

In several cases, women became so involved in their work that they had little time for personal life. These women experienced not a simple disillusionment with the career—in which they were in fact deeply involved—but the extra burdens of managing a family along with the normal career pressures for a high level of commitment and competitive fervor. "It was stirring work," wrote Jane Allen after quitting her job, "which at times closed in on my attention to the exclusion of everything else. I could feel myself becoming the narrow, hard, efficiency-bitten drive wheel of my department." [73] Or as another woman put it:

> Before I had a job I had been screaming for self-expression at the head of the pack. I did not stop work because I had ceased to believe in expression—self or otherwise. My reason was a deep desire to catch up with my coat tails to find out what I was expressing and to whom.[74]

These women, unlike men in the same position, were sensitive and perhaps guilty about becoming hard-bitten careerists and about neglecting their families. Some of them quit work not because they did not like their job or because they had rejected the idea of economic independence, but because they could not come home from the office rat-race to find their slippers and a warm dinner ready. And if fewer career women went home in the 1920s and 1930s than the publicity surrounding their exit would suggest, even some of these did not wholly internalize domestic values. The surrender to home life did not always mean that the appeal of economic independence and useful work had disappeared, or that the role of the happy homemaker was accepted easily. Even as the feminine mystique spread in the 1940s and 1950s, feelings of discontent and deep conflicts were bound to continue among women in careers and potential career women. More and more women went to college and many of them were touched with the possibilities of a future beyond domestic life. Hence the still small but growing number of women who took their doctorates or entered the business world.[75] Economic and social forces drew more rather than fewer women out of the home; many who stayed home had been touched by the desire for something more. As one college graduate put it, "I have needed all my philosophy courses to reconcile myself to accepting the monotony of household duties so that I will have some free time daily to express my own personality." [76] The feminine mystique did not arise in a vacuum, but to meet the real conflicts these women experienced. Domesticity had not conquered the minds of American women, even in the 1950s.

VI

What was missing all through these years was not a base of discontents or significant numbers of career women, but a feminist movement to interpret these discontents as collective phenomena, rooted in fundamentally inegalitarian social and economic structures. Nor were there many intellectuals who viewed the American social and economic structure from the outside with a critical perspective. Fervent protests about women's condition were few.[77] Some college women and academics advocated the adjustment of women to housework rather than the transformation of social and economic structures. Several alumnae agreed that college should "teach women to be household managers and mothers." [78] Yet from a feminist point of view, some of the colleges apparently strove to do a good job. As a result, the alumnae, wrote Dr. Dorothy Lee of Vassar's anthropology department, were forced to go through a long and bitter conflict before unlearning what they had learned in college, before they could find the value of office work or homemaking. The colleges had taught them that it was better to read Plato than to wash diapers, to prefer a lecture on T.S. Eliot to staying at home with the babies (indirect evidence, at least, that colleges continued to play a role in career choices and tensions). Dr. Lee urged that the colleges eliminate the tensions by training women for a domestic future. How should a wife react when her husband fumed in a traffic jam? When he came home to announce that he had been fired? These were the great questions that taxed modern woman's mind. Dr. Lee urged that she be taught "how to come out of this situation emotionally refreshed, not cross and wilted. In this way she can learn to find continuity and personal maturity in homemaking; her life as a housewife will be fulfilling and not just a series of drab chores." [79]

Obviously, if such medicine were necessary, it was clear that the domestic psychology had not been completely internalized by the alumnae themselves. Yet among academics the tide seemed to be running against feminism in the late 1940s and the 1950s, even if not all yielded to Dr. Lee's pragmatism. It is not surprising that many intellectuals—especially the Freudians in psychology and the functionalists in sociology—came forward with tools for a more efficient "adjustment" of women to the home. In the 1940s and 1950s, the United States lacked a solid core of genuinely radical intellectuals who were ready to do battle with the fundamentals of the American system. If it sometimes seemed that the feminine mystique monopolized the pages of popular magazines, it was not because of the unmitigated hold of that ideology on women themselves, but because of the absence of a loud, clear challenge from critical intellectuals and a feminist movement.

All too often American academics served the cause of adjustment rather than social change. Sociologists and psychoanalysts assumed that individuals had to adjust to roles and institutions that were conceived in fundamentally static ways. The family, with its sexual division of labor between husband and wife—each with sexually defined emotional characters—was defended as a logical and functional system.[80] It was as much this conservatism of academic thought as the alledged disillusionment among anonymous women that allowed the surge of domestic ideas in the late 1940s and 1950s.

This suggests an important general point for students of women's history. The history of the organized feminist movement and feminist thought is separable from the attitudes of women and, in particular, from the history of career women. In the 1920s older feminists looked with dismay on the devotion of younger women to sex and self. But the rejection of the feminist movement and of the ideal of service to society by younger women was not by itself a rejection of economic independence. As one young woman stated her credo, "We're not out to benefit society ... We're out for Mary's job and Luella's art, and Barbara's independence and the rest of our individual careers and desires."[81] This privatized individualism naturally did not sit well with older feminists who had been animated by a broader ideal of social service and a political goal—woman suffrage. But in its way, the attitude of the younger generation may have been a necessary reaction to the feminist movement's neglect of the personal side of things and especially of self-fulfillment.

Just as feminists in the 1920s viewed the flapper as a sign of the decline of the movement, so recent writers, reading only the literary evidence or misreading the statistical evidence, have exaggerated the depth of disillusionment and actually misstated the facts of the history of career women after 1920. Moreover, no one has examined in detail the literary evidence itself. How much of the unhappiness women expressed during these transitional decades was concerned with the job and how much was simply a temporary surrender to the practical problem of running a home or to discrimination on the job? Through a synthesis of demography and traditional history, a more careful and systematic reading of the periodical literature, and the collection of oral histories and biographies of women who lived through the 1920s, 1930s, 1940s, and 1950s, we may be able to show a gradual progression in the spread of career impulses, proceeding despite many obstacles and finally erupting in one segment of the women's liberation movement of the 1960s.

In constructing this history, our models of economic and social trends as well as individual psychology must be dynamic and complex. The American economic and social system transformed the roles of American women, even as it limited women, denied them equal opportunity, and perpetuated the idea that their primary role was that of wife and mother. American capitalism profited from sexual discrimination in the workplace and women's unpaid labor at home. Yet the system also sent hundreds of thousands of women into the workplace or college. Formally, the American system promised equality; in actuality, women were faced with discrimination and painful role conflicts. But the important point is that there were conflicts, having two sides to them. The minds of working career women and potential career women were not monopolized by conservative ideologies. Indeed, the feminine mystique of the 1940s and 1950s arose in part to smooth over the contradictions which the American system itself created. As more and more women entered careers or came in touch with the possibility of economic independence, the strains intensified. In each succeeding decade since 1920, some women who were out in the world did "go home." Many more were in touch with the possibility of a permanent place in the world outside the home, often trying to combine this place with the home, in an unprecedented mixture of roles and identities.

NOTES

1. For a brief survey, see Robert W. Smuts, *Women and Work in America* (New York, 1971). William Chafe, *The American Woman: Her Changing Social, Economic, and Political Roles, 1920–1970* (New York, 1972), is a useful analysis, especially of career women. For the flavor of women's work at the turn of the century, read Dorothy Richardson, *The Long Day* (1905), in William O'Neill, ed., *Women at Work* (Chicago, 1972).

2. See Frances Donovan, *The Woman Who Waits* (Boston, 1920), especially

pp. 9–11, 223–27. Also Alice Beal Parsons, *Woman's Dilemma* (New York, 1926), pp. 272ff.

3. For three feminist statements on work from three different periods, see Charlotte Perkins Gilman, *Women and Economics* (New York, 1966); Parsons, *Woman's Dilemma;* and Betty Friedan, *The Feminine Mystique* (New York, 1963).

4. The term "social feminism" is used by William L. O'Neill throughout his *Everyone Was Brave: The Rise and Fall of Feminism in America* (Chicago, 1969). For comments on the twenties, see ibid., pp. 304 ff. On the battle over the Equal Rights Amendment, see Chafe, *The American Woman,* pp. 112–32. Also see Sophonisba P. Breckinridge, *Women in the Twentieth Century: A Study of Their Political, Social and Economic Activities* (New York, 1933), for a survey of women's organizations, and especially pp. 93–95, for an insight into the way reform activities absorbed women who might otherwise have had careers. R. Le Clerc Phillips, "The Real Rights of Women," *Harper's Monthly Magazine,* October, 1926, pp. 609–14, is important as a warning against feminine self-sacrifice.

5. O'Neill, *Everyone Was Brave,* pp. 304–05; Jessie Bernard, *Academic Women* (University Park, Pennsylvania, 1964), p. 40; Breckinridge, *Women in the Twentieth Century,* p. 188; Chafe, *The American Woman,* pp. 48–65; and U.S. Department of Labor, *Women's Occupations Through Seven Decades,* by Janet M. Hooks, Women's Bureau Bulletin No. 218 (Washington, D.C., 1947), pp. 154–89.

6. See for example, Lucy R. Tunis, "I Gave Up My Law Books for a Cook Book," *American Magazine,* July, 1927, pp. 34–35, 172–77; and Jane Allen, "You May Have My Job, A Feminist Discovers Her Home," *The Forum,* April, 1932, pp. 228–31.

7. Dorothy Dunbar Bromley, "Feminist-New Style," *Harper's Monthly Magazine,* October, 1927, pp. 552–60.

8. Phyllis Blanchard and Carolyn Manasses, *New Girls for Old* (New York, 1937), p. 237. See also, with a different slant, Nancy Evans, "Good-by, Bohemia," *Scribner's Magazine,* June, 1931, pp. 643–46.

9. Alice Beal Parsons, "Man-Made Illusions About Woman," in Samuel D. Schmalhausen and V.F. Calverton, eds., *Woman's Coming of Age: A Symposium* (New York, 1931), pp. 20–34. Quotation on p. 23.

10. Evidence from the films of the period is mixed. In some ways the 1930s offered a more positive image of the career woman than the 1920s. See Marjorie Rosen, *Popcorn Venus* (New York, 1973), pp. 144, 147, 154. Rosen argues that the positive image of women reporters in films of the depression decade insulated women from the reality of declines in professional occupations. See also Joseph Kirk Folsom and Marion Bassett, *The Family and Democratic Society* (London, 1948), pp. 616 ff., especially p. 623 for remarks on the negative image of career women in films of the period.

11. O'Neill, *Everyone Was Brave,* pp. 304 ff. Bernard, *Academic Women,* consistently dismisses discrimination and anticipated discrimination as important factors in women's declining proportion of academic positions.

12. Bernard, *Academic Women,* pp. 36–37, 61–62, 215.

13. O'Neill, *Everyone Was Brave,* p. 308.

14. Mary P. Ryan, *Womanhood in America: From Colonial Times to the Present* (New York, 1975), pp. 235, 255–57, 287–93. Also Bernard, *Academic Women*, pp. 209–10, and Chafe, *The American Woman*, pp. 92–93. Historical treatments of Victorian sexual morality can be sampled in Andrew Sinclair, *The Emancipation of the American Woman* (New York, 1966), pp. 127–36, and Daniel Scott Smith, "Family Limitation, Sexual Control, and Domestic Feminism in Victorian America," *Feminist Studies* 1 (1973): 40–57.

15. On the feminine mystique, Friedan, *The Feminine Mystique*.

16. Useful research in this connection includes Matina Horner, "The Motive to Avoid Success and Changing Aspirations of College Women," and Mirra Komarovsky, "Cultural Contradictions and Sex Roles," in Judith M. Bardwick, ed., *Readings on the Psychology of Women* (New York, 1972), pp. 58–67. Both show the conflicting pressures on college women. A fictional treatment of a young woman and the beauty ideal is Alix Kates Shulman, *Memoirs of an Ex-Prom Queen* (New York, 1973).

17. Lorine Pruette, *Women and Leisure: A Study of Social Waste* (New York, 1924), pp. 116 ff., 122 ff., 131 ff., and 199. Pruette remarked that the career goals of the girls were somewhat unrealistic. Nearly half hoped to make a career in the arts. See pp. 125–26. O'Neill makes the same point in *Everyone Was Brave*, pp. 322–23.

18. Blanchard and Manasses, *New Girls for Old*, pp. 175–77. The authors had no data from an earlier period as the basis for their discovery of a "disillusionment."

19. O'Neill, *Everyone Was Brave*, pp. 307–09; Ryan, *Womanhood in America*, p. 255; and Chafe, *The American Woman*, pp. 102–03.

20. Blanchard and Manasses, *New Girls for Old*, pp. 175–77.

21. Chafe, *The American Woman*, p. 102.

22. Folsom and Bassett, *The Family and Democratic Society*, p. 617.

23. Ibid., p. 616.

24. Mirra Komarovsky, "Cultural Contradictions and Sex Roles: The Masculine Case," *American Journal of Sociology* 78 (1973): 873–84, is an exception in that it includes, p. 833, comparisons of similar college groups in 1943 and 1971.

25. Mirra Komarovsky, *Women in the Modern World: Their Education and Their Dilemmas* (Boston, 1953), pp. 92–99; quotation from p. 97.

26. Quoted in Bernard, *Academic Women*, p. 228.

27. Table 1 is based on the numbers in Gertrude Bancroft, *The American Labor Force: Its Growth and Changing Composition* (New York, 1958), Table D-2, p. 209. I calculated the percentages and rounded off the last digit.

28. Hooks, *Women's Occupations Through Seven Decades*, p. 89; and Breckinridge, *Women in the Twentieth Century*, pp. 172, 174. Generally on businesswomen, see Hooks, pp. 180–89.

29. However, it was proof against any who were naive enough to expect that the achievement of woman suffrage in 1920 would bring equality with men in all occupations. See also, Anne W. Armstrong, "Seven Deadly Sins of Woman in Business," *Harper's Monthly Magazine*, August, 1926, pp. 295–303, which describes and in some ways surrenders to the pressures on businesswomen.

30. Table 2 based on figures in Bancroft, *The American Labor Force*, p. 209.
31. In the same decade, male professionals increased their numbers by about twenty-four percent. Based on figures in ibid.
32. On discrimination during the depression, see Chafe, *The American Woman*, pp. 107 ff.; Helen Buckler, "Shall Married Women Be Fired," *Scribner's Magazine*, March, 1932, pp. 166–68; and J. Stanley Lemons, *The Woman Citizen: Social Feminism in the 1920s* (Urbana, 1973), pp. 230ff..
33. Cynthia Fuchs Epstein, *Woman's Place: Options and Limits in Professional Careers* (Berkeley, 1971), Table II, pp. 200–01.
34. Breckinridge, *Women in the Twentieth Century*, pp. 188–90.
35. Epstein, *Woman's Place*, Table II, pp. 200–01.
36. Ibid., and p. 64, for signs that even in the "female" occupation of nursing women experienced anxieties about sex roles.
37. Table 3 is taken from Table 2/2,B, and Table 4/5 in Bernard, *Academic Women*, pp. 40, 70.
38. Epstein, *Woman's Place*, Table II, pp. 200–01.
39. Columns 1 and 2 of Table 4 are from Bernard, *Academic Women*, pp. 70–71. I calculated the decennial increases. It should be noted that the distribution of subject areas changed dramatically. Of five subject areas, the fewest doctorates in 1920 and the most in 1961 were awarded in education. Women showed the smallest numerical increase in the physical and biological sciences.
40. Bernard, *Academic Women*, p. 215.
41. Calculations based on the figures for adult women and women in career occupations in Bancroft, *The American Labor Force*, pp. 203, 209.
42. Bernard, *Academic Women*, p. 74.
43. The general fertility rates (births per 1000 women, ages 15–44) are given in George Grier, *The Baby Bust* (Washington, D.C., 1971), p. 73. Female doctorates awarded yearly from Bernard, *Academic Women*, p. 71.
44. Chafe, *The American Woman*, pp. 199–225.
45. See above, notes 11–14, on Ryan and O'Neill.
46. Paul H. Jacobson and Pauline F. Jacobson, *American Marriage and Divorce* (New York, 1959), Table 2, p. 21.
47. See Geoffrey Hawthorn, *The Sociology of Fertility* (London, 1970), pp. 25–26.
48. Jacobson and Jacobson, *American Marriage and Divorce*, p. 21, Table 2.
49. Figures for all professional women from Elizabeth Nottingham, "Toward an Analysis of the Effects of Two World Wars on the Role and Status of Middle-Class Women in the English-Speaking World," *American Sociological Review* XII (1947): 666–75, especially p. 670. Figures for school teachers from U.S. Bureau of the Census, *Census of Population, 1930*, Vol. V, *General Report on Occupations*, pp. 276–80, and U.S. Bureau of the Census, *Census of Population, 1940*, Vol. III, *The Labor Force, Occupation, Industry, Employment, and Income*, Part 1, U.S. Summary, p. 115.
50. Helen S. Astin, "Factors Associated with the Participation of Women Doctorates in the Labor Force," in Athena Theodore, ed., *The Professional Woman* (Cambridge, Mass., 1971), pp. 441–52. Quotation from pp. 444–45. See also Valerie Kincade Oppenheimer, *The Female Labor Force*

in the United States: Demographic and Economic Factors Governing Its Growth and Changing Composition, Population Monograph Series, No. 5 (Berkeley, 1970), especially pp. 8–15.

51. Mabel Newcomer and Evelyn S. Gibson, "Vital Statistics from Vassar College," *The American Journal of Sociology,* XXIX (1924): 430–42; Mabel Newcomer, *A Century of Higher Education for American Women* (New York, 1959), pp. 212–14; Rosewell H. Johnson, "Marriage and Birth Rates at Bryn Mawr," *Eugenics* II (1929): 30.

52. Ernest Havemann and Patricia Salter West, *They Went to College: The College Graduate in America Today* (New York, 1952), pp. 61–62.

53. Clyde V. Kiser, Wilson H. Grabill, and Arthur A. Campbell, *Trends and Variations in Fertility in the United States* (Cambridge, Mass., 1968), pp. 148–49. The percentages were ninety percent for the college graduates and ninety-five percent for those women with an eighth grade education.

54. James R. McGovern has already pushed the sexual revolution back to the 1910s in his "The American Woman's Pre-World War I Freedom in Manners and Morals," *Journal of American History,* LV (1968): 315–33. For evidence of a more positive view of women's sexuality in the late nineteenth century, see Carl N. Degler, "What Ought To Be and What Was: Women's Sexuality in the Nineteenth Century," *American Historical Review,* LXXIX (1974): 1467–90.

55. Johnson, "Marriage and Birth Rates at Bryn Mawr," and Newcomer, *A Century of Higher Education for American Women,* pp. 30–31. On Carey Thomas, see O'Neill, *Everyone Was Brave,* pp. 110–14; and on the success of Bryn Mawr graduates, Newcomer, *A Century,* pp. 196–97.

56. An excellent example of demographic work relevant to students of women's history is Richard Easterlin, *The American Baby Boom in Historical Perspective,* Occasional Paper 79 (New York, 1962). Easterlin offers an economic and demographic explanation of the baby boom.

57. Ryan and O'Neill may rely too much on the fears of older feminists for their picture of the effects of the new morality on younger women. See, for example, Ryan, *Womanhood in America,* pp. 255–56.

58. June Sochen, *Movers and Shakers: American Women Thinkers and Activists, 1900–1970* (New York, 1973), pp. 45ff., and Vassar Alumnae Collection, 1903, in Vassar College Library.

59. Phyllis Blanchard, "The Long Journey," *Nation* 124 (1927): 472–73, reprinted in Anne Firor Scott, ed., *The American Woman: Who Was She?* (Englewood Cliffs, N.J., 1971), pp. 164–66.

60. Anonymous, "The Harm My Education Did Me," *Outlook,* November 30, 1927, pp. 396–97, 405.

61. Bromley, "Feminist-New Style," p. 555.

62. Ryan, *Womanhood in America,* p. 270. On a broader scale, seeking to explain the surge in European illegitimacy in the eighteenth century, Edward Shorter has linked women's sexual autonomy to their involvement in a wage economy and their freedom from patriarchal controls. As their sense of self increased, young women engaged in sex more frequently and demanded greater fulfillment. See Shorter, "Female Emancipation, Birth Control, and Fertility in European History," *American Historical Review,* LXXVIII (1973): 605–40. How economic activity af-

fected career women in modern America is not clear, but Shorter's frankly speculative article suggests how complex is the relationship between work and sexual behavior.

63. For a contrasting view, see Bernard, *Academic Women*, p. 311, n.14, which reveals Bernard's curious view that career-home conflicts are hardly more onerous for women than for men.

64. See Tunis, "I Gave Up My Law Books for a Cook Book"; Allen, "You May Have My Job"; Anonymous, "Lady in the Shoe," *Harper's Monthly Magazine* (1939): 629–34; Judith Lambert, "I Quit My Job," *The Forum*, July 1937, pp. 9–15; Katherine Gauss Jackson, "Must Married Women Work," *Scribner's Magazine* (1935): 240–42; Harriet Bradley Fitt, "In Praise of Domesticity," in Herbert Elmer Mills and His Former Students, *College Women and the Social Sciences* (New York, 1934), pp. 265–79; and Chafe, *The American Woman*, pp. 99–106.

65. Anonymous, "Lady in the Shoe." Folsom and Bassett, *The Family and Democratic Society*, p. 623, offer an interesting example of slanted publicity. In 1938 a photo of the "Ideal American College Girl" appeared in the press with the caption, "Ideal College Girl Puts Marriage Before Career." Only in small print was it revealed that putting marriage first was a requirement for entering the "Ideal Girl" contest.

66. On discrimination, see, for example, Breckinridge, *Women in the Twentieth Century*, pp. 238–41; Chafe, *The American Woman*, pp. 60, 107 ff., 271, n.23; Nottingham, "Toward an Analysis," pp. 671–72; Marion O. Hawthorne, "Women as College Teachers," *The Annals* CXLIII (1929): 146–53; Alice I. Bryan and Edwin G. Boring, "Women in American Psychology: Factors Affecting Their Professional Careers," *The American Psychologist* 2 (1947): 3–20, especially pp. 8 ff. In addition to on-the-job discrimination, there were the usual antifeminist attacks such as John Macy, "Equality of Woman with Man: A Myth," *Harper's Monthly Magazine* (1926): 705–13; and harsh attacks on women's colleges and college women from men who worried that the "best" people were not reproducing in sufficient numbers. See Henry Carey, "Career or Maternity: The Dilemma of the College Girl," *North American Review* (1929): 737–44; and Willis J. Ballinger, "Spinster Factories: Why I Would Not Send a Daughter to College," *The Forum* (1932): 301–05. See also n. 32 above for additional references on discrimination during the depression. On the anticipation of discrimination, see Bernard, *Academic Women*, pp. 174, 181–84.

67. Tunis, "I Gave Up My Law Books," p. 174.

68. Ibid.; Jackson, "Must Married Women Work," by a career woman who would have felt "more a woman" if she could have turned out a proper souffleé; and Eva Von B. Hansl, "What About the Children? The Question of Mothers and Careers," *Harper's Monthly Magazine* (1927): 220–27.

69. It should be mentioned that some of these women might have found home life more attractive because they were of a class that could afford a nice house in the country.

70. Edith Clark, "Trying To Be Modern," *Nation* 125 (1927): 153–55, in Scott, ed., *The American Woman*, pp. 141–46. Quotation on p. 146.

71. Anonymous, "Lady in the Shoe;" Lambert, "I Quite My Job;" and

Caroline Ware, *Greenwich Village, 1920–1930, A Comment on American Civilization* (New York, 1965), p. 260. The avant-garde men of Greenwich Village were more backward in practice than in theory when it came to helping around the house.

72. The necessity to relocate for the husband's job damaged the careers of Fitts, Tunis, and Clark.

73. Jane Allen, "You May Have My Job," p. 229.

74. Anonymous, "Lady in the Shoe," p. 634.

75. To information given earlier about whether women in the professions and business might be added the figures on college women. The total number of women in college was as follows:

1920	282,942
1930	480,802
1940	600,953
1950	805,953

Women as a proportion of total enrollment declined for the same years as follows; 47.3 percent, 43.7 percent, 42.1 percent, and 30.3 percent. These percentages show how women were losing ground to men. But another way of looking at the same figures is to use college women as a proportion of young women. Taking the age group of women twenty to twenty-four as a rough base, the proportion of women in college rose, from sixty per 1000 women twenty to twenty-four in 1920, to eighty-seven in 1930, 102 in 1940, and 137 in 1950. This does not negate the fact that women were denied equal opportunities in college. It does suggest that more and more women were put in touch with the possibilities of a future broader than homemaking. Sources for college enrollments: Bernard, *Academic Women*, pp. 68–70; for females aged 20–24, Bancroft, *The American Labor Force*, p. 203.

76. Havemann and West, *They Went to College*, p. 64.

77. But see Della D. Cyrus, "Why Mothers Fail," *Atlantic Monthly* (1947): 57–60; and Edith M. Stern, "Women Are Household Slaves," *American Mercury* (1949): 71–76, reprinted in Aileen S. Kraditor, ed., *Up From the Pedestal: Selected Writings in the History of American Feminism* (Chicago, 1970), pp. 346–53.

78. Havemann and West, *They Went to College*, pp. 64–65.

79. Dorothy D. Lee, "What Shall We Teach Women?" *Madamoiselle*, August, 1947, pp. 213, 354, 356, 358.

80. See for example, Friedan, *The Feminine Mystique*, pp. 117–41. An early document that mixed psychoanalysis and an adjustive approach against feminism was Floyd Dell, *Love in the Machine Age: A Psychological Study of the Transition from Patriarchal Society* (New York, 1930). For more recent examples, see Bernard, *Academic Women*, pp. 200–01, 305–06, n. 27, which accepts as "functional" the sexual and emotional division of labor in the family; and Chafe, *The American Woman*, pp. 212–16, on role theory.

81. Anne O'Hagan, "The Serious-Minded Young—If Any," *The Woman's Journal* XIII (1928): 7, quoted in O'Neill, *Everyone Was Brave*, p. 307.